THE CORNBREAD GOSPELS

THE
CORNBREAD
GOSPELS

CRESCENT DRAGONWAGON

Illustrations by Andrea Wisnewski

WORKMAN PUBLISHING • NEW YORK

Library of Congress Cataloging-in-Publication Data is available.

ISBN-13: 978-0-7611-1916-6

Interior design by Barbara Balch
Front cover photographs © by Christopher Hirsheimer (cornbread in pan, corn muffin), Renee Comet/Jupiterimages (pancakes), Burke/Jupiterimages (cornsticks), James Baigrie/Jupiterimages (cornbread squares)
Back cover photographs © by Christopher Hirsheimer

Text credits: page 9, from *Gap Creek*, by Robert Morgan. © 1999 by Robert Morgan. Reprinted by permission of Algonquin Books of Chapel Hill; page 23, from *Lunch at the Picadilly*, by Clyde Edgerton. © 2003 by Clyde Edgerton. Reprinted by permission of Algonquin Books of Chapel Hill; page 70, from "Cornbread Poem" © 2004 by Max Yoho, in *Felicia, These Fish Are Delicious*, Dancing Goat Press; page 77, by Jan Epton Seale, "In Praise of Mesquite," www.prairiepoetry.org.; page 308, from *Writing Past Dark: Envy, Fear, Distraction, and Other Dilemmas in the Writer's Life*, by Bonnie Friedman, 1993, HarperCollins Publishers.

Workman books are available at special discounts when purchased in bulk for premiums and sales promotions as well as for fund-raising or educational use. Special editions or book excerpts can also be created to specification. For details, contact the Special Sales Director at the address below.

Workman Publishing Company, Inc.
225 Varick Street
New York, NY 10014-4381
www.workman.com

Printed in U.S.A.

First printing October 2007
10 9 8 7 6 5 4 3 2 1

To Kay Kelley Arnold,
friend and mentor, honest as cornbread,
and in memory of
Judge Richard Arnold,
who loved her well, truly, and proudly
for all the years they shared the bread of life.

ACKNOWLEDGMENTS

First: very cornbread-specific thanks go to Zoë Caywood, Darra Goldstein, most especially the ultra-generous Ronni Lundy (queen of Southern cornbread and my friend of a decade plus), Carmen Sanchez, Suzanne Wickham-Beaird, the late Sylvia Teague, John Edgerton, Brinna Sands, Pam Anderson, Patsy Bruce, Lisa Cone (and her late mother, Mary), Jessica Harris, Chef Tommy Ryan of Durgin-Park, Patsy Watkins, Marilyn Kennedy, Maria Petra Vasquez, Marilyn Tausend, Layla Torres and John Sutton, Diane Kellner of Gap Mountain Breads, Diane Kolchilas, Aglaia Kremezi, Raghavan Iyer, Carol Field, Leslie Shaw, Sri Owen, Patsy Barker. On behalf of this book's readers as well as myself, I especially thank those of you who gave me recipes that had never before left your families.

Valuable data and historical insight was provided by David Dudek, research librarian of the Miller Library at Washington College; Mary V. Thompson of the Mount Vernon Ladies' Association; food historian Sandra Oliver; and Amy Steigman of the Tortilla Industry Association. Betty Fussell plowed the cornfield. Thank you to farmer-photographer-author Michael Ableman for your soulful respect and knowledge of Hopi agricultural practices; and to columnist Bob Lancaster, who added much to my understanding of cornbread in a single throwaway line twenty years ago. Though not cited directly here, authors Jack Weatherford (*Indian Givers*) and Gary Paul Nabhan (*Coming Home to Eat*) gave me insights I could not have gleaned elsewhere. The Greek Food and Wine Institute (especially

Lisa Cutick), and Spiros Abatzopoulos, Commercial Attaché of the Greek Consulate in New York, really went above the call of duty in helping me track down Greek cornbread. Laurie Danforth—I will never forget the great Tamale Boogie.

And Mishala Jones . . . for testing and moose-sighting and driving wretched Blazer (R.I.P.) across country and so much else we both carry in our hearts . . . thank you thank you thank you, and please keep Vermont on the list.

The distinctions between personal and professional blur when I think of the kindness, perspicaciousness, and hard work of my agent, the hard-headed, tender-hearted Edite Kroll. Thank you, Edite, for so many reasons. And without the divine Ms. Suzanne Rafer, this croissant might well have been altogether too flaky. Jen Griffin: thank you and we miss you. Kylie Foxx, brave girl, you stepped boldly into the breech with determination and thoughtfulness: thank you. This book would be much less without the illustrations of Andrea Wisnewski, who I knew would be perfectly perfect for this project from the very first samples sent by primo designer Barbara Balch. Janet McDonald: I never thought I would ever have occasion to say, "Wow, this copyediting is not only meticulous, it's thoughtful and interesting." But yours was, and I'm saying it to you. Thanks! All of you have been tremendously patient with me. Lastly, in an era of dinosaur-size impersonal publishers, I am truly grateful that Peter Workman publishes not just books, but

authors; he returns phone calls; and recognized something in me way back that, despite everything, has kept him publishing me for more than thirty-five years.

For products, materials, and ingredients, I am grateful to Lodge Manufacturing, 505 Chile Company, Scharffen Berger Chocolate, War Eagle Mill, King Arthur Flour, Melissa Guerra, Cuisinart, Cocina de Vega, and KitchenAid. Frasier Cooper-Ellis makes my life, cornbreads, and neighborhood sweet by tapping "the family trees." And thanks for a miscellany of things that season this book go to Max Yoho; the CopperWynd Resort in Scottsdale, Arizona; Cina Nutumya; Jan Epton Seale; Claudia F. Manz; and Madge Griswold. South Pittsburg, Tennessee, and its fine folks—thank you for the warm and welcoming National Cornbread Festival; you helped put cornbread at the center of the universe (where it belongs) before I had even conceived of this book.

For me, between the starting and conclusion of writing this book, there was a major personal before-and-after. Deep, once-in-a-lifetime extraordinary thanks go to those who populated the before, both of this book and my life: the friends and neighbors of my former community, Eureka Springs, Arkansas. Especially grateful hugs not only to everyone I thanked at the beginning of *Passionate Vegetarian*, but to these dear friends who helped me launch boldly into my new life: Cheri White, Debbie Dye, Renae Sterling, K. J. Zumwalt, Charlisa Cato, the remarkable Galyen family, Michael and Jae Avenoso, John Willer and Mary Springer, the extraordinarily competent Patti, and, with belated and genuine thanks for dragon beautification, Stan and Jeff. Becky Sisco, you will probably be surprised to learn that an offhand comment of yours in a sense sparked this whole book. I thank you, too.

In my larger Arkansas life and being, from the bottom of my heart I thank the life-saving and funny W. F. Symes; the wise, wise Kay Kelley Arnold; and Wenonah Fay Holl, who has held me to a larger life in more ways than I'm sure she imagines. Corrinnia and Rick Briggs: your great gift and presence is beyond reckoning, still and to this day. In your individual and sui generis ways, Susan and Rick Smith, Jean Gordon, Brenda Moosey, Bill Worthen, Jim "You must write your memoirs, my dear" Rule, Anna Cox, Connie Fails, all receive my deep gratitude. Ken Frazier, any man who looks at a heap of steamed greens at breakfast and

says, "Have I died and gone to heaven?" is much more than noteworthy in my book. Thank you. And yes, most certainly you, too, Steven Weintz: don't try and weasel out of it.

For believing: thanks are due Shannon Chamberlin, Walter Smiley, the gentle and persistent visionary Pat Lile, Archie Schaeffer, Carolyn Walton, the very dear Mary Gay Shipley of That Bookstore, Anne and Ralph Broadwater, Brian Maynard, Donna Jackson, Larry Stone, Justin Newby, and Jerry Bedford.

Bianca Zafferano, Lei Ann Marshall-Cohen, and Karen Kahn gave me, as only they could, the images and stories of the boy who grew up to become my great sweetheart. Linda Mannheim, you were the conduit for the right wisdom at the right time. Elizabeth Karmel, Wayne Petersen . . . how "there" you managed to be astounds me to this day.

Vernon Gross, you helped me bridge before and after, in a manner peculiar, sweet, and (thankfully) ongoing. We'll always have Memphis.

For extraordinary and kind forbearance and understanding, I must mention my brother, Stephen Zolotow, as well as Paul Silberberg, and Leah Scherer. Their help in this transitional phase was and remains enormous. Thank you. May I someday repay your patience and belief, with interest.

The afters, of my new life in southeastern Vermont, include Deborah and Michael Krasner, Michelle and Pete, Sandy and Bill Curry, Gary Clay, Elisa Leigh (who also stepped in as an eleventh-hour recipe tester when I broke my foot), Elizabeth Pittman, Andy and Kate, Lisa and Alan, Judith Reichsman and Stephanie Petkanas, Silvestre, Beth Ami Maglin, Averill and Bob. Peter Stamm, I am grateful to you not only on my behalf but that of Dot. Larry Burdick: thanks for offering an office away from home (all this, and chocolate, too). The folks at Walker's and Harlow's, Ray Massucco (bless you, Ray), the Rockingham Library staff (past and present) as well as that of the Putney Library, the Co-operators of Putney and Brattleboro—I cannot overstate your assistance. And oh, Gaelen and Richard . . . thank you for help, and joys both vernal and blizzardly. Carol G., you know I love you for yourself—really!—but oh, your darling Zoë: it's my privilege to be her CresAunt.

There are also some who are neither before or after, but both, and from what I can tell, always and ever presently: George West,

Starr Mitchell, Billy Haymes, Chou-Chou (Marcia) Yearsley, Charlotte Zolotow, Dorothy Arnof, Jane Maas, Jan Brown, Patti Summerville (again), Crow Johnson . . . the late Elsie and Louis Freund, Maurice Zolotow, and of course Ned. I hope, if I travel with you in mind and heart as you do with me, that your journey is as much sweeter and more interesting for you as you have made mine.

No one could write about corn without acknowledging, in the largest, deepest way, the contribution of countless generations of America's natives. Without them, there would be no maize. I hope my grateful respect to those ancient nameless ones who, through most careful observation and with great generosity, co-created maize can somehow come wafting up to them across time and space, rising like smoke from a smudge of sage.

Lastly, David Richard Koff: with whom I didn't fall, but walked, slowly, into love. As we walk still, and walk onward, and make our path by walking, please know that I consider this, our mutual reawakening, a daily miracle, astonishing as bread.

(And Mollie adds, "If you takes me meaning, sir.")

I hope, as each of you read your name, you feel the specific and individual hum of gratitude, respect, and love I have for you. Thank you for tethering me to life, before, after, and during. And right, right now.

Crescent Dragonwagon
Saxtons River, Vermont

CONTENTS

INTRODUCTION
The Gospel Truth About Cornbread

What if, in a world where news is too often bad, where the future, never certain, seems especially tenuous and fraught at the present moment, there were a happiness-giving magic word that automatically brought forth love, enthusiasm, recognition, and pleasure?

There is such a word. Cornbread.

"Cornbread? I *love* cornbread!"

I discovered cornbread's true power about six years ago, when, in response to being asked "And what are you working on now?" I'd say, "I'm writing a book about cornbread." Instantly, almost invariably, I'd get a response nearly shocking in its suddenness, conspiratorial delight, and universality. And this was no default have-a-nice-day-okay-let's-

move-on-to-the-next-thing smile: this was real, as unfaked—and as unfakable—as real cornbread.

That ability to call forth joy, and memory? That's cornbread's mojo.

Oddly, those who know and love cornbread seem to feel their fondness is unusual. The fervency with which they express it, along with the fact that someone else shares these same deeply personal feelings, seems to surprise even them. But cornbread-love, like all love, is universal and deeply individual. Even now, when I have grown to half-expect it, this rapturousness at the word itself is as unlikely an illumination as a sharp ray of sunlight, all the more abrupt and lit-up because it is piercing gray November clouds.

ABUNDANCE AND RHYTHMS

"Cornbread" is also a password of admittance into an astonishing number of private clubs. Since just talking about cornbread makes people happy, perhaps it's natural that once the subject's arisen, they keep talking. Spontaneous exclamations and smiles of recognition are followed by a story, usually involving a family member. Sometimes this in turn is followed by a recipe: described, recalled, scribbled on the back of a card or napkin, e-mailed a week or two later. Many of those recipes are here, now. What was once someone's personal cornbread gospel is now ours, and I know that because of that

generosity and good grace, the lives of all concerned are richer.

We share that richness here. Together in this book we'll bite into homemade corn tortillas, hot, pliable, and seductive, straight from the griddle. We will carefully get buttery cast-iron skillets smoking hot, and then pour in the cornbread batter we've made. We'll hear it sizzle invitingly as it hits the hot skillet, and we'll discover and rediscover, after baking, that that instant of contact results in the most amazingly good crisp-crunchy golden brown crust, a revelation and a joy to bite into. We will make the simplest of corn pones, both American- and Colombian-style (the latter are called arepas), their shapes embossed with the loving imprints of the fingers that patted them out. At first bite these may seem plain to us . . . but then we take one more and then another until . . . oh! Where *did* that platter of pones go?

Some of our cornbreads, confetti'd with the Southwestern kick of chiles, will do a quick salsa-merengue in our mouths. We'll find we love this, as we also love the waltz of maple-sweetened cornbread from Vermont, the hip-hop of eggy high-rising Southern spoonbreads, the do-si-do of cornbreads jeweled with fresh corn cut off the cob, and the slow fox-trot of moist pudding-like cornbreads rich with sour cream and canned creamed corn.

We'll taste not only the abundance and rhythms and stories of cornbreads themselves, but the delectable choices about what to eat with them: chilies, stews, hot pots; beans; greens. And then there are the what-to-eat-with-its that actually incorporate cornbread: dishes like Golden Gazpacho (page 266) and Southwestern-Style Cornbread Casserole with Chorizo (page 281). And though, because cornbread is so good, you don't often have leftovers unless you set out to, we'll also investigate what to make with the occasional overflow of this cornbread generosity, such as cornbread dressings and luscious cornbread bread puddings, both sweet and savory.

Breakfast, lunch, and dinner; as an afterschool snack; sweet or savory or neutral; at feasts ranging from Thanksgiving to Kwanzaa, in cities ranging from Bombay to Boston . . . we will discover, bite by bite and recipe by recipe, why and how cornbread is almost always a part of every meal, every occasion, somewhere in the world.

LOVE, HOME, AND HISTORY

I started out knowing I was neither the first nor the last to love cornbread; I also knew that as a writer, I tend to fall in love with my subject. True, *I* was utterly hoodooed by cornbread. But so, I discovered, was almost everyone else. Until I unexpectedly found this out, I had no idea how widespread cornbread's enchantment was. None of the subjects of my previous books, culinary and otherwise, evoked this instant, intense response, this ability to walk right into the lives and stories of others, regardless of their background, nationality, education, or age.

Why, I began asking myself, is cornbread so powerful to so many?

I've pondered this during the almost-six years I've worked on *The Cornbread Gospels*. What I think now is that while there are many answers, the most universal is this: Cornbread is not usually restaurant food. It is rather, as a London Pakistani taxi driver once told me, "a homely food." (Yes, they eat cornbread—with greens—in Pakistan and North India, too. Cornbread-love is a worldwide thing.)

Home. That potent place, both physical and not, from which we all come; for which we all long; which we all try to create, recreate, or imagine; but from which, through circumstances that may be beyond our making or control, we may be exiled. As human beings have always been exiled, right back to Adam and Eve.

Home. If cornbread, even momentarily, takes us back to the home we had, or the home we wish we had had, or the best parts of the home we did have, no wonder it is powerful. No wonder we want to tell our stories. And no wonder cornbread tastes so very good to us, no wonder we love to talk about it almost as much

as we love to eat it. As the writer Betty Fussell says, "Corn breeds its own poets, lunatics, and lovers." And so, of course, does home. When you put the two together, it's compelling.

Cornbread has opened doors I couldn't have imagined. Doors into homes and lives, all over the world. Doors to an arepa factory in the Florida Everglades and the home of a Colombian children's book writer in Vermont; a tortilleria in East Los Angeles; a Hopi reservation in Arizona; a cornbread festival in Tennessee; mills in Rhode Island, Arkansas, North Carolina, and Oregon; to a mail-order tortilla-making supply company in Texas. Doors to the kitchen of an haute resort in Scottsdale, Arizona. Doors to family reunions, church picnics, and potlucks from Mississippi to Maine, Florida to Washington. Doors to literature, history, ethnobotany, and folk culture. Doors to memories, written and oral: *this is the cornbread that Truman Capote grew up eating . . . this is the cornbread that my grandfather*

fixed every Sunday, he was the designated cornbread maker . . . this is the cornbread that my mother was raised on in east Texas and I still think it's the best I ever ate. Doors that opened other doors.

And behind almost every door, a recipe.

How could it be otherwise? No other single food has been the subject of more passionate discussion, on and off the record, than cornbread. Thomas Jefferson, Benjamin Franklin, Frederick Douglass, Henry David Thoreau, and Mark Twain are just a few of those who wrote heatedly about cornbread. No other single food has more purely American historical and cultural connections, from the worship of Mother Corn, the Corn Goddess, by Native Americans, to the survival of the Pilgrims, to the New World's gradual, then vigorous disputation of the Old World's smug insistence that maize was fit only for cattle, to its darker history, that of staple food to those once enslaved in this country. No single food native to America has become more essential to the survival of so many different nationalities around the globe.

Our Cornbread, Now and Forever, Amen

Say "cornbread," with open eyes, heart, mouth, and mind, and you will find it is so inextricably bound with so much that is essential to human life that it leads to everything, everywhere. No other single food

CORN, SPIRIT, AND SUSTENANCE

Most Native Americans knew one staple grain: corn. Corn-and-creation myths abound, varying from tribe to tribe, but all are underlaid by reverence. For Native Americans, the connection between physical and spiritual worlds lay in the connection between human beings and "Mother Corn."

Those who immigrated to America had grown up in a place where wheat was the staple grain. In the New (to them) World, often corn was all that stood between them and starvation, and they were grateful. Yet, this life-saving corn was so very *not wheat;* the way it grew, its taste, its cooking properties were all utterly different. Every bite, no matter how delicious and how essential to survival, reminded them of what they had left. So, along with gratitude, the newcomers also felt that cornbread tasted of homesickness.

But gradually, as newcomers sank their own roots into American soil, as generations of children were born here, the New World became not so new. It became home, and corn became *ours.* With the expansion and settlement of this continent—from south to north, from north to south, and then from east to west—regional variations in cornbread began to spring up. The preexisting local Native American ways with corn, along with regional climate variations and economies, all shaped and flavored the regional cornbreads baked by these new Americans.

Thus corn and cornbread, as it had always been for the Native Americans, became the American taste of home.

that I have come across has remotely this much power.

Cornbread has been good to me. First, every time I make it, I marvel with each bite, astonished yet again by its sheer simple goodness. How could I do otherwise than to share this goodness? People who invite me to potlucks add, "And, oh, would you bring your cornbread?" Innumerable guests at the restaurant I once owned asked, "Will you give me the recipe for this cornbread?" A reader of my cookbooks told me that so deeply enshrined is "my" cornbread as her family's cornbread that her son called home (to Springfield, Missouri), from college in San Francisco, so she could dictate the recipe to him.

I learned to make "my" cornbread from a once-neighbor some thirty-five years ago. Her name was Viola. She was a soft-voiced Southerner living in New York; her skin was so black it had almost a blue cast to it. Hence the quote marks around "my": How could such a recipe be mine, any more than it was hers, or that of the person (mother? grandmother?) who taught it to her? No matter who the *me* is, no one person can truly claim a cornbread as "mine." The recipes, and their main ingredient, go too far back to calculate origin or ownership.

Cornbread belongs to *us*, the human race. And that is the gospel truth.

Now all of this would have been more than privilege enough for me. But this project has given me another gift, which extends into the future.

From now on I will be able to say, "I once wrote a book about cornbread." And then I will get to see those lit-up smiles, and to listen, once again, as the stories, the recipes, and the intimate, particular, personal tellings of the cornbread gospels unfold.

Chapter 1

SOUTHERN CORNBREADS

Soul in a Skillet

N owhere in America are people as passionate, proud, and particular about cornbread as in the South. And though Southerners often disagree region to region as to exactly what constitutes good cornbread, they are generally adamant on two points: 1) Yankees just can't, can*not*, make good cornbread, and 2) their mother/grandmother makes or made the very best cornbread ever. At times Southerners can get downright belligerent. Mark Twain did, (in)famously:

"Perhaps no bread in the world is quite as good as Southern corn bread, and perhaps no bread in the world is quite so bad as the Northern imitation of it." So much are cornbread and the region intertwined that I don't know of a single narrative that takes place in the South, fiction or non, in which you *don't* come across characters eating, making, serving, or referencing cornbread at least once.

Before we go further, in the interest of full disclosure, my vantage point is this: I was born Yankee, but I spent most of my teenage and adult life in the South. Thus, I love many cornbreads, some Southern *and* some Northern. Too, though there are *general* differences between the two (see pages 34–36), the delicious, contrary cornbread world is filled with exceptions to the rule.

But I can say with certainty that no part of America cares more about cornbread than the South. Cornbread is the South's daily bread, or at least it was until the recent past. And, though it was everyday fare, it was also part of every important Southern occasion: holidays, church picnics, dinners on the grounds, family reunions—cornbread was always present.

(Weddings are the only general exception to this rule, though many a contemporary wedding brunch is graced by a baked casserole of cheese grits or a spoonbread. But other than this, or at weddings during very impoverished times, or at hippie/alternative nuptials, no cornbread.) The ever-present cornbread might be stripped-down and simple, like Truman Capote's Family's (page 13), Sylvia's Ozark (page 18), or Ronni's Appalachian (page 21); or it might rise to great heights (elaborate, soufflé-like spoonbreads, see pages 183–198). But look on the table, and in some form, there it is.

CELEBRATION, SUBSISTENCE

That cornbread is associated with celebration, abundance, and family in the South is indisputable. But look at the whole story of Southern cornbread—complex and rich, if at times less sunny—and you see the best and worst of the South's culture and history. Cornbread in the South speaks of kitchen acumen; the ability to make a great meal from simple ingredients; hospitality, joy, pride, and just plain good eating. But Southern cornbread also tells the story of lack; subsistence in a not-so-very-long-ago time; of stigma, class, race, and shame.

I learned this when, more than twenty-five years ago, I first opened an upscale restaurant in Arkansas with my late husband. The fact that we served, among many other things, cornbread, was a cause of both consternation and wonderment to some local-born-and-bred Ozark Arkansawyers, to whom cornbread was anything *but* white-tablecloth food.

This astonished me only until I thought, "Well, who among us doesn't discount the wonders in our own lives because they are common and everyday to *us*?" Still, I was puzzled and intrigued enough to begin digging more deeply into cornbread's Southern roots. I found a two-sided history, and began to understand a little more.

I hadn't fully realized, at the time when we proudly, and generally to great acclaim, brought forth our Dairy Hollow House Skillet-Sizzled Cornbread (page 12) in the restaurant's bread-baskets, that while cornbread was traditional much-loved Ozark family fare, it was *also* what you ate when the family had no money. Leftover cornbread was what the poor had for breakfast, lunch, and dinner, what the poor kids brought to school in a lunch pail: a line of demarcation.

"It is constantly surprising, this vegetable snobbism," wrote M. F. K. Fisher in *The Art of Eating*. "It is almost universal." But then she went on to describe ". . . corn meal mush and molasses, a dish synonymous to many Americans with poor trash of the pariah-ridden South."

How did cornbread become "synonymous" with those Fisher writes off as "trash"? Go back to slavery times, when cornmeal (far cheaper than wheat flour) comprised the bulk of slave rations. According to one former slave, Louis Hughes, it was eaten so continually that slaves called it "Johnny Constant." (At Christmas, on

"During the terrible winter . . . we almost run out of cornmeal. Mama liked to say, 'Now you can do without a lot of things, but a family can't do without cornmeal. If you run out of meal you don't have any bread and you don't have any mush. And you don't have anything to fry fish in, or squirrels. When the meat runs out, and the taters runs out, the only thing that will keep you going is the cornbread. You can live a long time on bread and collard greens, if you have collard greens. And you can live a long time on bread alone if you have to, despite what the Bible says.'"

—ROBERT MORGAN, *Gap Creek*

the Virginia plantation of his childhood, slaves each received a "gift" of a pint of flour, from which they made a biscuit: "Billy Seldom.")

Frederick Douglass, also born a slave, in Maryland, describes how cornbread was prepared, midday in the field:

The slaves mixed their meal with a little water, to such thickness that a spoon would stand erect in it. After the wood had burned away to coals and ashes, they would place the dough between oak leaves and lay it carefully . . . completely covering it; hence, the bread is called ash cake. The surface of this peculiar bread is covered with ashes, to the depth of a sixteenth part of an inch, and the ashes, certainly, do not make it very grateful to the teeth, nor render it very palatable.

This cake, supplemented only by a little pork, salt herring, and whatever vegetables they could grow when not working the fields, was what most slaves lived on. Their heavily cornmeal-centered diet, monotonous no less than nutritionally bereft, contrasted mightily with the light, buttermilk-rich and egg-leavened cornbreads proudly served at the master's table (invariably prepared by a slave cook). Thus, the roots of cornbread's double history.

CORNBREAD'S CONUNDRUM

So great and divisive an evil as slavery could not stand in a country whose ideals were formulated on freedom. During the Civil War, cornmeal again played a critical but ambiguous role. Along with and part of the horror of enslavement, the slaves lived with monotony, poor nutrition, and the knowledge that corn was all that kept them from starvation. Though free, the soldiers of the Civil War, especially on the Confederate side, also lived on cornmeal: sometimes made into cornbread, sometimes simply cooked in water as porridge or mush, and sometimes eaten raw. "Johnny Reb fought the Yankees for four years on rations composed mainly of cornbread and beef. There were, to be sure, admixtures now and then of field peas . . . of flour, pork, potatoes, rice, molasses, coffee, sugar, and fresh vegetables, though it was for the last that the soldiers always suffered most. But (corn) meal . . . was the staple fare," wrote Bell Irvin Wiley in *The Life of Johnny Reb: The Common Soldier of the Confederacy.*

War and defeat impoverished the South. Postwar reconstruction was a long, slow process. The South, at least certain pockets of it, continued to live close to the bone for a long, long time, even after the ghosts of the Civil War had faded to a whisper elsewhere in the country. When I first moved to the Ozarks, in 1972, a lot of the older natives were still alive. One, who'd been young in the late 1920s, told me that when the Depression hit seventy-some years after the end of the Civil War, "Hell, we didn't know the difference . . . we'd *always* been depressed."

But here's the thing—the magic of the South, human resilience, and, yes, cornbread— he didn't sound in the least depressed in the way we use the word now. He sounded *proud*, as so often do those who survive hard times.

Slowly, cornbread's character in the South began to change. Gradually, times began to get better, and cornbread's associations began to become positive. As cornbread became a *chosen* food, not just the only option, its inherent goodness shone through. It became enriched with the occasional egg or fat or buttermilk; other dishes became available to eat *with* it, and it was not eaten raw, nor baked in leaves and ash, but cooked in a skillet, in an oven. The rough past began to glow. Cornbread was good, and so was pride in the accomplishment of not only surviving, but surviving well, despite long odds. In 1988, Bob Lancaster wrote in the *Arkansas Times* that Southerners could "make a filling, gratifying supper out of cornbread and not much else. Forgive the nostalgia, but my mother did it at least a thousand times—and I didn't come along until after the hard times. Cornbread and sweet milk—with a green onion on the side in season. If I had thought about it, which I don't recall ever having done, I would have supposed that this was a meal for the privileged rather than the poor, and I would have been right."

He would have been, but "a meal for the privileged *and* the poor" is closer to the truth. When diners at Dairy Hollow House folded back the napkin lining the restaurant breadbasket and found cornbread, there were almost always audible cries of delight, and cornbread stories. (This was one of the moments at which, daily, I began to hear over and over the magic words I began this book with: "Cornbread? I love cornbread!") Gradually, I believe, the locals who had at first scoffed at us for serving so homey a food in a high-priced restaurant came to see the point. Something

like: *Yes, this is what we eat, and people are coming here to visit our place, to see what makes us us. Yes, cornbread's what you serve your people, but it's more than good enough for those high-falutin' strangers, too . . . probably a hell of a lot better than what they got at home. Imagine them not knowing cornbread! They finally have sense to appreciate what* we *knew all along!*

What we eat develops from the physical and human environments, an inextricable convergence. Every bite, whether we know it or not, is a word in the ongoing story of the world: place, people who live there, choice, accident, history—good and bad, easy and hard. That's life; that's food. Love, pride, strong opinions; sustenance, survival; celebration, war and peace, division and healing: this is the true delicious conundrum and communion in every satisfying bite of Southern cornbread, one universal telling of the cornbread gospel.

Dairy Hollow House Skillet-Sizzled Cornbread

MAKES 8 WEDGES

This is the cornbread I served when I owned and ran Dairy Hollow House; it was its single most requested recipe. It is the first Southern food I ever learned to fix and the one that started me on my cornbread journey. I learned how to make it in the Fort Greene section of Brooklyn, New York, in 1969, when I was very young and living in a brownstone with seven other people. Viola, the soft-spoken lady friend of a kind neighbor, taught it to me. Viola was from Georgia, and it was she who initiated me into baking cornbread in an already-hot skillet.

I've served this cornbread to a president (Bill Clinton) and a princess (Princess Elizabeth of Yugoslavia). Countless people have told me it's become their house cornbread and signature dish—the one they take to potlucks and serve to company. While I love cornbreads of all kinds, I come back to this one over, and over, again.

Vegetable oil cooking spray
1 cup unbleached white flour
1 cup stone-ground yellow cornmeal
1 tablespoon baking powder
1/4 teaspoon salt
1/4 teaspoon baking soda
1 1/4 cups buttermilk
2 tablespoons sugar
1 egg
1/4 cup mild vegetable oil
2 tablespoons butter, or
    mild vegetable oil

1. Preheat the oven to 375°F. Spray a 10-inch cast-iron skillet with oil and set aside.

2. Sift together the flour, cornmeal, baking powder, and salt into a medium bowl.

3. In a smaller bowl, stir the baking soda into the buttermilk. Whisk in the sugar, egg, and the 1/4 cup oil.

4. Put the prepared skillet over medium heat, add the butter, and heat until the butter melts and is just starting to sizzle. Tilt the pan to coat the sides and bottom.

5. Pour the wet ingredients into the dry and combine them quickly, using as few strokes as possible. Scrape the batter into the prepared pan and bake the cornbread until it is golden brown, about 20 minutes. Let cool for a few moments, and slice into wedges to serve.

·M·E·N·U·

DINNER AT THE INN: DAIRY HOLLOW HOUSE DAYS

Oven-Roasted Shiitake Mushrooms with Garlic and Coarse Salt

*

Pumpkin Bisque or Gumbo

*

BREADBASKET:

Dairy Hollow House Skillet-Sizzled Cornbread

Glazed Maple Oatmeal Cornmeal Rolls (page 176)

*

Butter * Blackberry Preserves

*

Slaw of Carrots and Red and Green Cabbage, with Curried Vinaigrette

*

Roasted Chicken, Herb-Stuffed Trout, or Trio of Stuffed Vegetables

*

Roasted Potatoes, Carrots, and Onions * Slow-Cooked Green Beans with Cherry Tomatoes and Olive Oil

*

Chocolate Torte, or Mixed Sorbets

TRUMAN CAPOTE'S FAMILY'S CORNBREAD

MAKES 8 WEDGES

Everything about this straight-up cornbread—not sweet, not fancy but for its two eggs—points to it being an early creation, not far from sustenance. For that, maybe because of that, it has a purity that is hard to beat, as well as a winning, light texture.

This is adapted from the recipe of Sook Faulk, who gave it, and other family recipes, to her niece Marie Rudisill (Truman Capote's aunt) in 1946, with "the understanding that [she] would share them with Truman Capote, [her] sister's child, who had been brought up in Sook's hometown, Monroeville, Alabama."

1 tablespoon butter or bacon drippings

2 eggs

2 cups buttermilk

1 teaspoon sugar

1 teaspoon salt

1 teaspoon baking soda

2 cups stone-ground white cornmeal

1. Preheat the oven to 450°F. Place the butter or drippings in a 10-inch cast-iron skillet, and place it in the oven.

2. Combine the eggs and buttermilk in a small bowl or measuring cup, whisking together well with a fork.

3. In a medium bowl, combine the sugar, salt, baking soda, and cornmeal, stirring well to combine.

4. Stir the egg mixture into the dry ingredients, beating just until the dry ingredients are moistened, no more.

5. Pull the skillet from the oven. It should be good and hot, with the fat sizzling. Swirl the pan to coat it. Quickly transfer the batter to the hot skillet and return the skillet to the oven.

6. Bake until browned and pulling away from the skillet, 20 to 25 minutes. Serve, hot, in wedges from the pan.

"PERFECT" NEW SOUTH-STYLE CORNBREAD

MAKES 6 THIN WEDGES

P am Anderson was at one time the executive editor of *Cook's Illustrated,* the magazine that fanatically tests every recipe, and every assumption about that recipe, countless times. In 1998, she published a book called *The Perfect Recipe.* I was curious to see her take on cornbread, since she'd tried using every possible variety of cornmeal, a wide range of fats and cooking methods, and liquids from sour cream to sweet milk to buttermilk.

I've adapted her favorite recipe here. Like a spoonbread, it calls for saturating the cornmeal with boiling water before mixing it into a very simple batter. The method gives this bread the simple, straight-up wholesomeness of a pure Southern cornbread, but with a moister crumb.

Vegetable oil cooking spray
1 tablespoon butter

1 cup stone-ground yellow cornmeal

⅓ cup boiling water

1 teaspoon sugar

½ teaspoon salt

1 teaspoon baking powder

¼ teaspoon baking soda

¾ cup buttermilk

1 egg

1. Preheat the oven to 450°F. Spray a 10-inch cast-iron skillet with the oil, add the butter, and place the skillet in the oven.

2. Place ⅓ cup of the cornmeal in a small, heat-proof bowl and pour the boiling water over it, stirring well with a fork.

3. Combine the remaining ⅔ cup cornmeal with the sugar, salt, baking powder, and baking soda in a medium bowl.

4. Whisk the buttermilk into the moistened cornmeal, then add the egg, beating well. Combine the wet and dry mixtures, stirring until not quite blended.

5. Take the by-now-very-hot skillet from the oven and pour the melted butter from the skillet into the batter. Stir a few times, until the ingredients are blended, and pour the batter into the hot buttery skillet.

6. Immediately return the skillet to the oven. Bake the cornbread until it is golden and quite crusty, about 20 minutes. It will pull away from the edges of the skillet more

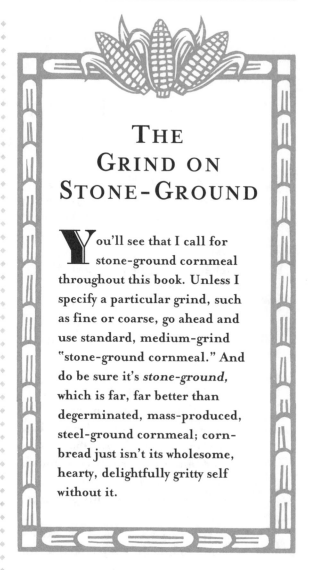

THE GRIND ON STONE-GROUND

You'll see that I call for stone-ground cornmeal throughout this book. Unless I specify a particular grind, such as fine or coarse, go ahead and use standard, medium-grind "stone-ground cornmeal." And do be sure it's *stone-ground,* which is far, far better than degerminated, mass-produced, steel-ground cornmeal; cornbread just isn't its wholesome, hearty, delightfully gritty self without it.

than is usual. Turn the cornbread out on a rack, let it cool for 5 minutes, and then serve, still warm.

How to Season
a Cast-Iron Skillet

A cast-iron skillet, properly seasoned, plays a major role in the preparation of the cornbreads in this chapter. What's more, it is as much a part of every working kitchen as is a good, sharp chef's knife. If you lack either, please remedy the situation at once.

A seasoned cast-iron skillet is solid black, with a smooth, dully shining surface that is not quite but almost nonstick. You might inherit one. You might find one in ideal shape at a flea market or yard sale. But you might have to buy a new one, or an old one that has rusted, and in these cases you *must* season it by following a process I am about to describe. This prepares it for use.

Never use a new cast-iron skillet (or an old one with rust spots) without first seasoning it! Seasoning seals, smooths, and finishes the straight-from-the-factory cast iron and brings about the natural, (mostly) nonstick cooking surface. Seasoning also prevents rust and assures that foods cooked in the pan will not react (or will react very little) to the iron—no discoloration or metallic taste.

Of course, even if you follow the process exactly, your skillet will not at first have the perfect, dull-shiny smooth black surface you may recall from your grandmother's kitchen. It takes not only seasoning, but repeated use over time, to get your cast-iron skillet just right. But it will go from gray, to brown, to deeper brown, and eventually become its own beautiful black self. This is an ongoing process.

Here we go. You'll need to have some solid vegetable shortening, such as Crisco, on hand.

1. Remove any labels from your new skillet (or other cast-iron cookware). Then wash the skillet in hot, soapy water, scrubbing it vigorously with a stiff brush or scrubbie.

2. Rinse it, and dry it out completely.

3. Melt a few tablespoons of vegetable shortening in a small pan, and let it cool slightly. Dip a paper towel in the melted shortening and use it to wipe the entire surface of the cookware, inside and out, top and bottom. Rub the shortening into all these surfaces, coating the pan lightly but thoroughly.

4. Line the lower rack of your oven with aluminum foil (this will catch any dripping shortening). Preheat the oven to 350°F.

5. Place the skillet upside down on the upper oven rack, and bake it for one hour.

6. Turn the oven off, but let the cookware cool gradually inside before removing it from the oven.

Once your skillet has been seasoned, never wash it in a dishwasher. You can generally keep it clean with nothing more than hot water and a scrubbie or brush, but if you like, you can use a little dish liquid in the hot water. Just be sure to rinse it thoroughly, and above all, dry it well, after washing. After it's dry, give it a quick spray or mini-pour of vegetable oil (use oil, not shortening, for maintenance) and rub that in with a paper towel. This will keep your skillet increasingly happy.

If your skillet ever seems *unhappy* (that is, if it gets rusty, smells metallic, or imparts a metallic taste), don't worry. Just give it a good wash and scrub with soap and hot water, scouring off any rust, and season it again.

Cast iron likes to be stored in a cool, dry place where there is some air circulation. Mine hangs from hooks. Store the lid separately. Or, if space is at a premium, put a folded paper towel between the lid and the skillet, which allows some air circulation.

Sylvia's Ozark Cornbread

MAKES 8 WEDGES

Sylvia Teague, who lived in Eureka Springs for many years, was a recipe taster on my previous cookbook, *Passionate Vegetarian*. Friend and all-around trouper extraordinaire with an amazingly perspicacious palate, she was large-boned, rather quiet, and serious until you knew her—then: ribald, sly, wry, dry, and just uproarious.

This delicious, ultra–low-fat buttermilk cornbread, very easy, was the Teague family cornbread for decades—a straightforward, very tasty plain formula. This is so healthful and quick to make that you could eat it daily—as Ozark natives did (with bacon fat instead of oil) for generations.

Vegetable oil cooking spray

1 tablespoon butter

2 cups stone-ground yellow cornmeal

1 teaspoon baking soda

1 teaspoon salt

2 cups buttermilk, preferably measured into a 4-cup measure

2 eggs

1 tablespoon mild vegetable oil

1. Preheat the oven to 400°F.

2. Spray a 10-inch cast-iron skillet with oil, add the butter, and put it into the oven to heat. Meanwhile, stir together the cornmeal, baking soda, and salt in a medium bowl.

3. In a smaller bowl, or in the 4-cup measure, beat the buttermilk with the eggs and oil.

4. Combine the two mixtures. As always, be careful not to overbeat, stirring until wet and dry are just combined.

5. Scrape the batter into the hot skillet and bake the cornbread until it is golden brown and crusty at the edges, 23 to 27 minutes. Serve hot, in wedges.

TWO-PART HOMINY

Incomprehensibly, to me and my late friend Sylvia Teague, some people don't *like* playing with words. Not our problem, as this e-mail exchange, while I was working on this book, illustrates.

Dragon:
You write that you are "deep in cornland." If you work too long, do you flake out . . . does your voice get husky? Do you feel each day is just back to the same old grind, or is this what you were born and bre(a)d for? Tell: I'm all ears.

Now, I'm sure you're putting Chex by each fact, and avoiding syrupy adjectives. You're not stalking around the house at night, are you? No, you've got too much grit to fritter away your time like that.

In peace and hominy, love,
S.

Sylvia,
I Karo for you, deeply . . . there is more than a kernel of truth to this. I look at you, your hair like silk, my heart goes flap, Jack!, and I turn to mush. You are one hot tamale! Forgive this cobbled-together message, but I want you to know I took a pol(l)'n'ten outta 'leven people think it would be amaizeing if you came to town more often. Let me pop the question: when?

I masa you, my friend.
Love,
CD

LEORA'S SWEET MILK-BUTTERMILK CORNBREAD

MAKES 8 WEDGES

During one of the cooking classes I taught at the Biltmore Winery and Estate in North Carolina—at which I demo'd the Dairy Hollow House Skillet-Sizzled Cornbread (page 12) and Ronni's Appalachian Cornbread (opposite)—I mentioned being at work on this book. After class, a woman named Virginia Brown came up to me and said, "You know, this really is good cornbread, just about as good as my grandmother Leora's . . . I'll e-mail it to you." And she did. Thanks, Virginia!

Though the original was baked in a 10-by-16-inch glass baking dish, I prefer to bake it in a skillet.

> Vegetable oil cooking spray
> 1 cup stone-ground white cornmeal
> 1/2 cup unbleached white flour
> 1 1/4 teaspoons baking powder
> 1/4 teaspoon baking soda
> 1/4 teaspoon salt
> 1 1/2 teaspoons sugar
> 2 tablespoons butter
> 1 cup milk
> 1 cup buttermilk
> 1 egg
> 3 tablespoons mild vegetable oil

1. Preheat the oven to 425°F. Spray a 10-inch cast-iron skillet with oil and set aside.

2. Stir all the dry ingredients together in a large bowl, combining them well. Set aside.

3. Now, add the butter to the prepared skillet and put it in the oven, to heat the skillet and melt the butter. Work quickly from here on out; you don't want the butter to burn.

4. Whisk together the wet ingredients in a medium bowl. With as few strokes as possible, combine the wet and dry ingredients.

5. Remove the hot buttery skillet from the oven. Transfer the batter into the hot buttery skillet. Return the hot buttery now-filled-with-batter skillet to the oven.

6. Bake the cornbread until it is barely browned, 25 to 30 minutes. Serve, hot, in wedges from the pan.

Ronni's Appalachian Cornbread

MAKES 8 WEDGES

This is probably my favorite of the "plain" cornbreads. It's the stripped-down cornbread my friend Ronni Lundy, born in Corbin, Kentucky, grew up eating. Ronni is the author of *Shuck Beans, Stack Cakes, and Honest Fried Chicken*, in which this recipe first appeared.

When I told her I was writing a book about cornbread, Ronni sniffed haughtily. "Well," she said, with disdain, "*I* could write a book about cornbread. It would only be one page long, however."

¼ cup butter or bacon drippings

2 cups fine stone-ground white cornmeal

1 teaspoon salt

½ teaspoon baking soda

½ teaspoon baking powder

1 egg

1½ cups buttermilk

1. Preheat the oven to 450°F.

2. Place the butter or drippings in a 10-inch cast-iron skillet and pop the skillet in the oven to heat.

3. Combine the dry ingredients in a large bowl. In a small bowl, beat together the egg and buttermilk. Add the wet mixture to the dry, using the absolute minimum number of strokes needed to moisten dry with wet.

4. Remove the hot skillet from the oven and swirl it around so the butter or drippings coat the bottom and lower sides of the skillet. Then pour the remainder of the hot butter or drippings into the batter, and stir a couple of times.

5. Turn the batter into the hot skillet, put the skillet back into the oven, and bake the cornbread until it is golden brown, 20 to 25 minutes. Serve, hot, in wedges from the pan.

> "At a little distance stood Mr. Lee's mill, where the people came in large numbers to get their corn ground. I can never tell the many things thought and felt, as I sat on the bank, and watched the mill and the turning of its ponderous wheel."
>
> —FREDERICK DOUGLASS, *My Bondage and My Freedom*

Nora's Memaw's Alabama Cornbread

MAKES 6 THIN SQUARES

"Sure, you can use my grandma's cornbread in your book," said my friend Nora, an Atlanta freelance writer, who grew up on and off with her grandparents in a small town about an hour outside of Birmingham. "But you have to write down *exactly* how you do it. And no last name; very few of my friends even know I cook, and I don't really—just my memaw's cornbread." I wrote it down faithfully, but Nora made a few disclaimers: "Well, *she* used to make it not *quite* this way. She used to use bacon fat when I was a kid, but I can't bring myself to, and lately, even she's started using oil."

Vegetable oil cooking spray
1 cup stone-ground white cornmeal
1/2 cup unbleached white flour
1 1/2 teaspoons baking powder
1/2 teaspoon baking soda
1/2 teaspoon salt
1 1/2 teaspoons sugar

1 cup milk
1/2 cup buttermilk
1 egg
1/4 cup mild vegetable oil
Butter, for serving (optional)

1. Preheat the oven to 450°F. Spray a 10-by-16-inch baking dish ("Memaw always used glass") with oil.

2. Combine the dry ingredients in a large bowl, whisking or stirring well to mix. In a small bowl, beat together the milk, buttermilk, egg, and oil. Add the wet mixture to the dry, using the absolute minimum number of strokes needed to moisten dry with wet.

3. Transfer the batter to the prepared baking dish and bake it until the top of the cornbread is golden brown and springs back when touched, about 20 minutes. If it's not nicely brown after 20 minutes, transfer it to the top rack of the oven and give it 5 more minutes.

4. Serve, hot from the pan if possible, with butter.

Patsy Bruce's Tennessee Cornbread

MAKES 8 LARGE WEDGES

This cornbread, like many Southern cornbreads, is baked in a skillet and encorporates buttermilk. But here the resemblance ends. This is the cornbread songwriter Patsy Bruce ("Mamas Don't Let Your Babies Grow Up to Be Cowboys" is one of hers) grew up eating. It's quite eggy, which gives it almost a spoonbread-like character. And it is *fast*! Self-rising flour and self-rising cornmeal (both of which are already salted and leavened) are used, so the number of ingredients is reduced, hence prep time is lessened.

P.S. If you, like me, prefer stone-ground meals, try the substitute for self-rising cornmeal in the Pantry.

¼ cup mild vegetable oil

½ cup self-rising flour

1½ cups self-rising cornmeal (see Pantry, page 350)

3 eggs

2 cups buttermilk

"We need real corn bread. We need a homemade tortilla. May we, with powerful spirits, diminish the force of fast food. Give victory to the forces that fight with the forces that will put man-made genes into the food that has until the last decade been sanctified by the breath of the Holy Spirit of the Holy Universe of Soft Green Fields. Amen, and amen."

"Amen," says Aunt Lil.

"That was a long blessing," says Mrs. Cochran. "I like that part about corn bread. I like anything about corn bread. They've completely ruint corn bread. I had nineteen recipes for corn bread that came out of the *Farmers' Almanac.*"

—CLYDE EDGERTON, *Lunch at the Piccadilly*

I. Preheat the oven to 500°F.

2. Place half of the oil in a 12-inch cast-iron skillet and the other half in a large bowl. Put the skillet on the stove, over medium heat.

3. Combine the flour and cornmeal well in a medium bowl and set aside. To the oil in the large bowl, add the eggs and beat well. Add the buttermilk and stir in the dry mixture until nearly smooth. The batter will be thinner than usual for cornbread, more like the consistency of pancake batter.

4. Pour the batter into the hot oiled skillet, and pop the skillet into the oven. Bake the cornbread until it is brown and crusty, 15 to 20 minutes.

LISA CONE'S MAMA'S CORNBREAD

MAKES 8 WEDGES

Mary Cone was at various times in her life a dirt-poor east-Texas Depression-era child, a flirtatious and feisty young woman, a mother, and a businesswoman. By the time I knew her, she was an old lady, a compulsive mystery reader and crossword addict. She was also helping out and being helped by my friend, her daughter Lisa, at Waterfall Hollow Farm in Berryville, Arkansas, the family's pasture-finished natural beef business (www.waterfallhollowfarm.com).

The last time I visited the farm, which was also the last time I saw Mary, she wrote out for me the cornbread recipe she had grown up on. It is thin and crisp, ideal for crumbling into stews, chilies, and buttermilk.

1 cup stone-ground white cornmeal
1/2 teaspoon baking soda
1/4 teaspoon salt
1 egg
1 cup buttermilk
2 tablespoons mild vegetable oil

1. Preheat the oven to 450°F.

2. Quickly combine all ingredients except the oil in a large bowl, whisking well.

3. Put the oil in a 10-inch cast-iron skillet and heat the skillet, either on top of the stove or in the oven. When the skillet is good and hot ("the oil should be smoking," Lisa told me), pour in the batter.

4. Now, here's the unusual part: Let the poured-in batter sit in the skillet for 20 minutes on a heat-proof surface. Then, transfer the skillet to the oven and bake the cornbread until it is brown and crusty, 20 to 25 minutes.

WHITE RIVER CORNBREAD

MAKES 8 THIN WEDGES

Arkansas has several distinct bio-regions. Across the state from the hilly Ozarks (in Arkansas's northwest corner), to the east and a bit to the south, are the flat, moist lands just above the Mississippi Delta. In 1980, the Arkansas Symphony Guild produced a fund-raising cookbook called *Concerts from the Kitchen,* which contained "Cornbread for Georgetown, Arkansas." This tiny community (present population 129; population in 1980, 75) is on the White River. "This recipe originated with an old cook employed on a nearby plantation," noted the book's author, Marilyn Criner. The original recipe called for "fat," presumably bacon drippings, but I use butter.

> **2 tablespoons butter, mild vegetable oil, or bacon drippings**
>
> **1 cup stone-ground white cornmeal**
>
> **2 tablespoons unbleached white flour**
>
> **¼ teaspoon baking soda**
>
> **1 teaspoon baking powder**
>
> **½ teaspoon salt**
>
> **2 eggs**
>
> **1 cup buttermilk**

1. Preheat the oven to 425°F. Place the butter in a 10-inch cast-iron skillet and place the skillet in the oven.

2. Combine the cornmeal, flour, baking soda, baking powder, and salt in a large heat-proof bowl and stir well.

3. Beat the eggs and buttermilk together in a medium bowl. Add them to the dry mixture and whisk a few times.

AN EXCELLENT PROVIDER

Every part of the corn plant—the second most plentiful cereal grown on earth for human consumption—serves us in some way. The husks of corn are traditionally used in making tamales, the kernels for food, the stalks for cattle and hog food (silage), and the silks for medicinal tea. You can fry in corn (corn oil), bake with it (cornmeal, of course), snack on it (popcorn, tortilla chips), sweeten with it (corn syrup), thicken with it (cornstarch),

and get drunk on it (bourbon).

One cup of raw white corn has about 130 calories, 2 grams of fat, 5 grams of protein, 29 grams of carbohydrate, and 4 grams of fiber, with no cholesterol. Corn is also rich in the antioxidants lutein and zeaxanthin, which are associated specifically with eye health, as well as a lowered risk of many chronic diseases. And corn oil is high in the essential fatty acid linoleic acid, as well as vitamin E.

4. Carefully remove the hot skillet from the oven. The butter should be smoking. (If it isn't smoking yet, continue heating it on the stove until it is.) Pour about half of the hot butter from the skillet into the bowl containing the batter. Set the skillet down, whisk the batter just until the ingredients are combined, and immediately pour it into the hot skillet.

5. Return the skillet to the oven and bake the cornbread until it is firm to the touch but not brown on top, 10 to 15 minutes.

6. Turn the oven to broil and broil the cornbread for a few minutes, watching closely, just enough to brown the top slightly.

7. Serve hot, cut into wedges.

MISSISSIPPI-TENNESSEE DELTA-STYLE CORNBREAD

MAKES 8 WEDGES

David Johnston, an East-Tennessean and Dairy Hollow guest, disapproved of our cornbread, although he was highly cordial about everything else. "Notice that *my* recipe does *not* call for sugar," he noted on the top of the file card he sent me after he returned home. Then, echoing Mark Twain's famous line, he added, *"Real* cornbread does *not* contain sugar."

If you want to make cornbread like they do it in the Delta, use bacon drippings, though I myself go for half oil, half butter.

Vegetable oil cooking spray

1/4 cup mild vegetable oil, melted butter, or bacon drippings

2 cups self-rising cornmeal (see Pantry, page 350)

1 1/2 cups milk

1 egg

1. Preheat the oven to 350°F.

2. Spray a 10-inch cast-iron skillet with oil and place 2 tablespoons of the fat of your choice in it. Put the skillet in the oven to get good and hot. Let it stay there a couple of minutes before you start mixing the batter, which is so quick to put together you need to give the skillet a head start.

3. While the skillet heats, combine the self-rising cornmeal, milk, egg, and the remaining 2 tablespoons of fat in a medium bowl. Don't overbeat.

4. When the oil and skillet are both smoking-hot, remove the skillet from the oven and pour in the batter.

5. Return the skillet to the oven and bake the cornbread for 20 minutes, then crank the heat to Broil until the bread is extra crusty and deeply golden on top, 1 to 2 minutes.

"Mrs. Pickett smoked a lipstick-stained cigarette between bites of cornbread and butterbeans. She'd stare at me and shake her head as if confused. 'You're the skinniest thing I've ever laid eyes on; you better eat up 'em butterbeans, girl.'"

—BARBARA ROBINETTE MOSS,
Change Me Into Zeus's Daughter

TWO GRANDMAS' CREAMED CORN CORNBREAD

MAKES 8 WEDGES

This is adapted from a recipe from the excellent, story-rich *Kwanzaa: an African-American Celebration of Culture and Cooking,* by Eric V. Copage. Typical of many African American cornbreads, it's a little sweet and extremely moist. Creamed corn gives it a comforting pudding-like texture.

Vegetable oil cooking spray
¼ cup (½ stick) butter
1 cup stone-ground yellow cornmeal
¾ cup unbleached white flour
2 tablespoons sugar
1 tablespoon plus 1 teaspoon baking powder
½ teaspoon salt
1 cup canned creamed corn (see Pantry, page 351)
1 cup milk
1 egg

1. Preheat the oven to 450°F. Spray a 9-inch round cake pan with oil and add half of the butter. Put the pan in the oven to let it get very hot.

2. Meanwhile, combine the cornmeal, flour, and sugar in a medium heat-proof bowl, then sift in the baking powder and salt.

3. Whisk together the creamed corn, milk, and egg in a small bowl.

4. Add the wet mixture to the dry, stirring until all is combined but taking care not to overbeat.

5. By now your pan should be nice and hot. Remove it from the oven, lowering the oven temperature to 400°F. Carefully pour about half of the by-now-melted butter from the hot pan into the batter. Stir the batter a couple of times, and then pour it into the hot pan.

6. Bake until the cornbread is golden brown, 20 to 25 minutes. Remove the cornbread from the oven and let it stand for 15 minutes before serving.

VARIATION:
"ALL THAT JAZZ" SOUL FOOD VEGAN CORNBREAD

I met a lovely dreadlocked young woman selling vegetarian food from a booth at the Eighth Annual Central Avenue Jazz Festival in Los Angeles. She was kind enough to give me this recipe, which, she explained, is "Just like my grandma's but vegan." Follow the recipe above, but instead of the egg use reconstituted egg replacer, either homemade (see Eggscellence, page 352) or commercial, to equal one egg; instead of the 1 cup dairy milk use ¾ cup soy milk; and instead of the butter use 5 tablespoons (¼ cup plus 1 tablespoon) canola oil or vegan margarine. Add an extra 2 tablespoons canned creamed corn (see Pantry, page 351).

WENONAH FAY'S MAMA'S "PLAIN BREAD" (CORN PONE)

MAKES EIGHT 2- TO-3-INCH PONES

The cornbread of childhood stays with a person a long time. Wenonah Fay Holl, my good old friend who now lives in Little Rock, grew up on and with the following, in Conway, Arkansas. But this stripped-down bread had its precursor in Indian days, and it was a constant for blacks during slavery times. In some places it was known as ashcake and hoecake; and, traveling north and east, it was johnnycake or jonnycake (sometimes as elaborate as the preceding recipes, other times just as simple as what follows). But it was always Mama's Plain Bread in Wenonah Fay's family, and the individual cakes were pones.

"This was a fixture of my growing-up years," Wenonah Fay wrote me (she was eighty-seven at the time). "There was not much to it but meal and boiling water. And this is the only time Mama used *white* cornmeal. It was made into little pones, about an inch thick and a size that would fit nicely in the palm of her hand, with the prints of her fingers on top. The pones were baked in a HOT oven, and I never remember having them except when we had cabbage. But we had cabbage fairly often. And her cabbage was so good . . . steamed crispy fresh. And the pones served hot from the oven with lots of butter . . . oh, my!"

"Your choice of fat," the recipe tells you. This could be butter, mild vegetable oil, or bacon drippings. Most probably the Native American precursor would have been something like bear fat.

And the cornmeal really ought to be white. Just ask Wenonah Fay.

Vegetable oil cooking spray

About 2 cups boiling water

2 cups stone-ground cornmeal, preferably white

1 teaspoon salt

1 tablespoon butter, mild vegetable oil, or bacon drippings

Butter, for serving (optional)

Skillet-Fried Cabbage (page 297), for serving (optional)

1. Preheat the oven to 375°F. Spray a baking sheet with oil.

2. Pour the boiling water over the remaining ingredients in a heat-proof bowl, and let the mixture stand for 5 to 10 minutes—long enough so the cornmeal can soften slightly, plus cool enough so that you can handle it.

3. Now, you'll want to shape it into small, patty-like cakes, about 2 to 3 inches round and ⅓ to ¾ inch thick. Their consistency will not be smooth and seamless but rather rough and uneven. It's possible you might need to add another tablespoon or so of boiling water to achieve this.

4. Place the pones on the prepared sheet. Then, with a wet hand, press your three middle fingers across the top of each pone, leaving three little indentations . . . a love note or valentine to those who will eat them.

5. Bake until golden brown, 12 to 15 minutes. Serve hot, with butter and skillet-fried cabbage, if desired.

JESSICA HARRIS'S HERBED CORNBREAD

MAKES 9 SQUARES

In her terrific book *A Kwanzaa Keepsake*, Jessica Harris points out that, like tomatoes and peppers, corn and cornmeal are New World additions to the traditional African diet. However, she says, they "have been so gleefully adopted that it is virtually impossible to think of the cooking of the African Atlantic world without them." This excellent cornbread, adapted from hers, features an accent of thyme and uses canned or frozen corn.

Vegetable oil cooking spray

¾ cup stone-ground yellow cornmeal

¼ cup unbleached flour

2 tablespoons sugar

1 tablespoon baking powder

½ teaspoon salt

1 teaspoon dried thyme leaves, crumbled between the fingertips

⅓ cup milk

2 teaspoons to 1 tablespoon finely chopped pickled jalapeño peppers

1 egg

3 tablespoons butter, melted

¼ cup corn kernels, cut from 1 ear of fresh corn (see Shuck and Jive, page 49); or frozen corn kernels, measured and defrosted; or canned, very well-drained

1. Preheat the oven to 425°F. Spray an 8-inch square baking pan, preferably glass or glazed ceramic, with oil.

2. Combine the cornmeal, flour, and sugar in a large bowl, and sift in the baking powder and salt.

3. Whisk together the thyme, milk, jalapeños, egg, and melted butter in a smaller bowl. Stir into the dry ingredients gently so that the mixture is thoroughly moistened, but don't overbeat it. Stir in the corn kernels, distributing them evenly throughout the batter.

4. Transfer the batter into the prepared pan, place it in the oven, and bake until the top is lightly browned and a toothpick comes out clean when inserted into the middle, about 20 minutes. Serve hot.

"If God had meant for cornbread to have sugar in it, he'd have called it cake." —MARK TWAIN

CORNBREAD AT KWANZAA

Invented in 1966, Kwanzaa is an African American holiday held annually for seven days, beginning each December twenty-sixth. It was started by the often-controversial Ron Karenga, a "cultural nationalist" who served as chair of the Department of Black Studies at California State University at Long Beach from 1987 to 2002 and still teaches there. Part of the movement toward reclaiming and celebrating black identity, in turn part of the Civil Rights and freedom movement, Kwanzaa ("first fruits of the harvest" in Swahili) was created at one of the crests of this ongoing movement's power, vitality, and energy. Though it was Karenga's conscious ideological attempt to integrate the diversity of African roots with the need for unity and shared identity, in the nearly forty years that Kwanzaa has been in existence, it has taken on a vigorous life of its own, and is now celebrated by more than thirteen million people worldwide.

Rooted in the first-fruits and harvest festivals that are part of every agrarian culture, and that have been part of African civilization since the days of ancient Egypt and Nubia, Kwanzaa today is family-oriented and often is observed in addition to religious holidays. Like many celebrations that occur around the time of the winter solstice, the year's shortest day, Kwanzaa punctuates the pending gradual return of daylight with symbolic and literal illumination. (The Ashanti say, beautifully, that solstice is "when the edges of the year meet.")

On each of the holiday's seven days, a family member lights a candle from the *kinara,* a seven-branched candelabra, and the family talks about one of seven principles of African American unity. The celebration culminates on December thirty-first with the *Karamu,* a feast. In America, this abundance of good food often includes not only African preparations, but traditional dishes from the Caribbean, South America, North America . . . wherever enslaved Africans were taken. Many African Americans incorporate Southern dishes into their feasts, because, as Stephen Johnson of Oakland, California, a longtime devotee of the holiday, explained to the *Pittsburgh Review-Tribune,* "We're of African descent, but a lot of us don't cook African food because it hasn't been passed on to us the way the Southern food has been passed on to us." Such pass-on dishes include rice and black-eyed peas, collard greens, fried okra, biscuits with coconut and/or sesame seeds, and sweet potato pie. All are popular at Kwanzaa feasts, and they might accompany an African dish like vegetable mafé, a very spicy vegetable stew with a peanut butter and tomato sauce. And of course, cornbread's appearance is essential.

· M · E · N · U ·

AN ABUNDANT KWANZAA KARAMU

Salad of Marinated Black-Eyed Peas
*

Greens, Old South Style or Greens, New South Style (pages 290 and 293)
*

Baked Catfish, Fried Chicken, and/or "Chicken-Fried" Tofu
*

Vegetable Mafé (page 317) over Cooked Millet or Cornmeal Mush
*

Candied Sweet Potatoes or Fried Plantains
*

Two Grandmas' Creamed Corn Cornbread (page 28)
*

Jessica Harris's Herbed Cornbread (page 31)
*

Sesame-Coconut Cornmeal Biscuits for Kwanzaa (page 153)
*

Fresh Fruit in Season

Just What, *Exactly,* Is the Difference Between Southern and Northern Cornbreads?

As we prepare to leave the South, passionate about proper cornbread ingredients and technique to the point of near-fanaticism and head to the North, also cornbread-loving but far more open to variations on a theme, it's worth looking more closely at the as-a-rules of basic Southern and Northern techniques and ingredients.

Just remember . . . every rule has an exception, as you'll see.

THE RULE: CORNMEAL AND/OR FLOUR. *Southern* cornbreads often use all cornmeal or mostly cornmeal with just a tiny amount of flour (sometimes as little as a tablespoon), white cornmeal more often than yellow. *Northern* cornbreads generally use half flour, half cornmeal, and occasionally use an even larger percentage of flour to cornmeal; say, $1^1/2$ parts flour to $^1/2$ part cornmeal. Yellow cornmeal is used more often than white. EXCEPTIONS TO THE RULE: In the *South,* most African American cornbreads, as well as some from Virginia, usually contain equal parts flour and cornmeal. And in the *North,* almost all Rhode Island jonnycakes use all cornmeal, preferably whitecap flint cornmeal.

THE RULE: LIQUID. *Southern* batters are almost always moistened with buttermilk, though in spoonbreads and a few other cornbreads, the meal is first presoaked with boiling water. *Northern* cornbreads usually call for "sweet milk" (i.e., regular, non-buttermilk milk). EXCEPTIONS TO THE RULE: Occasional regional variations both Northern and Southern break the rule; some recipes from both parts combine sweet milk and buttermilk; some forgo milk altogether or partly and use water.

THE RULE: SUGAR. *Southern* batters usually have no sugar (or other sweetener), often *emphatically* none. But occasionally just a little is added, "just enough to make it as sweet as sweet corn," as a gent who ran a sawmill and fixed cars in the Ozark backwoods once told a friend of mine. *Northern* cornbreads, though, are usually quite sweet; $^1/4$ cup to $^3/4$ cup sugar or even more is not uncommon. Other sweeteners, including honey or maple syrup, may also be used. No other difference brings down as much invective (from the Southern side) as this particular item. EXCEPTIONS TO THE RULE: African American Southern cornbreads as well as some Virginia cornbreads are often quite sweet, and almost all Rhode Island jonnycakes are *not* sweetened (and many Ocean State residents are prepared to heap as much scornful invective on their fellow cornbread-sweetening New Englanders as Southerners do).

THE RULE: FAT. Traditionally, bacon drippings and/or butter were the fat of choice in *Southern* cornbreads, as well as in the all-important skillet-heating. Today oil and/or butter are usually used, but, for some, only reluctantly: At one time the smokiness given by bacon fat was an essential prized part of the region's cornbread. Traditionally, *Northern* cornbreads call for butter, though lard was sometimes used in the old days. Today oil and butter are the usual choice. EXCEPTIONS TO THE RULE: In Rhode Island, some fry their jonnycakes in bacon fat. And, in my kitchen (which for thirty-five years was located in the South, but for four has been in the North), I always use Better (see the Pantry, page 346).

THE RULE: EGGS. *Southern* cornbreads most often have one egg, occasionally two, rarely three. Some Southern cornbreads—usually those intended for crumbling into stews or used in dressing, and in those recipes dating from subsistence times—have *no* eggs.

Contemporary *Northern* cornbread always, always has at least one egg, and often two or three. EXCEPTIONS TO THE RULE: The *South*'s spoonbreads: usually soufflé-like dishes, to which many eggs are essential. In the *North,* most varieties of Rhode Island jonnycakes are egg-free, as is steamed Boston Brown Bread (page 62). (And, referring to an egg as a cackleberry, something you'd expect might be a Southernism, is actually straight from Albert, my old-timer Vermont pal.)

THE RULE: LEAVENING. *Southern* cornbreads are most often leavened with a combination of baking soda and baking powder; the soda offsets the acidity of the buttermilk. But most *Northern* cornbreads use just baking powder, with sweet milk obviating the need for soda. EXCEPTIONS TO THE RULE: *Southern* spoonbreads, in essence soufflées, are leavened by beaten egg whites.

THE RULE: BAKING DISH AND METHOD. *Southern* cornbreads are almost always baked in a sizzling-hot round cast-iron skillet, occasionally a cornstick pan. You see a cornbread muffin not too often in the South. *Northern* cornbread batter goes into a room-temperature square pan or casserole dish, and muffins are made much more often than in the South. EXCEPTIONS TO THE RULE: Some *Southern* cornbreads, notably those from Virginia, are baked in square pans or casserole dishes. And in the *North,* a few very old recipes call for being baked in a "spider," a three-legged elevated cast-iron skillet with high sides. Traditionally the spider's legs were set directly in a fire that had burned down to hot coals, so the cornbread baked just above it.

THE RULE: CULTURAL APOCRYPHA. Until quite recently (the 1930s) cornbread served as *the* daily bread in the *South,* with biscuits running second. During times of poverty, cornbread was subsistence food. Southerners have a strong, almost compulsive emotional attachment to cornbread; types of cornbread and how one makes it serve as a regional badge of identity. In the *North,* cornbread is and was much more occasionally served. In the past homemade daily breads were likely to be yeast-risen wheat or "thirded" breads (see page 42), or muffins. Cornbread has always been more in the line of a treat, something special. While Northerners have strong affection for cornbread and enjoy it, it has little to do with identity. EXCEPTIONS TO THE RULE: One partially cornmeal-based bread made a regular appearance on *Northern* tables: Boston Brown Bread, a very moist, sweet, steamed bread that always contains a good percentage of cornmeal (see page 62) was often served weekly. Such bread would be incomprehensible in the South.

THE RULE: HOW YOU CUT AND SERVE IT. Most often *Southern* cornbreads are served in wedges, like a pie, served hot, straight from the skillet (unless baked in cornstick pans or as muffins). It's a daily bread, also used as the basis for dressing, and crumbled directly into stews, soups, and chilies. It's a classic accompaniment to slow-cooked greens and/or beans or black-eyed peas. An especially *Southern* serving method: Crumbled non-sweet classic cornmeal-only cornbread is placed in a glass, topped with either buttermilk or sweet milk, and eaten with a spoon. In the *North,* expect cornbread in squares or muffins, warm or at room temperature. It's used as a specialty bread, a snack, often an after-school snack, not a daily bread, and is frequently served with butter and honey or jam. EXCEPTIONS TO THE RULE: *Southern* corn pones are formed free-hand and baked in patties, often served with vegetables on the side (especially cabbage). The *Northern* Boston Brown Bread, already mentioned above, is typically steamed in a cylinder (such as a coffee can), sliced crosswise in thick circles, and served alongside classic sweet, tangy baked beans.

Chapter 2

NORTHERN CORNBREADS

What the "H" Is a Jonnycake, and Other Yankee Hanky-Panky

Most Northerners will tell you they love cornbread. And they do. If their love is gentle, accepting, it's no less sincere for not being the red-hot passion you find in the South. A Northerner is receptive to trying new cornbreads: You'll hear a Yankee say, "Oh, you add grated apples and maple syrup to yours? And sesame seeds? That sounds good." (This would be versus, "Listen, my great-grandmother Ella Roberts Mayfield made it this way, my grandmaw Anna Lee Souder made it this way, and my mama, bless her soul, made it this way. *And* they all used this very same skillet. Now do you really think I'd *profane* my great-grandmother's skillet by adding *apples*?")

Why is Northern cornbread-love so laissez-faire (not counting that of Rhode Islanders, who are almost as fanatical about their particular cornbread, Jonnycake—pages 224–299—as Southerners are)?

"Because," I can almost hear the deafening Southern response, "their cornbread isn't as good in the first place!"

But that, my friends, is not true. Northern cornbread *is* as good. "Oh, *good*," my Kentuckian friend Ronni Lundy will say dismissively, "Sure it's good. It's just not *real* cornbread."

I say it *is* real. Northern cornbreads have their own purpose, history, and raison d'être.

Take a look at pages 34–36, for the differences between the two regions' cornbreads. Generally, Northern cornbread is sweeter (like Vermont Maple–Sweetened Cornbread, page 54). It uses a larger proportion of wheat flour in addition to cornmeal (see Durgin-Park–Style Cornbread, page 41) and is almost never composed of straight cornmeal. And, yes, sometimes Yankees add ingredients that would make Great-Grandmother Mayfield get up out of her grave and smack you (see Quasi-Colonial Cornbread with Apples, page 45).

Northern cornbread today is something of a treat, a specialty: not exactly a sweet tea bread (like, say, banana bread) but not a daily go-with-anything-and-everything staple bread, either. It's natural to play with specialty breads, which are by definition non-staples; to fool with ingredients and add-ins (as in Cornmeal-Oatmeal Cranberry-Orange Loaf, page 60). Even when cornbread *was* a daily bread to New Englanders, back in colonial days, it was as Rye'n'Injun (page 162), a yeast-risen corn-rye-wheat bread that bears no resemblance to what most of us now think of as cornbread.

All cornbreads owe their existence to Native American foodways. When Europeans made their way to this continent's shores, the newcomers mixed what was familiar to them with the ingredients and methods they found here.

COLONIAL CORNBREADS

The newcomers who settled in the Northeast were like-minded people of English or Dutch stock. They came in search of religious freedom, and they tended to live clustered in communities. They arrived to make self-sufficient settlements, not fortunes; and to raise families. They were carpenters, farmers, ministers, leaders, and women and children, who added what has often been called "a civilizing influence." (By contrast, the first newcomers to the South, mostly male, were in search of fortunes to be made; and, generally independent-minded, they tended to spread out more, not settle in communities.)

The early colonists in the Northeast, with their literally Puritan mindset, did not suffer huge gaps between social classes among themselves. They did, however, regard their new home and its native people with incredible chauvinism. European goods and ingredients were superior to anything the strange, primitive savages might have to offer, in any area—from general worldview, to manners and customs, to foodstuffs.

The Pilgrims crossed the sea with the seeds of their own European staple grains, wheat and rye. But when these crops failed, rather than starve they turned to corn, a gift from the native people. Plymouth Colony governor William Bradford attributed this generosity to the divine: "And sure it was God's good providence that we found this corne, for else we know not how we should have done."

But the Dutch and English newcomers remained, if only in their minds, strongly and persistently convinced that wheat was superior. Yankees kept trying, doggedly, to make breads and desserts ("puddings") from the new grain in the same way they'd used the old-world grains. This was impossible: Although corn and wheat are both staple grains (along with rice, barley, and others), each has its own culinary qualities and attributes. Cornmeal was and is *cornmeal*, not substitute wheat (mostly because corn has no gluten, the protein structure in wheat, on which European baking traditions rest).

But that didn't stop those stubborn Yankees from trying. Whenever possible they cut the cornmeal with precious, expensive flour (see "Thirded" Colonial Cornbread, page 42) brought over from across the sea. (Hence the fact that in general, to this day, Yankee cornbreads contain a much higher percentage of flour than do Southern cornbreads.) Their tastes in baked goods also dictated an ample scoop, dollop, or pour of sweetening. The latter could be accommodated with relative ease: The Pilgrims quickly learned, from their native brethren, the trick of tapping maple sap and boiling it down for syrup.

What other factors influenced New Englanders' cornbreads? The climate. Which crops grew most quickly in the shorter growing season? Which would keep best through the long, cold winters? Pumpkins and winter squash were the transitional crops, and the summer's fruits were dried to last all winter. The only fresh fruits to last into winter were apples, which kept relatively well. However, the weather did have its upsides. Refrigeration was possible. For most of the year, even in hot summers, ice, cut in huge blocks from rivers and lakes, was stored in caves and shelters, where it was used to keep ingredients cool.

The weather affected both ingredients and cooking methods. Icehouses delayed milk's souring; thus, in the North, "sweet" milk or even cream (as in Sweet Cream and Honey Cornbread, page 47) often replaced the buttermilk usually used in the hot, humid South. Traditions in both places are largely followed to this day. Also, in a cool climate you *want* continual, steady warmth indoors throughout much of the year. Yankee cornbreads are thus usually baked longer than Southern ones, at a slightly lower temperature. And steaming bread for hours (see Classic Boston Brown Bread, page 62)—a practice unthinkable in the already steamy South—made great sense in colder climates. Slow cooking, whether by oven or stove, was a major advantage.

But any cornbread framework is necessarily loose. As in all things cornbread, there are exceptions to the rule. Yankee "Spider" Cornbread with a Custard Layer (page 50) does go into a hot Southern-friendly skillet; and some Northern cornbreads do use buttermilk, just as some Southern ones use a bit of flour and the slightest touch of sweetening.

When immigration brings human beings of different traditions together, their influence on each other is inevitable. It was impossible for the Pilgrims to stay the same; they had to evolve into something new. Here's how the poet Stephen Vincent Benét described it:

> *And those who came were resolved*
> *   to be Englishmen.*
> *Gone to the world's end, but English*
> *   every one.*
> *And they ate the white corn kernels,*
> *   parched in the sun,*
> *And they knew it not, but they'd not be*
> *   English again.*

For Englishmen (and women) became Americans, and America was soon no longer "the world's end" but "home." And cornmeal, once viewed with suspicion and scorn, gradually became an ingredient so beloved, and so identified with America, that in 1776 Benjamin Franklin wrote in its impassioned defense to a British newspaper, "Indian corn is one of the most agreeable and wholesome grains in the world; its green ears roasted are a delicacy beyond expression; and a *johny*, or *hoe-cake*, hot from the fire, is better than a Yorkshire muffin."

Thus does Yankee cornbread quietly offer its own gospel, leaving the preaching and conversion to those who have already partaken of its goodness.

"**Our Indian Corne, even the coarsest, maketh as pleasant a meal as rice . . . our Corne did proue well, & God be praysed, we had a good increase of Indian Corne, and our Barly indifferent good, but our Pease not worth the gathering, for we feared they were too late sowne. . . .**"

—LETTER FROM NEW ENGLAND, SENT BY EDWARD WINSLOW, PLYMOUTH, MASSACHUSETTS, BACK TO ENGLAND, DECEMBER 11, 1621

DURGIN-PARK-STYLE CORNBREAD

MAKES 9 SQUARES

The bread most associated with Boston is, of course, Boston Brown Bread (page 62). But at Durgin-Park, the restaurant most associated with Boston, the first bread to reach the table is cornbread—thick, golden squares of it, rough, crumbly, slightly grainy, moist, sweet, almost cakelike.

Durgin-Park, *the* ultimate old-school New England restaurant, has been located in Boston's Faneuil Hall Market Place since 1827. In all that time, incredibly, it's had only four owners. Stalwart Yankee dishes such as chowder, apple pan dowdy, New England boiled dinner, and at least three famous cornmeal-based dishes—cornbread, johnnycakes (with an H, unlike in Rhode Island, where an H is grounds for lynching), and Indian pudding—remain on the menu, unchanged.

When chef Tommy Ryan came on the job forty-three years ago, "Cornbread Helen" (aka Helen Goodman) had already been working "a good twenty-five, thirty years." He learned the recipe from her.

Numerous recipes floating around (in books, on the Internet) purport to be "the *real* Durgin-Park cornbread." All have more flour than cornmeal, are extremely sweet, and have almost no added fat. This is my take. Since there is so little fat, you *must* use at least whole milk. Half-and-half is even tastier.

Vegetable oil cooking spray
2 cups unbleached white flour
1 tablespoon baking powder
¾ teaspoon salt
1 cup stone-ground yellow cornmeal
½ cup sugar
2 eggs
1 tablespoon melted butter
1½ cups whole milk or
**   half-and-half**

1. Preheat the oven to 400°F. Spray a 9-inch square pan with oil.

2. Sift together the flour, baking powder, and salt into a large bowl. Stir in the cornmeal. Set aside while, in a smaller bowl, you whisk together the sugar, eggs, melted butter, and milk.

3. Combine these two mixtures, stirring just enough to combine the ingredients, then transfer the batter into the prepared pan.

4. Bake the cornbread until it is deeply golden, about 30 minutes. Cool for a few minutes, and cut into squares. Serve, still hot from the oven.

"Thirded" Colonial Cornbread

MAKES ABOUT 12 SQUARES

When the British came to America they were pining for wheat. In order to stretch their thin and dear wheat supplies, they made yeast doughs of one third wheat flour, one third cornmeal, and one third rye flour. The method was called "thirding," and it was used for both yeast-risen and "quick" breads (like pancakes).

This bread, though contemporary in its leavening agents, is thirded like breads of long ago, and it is can't-stop-eating-it delicious a few minutes out of the oven, with a little butter. It's still good that same day, goes quite nicely with vegetable soup or stew, and can be split, toasted, and gussied up with sharp Cheddar cheese melted on each half. The next day, when it dries out a little, crumble it and save it for bread pudding, stuffing, or—my favorite—French toast.

To make a moister bread, add ¼ cup sour cream whisked with ¼ teaspoon baking soda to the wet ingredients.

Vegetable oil cooking spray
¾ cup stone-ground yellow cornmeal
¾ cup whole-grain rye flour
¾ cup whole wheat pastry flour
1 tablespoon plus 1 teaspoon baking powder
½ teaspoon salt
3 tablespoons butter or mild vegetable oil
3 tablespoons blackstrap molasses
2 eggs
1¼ cups milk, measured into a 4-cup measure

1. Preheat the oven to 375°F. Spray an 8-by-11-inch baking pan with oil.

2. Sift together the cornmeal, rye flour, whole wheat pastry flour, baking powder, and salt into a medium bowl. Set aside.

3. Measure the butter or oil by tablespoon into a small skillet or saucepan, then, using the same thus-greased tablespoon, measure in the molasses. Place on low heat to thin the molasses and melt the fat.

4. Beat the eggs into the milk in its measuring cup, and then stir in the warmed molasses and butter.

5. Combine the wet and dry ingredients with as few strokes as possible (the batter will be much darker than typical cornbread batter). Transfer it to the prepared pan.

6. Bake the cornbread until it is firm and

THE WORLD'S MOST EGREGIOUS CORNBREAD

You might think, given the love I hold for cornbreads Northern and Southern, spicy and plain, in loaf, muffin, or pancake form, that I have never met a cornbread I didn't like. This is almost, but not quite, true.

I witnessed a crime against one of the world's great foods at a quasi-hip, pseudo-retro New York pancake house. The waiter set down a breadbasket on the table, before I'd even ordered.

(*Breadbasket?* At a pancake place? Is that carb overkill or what?)

I unfolded the basket's napkin. Inside there were large, damp squares of something crumbly and yellow. I guess you could call it "cornbread" after a fashion—but it was very sweet, very, very, very cakey, and dotted with . . . *chocolate chips.*

As Joseph Conrad said, "The horror, the horror!"

deeply brown, with browned edges slightly pulling away from the sides of the pan, about 30 minutes.

VARIATION: VEGAN "THIRDED" CORNBREAD

In addition to the obvious (soy milk for dairy, egg substitute such as Eggscellence, page 352, for eggs), add ¼ cup applesauce, which will soften the dense bread.

APPLE CIDER SYRUP

Apple cider syrup is an old New England sweetener. Sweet, a little tart, extraordinarily full-flavored, it is nothing more or less than a reduction of apple cider, the water boiled away to leave only the essence of apple. Commercially, it's made much in the same way maple sap is turned into syrup, in an evaporator, so it's not surprising that one of the few places it's produced is in Vermont.

Apple cider syrup has a honey-like consistency. It is excellent used not only in Quasi-Colonial Cornbread but over pancakes, French toast, or ice cream, or in marinades or salad dressings, where it adds a hauntingly delicious flavor.

QUASI-COLONIAL CORNBREAD

MAKES 9 SQUARES

Apple cider syrup gives this cornbread a special flavor note. Depending on what era of "colonial" we are talking about, this probably would have been baked not in an oven as such, its flour might well have been "thirded" (see page 42), and it would not have had the optional fresh corn kernels added. Hence, the "quasi" in its name.

Vegetable oil cooking spray

1/2 cup unbleached white flour

1/4 cup whole wheat pastry flour

1 tablespoon baking powder

2/3 cup stone-ground yellow cornmeal

1 teaspoon salt

1 egg

1 cup milk

3 tablespoons apple cider syrup (see Note)

3 tablespoons butter, melted, or mild vegetable oil

Kernels cut from 2 ears of fresh corn, about 1 cup (see Shuck and Jive, page 49; optional)

Butter, for serving (optional)

Apple butter, for serving (optional)

1. Preheat the oven to 450°F. Spray an 8-inch square baking pan with oil.

2. Combine the flours, baking powder, cornmeal, and salt in a large bowl and set aside. In a smaller bowl, whisk together the egg, milk, and apple cider syrup.

3. Stir together the wet and dry mixtures along with the melted butter or oil. Mix just enough to combine, stirring in the corn kernels at the end, if using. Transfer the batter to the prepared pan.

4. Bake until deeply golden, about 20 minutes. Cool for a few minutes, and cut into squares. Serve, still hot from the oven, with butter and apple butter, if you'd like.

NOTE: If you don't have commercially made apple cider syrup on hand (see Pantry, page 346), thaw 2 large cans of frozen organic apple juice concentrate, and boil them down to half their original volume, until the liquid becomes as thick as honey. As the juice cooks down, transfer it to a smaller pot, because it will grow more and more concentrated, decreasing dramatically in volume.

VARIATION: QUASI-COLONIAL CORNBREAD WITH APPLES

Substitute 1 cup apples (peeled, cored, and grated—not chopped) for the corn.

·M·E·N·U·

FALL FARM-STAND ORCHARD IDYLL

**Salad of Mixed Greens,
Red Cabbage Slivers, Scallions,
Apples, Maytag Blue Cheese,
and Toasted Walnuts,
with Apple Cider Syrup Vinaigrette
(page 299)**

*

**Chicken or Vegetable Soup with Fresh
Corn and Tomatoes**

*

**Quasi-Colonial Cornbread
with Butter and Apple Butter**

*

**Buttermilk Cornbread Pudding
with Apricots and Lemon
(page 328)**

CARROLL'S EXTRA-MOIST CORNBREAD

MAKES 9 SQUARES

This recipe is from my down-one-hill-and-up-the-side-of-another Vermont neighbor, Carroll Metrick. Carroll says, "The fewer pans, the fewer bowls and spoons, the better. That's how I cook." She discovered the prototype for this recipe in *The New York Times*, but she found that version a little too wet for her taste. I tweaked it slightly both method- and ingredients-wise, and now it meets with her approval, retaining its signature rich delicacy, still plenty moist, but less so than the original.

Carroll likes this cornbread split and toasted, with butter and maple syrup; but then, what cornbread wouldn't be good that way? Myself, the day I came up with the final version, I happened to have some sweet potato and lima bean soup going, and it was terrific with that.

Vegetable oil cooking spray

**1 cup reduced-fat sour cream
(or full-fat, if you prefer)**

½ teaspoon baking soda

¼ cup mild vegetable oil

**1 cup canned creamed corn
(see Pantry, page 351)**

2 eggs

1 cup stone-ground yellow cornmeal

1 tablespoon cornstarch

1½ teaspoons baking powder

¾ teaspoon salt

1. Preheat the oven to 350°F. Spray an 8-inch square baking pan with oil.

2. Place the sour cream in a large bowl and whisk in the baking soda to activate it. Then whisk in the remaining wet ingredients: the oil, creamed corn, and eggs. When thoroughly combined, sprinkle the cornmeal over the top.

3. Combine the cornstarch, baking powder, and salt in a small dish, and sift over the cornmeal. Stir the whole thing together with as few strokes as possible, to just combine the wet and dry.

4. Transfer the batter to the prepared pan. Let it stand at room temperature for 20 minutes, then pop it in the oven and bake until golden brown, about 40 minutes.

SWEET CREAM AND HONEY CORNBREAD

MAKES 9 SQUARES

Ultrarich, quite sweet (due to both honey and sugar), this is a truly yummy Yankee-style indulgence of a cornbread. Heavy cream is backed up by two eggs and plenty of butter; light it certainly isn't, but wonderful it is. The honey is warmed so it will combine with the other wet ingredients more readily; just run very hot tap water over the honey jar to liquefy the honey. If you're used to stripped-down cornbreads, this might be almost too rich for you.

Vegetable oil cooking spray
1 cup unbleached white flour
1 cup stone-ground yellow cornmeal
1 tablespoon baking powder
$\frac{1}{2}$ teaspoon salt
$\frac{1}{4}$ cup sugar, preferably unrefined
    (see Pantry, page 356)
$\frac{1}{2}$ cup whipping cream
$\frac{1}{2}$ cup milk
4 tablespoons ($\frac{1}{2}$ stick) butter,
    at room temperature
$\frac{1}{4}$ cup honey, warmed
2 eggs, lightly beaten

I. Preheat the oven to 400°F. Spray a 9-inch square pan with oil.

2. Combine the flour and cornmeal in a large bowl, then sift in the baking powder and salt.

3. Beat together the sugar, cream, milk, softened butter, and warmed honey in a smaller bowl. When well mixed, beat in the eggs.

4. Combine the wet and dry ingredients, stirring just until moistened. Transfer the batter into the prepared pan and bake until golden brown and intoxicatingly fragrant, 20 to 25 minutes.

"I lay five kernels of dried corn on every place setting at Thanksgiving dinner to remember the starvation the Pilgrims endured in 1621. That was their daily ration before the first crops came in. When you see it, you know how little it was. Of the one hundred two passengers on the *Mayflower,* only fifty-one survived. I am descended from two of them. So I give thanks to my ancestors, who struggled against all odds."

—CAROLINE LEWIS KARDELL,
HISTORIAN GENERAL OF THE GENERAL
SOCIETY OF MAYFLOWER DESCENDANTS IN
PLYMOUTH, MASSACHUSSETTS

LAND OF MILK AND HONEY CUSTARD-LAYERED CORNBREAD

MAKES 12 SQUARES

This is a magical, surprising cornbread. An improbably thin, eggy, milky batter bakes into a tri-part cornbread, with a thin but distinct layer of voluptuous custard sandwiched between a cornbready bottom layer and a light topping of the risen bran and fresh corn kernels.

This is my crossbreeding of two similar recipes from two very different places. The first is from my well-worn, old (1970! And with age spots and drizzles to prove it!) *Tassajara Bread Book*, by Edward Espe Brown. The second is from an almost-as-old and also much-dripped-on handwritten recipe card bearing the recipe I begged from a stranger at a Thanksgiving potluck in Eureka Springs, Arkansas.

Vegetable oil cooking spray

1 cup stone-ground yellow or white cornmeal

1/2 cup whole wheat pastry flour

1/2 cup unbleached white flour

2 1/4 teaspoons baking powder

1 tablespoon sugar, preferably unrefined (see Pantry, page 356)

1/2 teaspoon salt

1/3 cup honey

3 tablespoons butter

3 1/4 cups milk

2 eggs

Kernels cut from 2 to 3 ears of fresh corn, 1 to 1 1/2 cups (see Shuck and Jive, opposite)

1. Preheat the oven to 350°F. Spray a 9-by-11-inch baking pan with oil.

2. Stir together the cornmeal, flours, baking powder, sugar, and salt in a small bowl to blend well. Set aside.

3. Gently warm the honey and butter in a medium-size saucepan over medium-low heat until the honey thins slightly and the butter melts. Whisk in the milk, and then the eggs.

4. Combine the wet and dry mixtures, whisking a few times. Gaze suspiciously at the batter, which will look too thin. Stir in the fresh corn kernels.

5. Pour the batter into the prepared pan and bake until the top of the cornbread is golden brown and springs back when lightly touched, 45 to 50 minutes. Let cool for at least 30 minutes to give the custard a chance to fully set up before cutting into the cornbread, but do serve it warm.

SHUCK AND JIVE:
FRESH CORN OFF THE COB

Fresh corn, cut from the cob, is needed for many cornbreads, muffins, most corn fritters, and things like corn chowder, kernel-sparkled salads, or truly incredible from-scratch creamed corn or succotash. Removing the corn is not difficult, but *is* certainly more time-consuming than dumping out frozen kernels.

Since most kernel-corn—containing recipes taste good with frozen corn, why go to this trouble? Because fresh-kernel corn takes "good" to a whole other galaxy. It ramps up the corn flavor itself, a pronounced taste of *corn-ness* that frozen just can't achieve. And then there's the texture: tiny explosions of sweet milky corn juice as you crunch down on fresh kernels . . . summer in your mouth.

To make corn shucking and cutting slightly less messy (remember: each cob yields about $1/2$ cup off-the-cob kernels):

1. Shuck the corn, removing as much silk as you can. Working one cob at a time, hold the cob upright in a wide, shallow bowl or glass pie pan, stem end of the cob down. Take a sharp chef's knife and slide the blade down the cob, fairly close to the cob. You'll get about 2 or 3 rows of kernels with each slice. Rotate the cob and proceed down again, continuing to rotate until most kernels are removed. Then lift the cob over the shallow bowl and, using quick, short knife-strokes, cut off the remaining kernels at the ends of the cob, where there's a slight inward curve.

2. Save de-kerneled cobs to make corn stock, or toss them into the compost.

·M·E·N·U·

Cicada Sonata Summer Supper

Salad of Baby Arugula, Diced Yellow Tomato, Minced Scallion, and a Sprinkling of Crumbled Raw-Milk Gouda Cheese, with Kalamata Olive–Mustard Vinaigrette

*

Navy Bean, Tomato, or Zucchini Soup

*

Breadbasket:

Yankee "Spider" Cornbread with a Custard Layer

or

Land of Milk and Honey Custard-Layered Cornbread (page 48)

*

Fresh Strawberries, Raspberries, and Blackberries, with Brown Sugar, a Teensy Grind of Fresh Black Pepper, and a Splash of Kirsch or Aged Traditional Balsamic Vinegar of Modena

Yankee "Spider" Cornbread with a Custard Layer

Makes 8 wedges

Another excellent custard-centered cornbread that combines features of the North and South, and a wholly unique twist on preparation. The twist? A cup of milk is poured *over* the finished batter, resulting in a custard layer just underneath the top crust.

Originally this cornbread was baked in a spider, a footed, long-handled skillet designed to stand in the fireplace just above the coals for hearth baking. But now it's baked in a preheated skillet. Serve the "spider" bread still warm, but not hot, beside a bowl of stew or paired with an assertive salad.

Vegetable oil cooking spray

⅓ cup unbleached white flour

1½ cups stone-ground yellow cornmeal

¼ cup sugar

1¼ teaspoons baking powder

½ teaspoon baking soda

½ teaspoon salt

2 eggs

¾ cup buttermilk

2 cups milk

2 to 3 tablespoons butter or
mild vegetable oil

1. Preheat the oven to 350°F. Spray a 10-inch cast-iron skillet with oil, and set aside.

2. Sift together the dry ingredients into a medium bowl.

3. Break the eggs into a second medium bowl and whisk them well. Whisk in the buttermilk and 1 cup of the milk. Set aside.

4. Place the butter or oil in the skillet, and place the skillet over medium heat on top of the stove. As the butter or oil heats, quickly stir the wet ingredients into the dry using as few strokes as possible to combine them. (The batter is wetter than most cornbreads. You might need to whisk it a couple of times to incorporate wet into dry, but don't overbeat.)

5. Pour a little of the hot butter or oil from the skillet into the batter, give a stir or two, then pour the batter into the prepared hot skillet. Now, here comes the odd part. Pour the remaining 1 cup milk over the batter, without stirring it in.

6. Bake the cornbread in the oven until golden brown in spots on the top and quite golden around the edges, 50 minutes to 1 hour. The bread will still seem slightly wetter than most cornbreads, but if you poke a toothpick in the center, it'll come out clean. Let cool in the pan for at least 20 minutes before cutting, so the custard can set up a little.

"Spider bread . . . is sliced as a pie. A large piece of butter is placed on top of each slice and it is eaten with a fork."

—IMOGENE WOOLCOTT,
The Yankee Cookbook, 1939

MY FIRST CORNBREAD

About seven years ago, my mother, Charlotte, who's now in her nineties, was decluttering her kitchen. I saw, in the giveaway pile, *the bowl*: a large, heavy glass mixing bowl with a rosy-beige exterior and milky white interior. When you broke an egg against its side, as I did when I made cornbread in it as a girl, the sound was satisfying and the break clean.

First cornbreads date from childhood. Mine, baked in the same kitchen my mother was clearing out, was in Hastings-on-Hudson, New York, from a mix. When you opened the box, a cellophane bag with the mix itself rested neatly in a flimsy, very shiny aluminum pan, good for one use only. Could you get any more '50s, any farther from cast-iron skillets and from-scratch, than that?

Charlotte Zolotow, née Shapiro, was born in Norfolk, Virginia. She claims to remember almost nothing about it; her speech has no Southern inflection and her family moved north when she was young. I've always suspected, though, that she was more influenced by the region than she either knows or lets on. Her mother, aunt, and three cousins remained in Norfolk; she visited them often. One endearment she and her sister, my Aunt Dot, use to this day is "honeychile," and my mother's social style is what I came to recognize as the classic manner in which Southern women were (to some extent are) schooled: graceful, charming, genteel, effusive in thanks, indirect, quite certain (despite or because of this) to get their way, and capable of summing up others with wicked, deadly accuracy (generally only in private company, after a gin and tonic or two).

My mother, a good cook, specialized in entrées. I took to baking from the first, and took over the post as designated family cornbread baker early on, using the mix with its cunning mirror-shiny pan, one step up from a doll's baking dish. This cornbread, very sweet, rose with a slightly domed center. In our house it wasn't served with any of the tried-and-true cornbread matches: not chili, soup, greens, or beans. And it never accompanied meals. Instead, it was a snack, always served with butter and honey.

Don't these cornbread beginnings seem shallowly rooted, unsoulful, for someone who would grow up to be a cornbread aficionado?

Well. At the 2003 National Cornbread Festival in South Pittsburg, Tennessee, I met a couple named Stephanie and LeBron Colvin (see page 268), both Southerners.

By this point in my cornbread research I'd begun to question what are often promulgated as the clear-cut, decisive differences between Northern and Southern cornbreads (see pages 34–36). Yes, there were general "as a rules." But exceptions to these abounded.

When Stephanie told me about the sweet, square Virginia cornbread she had grown up on, *always served with butter and honey,* my cornbread roots deepened: Suddenly, through a few simple accompaniments, matter-of-fact in a suburban New York childhood, I was *not* just a "mix cornbread" girl. I had propers, identity, a culinary genealogy attaching me to my mother, and to her childhood in Norfolk, Virginia. That's cornbread root magic and mojo in action.

"Don't you *dare* throw that bowl out!" I told my mother. "It's odd, what children remember," she said, bemused. "I never dreamed that old bowl had any significance to you."

But it did. And she kept it. And one day I'll be making cornbread in it, this time from scratch, with my very young adopted niece, Zoë, who will make that satisfying crack as she breaks the egg against the side of the rosy-beige bowl.

Vermont Maple-Sweetened Cornbread

MAKES 9 SQUARES

Idyllic childhood summers and early fall days were spent at my Aunt Dot's farm in southeastern Vermont, where I now live. Maple syrup is part of many meals I associate with the farm. It makes its way into many Vermont cornbreads, too. This version is sweet but not too sweet, tender, and rises high into a bit of a dome in the middle. It's best hot from the oven with butter and, if you wish, a little extra syrup. Enjoy it with baked beans, also sweetened with a good dollop of maple syrup. And if you like the flavor of cornbread and maple syrup as much as I do, don't miss the Glazed Maple Cornmeal Rolls on page 176.

Vegetable oil cooking spray
1 cup unbleached white flour
1 cup stone-ground yellow cornmeal
1 tablespoon baking powder
1/2 teaspoon salt
2 eggs
1/3 cup pure maple syrup
2/3 cup milk
1/3 cup butter, melted, or mild vegetable oil

1. Preheat the oven to 400°F. Spray an 8-inch square pan with oil, and set aside.

2. Sift together the flour, cornmeal, baking powder, and salt into a medium bowl.

3. Break the eggs into a smaller bowl, and whisk them well. Whisk in the maple syrup, milk, and melted butter or oil.

4. Pour the wet ingredients into the dry and combine them quickly, using as few strokes as possible. Scrape the batter into the prepared pan and bake until golden brown, 20 minutes.

· M · E · N · U ·

A Sugaring-Off Supper

Coleslaw with a Tart,
Mustardy Vinaigrette

*

Vermont Maple-Sweetened
Cornbread

*

Brattleboro Baked Beans Borracho
(page 311)

*

Baked Apples Glazed with Maple Syrup

GOT TO DRAW THE LINE SOMEWHERE: MASON, DIXON, AND THEIR LINE

If you're like most Americans, "Mason-Dixon Line" doesn't mean what you probably think it does.

First off, Mason and Dixon were two surveyors, Charles Mason and Jeremiah Dixon. And the real, that is to say, original, historical line they surveyed between 1763 and 1767 demarcates the east-west Pennsylvania-Maryland border and that portion of the Maryland-Delaware border running more or less north-south . . . a much smaller area, and one with a much less pointed meaning, than most of us suppose.

For over time, "Mason-Dixon Line" has taken on a quite different connotation in common parlance. Most nonhistorians use the phrase to describe the border between free states and slave states prior to the Civil War, or once the war broke out, during, and after it, between states on the Union and Confederate sides.

This anecdotal, but not historical, dividing line is generally what is recognized as the Mason-Dixon Line: the border (as it turns out imaginary) separating North from South, and a division (also, as it turns out, imaginary) between the alleged two types of cornbread.

A ROUND AND ABUNDANT TABLE

Located in Norwich, Vermont, is one of America's best, most energetic, interesting flour and baking supply companies, King Arthur Flour—known as KA to its fans. The company's exuberance is remarkable when you consider that it has been in business since 1790, when it sold one product: premium wheat flour, imported from England (from which America had only just declared independence). Moreover, while Frank Sands is the fifth generation of his family to be part of the company, it's now seventy percent employee-owned. "That just seemed the right evolution for the company," Frank's wife, Brinna, wrote to me recently, "because its employees are so great and they really feel like they own it."

Unlike every other source for cornmeal mentioned in this book, KA does not, itself, own a mill. Rather, they buy (very selectively) flour and meal from about 16 mills across the country (nope, no more flour from England). Every flour and meal KA sells is milled to KA's own, very tight specifications, one reason its fans are so devoted.

Brinna's indispensable, substantial cookbooks, which include *The King Arthur Flour Baker's Companion* and *The King Arthur Flour Cookie Companion,* belong on every home-baker's bookshelf. The company's website, www.kingarthurflour.com, belongs on every home-baker's web "favorites" list. The mail-order catalogue is filled to overflowing with products, recipes, anecdotes, and profiles of customers, employees, and suppliers: It's irresistible! (For more information, call 800-827-6836 or visit the website.)

Mary Baird's Johnny Cake

MAKES 9 SQUARES

·M·E·N·U·

Stockbridge Summer Snack

Squares of Mary Baird's Johnny Cake, split and lightly toasted with Butter and Strawberry Jam

*

Glasses of Cold Milk

Y ou couldn't get a more impeccable Yankee pedigree, where bread-stuffs are concerned, than this third-generation cornbread from Brinna Sands' mother, Mary Baird, a great New England baker. Brinna's pedigree is conferred both by blood *and* marriage, the latter (to Frank Sands) making her part of the venerable King Arthur Flour clan (see opposite page). A fine baker, Brinna's definitive baking books include *The King Arthur Flour 200th Anniversary Cookbook*, from which this recipe is adapted. Like all her writing, its style is, one could say, both wry and rye.

Brinna's mother, Mary, learned this cornbread from *her* mother (Brinna's grandmother). Both grandmother and mother often prepared this quick, good bread. The extended Baird family summered each year in western Massachusetts. "There was a 'kitchen tent,'" says Brinna, who visited as a child, "and this was pretty easy fare for my grandmother to make for a big family for breakfast." Brinna fondly remembers how sticky and buttery she and the other kids would be after eating it. (See the menu above, and you'll get the picture.)

For Rhode Island jonnycakes, spelled without the "h" and griddled, see pages 224–229.

Vegetable oil cooking spray

1 cup unbleached white flour, preferably King Arthur brand

¾ cup stone-ground yellow cornmeal

⅓ cup sugar

1 tablespoon baking powder

¾ teaspoon salt

1 egg

1 cup milk

2 to 3 tablespoons butter, melted

1. Preheat the oven to 425°F. Spray an 8-inch square baking pan with oil, and set aside.

2. Sift together the flour, cornmeal, sugar, baking powder, and salt into a medium bowl.

3. Break the egg into a second medium bowl, and whisk it well. Whisk in the milk and melted butter.

4. Combine the wet and dry ingredients with as few strokes as possible, and transfer the batter into the prepared pan. Bake until golden brown, 20 to 25 minutes.

·M·E·N·U·

BEMIS HILL BRUNCH

Seasonal Fresh Fruit Cup

*

Toasted Slices of Gold-and-White Tasty Cornbread, topped with Sliced Tomatoes, Sautéed Bacon or Tempeh Bacon, Steamed Spinach, and Poached Eggs, with a Cheddar Cheese Sauce

*

Miss Kay's Dark Secret Cornmeal Cake (page 341) with Whipped Cream

*

Coffee
Black Tea * Spearmint Tea

GOLD-AND-WHITE TASTY CORNBREAD

MAKES 12 SQUARES

When I lived in Eureka Springs, Arkansas, I was fortunate enough to be able to dash over to Hart's Family Center and purchase five-pound bags of excellent stone-ground white or yellow cornmeal from Hodgson Mill, located in Teutopolis, Illinois.

Naturally, the bags have a cornbread recipe on the back—one entitled "Tasty Corn Bread." The version on the white cornmeal sack calls for white cornmeal, and on the yellow, of course, for yellow—otherwise they're identical. The recipe *was* tasty indeed, but I feel I improved on it by cutting back the oil ever so slightly and adding a bit of leftover canned creamed corn I didn't want to see go to waste. I prefer this one with the white meal, but either will do.

Try it with a bowl of tomato or vegetable soup for a lunch that radiates well-being.

Vegetable oil cooking spray

1 cup unbleached white flour, preferably Hodgson Mill brand

1½ **cups stone-ground white cornmeal,**
   preferably Hodgson Mill brand

¼ **cup sugar**

1½ **teaspoons baking powder**

½ **teaspoon baking soda**

½ **teaspoon salt**

1 **egg**

1 **cup plus 2 tablespoons buttermilk**

3 **tablespoons mild vegetable oil**

½ **cup canned creamed corn**
   (see Pantry, page 351)

I. Preheat the oven to 400°F. Spray a 9-inch square baking pan with oil, and set aside.

2. Combine the flour, cornmeal, sugar, baking powder, baking soda, and salt in a medium bowl.

3. Break the egg into a second medium bowl, and whisk it well. Whisk in the buttermilk, vegetable oil, and creamed corn.

4. Combine the wet and dry ingredients with as few strokes as possible, and scrape the batter into the prepared pan. Bake until golden brown, 25 to 30 minutes.

"I expand and live in the warm day like corn and melons."

—RALPH WALDO EMERSON,
Nature

CORN COLORATIONS

Although kernels of the usual corn varieties are bright yellow, white, or that random, lovely combination of yellow and white called "butter and sugar corn," occasionally one can find fresh sweet red-kernel and/or blue-kernel corn. Red and blue kernels have a more old-fashioned flavor, a texture some would say is more "real corn" than the super-sweet varieties most of us have become accustomed to, which are bred for high sugar content. All types of corn come in every color in the spectrum. As with other vegetables, the more intensely colored it is, the more nutrients it contains.

CORNMEAL-OATMEAL CRANBERRY-ORANGE LOAF

SERVES 8 TO 10

You can't get much more Yankee in the fruit department than the cranberry, a Massachusetts native. This is a not-too-sweet sweet bread that's perfect for tea, breakfast, maybe even dessert. Cornmeal gives a pleasant toothy crunch, the citrus a subtle accent, while the cranberries are little tart explosions of color and flavor in the pale gold. Its texture is light, firm, reminiscent of pound cake; yet it's very low in fat.

How do you "coarsely chop" a cup of cranberries, short of quartering them berry by berry? Throw them in the food processor and pulse chop just a few times, maybe three or four on-offs, scraping down the bowl sides in between.

Vegetable oil cooking spray
1½ cups unbleached white flour
⅓ cup stone-ground yellow cornmeal
1 teaspoon baking powder
¼ teaspoon baking soda
¾ cup plus 2 tablespoons sugar
½ teaspoon salt
2 eggs
3 tablespoons mild vegetable oil
½ cup plus 2 tablespoons buttermilk
Finely grated zest of 2 oranges (see Note)
1 cup cranberries, washed, picked over, and coarsely chopped (see headnote)
2 to 4 tablespoons walnuts, toasted and chopped (optional)
¼ cup oatmeal (rolled oats)

1. Preheat the oven to 350°F. Coat 1 large, 2 medium, or 3 small loaf pans with oil.

2. Sift the flour, cornmeal, baking powder, baking soda, sugar, and salt into a large bowl.

3. Whisk together the eggs, oil, buttermilk, and orange zest in a second, smaller bowl.

4. Combine the mix-ins—the cranberries, walnuts, and oatmeal—in a third bowl. Sprinkle 1 tablespoon of the flour mixture over them, and toss well.

5. Quickly combine the flour mixture and the egg mixture, using as few strokes as possible. Gently stir in the mix-ins. The batter should be stiff. Spoon the batter into the prepared pan(s). Bake for 45 to 55 minutes for the large pan, 35 to 50 minutes for the mediums, and 35 to 40 minutes for the smalls. Check two-thirds of the way through the baking period; if the loaves are browning excessively, tent them loosely with foil.

6. Let the baked breads cool for 10 minutes in the pan(s), run a thin knife around the edge of each pan, and turn the loaves out. Let finish cooling on a rack.

NOTE: When using citrus zest, try your best to get organic fruit, because it is free of the waxes and fungicides that are routinely sprayed on conventionally grown citrus fruit peels.

TOGUS BREAD

MAKES ABOUT 12 TO 15 SLICES

This sweet, rich, steam-cooked bread is almost certainly a legacy of the Algonquian-speaking peoples, who dominated most of northeastern America. Throughout the region, Native Americans made a sweetened steamed cornmeal bread, and the colonists adopted it as they did so many other things. Because it is nourishing and delicious, I've adopted and adapted it as well.

For instructions on steam cooking, see Steam On, pages 64–66.

Vegetable oil cooking spray

2 cups stone-ground white cornmeal, plus extra for dusting the molds

1/2 cup unbleached white flour

1/2 cup whole wheat flour

1 heaping tablespoon white sugar (or granulated maple sugar)

1 1/2 teaspoons baking powder

1/2 teaspoon baking soda

1/2 teaspoon salt

1 1/3 cups buttermilk

1/2 cup pure maple syrup, preferably Grade B

3/4 cup dried blueberries or cranberries

Boiling water, for steaming the bread

1. Have ready the mold(s), heat-proof trivet, and cooking vessel of your choice (see Steam On, page 64). Wash and dry the molds well, spray the insides thoroughly with oil, and dust the insides with cornmeal. Also have at hand some foil, and kitchen string or rubber bands to secure the foil to the top of the molds.

2. Stir together the cornmeal, flours, sugar, baking powder, baking soda (sift the leavenings if necessary), and salt in a medium bowl.

3. Whisk together the buttermilk and maple syrup in a small bowl.

4. Combine the wet and dry mixtures, stirring just enough to blend well but not overbeating. Stir in the dried fruit with a few quick strokes.

5. Scrape the batter into the prepared mold(s), filling each about two-thirds of the way full.

6. Tear off a piece of foil that is twice as large as the mouth of a mold. Fold it in half, and spray one side with oil. Place it oiled-side down on top of the mold, puffing it up a bit to allow for the bread's expansion as it steams. Repeat with any remaining molds.

7. Secure each piece of foil tightly with kitchen string or a rubber band. Place the trivet or equivalent in the cooking vessel. Place the mold(s) on top of the trivet.

8. Pour enough boiling water into the cooking vessel to come halfway up the sides of the mold(s). Secure the lid of the vessel and steam the bread according to the directions for the particular cooking vessel you are using.

9. Cook the bread for the length of time suggested, then test the bread with a long skewer: You want to get way down deep into the bread's interior. When done, the middle of the bread is moist, but not sticky. Visible wet batter means the bread should steam longer. If it's wet, keep steaming patiently, checking about every 20 minutes until the moist-but-not-sticky point is reached.

10. When the bread is done, remove it from the cooking vessel, and let it cool in the mold(s), uncovered, on a rack, for at least 45 minutes. Reverse the bread out of the mold(s)—it should come out quite easily—slice it, and serve.

> **"Boston brown bread, thick, sweetish, and beraisined . . . assuage[s] the nostalgic hunger of Boston's children far from home."**
>
> —SOPHIE KERR,
> *The Best I Ever Ate*

CLASSIC BOSTON BROWN BREAD

MAKES ABOUT 12 TO 15 SLICES

Classics and clichés generally get to be that way for a good reason—because they fulfill or express some basic principle. So it is with this New England mainstay, hard to beat with a traditional accompaniment like Brattleboro Baked Beans Borracho (page 311).

For instructions on steam cooking, see Steam On, pages 64–66.

Vegetable oil cooking spray

1 cup stone-ground yellow cornmeal,
plus extra for dusting the molds

2 cups whole wheat flour

1½ teaspoons baking powder

½ teaspoon baking soda

1 teaspoon salt

½ cup blackstrap molasses

¼ cup honey

2 cups buttermilk

1 cup raisins, currants, or pitted,
diced dates

Boiling water, for steaming the bread

1. Have ready the mold(s), heat-proof trivet, and cooking vessel of your choice (see Steam On, pages 64–66). Wash and dry the molds well, spray the insides thoroughly with oil, and dust the insides with cornmeal. Also have at hand some foil, and kitchen string or rubber bands to secure the foil to the top of the mold(s).

2. Combine the cornmeal, whole wheat flour, baking powder, baking soda (sift the leavenings in if they are at all lumpy), and salt in a medium bowl. Stir or whisk together well.

3. Run hot water over the jars of molasses and honey until the contents are nice and flowy. Place the molasses, honey, and buttermilk in a medium bowl and whisk together well.

4. Combine the wet and dry mixtures, stirring just enough to blend well but not overbeating. Stir in the raisins with just a few more strokes.

5. Scrape the batter into the prepared mold(s), filling each about two-thirds of the way full.

6. Tear off a piece of foil that is twice as large as the mouth of a mold. Fold it in half, and spray one side with oil. Place it oiled-side down on top of the mold, puffing it up a bit to allow for the bread's expansion as it steams. Repeat with any remaining molds.

7. Secure each piece of foil tightly with kitchen string or a rubber band. Place the trivet or equivalent in the cooking vessel. Place the mold(s) on top of the trivet.

8. Pour enough boiling water into the cooking vessel to come halfway up the sides of the mold(s). Secure the lid of the vessel and steam the bread according to the directions for the particular cooking vessel you are using.

9. Cook the bread for the length of time suggested, then test the bread with a long skewer: you want to get way down deep into the bread's interior. When done, the middle of the bread is moist, but not sticky. Visible wet batter means the bread should steam longer. If it's wet, keep steaming patiently, checking about every 20 minutes until the moist-but-not-sticky point is reached.

10. When the bread is done, remove it from the cooking vessel, and let it cool in the mold(s), uncovered, on a rack, for at least 45 minutes. Reverse the bread out of the mold(s)—it should come out quite easily—slice it, and serve.

STEAM ON:
GENERAL DIRECTIONS FOR COOKING LOAF BREADS WITH STEAM

What's that? *"Steamed* bread?" you say, perhaps raising an eyebrow skeptically. Well, while steamed bread is more of a production to make than its baked brethren, it's worth it. Why use this cooking method? Not only because it's traditional, but because of the wonderful sui generic texture of bread that is baked above water rather than in the dry heat of an oven. In earlier American days ovens were uncommon, and in many parts of the world that remains the case; steaming in hot water is the way folks got or get their daily bread. And good bread it is—flavorful and ultramoist without being gummy or packed with fat. You taste history, and it is delicious.

How to do it? First, you'll need something along the lines of a pudding mold. You say you don't happen to own a pudding mold? Well, how about a one-pound coffee can, or a couple of large soup or tomato cans? How about, even (with some attention), a regular old 9-by-5-inch loaf pan or some mini pans? Got 'em? Good.

Next you'll need something that acts as a heat-proof trivet: a few metal canning rings, some wadded-up foil, or a cake rack. The trivet keeps the pudding mold (or its improvised approximation) from coming in contact with the bottom of the pot, thus preventing the bread baking inside from burning.

Finally, you'll need a nice large pot, or, perhaps, a slow-cooker or pressure cooker, in which the almost-trivets and tightly covered molds are set. The pot is the one piece of equipment you really cannot improvise. It must be big enough to hold the breads in their molds, the trivets, the water the breads cook in, *and* it must have a tight-fitting lid. This is because this stovetop cooking method itself is nonnegotiable: The tightly covered batter-filled cans are half-submerged in simmering water, and then the pot lid traps the steam. A loose pot lid would allow the steam to escape; it would be like baking with the oven door ajar.

A few other points:

• Bread recipes calling for 3 cups of flour and meal, the quantity I've used in all the selections here (and in Mealiebrod, page 112), fills one 9-by-5-inch loaf pan, one 1-pound coffee can, three 20-ounce cans, or five 12-ounce cans. I prefer cans to loaf pans unless I am doing the bread in a large oval slow-cooker, because the taller the can, the more surrounding water you need, and the less you have to worry about its

boiling away (these breads cook for a long time).

• Be sure your molds *and* their foil are very well greased.

Now let's get down to the basics. There are three types of vessels in which you can steam your breads—two stovetop and one plug-in. Read on.

• *Using a large conventional pot on the stovetop.* Put the trivet or equivalent down first, then place the covered breads on them. You'll pour enough boiling water into the cooking vessel to come halfway up the sides of the molds. Cover the pot and steam: Typically, breads steamed in a large coffee can or loaf pan take 3 to $3^{1}/_{2}$ hours; breads steamed in smaller, shallower cans, like large soup or tomato cans or small loaf pans, take $1^{3}/_{4}$ to 2 hours. Test the bread(s) with a skewer, as directed in the individual recipes. It's pretty easy to identify an underdone bread. Just recover it and

Continued on next page

COOKING LOAF BREADS
WITH STEAM CONTINUED

go on steaming, checking it again after about 20 minutes.

• *Using a slow-cooker.* This is probably the most hassle-free way of steaming breads—I recommend the very large oval ones. Place the prepared batter-filled mold(s) on a heat-proof trivet or the equivalent on the bottom of the slow-cooker. Pour enough boiling water into the slow-cooker to come halfway up the sides of the mold(s). Cover the slow-cooker and steam the bread, using the High setting, for 2 1/2 to 3 1/2 hours (the shorter time is for tomato- or soup-can size molds or small loaf pans; the longer time is for large loaf pans). Remove the mold(s) from the slow-cooker, and test and cool as directed in the recipe.

• *Using a pressure cooker.* When you've placed the prepared batter-filled mold(s) on the rack of the pressure cooker or a heat-proof trivet, pour boiling water into the cooker to come halfway up the sides of the mold(s). Lock the pressure-cooker lid and bring to high, steam-emitting heat, then immediately lower to the mid range. For one large bread (in a coffee can or loaf pan), cook under mid-range pressure for 40 minutes; for smaller cans or loaves, cook for about 25 minutes. Turn off the heat and let the cooker return to normal pressure. Unlock the lid, remove the bread, and test. If the bread is done, cool as directed in the recipe; if not, re-cover the bread, bring the cooker back up to pressure, lower it to mid-range for 1 to 5 minutes (depending on how close to done the bread is), then turn off the heat and let the pressure come down to normal again. The pro of using a pressure cooker: cooking time is shortened. The con: it's more of a hassle to make adjustments if the bread is not quite done.

Chapter 3

SOUTHWESTERN CORNBREADS

Chiles, Tortillas, and Flame, Oh My!

So ubiquitous and well-loved are cornbreads accented with jalapeño or green chile that it's hard to remember a time when they weren't on the scene. But until the mid-1970s, they were largely unknown to most present-day Americans. In *Southern Cooking*, Craig Claiborne's book of that era, he described them, a little breathlessly, as "one of the great adventures in taste." And so they were, and are.

Yet although the habit of adding peppers and spice to what would otherwise be basic conventional American corn-breads (Southern or Yankee) may be relatively recent, its roots are ancient. The combination of chiles and corn goes far, far back: It is yet another gift Native Americans gave us newcomers. Corn tortillas and salsa, or chile-spiked bean pots, or bean-and-meat-pots—that is where contemporary "Mexican cornbread" really begins.

What most of us know as such was born in the Lone Star State, where Tex-Mex began its border crossing into the hearts, minds, and palates of Americans. These breads had fertile cultural and agricultural ground from which to spring: first, the felicitous, ancient flavor combination of corn and chile, and second, the hot and savory corn casseroles that turn up in parts of Mexico and Central and South America. (You'll find some of them on pages 91–96.) Most important of all was that phenomenon called fusion. Increasing numbers of Latino immigrants helped awaken palates to increasing amounts of heat, and cornbread—long a part of Texas cuisine—surfed the chile-jalapeño-salsa heat wave brilliantly.

Earlier, in the 1950s, the late Helen Corbitt, doyenne of Texas cooking, entertaining, and recipes, who ruled the influential culinary roost of Neiman Marcus's Zodiac Room restaurant for many years, first gave the imprimatur of upscale gringo respectability to these native flavors in her cookbooks, newspaper column ("Kitchen Klatter"), and, of course, the department store. More recently, a host of New Southwestern chefs—Stephen Pyles (Texas), Mark Miller (New Mexico), Jay McCarthy (Texas and Colorado)—as well as chefs who live outside the region yet are inspired by Southwestern or Mexican flavors, like Bobby Flay in New York and Rick Bayless in Chicago, have been at play with these seasonings and certainly have helped continue their popularization: The odds are good that almost any bread-stuff served in their restaurants will contain both corn or cornmeal, and some form of chile.

And so these cornbreads blend old and new, *right now* with an ancient *then*. And that is sweet indeed, and timeless.

Chou-Chou's Original Dallas Hot-Stuff Cornbread

MAKES 12 SQUARES

This is a particularly good, early Tex-Mex cornbread from my particularly good friend Chou-Chou. It is more elaborate than some, and quite rich, with a slightly sweet, almost cake-like texture. Chou-Chou makes hers with sliced pickled jalapeños straight out of a can and she uses $1/2$ cup instead of the $1/4$ cup I use. I have made it with fresh jalapeños, charred directly on the stove, then peeled and chopped (with seeds included, as I like things hot), which is the tastiest but most time-consuming way to go. When in a hurry, I use the jarred fire-roasted pickled jalapeños, such as the Mazetti brand; delish and simpler.

Chou-Chou remembers that back in her non-vegetarian days, she added crisp crumbled bacon to this cornbread.

Vegetable oil cooking spray
$1\frac{1}{4}$ cups unbleached white flour

$1\frac{3}{4}$ cups stone-ground yellow cornmeal
3 tablespoons sugar
1 tablespoon plus 1 teaspoon baking powder
$1/2$ teaspoon baking soda
1 teaspoon salt
3 eggs
$2\frac{1}{2}$ cups milk
$1/3$ cup mild vegetable oil
2 fresh garlic cloves, pressed
1 large onion, finely chopped or, if you prefer, grated
1 cup canned creamed corn (see Pantry, page 351)
$1/4$ to $1/2$ cup sliced jalapeño peppers (fire-roasted, sautéed fresh, or canned pickled)
$1\frac{1}{2}$ cups (6 ounces) grated sharp Cheddar or Jack cheese
1 tablespoon butter
Salt, for sprinkling the bread

1. Preheat the oven to 400°F. Spray an 11-by-15-inch baking pan with oil, and set aside.

2. Sift or stir together the flour, cornmeal, sugar, baking powder, baking soda, and salt in a medium bowl.

3. Break the eggs into a second medium bowl, and whisk them well. Whisk into them the milk, oil, and pressed garlic.

4. Combine the wet and dry mixtures, using a whisk (the batter will be thinner than usual).

Use as few strokes as possible. Stir in the onion, creamed corn, jalapeños, and half the cheese, mixing just until the ingredients are well combined.

5. Pour the batter into the prepared pan and top with the reserved cheese. Bake until golden brown, 35 to 40 minutes. Remove from the oven and dot with the butter (which will melt instantly) and a sprinkle of salt. Serve, hot, right away. But, as Chou-Chou says, "It is also fabulous cold the next day."

·M·E·N·U·

WHEN DAVID AND CD GOT THE STORM WINDOWS UP

Frijoles Charros (page 309)

*

Jane's Texas-via-Vermont Mexican Cornbread

*

Salad of Mesclun, Shredded Cabbage, Diced Honeycrisp Apple, and Scallion, with a Cilantro-Honey Vinaigrette

*

Ginger Cookies

*

Baked Apples with Cinnamon and Maple Syrup

*

Black Tea with Warm Milk and Mexican Honey

Jane's Texas-via-Vermont Mexican Cornbread

MAKES 12 SQUARES

Jane is the Texan sister-in-law of my Vermont neighbor Peter Stamm. Her Southwestern cornbread, made without wheat flour or sweetener, lets the corn-ness come through loud and clear, even with all the embellishments. It's ultrarich: it contains three eggs and quite a bit of oil, which, with the creamed corn, make it very moist. The finished product has nice crunchy edges and a golden brown top: It's almost impossible to stop eating.

Vegetable oil cooking spray
1½ cups stone-ground yellow
   cornmeal
1 teaspoon salt
2 teaspoons baking powder
½ teaspoon baking soda
⅓ cup plus 1 tablespoon
   mild vegetable oil

3 eggs
1 cup buttermilk
1 small onion, diced
1 cup canned creamed corn
   (see Pantry, page 351)
2 to 3 fresh jalapeños, diced
1 cup (4 ounces) grated Cheddar
   cheese

1. Preheat the oven to 450°F. Spray an 11-by-15-inch baking dish with oil.

2. Put the cornmeal in a medium-size bowl and sift the salt, baking powder, and baking soda into it. Stir well.

3. Whisk together the ⅓ cup oil, eggs, and buttermilk in a large glass measuring cup. Place the remaining tablespoon of oil in the prepared pan, and place the pan in the oven. Have the remaining ingredients prepped and ready to roll.

4. Combine the wet and dry mixtures together, stirring with a fork or whisking a few times to get rid of any large lumps, but don't overbeat. The batter will be somewhat thinner than most cornbreads.

5. Quickly stir in the onion, creamed corn, jalapeños, and cheese. Remove the hot pan from the oven and transfer the batter into it, then return the pan to the oven.

6. Bake the cornbread until golden and crusty around the edges, 20 to 22 minutes.

Patsy Watkins's Rockin' Cornbread

MAKES 8 WEDGES

Patsy Watkins, chair of the University of Arkansas School of Journalism, makes a jalapeño cornbread that is similar to my very own Dairy Hollow House Skillet-Sizzled Cornbread (page 12). Patsy is very particular that the jalapeños be pickled for the piquancy of the vinegar.

Vegetable oil cooking spray
1 cup unbleached white flour
1 cup stone-ground yellow cornmeal
1 tablespoon baking powder
¼ teaspoon salt
¼ teaspoon baking soda
1¼ cups buttermilk
1 egg
2 tablespoons sugar
¼ cup mild vegetable oil
¾ cup frozen corn kernels, thawed
About ¾ cup grated extra-sharp Cheddar and/or Monterey Jack cheese
⅓ cup chopped pickled jalapeños
2 tablespoons butter or mild vegetable oil

1. Preheat the oven to 375°F. Spray a 10-inch cast-iron skillet with oil, and set aside.

2. Sift together the flour, cornmeal, baking powder, and salt into a medium bowl.

3. In a smaller bowl, stir the baking soda into the buttermilk. Whisk in the egg, sugar, and oil. Then stir in the corn, cheese, and jalapeños.

4. Put the prepared skillet on the stove over medium heat, add the butter, and heat until the butter melts and is just starting to sizzle. Tilt the pan to coat both the sides and bottom.

5. Pour the wet ingredients into the dry and combine them quickly, using as few strokes as possible. Scrape the batter into the hot, prepared pan and bake until golden brown, 20 to 25 minutes. Let cool for a few moments, and slice into wedges to serve.

Con Queso

Cornbread and dairy products go together almost as well tastewise and nutritionally as the ancient combo of cornbread and beans (like beans, dairy products supply amino acids corn is lacking, and vice versa). We've already come across milk and buttermilk in countless recipes Northern and Southern; in the Southwest, dairy often appears as cheese.

The food Hernán Cortés and his army found in Mexico City in 1519 was based on corn and beans, enriched with local ingredients from chiles to chocolate. But there were no dairy products, because there were no cows. Cortés changed that: Part of his entourage were offspring of the cattle Christopher Columbus had taken to Hispaniola on his second New World voyage in 1493.

The land was hospitable to cattle, especially the region now called El Norte, which extends along 1,800 miles of United States border and is quite distinct geographically and historically. Successive waves of immigrants left their mark: Spanish, Sephardic, Chinese, Mormon, and Mennonite people all settled in northern Mexico. Most brought their own traditions of dairying. Over time, El Norte became famous for cheese.

Thus cheese, especially in El Norte, began to find its way into many traditional dishes, almost always including or served with corn tortillas. *Queso fundito* (cheese fondue), *sopa de queso* (cheese soup), cheese enchiladas, quesadillas . . . all went into Tex-Mex, and eventually Southwestern-style, cornbreads.

CHIPOTLE CORNBREAD

MAKES 8 WEDGES

Chipotle chile peppers are actually jalapeño peppers that have been dried and smoked. They are often packed in adobo sauce, which is full of herbs and spices and adds lots of flavor in and of itself. Together, they lend this cornbread a slightly complex, smoky-sweet-hot flavor.

If you like, bacon drippings can be used in place of the butter; the bacon's smokiness plays up that of the chipotles.

This is excellent with almost any kind of bean stew.

Vegetable oil cooking spray

⅓ cup butter

1 cup coarse stone-ground yellow cornmeal

1 cup unbleached white flour

2 teaspoons sugar

2 teaspoons baking powder

½ teaspoon salt

2 eggs, lightly beaten

⅔ cup milk

4 canned chipotle peppers (stems removed and discarded) plus 2 teaspoons adobo sauce, puréed

1. Preheat the oven to 400°F. Spray a 10-inch cast-iron skillet with oil and dollop in the butter.

2. Combine the cornmeal, flour, sugar, baking powder, and salt in a large bowl.

3. Whisk together the eggs, milk, and puréed chipotle-adobo mix in a small bowl.

4. Place the prepared skillet in the oven to heat up for a few minutes, allowing the butter to melt.

5. Combine the cornmeal mixture and the egg mixture, stirring until everything is just mixed. Then pull the skillet from the oven and pour about half the melted butter from the skillet into the batter. Stir the butter in, and working quickly so the skillet remains almost smoking hot, transfer the batter into it. Put the whole shebang back in the oven and bake until it's deep golden brown, 20 to 25 minutes.

"Two teaspoons of baking powder?
Well, I like it rather flat.
I substituted cayenne pepper;
it should get a rise from that!"

—MAX YOHO, FROM
"CORNBREAD POEM" © 2004
(*Felicia, These Fish Are Delicious,*
Dancing Goat Press)

SERIOUSLY SPICY MAIN DISH CORNBREAD

SERVES 6 TO 8 AS A SIDE DISH,
4 AS AN ENTRÉE

I have to say that I love, love, *love* this particular cornbread, a kickin', very hot meal in a pan. Is it really a full meal? You bet. Serve it with either a salad or the simplest of soups (like heated-up tomato juice with a bit of golden miso stirred in at the end, and the juice of a lime), and, honey, *you have dined*. Fresh mango for dessert, maybe with lemon sorbet, or just ice-cold watermelon wedges. Tecate or Dos Equis to drink.

¼ cup mild vegetable oil

1 onion, chopped

1¼ cups stone-ground white cornmeal

⅓ cup whole wheat pastry flour

1 teaspoon sugar

¾ teaspoon salt

¼ teaspoon baking soda

1 teaspoon baking powder

1 cup buttermilk

1 egg

¾ cup canned creamed corn
(see Pantry, page 351)

2 cups well-drained cooked kidney beans

½ cup sliced pickled jalapeño peppers, well drained

1 cup (4 ounces) grated sharp Cheddar cheese, or a Cheddar-Monterey Jack mixture

1. Preheat the oven to 400°F.

2. Place a 10-inch cast-iron skillet over medium heat, and add 1 tablespoon of the oil. Add the onion and sauté it until it's limp and transparent, about 5 minutes.

3. As the onion sautés, combine the cornmeal, pastry flour, sugar, salt, baking soda, and baking powder in a medium-large bowl. Stir them together well.

4. Whisk together the buttermilk, egg, and creamed corn in a small bowl. In a second small bowl, stir together the beans and jalapeños.

5. By this time the onions should be soft, and the oven nice and hot. Remove the skillet from the stove and scrape the onions into the bowl with the beans. Add the remaining vegetable oil to the skillet, and place the skillet—containing only the oil—in the oven.

6. Wait a minute or so, until the skillet gets good and hot; the oil should be almost

smoking. Then, working quickly, stir together the cornmeal mixture and the buttermilk mixture until barely combined. Stir in the bean mixture with just a couple of strokes. Carefully remove the hot skillet from the oven. Pour the hot oil from the skillet into the batter and stir into the batter briefly. Place the hot skillet down on your stovetop or other heat-proof surface, and transfer the batter into the skillet. Pop the whole thing into the oven.

7. Let bake for 20 minutes, then carefully pull the cornbread out of the oven. Sprinkle it with the cheese and lower the temperature to 350°F. Let the cornbread bake until firm and golden, another 20 to 25 minutes. Let stand in the pan for at least 10 minutes before cutting it, otherwise it will fall apart on you.

SONORAN SKILLET CORNBREAD WITH MESQUITE MEAL

MAKES 8 WEDGES

Think of mesquite at all, and you probably think of mesquite-grilled something-or-other. But this unprepossessing tree (a member of the locust family, like carob, or Saint John's bread) yields much greater culinary treasure: its long brown seed pods, which, when ripe, can be ground to make a flourlike meal. Mesquite meal is almost stunningly delicious, as well as nutrient-rich. Quite sweet (though low on the glycemic index), relatively high in protein, it's been used by natives of vast parts of the Southwest and Central Americas. I guarantee you have never tasted anything quite like it: Rich, haunting undernotes, a bit nutty, yet also reminiscent of chocolate and cinnamon, it's a buff-brown colored, slightly granular flour (in short, a meal). It has become one of my favorite unusual ingredients to play with. (For more information, see the Pantry, page 355.)

Mesquite meal makes an already good, more-or-less classic skillet cornbread that much more delicioso. To purchase this flavorful flour, go to www.cocinadevega.com.

**1 tablespoon butter or
    bacon drippings**

2 eggs

2 cups buttermilk

1 tablespoon sugar

1 teaspoon salt

½ teaspoon baking soda

1 teaspoon baking powder

**1¼ cups stone-ground blue or
    yellow cornmeal**

½ cup mesquite meal

**3 tablespoons unbleached white or
    whole wheat pastry flour**

1. Preheat the oven to 375°F. Put the butter or bacon drippings in a 10-inch cast-iron skillet, and place it in the oven.

2. Combine the eggs and buttermilk in a small bowl or measuring cup, whisking together well with a fork. Combine the sugar, salt, baking soda, baking powder, cornmeal, mesquite meal, and flour in a medium bowl.

3. Stir the egg mixture into the dry ingredients, beating with a whisk until the dry ingredients are moistened and incorporated. Do not overbeat. The batter will be on the thin side.

4. Pull the skillet from the oven. It should be good and hot, with the fat sizzling. Quickly transfer the batter to the hot skillet, and return the skillet to the oven.

5. Bake until firm, fragrant, and browned, 20 to 25 minutes. Serve in wedges from the pan.

"If all we had were mesquites,
we'd still have roosts for birds,
holes for bugs, flowers for bees.
We'd still have furniture,
fence posts, and fires,
coffee and flour and jelly.
The past would still have
its wagon wheels, spokes,
gumdrops and glue.
The future would be sure
with places for kids to climb,
and rest for all in dappled shade."

—Jan Epton Seale,
"In Praise of Mesquites,"
www.prairiepoetry.org

PIKI: FOOD OF
PEACEABLE PEOPLE

One bite of piki, its gossamer-thin, shatteringly fragile blue-gray rolled layers—crisp and then instantly tender in your mouth, full of grainy corn flavor yet so light and delicate the word *bread* seems not to apply—and you know you are eating something quite unlike anything else; something almost otherworldly. But piki is and isn't just food, just as it's wholly of this world yet also spiritual. This old dish—Hopis have been making piki since at least 1,500 years before the birth of Christ— is life's connective tissue for this venerable lineage of humanity, whose name means "the peaceable people." Piki is one reason this lineage has continued unbroken for so long. It links here-and-now with past and future, generations before with generations to come. Piki, its mysterious blue-gray color deepened by the use of culinary ash, is both everyday food and feast food. For the former, the thin batter-breads are formed into slightly more sturdy rolls, about ten to twelve inches long and two inches wide. These are eaten not with the bowl-scraping roughness we use for bread or tortillas (piki are far too delicate) but as an accompaniment to stews. For special feasts, celebrations, and ceremonies, the dough is made into folded piki, each about eight inches square.

Long before piki is rolled or folded, before the batter is even mixed up, the process begins: with a piki stone. Some piki stones, usually about three feet long by two feet wide and always of dense, flat basaltic or volcanic rock, have been in families for years.

Corn, the primary crop raised by these great agriculturalists, is so much at the center of Hopi life, one might even say it *is* life. Blue cornmeal is the first solid food to cross the lips of infants at their clan-naming ceremony. A special, slow-cooked sweetened moist corn cake is served when girls reach puberty. In traditional Hopi weddings, corn plays countless roles, serving as the main ingredient in most of the feasts that take place in the week-long celebration. Corn is also dower-price (paid to the groom's family, for in this matrilineal culture, he will leave them and become part of his bride's family), proving ground (the bride shows that she's worthy of having her groom's birth family give him up, by spending up to four days hand-grinding corn at her mother-in-law's home), ceremonial nourishment (the bride's family brings piki to the groom's family, to help sustain them as they weave the wedding clothes), and makeup (the night before the actual vows, the bride's family gently powders her face and arms with fine cornmeal while she holds dried corn ears in her hands). And when the bride finally approaches her husband, on the wedding day itself, she carries a basket of blue corn meal, wrapped in a cloth. It should not surprise us, then, to learn that at the last of life's great thresholds, ears of corn accompany the body to its final rest. And so does piki, to nourish and sustain the deceased as they travel into the spirit world.

Taste this remarkable, ethereally light bread, by visiting www.hopimarket.com. Click on "unique crafts." There you will find piki. You can call 520-737-9434 and talk to Melcina (she prefers to be called Cina) Nutumya, who is a full Hopi of the Butterfly clan. She makes and ships the bread to order, each roll carefully wrapped in film and light as air.

In fact, when my box of piki arrived from Cina by express mail, Pat, of my Vermont post office, handed it to me, saying, "Looks like someone sent you an empty box." Piki, that lightweight, is strong enough to bind a culture that has outlasted the fall of the Roman Empire and is still quietly going about its business.

CopperWynd Chipotle Cornbread

MAKES 9 SQUARES

From the CopperWynd Resort in Scottsdale, Arizona, this cornbread is a fine, spicy, moist classic Southwestern-style cornbread in the best border cuisine tradition: hot with canned chipotles in adobo, chunky with whole corn kernels, sugar-sweetened and buttery rich, mellowed and moistened by buttermilk. It's awfully good along with any sweet-smoky-savory beans, but it's de rigueur for the CopperWynd Chocolate Bread Pudding on page 332. Being the whole-grainy girl that I am, I like substituting whole wheat pastry flour for the unbleached white.

Vegetable oil cooking spray

1 cup stone-ground yellow cornmeal

1 cup unbleached white flour

1/3 cup sugar

1 1/2 teaspoons baking powder

1/2 teaspoon baking soda

1/2 teaspoon salt

2 eggs

1 1/4 cups buttermilk

1/3 cup diced canned chipotle peppers in adobo sauce, sauce included (remove any tough stems)

1/4 cup melted butter

Kernels cut from 1 ear of fresh corn (1/2 cup; see Shuck and Jive, page 49), or 1/2 cup frozen corn kernels, measured and thawed

1. Preheat the oven to 425°F. Spray a 9-inch square pan well with oil.

2. Whisk the cornmeal, flour, sugar, baking powder, baking soda, and salt in a medium bowl, combining well.

3. Beat together the eggs, buttermilk, chipotles, and melted butter in a separate bowl.

4. Combine the wet and dry mixtures, stirring until just combined, then add the corn with a couple of stirs.

5. Into the pan goes the batter, and then into the oven goes the pan. Bake the cornbread until it is pale golden, with its edges pulling away from the side of the pan, about 15 minutes. Serve warm if accompanying an entrée.

"Shortcake" of Savory Onion-Topped Cornbread

MAKES 6 LARGE WEDGES

Marilyn Kennedy from Broken Arrow, Oklahoma, sent me her cornbread recipe, which is certainly not your typical Southwestern green chile cornbread. It's herb-scented and cheese-accented, something of a mix of savory bread pudding, cornbread, and shortcake. I've adapted it here.

Vegetable oil cooking spray

2 tablespoons butter

2 large onions, chopped
(to equal about 2½ cups)

1 cup (8 ounces) full-fat or reduced-fat
(not fat-free) sour cream

2 teaspoons cornstarch

¾ cup (3 ounces) shredded extra-
sharp Cheddar cheese

1½ cups self-rising cornmeal
(see Pantry, page 350)

2 tablespoons sugar

¼ teaspoon dried dillweed

2 eggs

·M·E·N·U·

Bright Supper for a Gray November Night

Mesclun or Baby Greens Salad
with Mustard Vinaigrette

✳

Uncannily Good Santa Fe–Style
Quick Green Chile Soup-Stew
(page 321)

✳

"Shortcake" of Savory Onion-Topped
Cornbread

✳

Dark, Extra-Gingery Gingerbread,
with Darra's Hot Citrus Sauce
(page 343)

1 can (8.34 ounces) creamed corn
(see Pantry, page 351)

⅓ cup milk

2 tablespoons vegetable oil

⅛ teaspoon Tabasco or other prepared
hot sauce

1. Preheat the oven to 400°F.

2. Place a large nonstick or oil-sprayed skillet over medium heat. Add the butter and when it has started sizzling, add the onions. Sauté until softened, translucent, and almost limp, 5 to 7 minutes. Remove from the heat and let the onions cool slightly.

3. Meanwhile, whisk together the sour cream and cornstarch in a small bowl or measuring cup. Stir in ¼ cup of the Cheddar cheese, and the slightly cooled sautéed onions.

4. Combine the self-rising cornmeal, sugar, and dillweed in a large bowl. Set aside.

5. Combine the eggs, creamed corn, milk, vegetable oil, and hot sauce in a medium bowl. Stir this mixture into the cornmeal mixture in the large bowl. Mix until just blended; do not overbeat.

6. Turn the batter into the skillet. Dollop the onion mixture evenly over the top, starting at the outside edges and working inward, and sprinkle with the remaining ½ cup cheese. Bake until the shortcake is firm and the cheese is melted and golden, 25 to 30 minutes. Serve hot, and get ready for major accolades.

CORN TORTILLAS

MAKES 8 TO 12 TORTILLAS, DEPENDING ON SIZE

And the last shall be first. That is, as we conclude our Southwestern corn celebration, we now come to the mother-root of all cornbreads, the corn tortilla, America's real, original, native, ancient, contemporary much-loved cornbread. And also its first. In any true telling of cornbread gospels, tortillas are the Book of Genesis.

As you'll see from the recipe below, this is the simplest of cornbreads: just four ingredients. That said, tortilla making is an art and craft and requires a little bit of practice to perfect. Don't lose heart at the length of these directions: you'll get it after the first couple of tortillas; I'm just going to hold your hand as we walk through it this first time.

> 2 cups masa harina
>   (see Masa Class, page 85)
> ½ teaspoon salt
> 1¼ cups very warm but not boiling
>   water
> **Additional water and masa
>   as needed**

1. Place the masa harina in a bowl with the salt, and add the hot water all at once. Stir together with your hands; almost instantly the masa harina will absorb the water. Knead it, by hand, for 3 or 4 minutes. You want a soft dough, moist, but not in the least sticky. When you're finished kneading, virtually all the masa should be in a nice ball, no unincorporated bits of dough or flour, and none sticking to your hands. If this hasn't happened, amend with small amounts of additional water or masa harina until the right texture is achieved (if you're uncertain as to whether the right texture has been reached, cover the dough and let it rest; when it's time to make tortillas, one tortilla will tell you whether the masa is wet, dry, or just right—see step 4). Also note: Masa dough is incredibly forgiving; you cannot overknead it. Any scraps of masa can easily be kneaded back in and re-formed into new tortillas.

2. Cover the prepared masa and let it rest for 10 to 15 minutes.

3. In the meantime, cut two circles from heavy-duty plastic (a gallon-size zip-top freezer bag works well) to fit your tortilla press (see What It Takes to Make a Tortilla, page 86). Set aside.

4. Place a cast-iron skillet or griddle on the stove and turn the heat to a good, steady medium-high. As the skillet heats, pinch out a golf ball–size lump of the masa dough, and roll it between your palms until it forms a ball. The dough should neither stick to, nor crumble in, your hands.

*Bueno como el pan
(as good as bread)*
—A SPANISH COMPLIMENT

5. Open your tortilla press. Lay one circle of plastic on the bottom plate. Put the ball of dough on this, flattening it slightly with the heel of your hand. Top it with the second circle of heavy plastic.

6. Lower the hinged upper plate onto the bottom plate. Once it's shut, quickly raise the tortilla press's handle, then lower it until it catches. Don't push it all the way down at first; until you get the hang of it, which you will soon enough, making super-thin tortillas can be tricky.

7. Open the tortilla press. Wow! Prepare to impress yourself. Your tortilla will be beautifully round, 5 or 6 inches in diameter, and of a consistent thickness—a little thicker than commercial tortillas. Your tortillas might also be smaller in dimension than the factory-mades, depending on what size masa ball you used.

8. Leaving the tortilla on the press, gently peel the plastic layer off the upper side of the tortilla. Lift the raw tortilla, still on its lower circle of plastic, from the press. Gently reverse it, plastic and all, onto the palm of your less-dominant hand (in other words, the right-handed would place the tortilla in their left palm). The plastic-covered side of the tortilla is now up; the tortilla itself is resting gently on your palm.

9. Move next to the stove, facing the skillet, and very gently peel the plastic up and off the tortilla. (This is the only tricky part until you get used to it, and it isn't very tricky.) I've found this works a little more easily than peeling the tortilla off the plastic.

10. Slide the tortilla off your hand, briskly but gently—no dramatic pizza dough–like flippings—into the skillet, which by now should be very, very hot (you may want to lower the heat just slightly, but not much).

11. Let the tortilla cook in the hot skillet or on the griddle for 35 to 40 seconds on the first side; as you're doing this, proceed to shape and flatten the next tortilla. Gently lift the tortilla in the skillet. The underneath of a tortilla made from yellow masa harina will have become a paler yellow; whether white or yellow, it should be nicely freckled with golden-brown spots. If it is, turn it over with a spatula or two forks, or, if you have deft hands, with your fingers. Cook the second side for about 40 seconds (with luck it may puff slightly); then turn back to the first side for another 20 to 30 seconds. The whole process should not take much longer than a minute and a half to 2 minutes; less time if your tortilla is on the thin side, more if it's thicker. And of course, once you get the hang of it, you can have more than

one going at a time, and even more than one skillet.

12. Remove the tortilla(s) from the griddle as they're done, and repeat, the process with the remaining dough. To keep the tortillas warm for up to 20 minutes, wrap them in a clean dish towel, adding each tortilla as it's done. For longer than that—up to 1 hour—wrap the towel-swaddled tortilla stack in aluminum foil and place it in a very low oven.

NOTE: Black spots on your tortillas mean your skillet is too hot. A stiff, not pliable tortilla that is not blackened, however, means your skillet was the right temperature, but that you left the tortilla in it too long.

To learn how to make tortillas all the way from scratch, starting with the dry corn itself, go to www.cornbreadgospels.com.

ALL ABOUT TORTILLAS

MASA CLASS: WHAT'S MASA HARINA?

Tortillas are made from their own special type of corn flour, called masa harina. Please note: corn *flour,* not corn *meal.* Masa harina's consistency is flour-like, not meal-like, and its special texture, distinctive flavor, and one-of-a-kind scent—a scent instantly recognizable as that of tortillas—derive from the fact that the corn it is ground from is precooked and treated with lime. (For the full story on this ancient liming process, called nixtamalization, see the Pantry, page 355.)

Just as you can purchase ready-made tortillas of either white or yellow cornmeal, so you can purchase white or yellow masa to make tortillas at home. If you were blind-folded, you probably couldn't distinguish the taste difference between the two, so preferences are based on which one looks more appealing to you and what color tortilla you grew up eating (if you grew up eating tortillas).

Masa is easy to find in America today. Maseca, the most popular brand in Mexico, is in almost any U.S. supermarket in a community where there is a sizable Latino population. And you'd be hard-pressed to enter any American supermarket and *not* find the Quaker brand, labeled simply Masa Harina. Another excellent brand sometimes available is White Wings (in Spanish, La Paloma) Masa para Tortillas. If you can't find it locally, order it through www.melissaguerra.com.

These three and many other masa harinas are mass-produced, "enriched, degerminated" products, not whole-grain. At a health food store or natural food market, you can sometimes find organic stone-ground whole-grain masa harina, which works like a charm and is both tastier and better for you. (You can also find it on the web, at www.bobsredmill.com.) Whatever you do, do NOT, under any circumstances, attempt to use cornmeal instead of masa harina in tortilla making. It will not work.

Now, just to clear up one other possible source of confusion. While "masa harina" refers to the corn flour we've been talking about, just plain "masa" is the name for the corn dough itself, from which tortillas are made. You can make or procure masa in several different ways, but in this book, we're going to keep it simple, and just stick to the recipe opposite, using masa harina.

WHAT IT TAKES
TO MAKE A TORTILLA

The rhythmic sound of corn tortillas being patted out is sometimes called the heartbeat of Mexico. But if you didn't grow up making them, it will be a while, if ever, before you are patting them out by hand. Instead, you will want to employ a few low-tech items and supplies:

- a large, well-seasoned, heavy cast-iron skillet, griddle, or *comal* (a traditional flat cast-iron griddle without sides, about 9 inches in diameter; in earlier times, these were made of very flat heated stones). You can't use a lightweight pan because you'll need steady, even heat for awhile. A lighter skillet will warp; a nonstick skillet will get that funky, troubling, been-on-the-burner-too-long smell.

- a tortilla press, which is two hinged-together large heavy flat metal plates, between which you flatten the tortillas to a consistent thinness by pressing down on a handle. You probably think you can get by with a rolling pin and your fingers; well, you probably can't, and certainly not at first. Tortilla presses are easily found. If you can't find them at your local kitchenware store or Mexican market, order them through www.melissaguerra.com.

If you really don't want to use a press, use two plates, pressing the dough out between the *backs* of the plates. This, in effect, creates a quasi-tortilla press. Obviously, you want to choose plates with backs that are more or less flat. It'll work, but a press is much easier.

- heavy-duty plastic bags, such as gallon-size zip-tops made for use in the freezer. Cut one bag open into two squares. Trim the squares to just slightly bigger than the tortilla press. (Now don't ask, "So what did the Mayans use for plastic?" Remember, nobody loves a smart-ass.)

With these items, a stove, technique, and your masa, you're ready to go.

SERVING AND REHEATING
HOMEMADE TORTILLAS

Once you've made homemade tortillas you'll want to either serve them immediately, or keep them warm as follows: Stack them one atop the other as they come off the griddle, covering them with a towel or napkin to hold the warmth. They are traditionally served in a covered tortilla basket, still wrapped, and are rewrapped after each diner has taken his or hers.

Though they are far superior when freshly made, you can successfully rewarm homemade room-temp tortillas with pretty good results in one of two ways. Either stack 5 or 6 on top of each other, wrapping them securely in foil, and pop them into a 275°F to 300°F oven for 10 to 12 minutes. Or, if you just have a couple, get the griddle nice and hot again and give each tortilla a quick reheat for 10 to 15 seconds per side.

CLASS PROJECT

I have a core belief that every American owes it to him- or herself to make, at least once, the really, really, really serious, from-scratch tortillas the way the Native Americans did it. Why? Because, besides making an *amazing* tortilla, you put your hands in, and on, the lifeblood of America; you take communion with your own history, making your own masa directly from corn, by soaking dried corn overnight in water that you have treated with either commercially available or homemade lime, hulling the corn (easier than it sounds), and grinding it (in a small mill or food processor). This is obviously far more labor intensive than making corn tortillas from ready-to-use masa harina, and I know, pragmatically, that very few of you might wish to take the time and trouble to do this. If you are one of the few, though, I want to tell you how to do it—without taking up the time and energy of your fellow readers. So instead I've put the complete from-scratch directions on the Internet. How's that for handy? Just go to

www.cornbreadgospels.com and there, my dears, you will find it (along with a few other things that I just couldn't fit in this book).

For those of you who are teachers, or have children in the fourth or fifth grade, I have to tell you, making corn tortillas from the corn up is one major blast of a class or home project (supervised, of course), and it teaches one piece of American history as almost nothing else can. So go on and check it out.

WHIM AND SUSTENANCE

In Mexico, the farther south you get from the border, the more the corn tortilla, not the flour tortilla, rules, as it has for thousands of years. It nourishes: Each day, the average contemporary Mexican eats a little over a pound of dough made of corn, mostly in the form of tortillas. In the countryside, this jumps to seventy percent of the daily caloric intake. And lest you recoil in anti-carb horror, consider that the tortilla is far more nutritious than plain old corn itself, thanks to nixtamalization (see Pantry, page 355), a process used since the ancient native inhabitants of the Americas first began domesticating wild corn. And although there are countless and seductive regional variations in seasonings and accompaniments, the process of making masa, the corn dough that is the basis of tortillas, has been the same throughout the country as a whole since before the Spaniards arrived.

The average six- to seven-inch corn tortilla has about sixty calories and a gram or so each of fat and protein. (The protein content is considerably amplified in beautiful synergy when the tortilla is eaten with beans.) The same tortilla also offers its eater twelve grams of carbohydrate, forty-four milligrams of calcium, and no gluten, a component of wheat and rye flours to which a surprising number of people are allergic.

But lest you think that corn tortillas, being daily bread, are strictly about sober sustenance in Mexico, consider the panoply of that country's appetizers, most of which use corn masa, griddled or fried, with a touch of herbs, shredded meat, cheese, chile, or some other combination infinitely varied but always savory. They're called *antojitos,* which means "little whims."

Thus the corn tortilla, to our neighbors to the south, is not only daily bread, but heart and soul, pleasure and laughter.

THE NEIGHBORHOOD TORTILLERIA

Thanks to the all-American reinvention that is immigration's greatest gift, many once south-of-the-border neighbors now live down the block. A vibrant Latino population means that, today, you'd be hard-pressed to find an American supermarket without both wheat and corn tortillas. But if you think supermarket tortillas are pretty good, even just okay, then, my friend, believe me—you've never had a fresh one, and you have a treat ahead of you.

The next best thing to making your own is to find yourself a neighborhood *tortilleria,* or tortilla bakery. Virtually every village in Mexico has at least one; and the same is true in almost every Mexican American community in America. Find the nearest Latino area and drive around; the odds are excellent that you'll find not only Mexican grocery stores, but a tortilleria or two (or many more, if you're in a large metropolitan area). Why? Because often cooking the foods of their homelands is the first or second step for American immigrants. The capital with which these brave new arrivals start these tiny businesses is small, and it rarely goes to décor or upscale location.

Besides fresh tortillas, usually incredibly reasonably priced and infinitely better than those mass-produced and sold at the supermarket, a tortilleria often sells masa—fresh corn dough—for you to make your own warm-from-the-griddle tortillas at home.

In which case you don't even have to mix masa harina and water: Just buy the dough and follow the recipe for Corn Tortillas (page 82), picking up at step 3.

Chapter 4

GLOBAL CORNBREADS
The Whole World in a Pan

Where corn has grown, so, inevitably, has cornbread. Corn has always traveled. First, with the careful, observant help of indigenous people, it crossbred itself into existence around 3000 B.C., in Mexico's Balsas River Basin region. But from there it quickly spread throughout southwestern North America and then farther, into Central America, then South America. When, about A.D. 1000, Native Americans began to migrate from the southwest to the north and east, they took corn with them and, by selection, developed corn strains adapted to colder climates. Corn was global long, long before corporations, pop stars, and the brand names we now call "global" even remotely existed. But unlike McDonald's, Wal-Mart, or Pepsi, corn did not force uniformity wherever it landed. On the contrary, adaptability to the region in which it found itself was its secret. Corn, with human help, adapted and modified; it could, and did, grow almost anywhere. And with each regional border crossing, corn intermarried with local foodways, ingredients, and traditions.

When we say "cornbread" in America today, our first thoughts are of the iterations presented in previous chapters: skillet-sizzled, buttermilk-moistened Southern cornbread; sweet cake-like Northern cornbread; spicy, smoky Southwestern cornbread. But global cornbreads go in some other directions, and we follow their paths here.

Just below the border, in Mexico, we encounter the closest cousins of contemporary North American cornbreads. *Pan de elote* (literally "bread of corn," see opposite page) has recognizable similarities, incorporating wheat flour and fresh corn kernels. Then we spin off into the sweet-savory pudding-like *budins* (see page 93), and into the leaf-wrapped meal-in-a-casing-of-steamed-cornbread, tamales. We find *humitas* (see page 94), also steamed, in Colombia, Peru, and Bolivia. And arepas (see pages 98–102), similar to our hoecakes, are the definitive daily bread of Colombia and adjacent Latin American countries.

From South America we trace corn's transit to Europe, which began when the ships of Columbus's first fleet returned to Spain in 1499. The Spaniards, who had originally sought more profitable trade routes to the East Indies spice islands, wound up achieving something quite different. First, they carried new ingredients, most importantly corn—but definitely not the spices that had prompted their journey—back to Europe. But second, they introduced some of those very same spices *to* the New World, such as the soft canela (Ceylon) cinnamon and black pepper for which they'd originally set sail. Through the years, these flavors, as well as haunting Middle Eastern anise, mixed with native New World ingredients, creating singular dishes that spoke uniquely of place and time.

TAKING ROOT EVERYWHERE

Meanwhile, New World corn began to take root in Old World Europe. And so we meet Portuguese cornbread, called *broa* (see page 103)—yeast-risen, round, dense—which seems made to soak up the big garlicky flavors of *caldo verde* (see page 318), that country's national soup. The Italians took to cornmeal as polenta and the Romanians as *mamaliga*—in both cases, cornmeal mush, not bread—and the French shunned corn except as a cattle fodder. But it was used in a very simple Cretan flat bread until quite recently, and in time the Greek army began to use 15 or 20 percent cornmeal in the soldiers' bread. And, though the Greeks were slow to incorporate it into their home baking, Greek bakeries have started to carry cornmeal-laced breads with notes of olive, walnuts, feta cheese, and greens.

When Portuguese traders carried maize to India in the late 1500s, it was adapted immediately, becoming the griddled flat bread *makki ki roti* (see page 109). This is served with deeply spiced *sarson ka saag* (see page 294), an irresistible dish of slow-cooked mustard greens, a combination that echoes, in a different accent, the American South's beloved cornbread and greens.

Around the same time, Turkish traders introduced cornmeal to Africa. There it was widely accepted, though it was mainly used as mush (as in Italy and Romania). But the southern part of the continent created a moist, simple, steam-cooked staple bread. And thus our next-to-last stop on our global cornbread tour is South African *mealiebrod* (see page 112). Although it is far from American cornbreads in taste, flavor, and texture, mealiebrod is another example of cornbread's significant global role. Our last port of call? Not just international . . . *interspecies.*

Baked, griddled, leaf-wrapped, steamed . . . cornbread anywhere, any time, any way, is an honest and earthy gift of sustenance, carried from the Americas to the whole round world.

PAN DE ELOTE (REAL MEXICAN PAN CORNBREAD)

SERVES 6 TO 8

This simple recipe is for *real* Mexican pan cornbread (unlike the jalapeño or chipotle cornbreads we often, in America, call "Mexican"). It's a slight variation of one that appears in Marilyn Tausend's *Cocina de la Familia*, a delightful book that traces family recipes from their origins in Mexico to their new American homes. In this case, the family is that of Maria Petra Vasquez, a native of Nuevo Leon, Mexico, who's made her home for many years in Garden City, Michigan. The recipe, using whole fresh corn or frozen corn kernels and wheat flour, is one her mother made. Her mother used lard; Petra prefers butter, and so do I. (I also use a little less in my version, and I've used cornmeal to replace part of the flour, too, with excellent results.)

Vegetable oil cooking spray

¾ cup unbleached white flour

⅓ cup stone-ground yellow cornmeal

2 teaspoons baking powder

1 teaspoon salt

1 cup milk

½ cup sour cream or reduced-fat
(not fat-free) sour cream

2 eggs

3 tablespoons butter, melted and
cooled

2 cups corn kernels, either frozen
and slightly thawed, or cut from
about 4 ears of fresh corn
(see Shuck and Jive, page 49)

I. Preheat the oven to 325°F. Spray an 8-by-11-inch baking pan with oil, and set aside.

2. Combine the flour, cornmeal, baking powder, and salt in a medium bowl. Stir together well.

3. Combine the milk, sour cream, eggs, and melted butter in a second medium bowl. Whisk together thoroughly.

4. Quickly combine the flour mixture and the milk mixture. Do not overbeat. Stir in the corn kernels, and scrape the batter into the prepared pan.

5. Bake until the bread is a deep golden brown and tests clean with a toothpick, 35 to 45 minutes. Let the bread cool for 5 minutes before slicing, but do serve it warm.

VARIATIONS:

Petra Vasquez occasionally adds 1 teaspoon grated onion, stirring it into the batter with the corn.

CHILE VERDE Another option is to add 2 tablespoons chopped fresh roasted poblanos.

·M·E·N·U·

YUCATÁN SUNDOWN

**Black Bean Soup
or Pinto Bean Stew**

*

**Green Salad with
Sliced Avocado and Tomato with
Cilantro-Lime Honey Vinaigrette**

*

**Budin de Elote with
Grated Monterey Jack Cheese**

*

**Fresh Sliced Mangoes
and Pineapples**

BUDIN DE ELOTE (MEXICAN-STYLE CORN SPOONBREAD)

SERVES 4 TO 5 AS AN ENTRÉE, 6 AS AN ACCOMPANIMENT

This Mexican-style spoonbread pudding (*budin* is Spanish for "pudding") can be served alongside any main dish, but it is hearty enough and rich enough in protein to serve as a vegetarian main course in itself. Thick, Mexican-style crème fraîche (*crema*, available in Mexican groceries) or sour cream or even whipped cream seasoned with salt and freshly ground black pepper are the most common traditional accompaniments; however, I think it's knock-you-out good with a pleasantly warm green chile sauce, either homemade or commercial. (My favorite is a brand called 505 Southwestern Medium Hot Green Chile Sauce: www.505chile.com or 1-888-505-CHILE.)

Vegetable oil cooking spray
2 pounds frozen corn kernels, thawed
½ cup milk
3 eggs, separated
¼ cup sugar
1 teaspoon salt
½ cup stone-ground yellow cornmeal
3 tablespoons butter, melted
½ cup (2 ounces) grated Monterey Jack cheese
1½ teaspoons baking powder
¼ teaspoon cream of tartar (optional)

1. Preheat the oven to 450°F. Spray an 8-by-11-inch baking pan (preferably glass) with oil, and set aside.

2. Place the corn in a food processor with the milk. Pulse-chop to make a slightly texture-y purée. Set aside.

3. Setting aside the egg whites, whisk the egg yolks in a large bowl until thickened. Beat in the sugar, then the salt, cornmeal, melted butter, and cheese. Stir well. Add the pulsed corn kernels. Sprinkle the baking powder over the mixture, and stir it in with a few quick strokes.

4. Beat the 3 reserved egg whites in a large bowl with the cream of tartar, if using, until the egg whites are stiff and glossy, but not dry. Gently fold them into the corn mixture, and transfer the mixture to the prepared pan. Immediately put it into the oven.

5. Let the budin bake for 10 minutes, then lower the heat to 350°F and continue baking until the top is deeply browned but still soft, 40 to 45 minutes more. Scoop the budin out of the pan to serve it.

HUMITAS
(BOLIVIAN-COLOMBIAN-STYLE CORN PUDDING)

SERVES 6 TO 8

The Spanish Colonial influence is very visible in this corn pudding, accented by cheese and scallions on the savory side, and by sugar, raisins, cinnamon, and anise on the sweet. You might say "Huh?" when you first read the combination, but the flavors work beautifully. Accompany humitas with any pot of spicy beans. Although not traditional, Beans, Dragon-in-the-New-South Style (page 305) are right neighborly with humitas. This souffléed pudding is substantial enough to serve as an entrée.

Vegetable oil cooking spray
1/2 cup milk
4 cups corn kernels (either cut from about 8 ears of fresh corn, see Shuck and Jive, page 49; or frozen corn kernels, measured and thawed)
3 eggs, separated
1 cup stone-ground yellow cornmeal
1/4 cup unbleached white flour
1 teaspoon baking powder
1 teaspoon paprika or mild powdered red chiles
3 tablespoons sugar
1/2 teaspoon cinnamon
1/2 teaspoon salt
4 to 6 scallions, white and 1 inch of green, diced
1/2 teaspoon aniseed
1/3 cup raisins
1 1/2 cups (6 ounces) grated Monterey Jack cheese
1/4 teaspoon cream of tartar

1. Preheat the oven to 400°F. Spray a 1 1/2-quart baking dish with oil.

2. Combine the milk with 3 cups of the corn in the food processor and pulse-chop, then buzz, to make an almost-smooth purée. Beat in the egg yolks, reserving the whites for later use.

3. Meanwhile, combine the cornmeal, flour, baking powder, paprika, sugar, cinnamon, and salt in a large bowl.

4. Stir the corn mixture into the dry ingredients. Then add the remaining cup of whole kernel corn, the scallions, aniseed, raisins, and half the cheese. Combine well.

5. Beat the 3 reserved egg whites with the cream of tartar in a large bowl until the egg whites are stiff and glossy, but not dry. Gently fold them into the corn mixture, and transfer

the batter to the prepared pan. Sprinkle with the remaining cheese.

6. Bake the humitas until it is golden brown, fragrant, firmed, and puffed, 25 to 30 minutes.

Variation: Humitas in Petite Pumpkin Cups

Baking the humitas in miniature pumpkin cups makes for a delightful presentation and gives the humitas a lovely edge of sweet cooked pumpkin; you scoop a bit of the pumpkin up with each bite of pudding.

Preheat the oven to 375°F. Slice the tops off 8 small pie pumpkins or the tiny variety called "Munchkins." Then dig out all seeds and loose fibers. Steam the pumpkins, cut side down, over boiling water for 3 to 5 minutes—just long enough to warm and very slightly soften the pumpkin flesh. Remove the pumpkins from the steamer, and sprinkle the interior of each lightly with salt and freshly ground pepper. Set aside.

Prepare the humitas mixture as given, but instead of placing it in the pan, divide it among the pumpkins, sprinkling a bit of the cheese atop each (bake any extra batter in a ramekin). Place the filled pumpkins in an oiled rimmed baking sheet and bake until the filling is firmed, puffed, and golden and the pumpkin is lightly brown and can be pierced with a fork with a slight effort, 35 to 45 minutes.

> "It had always been a pleasure to him to work in the corn, to help make the green shafts shoot up, and contrast their deep, full green with the harsh faded desert. . . . When the stalks were waist high, he took her to the field . . . a soft breeze made the leaves swing and whisper. He showed her . . . the individual hills, the slender plants and their promise . . ."
>
> —OLIVER LA FARGE, *Laughing Boy*

New Spain-Style Corn Pudding

SERVES 6 TO 8

This is the Mexican version of the humitas recipe on page 94, and you can see the colonial Spanish influence even more clearly in the use of all the dairy products: both soft and hard cheeses, and buttermilk, which adds an especially pleasing, savory quality.

Try a scoop of this as the centerpiece of a vegetable plate, with a bit of salsa or green or red chile sauce spooned over the top.

Vegetable oil cooking spray

3 cups corn kernels (either cut from about 6 ears of fresh corn, see Shuck and Jive, page 49; or frozen kernels, measured and thawed)

4 ounces crumbled fresh goat cheese, or Neufchâtel or cream cheese, at room temperature

1¼ cups buttermilk

3 eggs

1 cup stone-ground yellow cornmeal

1 tablespoon sugar

½ teaspoon salt

1 teaspoon baking powder

¼ teaspoon baking soda

¼ teaspoon cinnamon, preferably canela (see Pantry, page 348)

3 tablespoons melted butter

4 to 6 scallions, white and 1 inch of green, diced

⅓ cup chopped fresh roasted poblanos or well-drained canned chopped green chiles

1 to 1½ cups (4 to 6 ounces) grated Monterey Jack or Cheddar cheese

1. Preheat the oven to 350°F. Spray a 1½-quart baking dish with oil.

2. Combine 1½ cups of the corn, the goat cheese or Neufchâtel or cream cheese, and ¼ cup of the buttermilk in a food processor, and pulse-chop to a slightly textured purée. Whisk in the remaining 1 cup buttermilk and the eggs, beating well. Set aside.

3. Combine the cornmeal, sugar, salt, baking powder, baking soda, and cinnamon in a large bowl.

4. Pour the puréed corn mixture into the dry mixture, combining until well blended. Stir in the melted butter, scallions, poblanos, Monterey Jack or Cheddar cheese, and the remaining 1½ cups whole kernel corn.

5. Transfer the batter to the prepared baking dish. Bake the pudding until it is light golden brown and just barely firm, 50 to 55 minutes.

HUMITAS IN PERU,
VIA SOUTHERN CALIFORNIA

Carmen Sanchez's humitas are nothing like the ones on page 94. Hers are Peruvian: more like tamales, steamed in neatly wrapped green corn husks and made with slightly stale corn.

Carmen, a friend of my friend Suzanne Wickham-Beaird, once explained to me that there are no cornbreads as such in Peru, but humitas are eaten often. What you do is husk ears of corn, saving the husks, then cut the kernels off. But the corn should be a bit older, "more stale." Carmen demonstrated with her hands slicing off the kernels, then made a face. "If it spits juice at you, it's too juicy." You allot the kernels of three ears of corn per person, and you put them in the blender with "poquito leche," a tiny bit of milk, and process to make a slightly grainy mix, still a bit sticky. No eggs, no cornmeal, no masa. You transfer the mixture to a bowl. Now, if you want sweet humitas, you add a little light brown sugar, a few dashes of cinnamon, and a handful of raisins. If, on the other hand, you want salty, you add grated queso, or maybe a little shredded cooked chicken.

You lay out your corn husks, pulling a thin strip of husk from one end to act as a ribbon. Then, you make a mound of humitas dough on the husk, fold the short sides over, roll it up the long way, and tie it with the strip of husk.

The finished humitas then cook in the top of an oiled double boiler covered, for 20 to 25 minutes, or until hot and cooked through.

Though travelers might not speak the same language, cooks always do.

ALL ABOUT AREPAS

Arepas (pronounced ah-RAY-pahs) are to parts of Latin America, particularly Colombia and Venezuela, the basic, go-with-anything starch that supports, and sometimes serves as, almost every meal. Their origins go way, way back: They were to the Indians of Colombia and Venezuela what corn tortillas were to the Aztecs. And, again like tortillas, since their origins were as staple/survival food, for many centuries they were looked down on as the food of the poor. Fortunately they have been rediscovered, today, as comforting, delicious, and satisfying, for anyone and everyone.

The corn cakes, made from yellow or white corn, are about a half-inch thick, firm and slightly crisp on the outside, and moist within. A young man of fourteen at the time, Nathan Harwood, for whom arepas were a brand new experience, probably described their excellent flavor and texture with greatest accuracy: "The outside, the crisp part, tastes kind of like popcorn, and the inside, the moist part, is sort of like really good, slightly firm cream of wheat." (Nathan, his brother, Mark, his mom, Alice, and I almost polished off a double batch of arepas, which would be about sixteen to eighteen, in one sitting.)

Arepas are made from masarepa (sometimes called *arepa harina*). Masarepa is not your plain old regular cornmeal. It begins with whole kernels of hard flint corn, which, instead of just being ground (this would yield your conventional cornmeal) are *cooked,* soaked overnight, and then ground. That precooked, soaked, ground corn, if you were making your arepas by the ultimate from-scratch method, would be in itself the masarepa dough. Instead, we're going straight to the easy way, the way Leyla Torres taught me, on a beautiful late summer Vermont day.

Leyla's Arepas

MAKES ABOUT 8 AREPAS

Leyla's arepa recipe is traditional, but one of her cooking methods—oven-broiling, on a small rack set atop the oven rack—is not. It's a genius touch; it allows air to circulate all around the arepas, drying them out slightly (desirably so) and giving them a pleasantly crunchy exterior.

The recipe calls for masarepa flour, either white or yellow. Goya, one of the most widely distributed Hispanic food brands in America, makes it; you'll find it in any supermarket that serves a population with a strong Latino component, or at smaller Hispanic groceries. Please don't try substituting conventional cornmeal; it won't work here. (By the way, traditional arepas, as eaten in Colombia and Venezuela, are unsalted, possibly because they're usually eaten with salty, spicy food. But in North America, they are nearly always made with salt and/or cheese added to the dough. Just omit the salt if you prefer.)

See page 101 for serving suggestions and accompaniments.

"Mama packed a picnic lunch of roast chicken, corn cakes, tangerines, lemonade, and plates together with cups and paper napkins. Grandma Felisa made her delicious salsa picante and placed it in the picnic basket. . . . Papa put the map in the car and checked to make sure there was enough gas. Fernando gathered up his paper and crayons so he could draw during the trip; and his younger sister, Flora, brought her pull-toy bear . . ."

—LEYLA TORRES, *The Kite Festival*

2 cups masarepa flour, yellow or white

3 cups water, at room temperature or slightly warm

1 to 2 teaspoons salt, or to taste

Butter, mild vegetable oil, or vegetable oil cooking spray, for greasing the metal rack

1. Combine the masarepa, water, and salt in a large bowl, mixing well to incorporate everything into a nice dough. Give a couple of kneads to break up any lumps of unmixed dry

ingredients. Cover the bowl and let it stand for 5 minutes.

2. Place an oven rack on the next to last rung of the oven closest to the broiling element and preheat the oven to Broil.

3. Using your hands, scoop out about ½ cup of dough, which will have a consistency much like Play-Doh. Shape the dough into patties, about 4 inches across and ½ inch thick. (If you have kids in the house, this is an activity they can easily participate in.) Try to make the arepas the same thickness throughout, not sloping down toward the edges.

4. Lightly coat a metal rack, smaller in dimension than the oven rack (like the kind you might cool cookies on), with butter or oil. Place the arepas on this rack, and place the whole shebang in the preheated oven on the rack you positioned in step 2. Let 8 to 10 minutes pass, then remove the rack and check the tops of the arepas. They should feel crunchy and firm to the touch and should come off the rack easily. If they're ready, flip the cakes over, then return them, still on their smaller rack, to the oven, giving the second side another 8 to 10 minutes.

5. Serve, hot and golden, as soon as possible.

VARIATIONS:

AREPAS ON THE GRILL When cooking outdoors, give your arepas a smoky taste by grilling them once the grill is good and hot.

Cook them over indirect lower heat, on a greased rack. Allow 7 to 8 minutes per side, testing for doneness by the same criteria as with the oven-baked ones.

RICHER AREPAS Leyla often adds a tablespoon of butter or oil to the dough. This adds a delicious flavor, aids crispness and browning, and prevents sticking.

LEYLA'S AUNT EMMA'S RICOTTA CHEESE AREPAS When the dough is mixed, add ½ to ⅔ cup whole-milk ricotta cheese, in little dabs. Stir it in gently, so there are still little discernible bits of ricotta. Bake as directed. "They are delicious; I love them," says Leyla.

LEYLA'S AREPAS WITH TOFU Because Leyla has a lactose sensitivity, she came up with these. When the basic dough is mixed, add ½ to ⅔ cup crumbled firm conventional tofu (not silken). Stir it in gently; again, you want little discernible bits of tofu. Bake as directed.

AREPA
ACCOMPANIMENTS

Pretty much everyone can figure out what to eat with cornbreads, muffins, and tortillas, but what to eat with arepas? In Latin America, they're often eaten for breakfast. Hot arepas, well buttered, may accompany a big pile of eggs scrambled with onions and garlic. (*Café con leche* with this, of course.) But simpler and far more common is an arepa as a solo breakfast act, eaten much like a bagel—with butter and cream cheese, *queso fresco*, Manchego, *queso blanco*, mozzarella, or similar white, mild cheese. (This idea has transmogrified, in Miami and South Florida, from *with cheese*, to cheese *included.* Commercial arepa manufacturers in that area add a slice of cheese, sandwiched between two thin disks of masarepa dough, the whole thing to be heated up at home.)

In Bogotá, arepas, hot and slightly smoky from the open-air grills, are sold on every street corner. Classic anytime snack food, they're usually offered with chorizo sausage, or with carne asada, marinated spicy flank steak moistened with a bit of hot sauce, called *ají,* pronounced ah-HEE. In Venezuela, the beef is shredded; in Colombia, it's in large pieces, pounded thin for tenderness.

One step up from street food are *pollerías,* popular restaurants where the centerpiece is very tender, garlicky roast chicken. "And you are always asked, when you order it," says Colombia-born children's book author Leyla Torres, "whether you want arepa or potato with it." This is the chicken Leyla had in mind for the picnic in her children's book, *The Kite Festival* (see quote, page 99).

Continued on next page

AREPA
ACCOMPANIMENTS CONTINUED

At many Colombian cafés, you can order a special plate, the *bandeja paisa* (meaning "tray of the countryside/region"), which includes what Leyla describes enthusiastically as "all the essentials of your life!"—kidney beans, arepa, rice, fried eggs, browned ground beef, pork rind, fried slices of plantain, a slice of avocado. Or, an arepa might accompany *sancocho,* a spicy, vegetable- and meat-packed stew. I offer you two versions (one vegetarian) of this amazingly hearty stew on pages 322 and 323.

In Venezuela, arepas, made a bit thicker than in Colombia, are the mainstay of *areperas,* small restaurants or cafés. There you choose from a variety of fillings: cheese, beef, pork, chicken, eggs, beans, and so on. The hot-from-the-grill arepa is split down the middle (as you would a hamburger bun), a bit of its steaming moist center is scooped out, and it's stuffed with your choice of filling. *La reina pepiada,* an arepa filled with chopped carne asada, avocado, and cheese, is both traditional and much-loved, any time of the night or day. In fact, the dish is a late-night favorite; go to an *arepera* at 2 A.M. and you'll see tired workers getting off late shifts mingling with young, sweaty, well-dressed young people, finishing off a night at the clubs with some arepas.

However, when foods leave their native places and move into new territory, they inevitably commingle with the foods of the new place. To eat arepas with something sweet rather than savory would out-and-out repel most born-and-bred arepa eaters. But Leyla's American husband, John Sutton, loves his arepas with butter and honey or guava jam.

Me? I'll pretty much take an arepa anytime, anywhere, and any way.

BROA
(PORTUGUESE CORNBREAD)

MAKES ONE 9- OR 10-INCH ROUND LOAF

This bread was originally a mainstay of medieval Portugal's poor. Early on it was made of humbler, cheap millet flour, with a bit of the more expensive wheat flour added. When corn—high-yielding and easy to grow—arrived from the New World toward the end of the fifteenth century, it changed the face of Portuguese agriculture. Corn cultivation completely replaced that of millet, and broa became a bread of cornmeal and wheat flour, as it is today.

A simple, plain, fairly dense, round, yeasted loaf, broa is on the dry side, the better to soak up the caldo verde, the soup of kale, beans, and *linguica* or chorizo sausage with which it is most often served. My version of caldo verde appears on page 318.

1 cup boiling water
1½ cups stone-ground white cornmeal
1¼ teaspoons salt
2 tablespoons olive oil
1 tablespoon active dry yeast

· M · E · N · U ·

SOOTHING A STORMY MONDAY, PORTUGUESE-STYLE

Broa
*
Caldo Verde (page 318)
*
A Poached Egg, optional,
in each bowl of soup
*
Flan * Crème Caramel

¼ cup lukewarm water, preferably filtered or spring
1 teaspoon sugar
2 cups unbleached white flour, plus a bit for kneading
Vegetable or olive oil cooking spray or additional olive oil

I. Pour the boiling water over the white cornmeal in a small, heat-proof bowl. Add the salt and olive oil and stir well to moisten the cornmeal. Allow the mixture to sit until lukewarm, about 20 minutes.

2. Toward the end of the 20 minutes, sprinkle the yeast over the ¼ cup lukewarm water

> **"Very few of us know all the breads of all the countries, uncountable the odd shapes, the subtle flavors, the cunning additions of raisins and currants and citron and poppy seed and sesame and caraway and chopped nuts and spices and salt crystals and sugar. Bread pale green with spinach, bread pale yellow with carrots, zestful orange bread, bread with cornmeal . . . bread for every taste, or every occasion, the backbone of the anatomy of food."**
>
> —Sophie Kerr, *The Best I Ever Ate*

(I usually leave it in the glass cup in which I measured the water). Add the sugar. Let stand until the yeast mixture is bubbly, about 7 minutes.

3. Transfer the cornmeal mixture and the yeast mixture to a large bowl, stirring well to combine. Beat in the flour a little at a time, kneading the last part in. Then knead the dough, which will be a little sticky, for about 5 minutes. You may work in a little additional flour if need be, but it will still be on the moist and tacky side. Transfer the dough to a large oiled bowl, cover with a clean towel, and let rise in a warm spot for about 45 minutes.

4. Punch down the risen dough. Remove it from the bowl and knead a few times, using just a bit more flour if you must.

5. Spray or oil a 9- or 10-inch cake pan (use a metal pan; glass will brown the crust too swiftly). Form the dough into a round loaf and, pressing it to fit, place it in the oiled pan. Cover first with a sheet of wax paper, then with a clean towel, and let rise in a nice warm spot for a second time, again until doubled. The second rise should run about 35 to 40 minutes. About halfway into that, preheat the oven to 350°F.

6. Remove the towel and carefully ease off the wax paper from any spots where it might have stuck (you don't want to deflate the dough). Bake the broa until it is firm-crusted and slightly brown, 40 to 45 minutes. Let it cool slightly on a rack before serving, in wedges.

Variation: Black Pepper Broa

Several years ago, *Bon Appétit* ran a broa as a cover recipe. The recipe inside was a classic one except for the addition of 1½ teaspoons coarsely ground black pepper. This makes a beautiful, interesting, if untraditional, broa, with a definite bite.

BOBOTA
(GREEK CORNBREAD)

MAKES 10 TO 12 SQUARES

obota is a truly succulent, very sweet modern-day Greek cornbread, intoxicatingly fragrant as it bakes. As far as I can tell, it seems to have originated in Thessaly, but is now popular all over the country, and you can find both from-scratch and mix-based versions. It is as much cake as it is bread, but it is cake with a decided Greek accent, moist and soaked in an orange and honey syrup. If you like baklava or *revani* (the syrup-soaked Greek walnut cake), you will swoon over this. Serve it as dessert.

   Vegetable oil cooking spray
   1 cup plus 2 tablespoons unbleached white flour
   1 cup plus 2 tablespoons stone-ground yellow cornmeal
   2 teaspoons baking powder
   1/2 teaspoon baking soda
   1/4 teaspoon salt
   4 eggs, separated
   1/2 cup butter, at room temperature
   1/3 cup sugar

Finely grated zest of 1 orange, preferably organic
1 cup freshly squeezed orange juice (seeds and large pieces of pulp removed, but not strained)
1 cup currants or raisins
1 recipe Orange-Honey Syrup (recipe follows)

1. Preheat the oven to 350°F. Spray a 7½-by-11¾-inch pan with oil, and set aside.

2. Sift together the flour, cornmeal, baking powder, baking soda, and salt onto a piece of wax paper. Set aside.

3. In a high-sided non-plastic bowl using scrupulously clean beaters, beat the egg whites until stiff. (See Beating Egg Whites, page 186.) Set aside.

4. Using the same beaters that you used on the egg whites, in a medium bowl, cream together the butter and sugar, beating until fluffy. Beat in the egg yolks one at a time. Add the orange zest.

5. Add the flour-cornmeal mixture and the orange juice to the creamed butter mixture, stirring until just combined. Using a rubber spatula, gently fold in the egg whites and currants or raisins.

6. Transfer the batter to the prepared pan, and put it in the oven. Bake until golden brown, firm, and slightly domed in the middle, 35 to 40 minutes. As the cake bakes, prepare the orange-honey syrup.

7. When the cake is done, remove it from the oven and prick the top all over with a toothpick. Pour the slightly cooled syrup evenly over the cake, dousing it. Let stand 1 to 2 hours before serving.

Orange-Honey Syrup

ENOUGH FOR 1 BOBOTA

- ½ cup sugar
- 3 tablespoons honey
- Juice from 1 orange plus water to equal 1 cup
- Finely grated zest of 1 orange, preferably organic
- 6 whole cloves

Combine all ingredients in a medium saucepan. Bring to a boil, turn the heat down to a simmer, and cook until the sugar is dissolved and the mixture is a thin syrup, about 4 minutes. Let the syrup cool to room temperature. Remove the cloves, and pour the syrup over the bobota.

Corn Thinbread
with Olives, Walnuts, Feta, and Sun-dried Tomatoes

SERVES 6 TO 8

When I decided to try pairing some of the big, bold, assertive salty-savory tastes of the Mediterranean with cornbread, I was picturing a thin cornbread with crispy-crusty edges. I wound up with this addictively good, highly unusual flat loaf, contrasting surprises in every bite: creamy-salty feta, chewy-unctuous sun-dried tomatoes, crunchy walnuts (decidedly sweet in counterpoint to the other saltinesses), bitter-salty oil-cured olives. Try it as part of an appetizer spread, as a starter in its own right, or served with a nice beany soup, or one in the minestrone line, flavored with basil, tomatoes, and vegetables. Or accompany it with a great big summer salad—butter lettuce from the garden, scallions, and red ripe tomatoes dressed with a lemon-y, garlicky vinargrette. This bread with such a salad is a fine supper indeed.

CORNBREAD IN CORFU

According to Diane Kochilas, perhaps the world's foremost authority on regional Greek cuisine, an extremely simple cornbread called *barbarella* was once a staple on the island of Corfu. You won't find a recipe for it because there isn't one: The cornmeal was boiled in water to become mush, then patted into thin cakes and baked (on a stone, in a wood-burning oven). It was served, warm, with an abundance of wild greens (watercress, mustard, nettle, dandelion, poppy, and more) sautéed with onions, olive oil, and a bit of paprika or chile and a slice of feta cheese. If there was a shortage of oil to sauté with, the greens might be steamed and kneaded right into the cooked cornmeal before it was baked. Until the infusion of prosperity brought by late twentieth-century tourism, Corfiot peasants subsisted on this barbarella. The bread received its name due to the mistaken belief that corn originated in Africa's Barbary Coast. (A very similar bread called *lipano* was eaten in northwestern Greece as well as in the neighboring southern Albania.)

While beating the bushes to find out exactly what barbarella was, I did learn from another pan pal, the extraordinarily knowledgeable Aglaia Kremezi, about the sweet Greek cornbread bobota, especially popular in Thessaly. Contemporary, as different from *barbarella* as day from night, *bobota* is served as a dessert or coffee cake, infused with a delicious, sticky, flavored syrup, much like Greek nut cakes (revani) or even baklava. My version of Aglaia's generously shared recipe, from her mother-in-law, Athanasia Moraitis, appears on page 105.

Vegetable oil cooking spray

1 cup unbleached white flour

1 cup stone-ground yellow cornmeal

1 tablespoon baking powder

¼ teaspoon baking soda

¼ teaspoon salt

2 tablespoons extra-virgin olive oil

1 cup buttermilk

1 egg

2 teaspoons sugar

2 tablespoons oil from oil-packed
sun-dried tomatoes

3 tablespoons diced oil-packed
sun-dried tomatoes

¼ cup pitted dry oil-and-salt-cured
black olives (pulled into pieces as
you pit them)

½ cup toasted walnuts, chopped

1 scant cup (4 ounces) feta cheese,
crumbled

1. Preheat the oven to 400°F. Spray a 15-by-11-by-1¼-inch jelly-roll pan with oil, and set aside.

2. Sift together the flour, cornmeal, baking powder, baking soda, and salt into a medium bowl.

3. Pour the olive oil into the prepared pan, and set the pan in the oven to heat.

4. Whisk together the buttermilk, ½ cup water, the egg, sugar, and the oil from the sun-dried tomatoes in a smaller bowl.

·M·E·N·U·

MEZZE MARVELOUS: PATMOS IN PUTNEY

Corn Thinbread with Olives, Walnuts, Feta, and Sun-dried Tomatoes

*

White Beans with Minced Celery, Parsley, Oregano, Lemon, Olive Oil, Garlic, and Salt

*

Yellow and Red Cherry Tomatoes in a Red-Leaf Lettuce–Lined Basket

*

Marinated Steamed Artichokes, Split in Half and Finished on the Grill

*

Steamed Beets Tossed with Lemon, Olive Oil, Tamari, and a Touch of Honey

5. Pour the buttermilk mixture into the flour mixture. The batter will be thinner than usual; whisk it a few times to smooth out the larger lumps. Then stir in the sun-dried tomatoes, olives, and walnuts, with just a few more strokes.

6. Carefully remove the hot pan from the oven. With a basting brush, distribute the hot olive oil more or less evenly over the pan. Scrape the batter into it, spreading it and patching in any spots where the pan shows through, making a thin, flat loaf. Sprinkle with the feta.

7. Bake until both the bread and feta are golden brown, the loaf edges especially so but not burned, 15 to 20 minutes. Let cool for a few moments. Serve warm or at room temperature, but not cold.

MAKKI KI ROTI (INDIAN CORN GRIDDLE CAKES)

MAKES 10 GRIDDLE CAKES

When I learned from Mr. Panseer, a North Indian airport limo driver, that Punjabis eat cornbread and greens (usually saag, see page 294), I, being the dyed-in-the-wool Southern girl I then was, about fell over. There are as many variations on makki ki roti as there are Punjabis. Sometimes they are made simply, as an accompaniment to something spicy; at other times, the breads are themselves spiced, with ginger, chiles, fresh cilantro, or all of these. And while in the north they are made with just cornmeal, in central India and Mumbai (Bombay) you'll find them made with a mixture of cornmeal or puréed fresh corn and *atta*, a low-protein wheat flour more usually used for making *chapattis*.

If you don't want to run out to your local Indian food store for atta, you can combine equal amounts of whole wheat flour, unbleached all-purpose white flour, and white cake or pastry flour. (If you do go, though, you can pick up some commercially made ghee—clarified butter—while you're there.) I have also used half whole wheat pastry flour and half unbleached white instead of atta with good results.

1 cup stone-ground yellow cornmeal

1 cup atta or chapatti flour (see headnote)

1 teaspoon salt

2 tablespoons melted butter, ghee, or mild vegetable oil

About 1/2 cup warm water

A little additional butter, as needed (optional but good)

1. Place the cornmeal, flour, salt, and butter in a medium bowl. Rub this combination

CROSS-CULTURAL CORNBREAD

Cornbreads almost identical to the American corn pone and hoecake are served daily in the Caucasus, the western part of the republic of Georgia, and also in the far north of India, in the Punjab. In Georgia, they're *mchadi*—unleavened corn cakes shaped into ovals (not rounds, like our pones), and baked on top of the fire on a *ketsi*, a clay griddle (of course, top-of-the-fire baking was the way it was first done in America, too). And in the Punjab, they're makki ki roti. Again, the dough is almost identical, but the cakes, griddled on a *tawa*, are rolled out more thinly (using a combination of meal-dusted hands and a rolling pin called a *belan*), to form a round cake slightly smaller in circumference than a corn tortilla. This traditional method is tricky, so I use my friend Raghavan Iyer's recipe for part cornmeal—part flour makki ki roti. Sometimes makki

ki roti are plain, sometimes they're jazzed up with grated radish and/or green chile and minced cilantro added to the dough.

What are these various traveling pones served with? In the mchadi-loving parts of Georgia they accompany unflavored yogurt, cheese, and just plain butter; beans; and vegetable or meat stews. Farther to the south and east, the Punjab's makki ki roti eaters, too, enjoy their corn cakes with a variety of foods. But one dish is de rigueur as an accompaniment: sarson ka saag, a slow-cooked, extravagantly spiced mixture of mustard greens (see page 294).

How'd corn get to Georgia and India in the first place? Portuguese sailors took it there thirty or forty years after 1492 (when Columbus sailed the ocean blue).

between your hands to disperse the fat. The mixture should have the texture of bread crumbs.

2. Add the warm water, drizzling in a few tablespoons at a time, and mix with your fingers. Keep working the flour-cornmeal mixture until you've formed a stiff dough. Knead this for 2 minutes (the dough will be grainy and dry).

3. Divide the dough into 10 equal pieces, shaping each into a round. Cover the rounds with a clean, slightly damp towel.

"I scarcely had time to wonder what would happen next, before Narayan appeared, looking pleased, carrying in one hand a tray of food, and in the other, a jug of drinking water. He spoke no English, merely adding to his very Sanskritized Hindi the kind of gestures that would help me understand him. 'Here,' he said, 'are vegetables, sweet peppers, cream custard, and hard corn-cakes. Mataji has cooked them . . .'"

—LIZELLE REYMOND,
My Life with a Brahmin Family

4. Heat a heavy nonstick skillet over medium heat. Working with one dough round at a time, carefully roll the rotis out on a very lightly floured board with a floured rolling pin to make circular breads, 4 to 5 inches across and about ¼ inch thick. You can try rolling out the rotis between two sheets of wax paper or heavy plastic, such as a cut-open zip-top bag.

5. Working with a few rounds at a time, place the rotis carefully in the hot pan, and let them cook until golden brown spots appear underneath the bread, 1 to 2 minutes. Flip the rotis over and repeat. Then brush the tops of the rotis lightly with just a bit of butter, flip them over a second time, and let them cook for about 10 seconds. Butter and flip one more time, for about 10 seconds more.

6. Remove the rotis from the skillet as they finish, and wrap them in towels or foil to keep warm.

VARIATIONS:
SPICED MAKKI KI ROTI

Buzz together in a food processor with a few tablespoons of warm spring water about 1 tablespoon coarsely chopped ginger; ½ onion, chopped; 2 garlic cloves, smashed or pressed; and, if you like, a green chile or two and 2 tablespoons of fresh cilantro. Pulse-chop to make a textured purée, and stir this into the cornmeal-flour-butter mix. Proceed as directed, bearing in mind that you will probably need little or no water to bring the dough together, given the water in the onion mixture.

FRESH CORN MAKKI KI ROTI

Delicious, but trickier to work with than the original Mumbai style. In a food processor buzz together 1½ cups fresh corn kernels (cut from 3 ears of fresh corn; see Shuck and Jive, page 49) with ½ teaspoon salt and 1 tablespoon butter, pausing to scrape down the sides with a spatula, until you've formed a slightly textured purée. Place 1 cup atta or equivalent flour mixture in a medium bowl, and stir the corn purée into it. Knead as directed in step 2, keeping in mind that you will likely need little to no water to bring the dough together, then proceed with the remainder of the recipe.

MEALIEBROD (SOUTH AFRICAN STEAMED FRESH CORNBREAD)

SERVES 6 TO 8

In parts of the world where ovens are not common, steamed breads often make an appearance. One of those places is South India, where there's a type of steamed bread made mostly of coconut and just a bit of flour. Steaming is also used in many parts of the African continent.

This traditional Zulu bread, widely accepted by the Boer settlers in southern Africa, folds in fresh corn (called mealies) with ample amounts of flour and a little cornmeal. It has no added fat. An extremely moist, dense bread, mealiebrod is an unusual loaf, but, especially to those who grew up on it, it is addictive. South Africans today eat it as a snack, with butter and jam, or as a breakfast bread.

For instructions on steam cooking, see Steam On, pages 64–66.

Vegetable oil cooking spray

Cornmeal, for dusting the molds

3 cups unbleached white flour

2 tablespoons baking powder

1¼ teaspoons salt

3 tablespoons sugar

3 cups ground fresh mealies (see Note)

¼ to ½ cup cold water

1. Have ready the mold(s), heat-proof trivet, and cooking vessel of your choice (see Steam On, pages 64–66). Wash and dry the molds well, spray the insides thoroughly with oil, and dust the insides with cornmeal. Also have at hand some foil, and kitchen string or rubber bands to secure the foil to the top of the mold(s).

2. Combine the flour, baking powder, and salt in a medium bowl. Stir or whisk together well. Whisk together the sugar and ground corn in a separate bowl.

3. Combine the two mixtures, stirring just enough to moisten the dry ingredients. Dribble in the water, 2 tablespoons at a time to make a fairly stiff batter, but avoid overbeating.

4. Scrape the batter into the prepared mold(s), filling each about two thirds of the way full.

5. Tear off a piece of foil that is twice as large as the mouth of a mold. Fold it in half, and spray one side with oil. Place it oiled-side down on top of the mold, puffing it up a bit to allow for the bread's expansion as it steams. Repeat with any remaining molds.

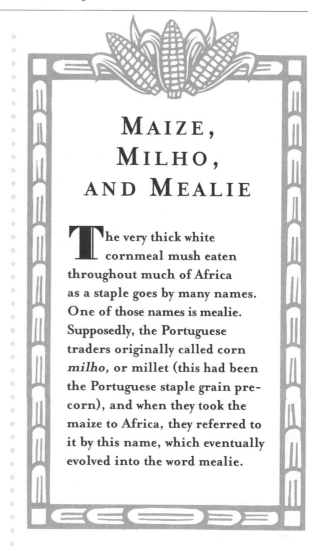

MAIZE, MILHO, AND MEALIE

The very thick white cornmeal mush eaten throughout much of Africa as a staple goes by many names. One of those names is mealie. Supposedly, the Portuguese traders originally called corn *milho,* or millet (this had been the Portuguese staple grain pre-corn), and when they took the maize to Africa, they referred to it by this name, which eventually evolved into the word mealie.

6. Secure each piece of foil tightly with kitchen string or a rubber band. Place the trivet or equivalent in the cooking vessel. Place the mold(s) on top of the trivet.

7. Pour enough boiling water into the cooking vessel to come halfway up the sides of the mold(s). Secure the lid of the vessel and steam the bread according to the directions for the particular cooking vessel you are using.

8. Cook the bread for the length of time suggested, then test the bread with a long skewer: you want to get way down deep into the bread's interior. When done, the middle of the bread is moist, but not sticky. Visible wet batter means the bread should steam longer. If it's wet, keep steaming patiently, checking about every 20 minutes until the moist-but-not-sticky point is reached.

9. When the bread is done, remove it from the cooking vessel, and let it cool in the mold(s), uncovered, on a rack, for at least 45 minutes. Reverse the bread out of the mold(s)—it should come out quite easily—slice it, and serve.

NOTE: To make the ground mealies, cut the kernels from 5 to 6 ears of fresh corn (see Shuck and Jive, page 49) and buzz them in the processor to make a not-quite-smooth, very liquid purée. You'll need 2 cups of this purée for the recipe above. Any extra? Swirl it into unsweetened yogurt, thin with a little vegetable stock, add a few diced scallions and a little fresh dill, and you have a simply lovely cold soup. Caveat: Do NOT substitute canned creamed corn here; this is the one case where only fresh will do.

MACAW MUFFINS
(FOR PEOPLE)
MAKES 12 MUFFINS

Macaw Muffins? Are these treats "for the birds"? Yes and no. Anyone who's ever purchased a bag of wild bird food knows that plenty of birds—including mourning doves, sparrows, and blackbirds—enjoy cracked corn. But some birds also adore corn*bread*. We're not just talking about scattering some leftover cornbread crumbs out on the lawn, but of cornbread baked specifically for parrots and their kin, notoriously picky eaters. After learning about the avian-cornbread connection and the fruit-and-carrot-studded corn muffins tropical birds love, I got to thinking that surely some form of this combination was one any human could love as well. Bingo! Moist and golden, sweet but not too much so, this cheering muffin is a delightful breakfast or snack, or just right with a bowl of soup for lunch. Though it'll please all human comers, I imagine it will especially (both because of the peanut butter, and because of the parrot connection) tickle any small humans in your family.

Now, a large, close-up avian creature is the last thing my complex, peripatetic life needs (especially given the huge particular needs of these gorgeous birds). But I admire them so. Always have.

So here is a Macaw Muffin for you, followed by one for your bird. While you *could* eat theirs and they *could* eat yours, you'll both be happier with the one prepared with your species in mind. This way, it'll be happy feasting for both of you.

After all, why should cornbread's global appeal be limited to just *homo sapiens*?

Vegetable oil cooking spray

¾ cup whole wheat pastry flour

1 cup stone-ground yellow cornmeal

¼ cup oatmeal (rolled oats) or quinoa flakes

½ teaspoon salt

1 tablespoon baking powder

2 eggs

3 tablespoons mild vegetable oil (preferably peanut, to back up the peanut butter flavor)

¼ cup peanut butter

3 tablespoons sugar

¾ cup plain soy milk

1 carrot, peeled and finely diced

1 apple, skin on, finely diced

½ cup raisins or currants

I. Preheat the oven to 400°F. Spray a 12-cup muffin tin with oil, or line with muffin papers.

2. Combine the flour, cornmeal, oatmeal or quinoa flakes, salt, and baking powder in a large bowl, stirring well. Set aside.

3. In a blender or food processor, buzz together the eggs, oil, and peanut butter until smooth. Add the sugar, and, with the machine running, add the soy milk. Scrape the sides of the processor if necessary to get off the last bits of peanut butter.

4. Stir the peanut butter mixture into the flour mixture, until just barely combined.

5. Gently stir in the carrot, apple, and raisins or currants. Spoon into the prepared muffin tins.

6. Bake until golden brown, 20 to 22 minutes. Serve warm.

MACAW MUFFINS
(FOR PARROTS)

MAKES 12 MUFFINS

Here's the thing: *You're a parrot.* You like to exercise your beak by gnawing on hard things. You dislike commercial parrot pellets. Green vegetables? Sure, they're good for you, but you don't always like them, either. Seeds? Great, but your owner insists they're an occasional treat. But it's true: You *do* feel peppier and calmer, and your feathers are shinier, when your diet is varied, seeds are limited, and fresh vegetables, fruit, and other healthy things are added to what you eat. Too, you love colorful food, the brighter the better. Lastly, you're wild about cornbread.

You have trained your owner to follow the recipe below, making a big batch, giving you some, freezing the rest, then warming up a bit each day for you.

This pleases you so much that you *may* refrain from biting her earrings or his watch.

Vegetable oil cooking spray

1 cup whole wheat pastry flour

1 cup stone-ground yellow cornmeal

¼ cup oatmeal (rolled oats) or quinoa flakes

¼ teaspoon salt

1 tablespoon baking powder

3 eggs, *with shells left on*

3 tablespoons mild vegetable oil or wheat germ oil

¼ cup peanut butter

1 tablespoon sugar

⅓ cup plain soy milk

1 apple, skin on, finely diced

½ cup raisins or currants

1 carrot, grated or finely diced

1 stalk celery, chopped

½ cup chopped red bell pepper

½ cup fresh spinach, parsley, or broccoli, finely chopped

½ cup frozen peas, rinsed in a strainer under hot water to thaw

½ cup frozen corn kernels, rinsed in a strainer under hot water to thaw

1. Preheat the oven to 400°F. Spray very well a 12-cup muffin tin with oil, or line with muffin papers.

2. Combine the flour, cornmeal, oatmeal (or quinoa flakes), salt, and baking powder in a large bowl, stirring well. Set aside.

3. Rinse the eggs in their shells. In a food processor, buzz together the eggs *(with shells)*, oil, and peanut butter. You want the shells wholly pulverized. Add the sugar and, with the machine running, the soy milk.

4. Stir the peanut butter mixture into the dry mixture, until just barely combined.

5. Gently fold in the fruits and vegetables. There will be less batter than usual, but enough to hold the mixture together. Spoon into the prepared muffin tin.

6. Bake until golden brown, 15 to 20 minutes. Serve slightly warm or at room temperature (never extremely hot or cold) to macaws, parrots, cockatoos, or other tropical birds. Some owners moisten them with a bit of warm water before serving.

Chapter 5

BABYCAKES

Muffins, Biscuits, Cornsticks, Gems, and Other Little Baked Corn Cakes

Cornbread and cornmeal-based babycakes—smaller cornbreads, such as muffins—are almost, but not quite, interchangeable. Because more of a small corn cake's exterior is exposed to direct heat, most are slightly crustier and usually hold together a bit better than their larger counterparts. Being discrete individual cakes (with the charm diminutive versions of full-grown anything always have), they are also less prone to crumble when being lifted to plate. They can be passed in a basket more successfully (that is, with less scattering of crumbs) than wedges of even the most exemplary cornbreads: a better choice any time you want fewer crumbs on the floor, the table, or the bottom of the basket.

Muffins are thus just a little dressier than their heftier big-pan kin. They bake more quickly than whole cornbreads, and, especially in their less-fancy nonsweet forms, go beautifully with almost anything.

In their sweet forms, muffins are like small cakes. And they're excellent made with cornmeal, a pleasing discovery as I did kitchen tinkering in the course of this book (previously my corn muffins had leaned toward spicy and savory). The goodness of sweet muffins, of many varieties made with all or part cornmeal instead of straight wheat flour, is one of the best surprises here.

All sweet muffins exist for pleasure more than sustenance. I often choose them as part of a breakfast or brunch I want to mark as celebratory: either having people over, or luxuriating in a lazy Sunday morning with weekend-in-the-country friends and houseguests who already *are* over. Or, I might want to mark a holiday or season with what I place on the table and in the muffin: thus August's fresh blueberry corn muffins give way to September and October's pumpkin-apple corn muffins, to be followed by November-December's cranberry-orange corn muffins. All are quick to make and honor the joy and wonder of being on this cyclical, blueberry-to-pumpkin, apple-to-cranberry spinning earth all together. To celebrate *right now*, today, with every bite, each crumb, every kiss, each muffin.

Corn gems were originally a leavened-by-eggs-only early American–style muffin-cake heavy and dense with lots of dried fruits and nuts. Nowadays gems are still leavened wholly or partly with beaten egg whites rather than baking powder or baking soda. They are thus more moist, with a more finely grained but slightly denser texture. The method of mixing them is quite different from that of a typical muffin, and the results are outstanding.

Cornsticks are another much-loved miniature cornbread. The cornbread or muffin batter is baked in a cornstick pan—a heavy cast-iron mold shaped like miniature ears of corn. Because a greater surface area is exposed to both the cast iron and the direct air of the oven, the adorable little cornsticks have an exceptional crunch and golden-brown color. While any cornbread batter can be baked in them, it's easy for batters to stick because the molds have so much detail, so the pans have to be very, very, very well greased, or the batter itself has to be on the rich (buttery or oily) side, or both. This chapter includes a recipe for a rich cornstick batter, but if you grease the pan well, you can use any kind you like. (Cornstick pans are made in America by Lodge Cast Iron in South Pittsburg, Tennessee—not coincidentally, home of the National Cornbread Festival. Most hardware and cookware stores carry cornstick pans, including Sur La Table—www.surlatable.com—and www.pans.com.)

And finally, we come to crackers. It's a pity so few of us make crackers from scratch at home. They are delicious, in a whole other category than packaged varieties, and no harder to fix than pie crust or cookies; in fact, some varieties are easier. (Of course, it is also true that many people no longer make pie crusts or cookies at home, either, another real pity—but don't get me started.)

Because of their rarity and rusticity (they definitely don't look like a factory made 'em), from-scratch crackers always attract attention. Serve them with all the savory things you can think of: dips and spreads, cheeses, olives. Tasty, inviting, their nonuniformity, to my eye, gives an extra measure of heart and soul.

Crackers, cornsticks, muffins, gems. These babycakes are quite different from each other. Some are sweet, some savory; some are moist and others crackly; some are Best Dressed, others Most Popular—but all are joy-inducing, indulgent, and very, very Likely to Succeed.

SIMPLY CORN MUFFINS

MAKES 12 MUFFINS

A classic. It accompanies almost anything, is receptive to a thousand variations, and is invariably well received. If you mastered only this recipe and Dairy Hollow House Skillet-Sizzled Cornbread (page 12), and took either to a few neighborhood get-togethers, you would find yourself queen or king of the potluck.

Vegetable oil cooking spray

1 cup unbleached white flour

1 cup stone-ground yellow cornmeal

1/2 teaspoon salt

1 tablespoon baking powder

1 1/4 cups buttermilk

1/2 teaspoon baking soda

2 eggs

1/4 to 1/3 cup sugar, preferably unrefined (see Pantry, page 356)

1/3 cup melted butter or mild vegetable oil

1. Preheat the oven to 400°F. Spray a 12-cup muffin tin with oil, or line with muffin papers.

2. Combine the flour, cornmeal, salt, and baking powder in a large bowl, stirring well. Set aside.

MUFFIN-MAKING MAGIC

MIXING: As with most cornbreads, the as-few-strokes-as-possible rule applies: Overbeaten muffins are rubbery, tough, and have an off-center bump on otherwise flat tops.

ADJUSTING FOR SIZE: Any muffin can be made in any type of muffin pan. Just adjust the timing: The smaller the muffin, the more quickly it bakes. Mini-muffins, which take about a tablespoon of batter each, bake in 10 to 12 minutes. Regular muffins take 2 to 3 heaping tablespoons of batter each and bake in 15 to 18 minutes. Giant mega-maxi-muffins take $1/2$ to $2/3$ cup of batter, and bake in 22 to 25 minutes. Muffin tops, taking 3 to 4 tablespoons of batter, bake in 13 to 16 minutes. (If using a muffin-top pan for a recipe with streusel, make a double batch of streusel to cover the greater surface.)

HEAT: Preheat the oven for at least 20 minutes so the muffins will bake in a timely fashion and have a nice crisp crust.

CAKEY VS. BREADY: You can make very delicious muffins, a bit more on the bready than cakey side, with a minimum of fat—$1/4$ cup or so—and relatively little sugar. However, this only works if you're planning on eating the muffins immediately. If you want your muffins to keep for a while, choose a higher-fat, sweeter muffin recipe.

ON STICKING: There's no reason for a muffin to ever, ever stick. If you have old, beat-up muffin tins, use paper liners. If your muffin pans are in relatively good shape, use liners or spray well with vegetable oil cooking spray. And if you have new, heavy-gauge nonstick, well, no worries.

3. Whisk together the buttermilk and baking soda in a medium bowl until the baking soda is dissolved. Whisk in the eggs, sugar, and melted butter or oil.

4. Stir the combined wet ingredients into the dry until the mixture is just barely combined. Spoon into the prepared muffin tin.

5. Bake until golden brown, 15 to 20 minutes. Serve warm.

VARIATIONS:

SWEET MILK CORN MUFFINS
Although I love the slight tang buttermilk gives to these muffins, they're also excellent made with regular milk. Simply substitute an equal amount of milk for the buttermilk, and omit the baking soda.

DOUBLE-CORN BASIC CORN MUFFINS
Use either the buttermilk or sweet milk version of the muffin. When you have just combined the wet and dry ingredients, stir in, with a couple of strokes, $1/2$ to 1 cup raw, cooked, or thawed frozen corn kernels. (If using fresh corn, you will need 1 to 2 ears; see Shuck and Jive, page 49.)

REDUCED-FAT SIMPLY CORN MUFFINS WITH CARROT
If you keep track of fat grams, you'll be pleased to know that you can cut the melted butter back to a mere 2 tablespoons and add 1 carrot, grated, and still end up with yet another delicious muffin, albeit one that won't keep as long.

JANICE CARR'S MIXED-GRAIN MUFFINS

MAKES 12 MUFFINS

For many years Dr. Leo Carr, a legendary chiropractor with a quietly piquant sense of humor and the body of a twenty-five-year-old up into his seventies (he practiced yoga for three hours each morning and rode his bicycle everywhere), ministered to the spines, shoulders, necks, and sacrums of *tout* Eureka Springs, Arkansas, from an immaculate Victorian house on Spring Street. It was also his home, shared with his partner, Janice.

For many years Janice's muffins, varied each time with different grain flours but always including cornmeal and unbleached white flour, were what came to mind whenever I thought "muffins." Thirty years later, I still love them. Her recipe always turns out utterly toothsome, high-rising, crusty-topped perfect muffins and offers a terrific opportunity to experiment with all the various whole-grain flours we're always being told to eat.

If you choose to use oat flour as part of the mix and want to make your own, simply buzz oatmeal in a food processor until pulverized (2 parts oatmeal yields 1 part oat flour).

Vegetable oil cooking spray

¾ cup unbleached white flour, plus extra as needed

¾ cup stone-ground yellow cornmeal

About 1 cup assorted whole-grain flours, in any proportion (this can include barley, quinoa, rye, rice, millet, or oatmeal flours)

2 tablespoons baking powder (yes, really that much)

1 teaspoon salt

⅓ cup butter, at room temperature

⅓ cup sugar

1 egg

1 cup milk

1. Preheat the oven to 400°F. Spray a 12-cup muffin tin with oil.

2. Stir together the white flour, cornmeal, whole-grain flours, baking powder, and salt in a medium bowl. Use a whisk or fork to combine everything well. Set aside.

3. Cream together the butter and sugar in a slightly smaller bowl, then beat in the egg.

4. Add the butter mixture to the dry ingredients along with the milk, stirring together just until combined. Depending on which flours you've selected, you might need to add more flour (either unbleached or one of the whole grains) or cornmeal to achieve proper muffin consistency: moist but still quite thick and a bit shaggy. Be prepared to add up to ⅓ cup additional flour or meal if needed.

5. Scoop the batter into the prepared muffin tin, and pop in the oven. Bake until the muffins are golden brown and crusty, 15 to 20 minutes. Serve them hot, if possible within a few minutes of their emergence from the oven. Now aren't these *good*?

CORN-VERSATION

"**O**h! A book on cornbread! I love cornbread!" As you already know, I heard this many times while putting this book together, but always from Americans . . . and after all, cornbread really is our native bread. So when I heard this from an Englishwoman, Diana Howe, my agent's former assistant, I was surprised.

"You do?" I asked. "Is cornbread eaten in Great Britain?"

"Oh, yes," said Diana. "Quite a bit, actually."

"Is it like the American kind? And is it sweet, or not?"

"Rather sweet . . . it's sort of like what you serve here, but not. It's actually more like what I suppose you'd call cornmeal muffins."

"And did you eat them growing up?"

"Oh, yes, and very happily so."

"And what were they served with?"

"Chowders, mostly, as I remember."

"*Fish* chowders?" I said. I was thinking about chowder controversy—Manhattan-style versus New England–style, oyster crackers or saltines, et cetera. To put two such argued-about foods as cornbread and chowder side by side seemed like a dangerous conjunction.

"Oh, *yes*," said Diana, clearly unaware of the ferment surrounding these two foods. She sounded happy, dreamily rhapsodic, the way people often get recalling the cornbreads of their childhoods. "All *kinds* of fish chowders: clam, haddock, salmon . . ."

I could just hear my mother, a devotee of salmon served at its absolutely most pristine and simple, saying, in tones of gentle horror, "Salmon—in *chowder*?"

So, chowder-loving cornbread eaters, or cornbread-loving chowder-eaters, try it if you like—but please, don't let me know what you think. I'm getting *way* out of the way.

"Company's Coming" Rich Corn Muffins

MAKES 18 MUFFINS

Southern in origin, these rich unsweetened muffins fairly proclaim Sunday dinner. In the old days, the liquid called for would have been soured "top milk," meaning the extra-creamy milk that rose to the top of the bottle. Reduced-fat sour cream (not fat-free) is a good substitute. Or, go ahead and use full-fat . . . after all, company's on the way.

Vegetable oil cooking spray
1 cup all-purpose flour
1½ cups stone-ground white cornmeal
1 teaspoon baking soda
1 teaspoon baking powder
1 teaspoon salt
¼ cup (½ stick) butter or solid vegetable shortening such as Crisco (or the natural-foods equivalent made with palm or coconut oil)
2 eggs, beaten
2 cups reduced-fat (not fat-free) sour cream

1. Preheat the oven to 425°F. Spray 18 muffin-tin cups with oil.

2. Sift the flour, cornmeal, baking soda, baking powder, and salt into a medium bowl. Using a pastry cutter or two knives, cut in the butter or shortening until the mixture is uniform, with fat in specks smaller than peas.

3. Combine the eggs and sour cream in a medium bowl, whisking together well. Using the bare minimum of strokes possible, combine the egg mixture with the flour mixture. Scoop into the prepared muffin tin. Bake until golden and firm, about 20 minutes.

·M·E·N·U·

Down-Home Dinner with the Preacher

Country-Fried Chicken with Gravy

*

Straight-from-the-Garden
Sliced Tomatoes

*

Mashed Potatoes

*

Slow-Cooked Green Beans

*

"Company's Coming"
Rich Corn Muffins or
Countryside Cornsticks (page 147)

*

Blackberry Cobbler

*

Iced Tea

OH, HAVE YOU SEEN THE MUFFIN MAN?

What exactly a muffin is depends on where you live, and when you lived there.

In England, until recently, a muffin was made of yeasted dough, as in (no-brainer) English muffins. Griddle-baked, formed in a round ring, it rose higher than pancake-like crumpets. It's this type of muffin, split, toasted, buttered, and served hot, to which novelist Evelyn Waugh referred when he said, "I think muffins one of the few things that make the English winter endurable."

During the nineteenth century, muffin sellers (the muffin men of the famous children's song) traveled the streets in English cities, trays of muffins on their heads, ringing large bells to summon customers. The bell-ringing became such a nuisance that in the 1840s muffin men's bell-ringing was prohibited by an Act of Parliament.

In Colonial days American muffins were almost identical to English ones. But over time muffins in North America became an entirely different breadstuff. With the advent of baking powder and baking soda instead of slow-acting yeast, muffins became "quick" breads. And once bakers began baking them in an oven, in deep cup-like tins, instead of griddling them, they became the recognizable precursors of today's muffins.

What of the word "muffin," so cozily appealing that it is sometimes used as a term of affection? There are two possible points of origin: it's probably either from the Low German *muffe,* or "cake," or the Old French word *moufflet,* an adjective used to describe the quality of certain breads, meaning more or less "soft."

Atlanta-Style Flat-Top Corn Muffins

MAKES 2 DOZEN MUFFINS

The first time I had these, in an Atlanta tearoom, I was perplexed by their simplicity, accustomed as I was to sweeter, more high-rising muffins. But these pure cornmeal (no flour) muffins, like other unadorned Southern-style cornbreads, grew on me.

Dry and crisp around the edges, flat, unsweet, they're intended to be eaten with, or crumbled into, something soupy—a bowl of beans, a cup of tomato-vegetable soup. Trust me, these will grow on you, too. Faster than fast to make, they're a good breakfast muffin, buttered or not and half crumbled into the yolk of your sunny-side-up egg.

2 teaspoons butter
2 cups stone-ground cornmeal,
**   preferably white**
1 teaspoon salt
Vegetable oil cooking spray or butter,
**   for greasing the muffin tins**
1 cup milk
1 egg
1½ teaspoons baking powder

1. Preheat the oven to 400°F. Bring 2 cups water to a boil and place the butter, cornmeal, and salt in a large heat-proof bowl.

2. Pour the boiling water over the cornmeal mixture, stirring or whisking well until lump-free.

3. Spray or butter one 24-cup or two 12-cup muffin tins, greasing them very well. (If you want to go all out, place a tiny chip of butter in the bottom of each muffin cup, too.) Put the prepared tins in the oven to heat up.

4. Combine and whisk together the milk and egg (I just pour 1 cup milk into a 2-cup measuring cup, break the egg into it, and beat with a fork). Pour this into the moistened cornmeal, and whisk very well.

5. Sprinkle the baking powder over the batter, then whisk it in thoroughly. The batter will be very thin for a muffin batter; don't worry.

6. Pull the hot muffin tin from the oven using oven mitts, and quickly divide the batter among the cups (since it's thin, I use a smallish ladle to do this). Pop the tin back in the oven (remember, it's still hot) and bake until the muffins are quite brown around the edges and slightly browned in the middle, about 25 minutes. Let the muffins cool at least 5 minutes; they'll come out of the pan much more easily.

NOTE: If you wish, make 12 muffins now and save the remainder of the batter for tomorrow. Cover and refrigerate the leftover batter, then, when you're ready to bake it, sprinkle an extra teaspoon of baking powder over the top, whisk it in, and follow the same drill, ladling the batter (it will be a little thicker today) into the heated greased muffin tin.

New World Pumpkin-Pepita- Poblano Muffins

MAKES 12 MUFFINS

Moist and deeply golden, these muffins are medium hot, studded with fire-roasted poblano peppers (roast, peel, and seed them before you start) and capped with an optional, very intriguing spicy, savory streusel topping. Pair them with something equally spicy or spicier, such as a chili, or let opposites attract: accompany them with a creamily bland leek and potato soup, or split pea–tomato soup.

What to do with the single cup of canned pumpkin you'll have left over from this recipe? Why, use it in the Uncannily Good Santa Fe–Style Quick Green Chile Soup-Stew on page 321, of course.

Vegetable oil cooking spray

1 batch Sweet-Hot Cheese Streusel Topping (optional, recipe follows)

1/2 cup whole wheat pastry flour

1/2 cup unbleached white flour

3/4 cup stone-ground yellow cornmeal

1/4 teaspoon salt

2 1/2 teaspoons baking powder

1/2 teaspoon baking soda

1 egg

3/4 cup buttermilk

1/3 cup dark brown sugar

3 tablespoons butter, melted and cooled slightly, or mild vegetable oil

3/4 cup cooked pumpkin or winter squash purée (fresh, canned, or frozen and thawed)

2 fire-roasted poblano peppers, peeled, seeded, and finely diced

1/3 cup tamari-roasted pepitas (optional; see Note)

1. Preheat the oven to 400°F. Spray a 12-cup muffin tin with oil.

2. Prepare and set aside the streusel topping if using.

3. Combine all the flours, cornmeal, salt, baking powder, and baking soda in a large bowl, stirring well. Set aside.

4. Now whisk together the egg, buttermilk, sugar, butter or oil, and pumpkin in a medium bowl.

"Sometimes, I would come to my field in the evening and stay all night because the porcupines were eating my corn. I'd sing all the way up and down the rows. My dad said that this corn is like children: You have to sing to it, and then it will be happy."

—ELDERLY HOPI FARMER,
QUOTED BY MICHAEL ABLEMAN,
FARMER AND AUTHOR OF
*Fields of Plenty: A Farmer's Journey
in Search of Real Food and the
People Who Grow It*

5. Stir the egg mixture into the flour mixture until not quite blended, then add the poblanos, with just a couple of strokes, so the mixture is just barely combined. Spoon into the prepared muffin tin. If embellishing with the streusel topping, divide it evenly over each cup. If not using the streusel, divide the pepitas evenly, sprinkling them over the tops of the muffins, pressing the seeds in lightly with your fingertips.

6. Bake until golden brown, 15 to 20 minutes. Serve hot.

NOTE: Pepitas are roasted pumpkin seeds, extra-good when roasted with tamari soy sauce instead of salt. They are available at natural foods markets. You can sometimes find a tamari-roasted pepita–sunflower seed mix, too, which you can feel free to substitute.

SWEET-HOT CHEESE STREUSEL TOPPING

ENOUGH FOR 12 MUFFINS

1 teaspoon butter
¼ cup (1 ounce) finely grated extra-sharp Cheddar cheese
1 tablespoon brown sugar
3 tablespoons unbleached white flour
⅛ teaspoon cayenne, or to taste
⅓ cup tamari-roasted pepitas (see Note, above)

Cream together the butter and Cheddar cheese, then cream in the brown sugar. Cut in the flour and cayenne. Add the pepitas. Reserve this crumbly mixture. Sprinkle each cup of muffin batter with a portion of the streusel. Bake as directed.

High Desert Blue Corn Muffins with Sage and Toasted Pine Nuts

MAKES 12 MUFFINS

Sage, an herb said to bring clarity and focus, has a strong flavor that can be intoxicatingly heady or excessive. Here, it is subtle and gently enticing. It's easier to cut sage with scissors than mince it with a knife: Just stack the sage leaves, scissor once or twice length-wise, then cut crosswise to make tiny ribbons. Blue cornmeal is widely available in natural foods markets, but you may also order it online from www.wareaglemill.com, www.bobsredmill.com, or www.cooking post.com.

Dissolving the baking soda in the buttermilk makes for an especially tender-textured, almost cake-like muffin. Serve these with any green chile–accented stew and dream of Taos.

> "Get outen the way, ol' Dan Tucker,
> You're too late to get your supper.
> Supper's done and the dishes washed,
> Nothin' left but a piece of squash."
> —"OLD DAN TUCKER,"
> AMERICAN FOLKSONG

Vegetable oil cooking spray
1 cup unbleached white flour
1 cup stone-ground blue cornmeal
1/2 teaspoon salt
1 tablespoon baking powder
1 1/4 cups buttermilk
1/2 teaspoon baking soda
2 eggs
1/2 cup unrefined sugar (see Pantry, page 356) or brown sugar
1/3 cup melted butter, cooled slightly, or mild vegetable oil
1 tablespoon finely scissored fresh sage, 7 to 9 medium leaves
1/2 cup pine nuts, lightly toasted

1. Preheat the oven to 400°F. Spray a 12-cup muffin tin with oil.

2. Combine the flour, cornmeal, salt, and baking powder in a large bowl, stirring well. Set aside.

3. In a medium bowl, whisk together the buttermilk and baking soda, dissolving the baking soda and admiring the slightly dramatic foaming. Now whisk in the eggs, sugar, melted butter or oil, and sage.

4. Stir the combined wet ingredients into the dry mixture, until just barely blended. Then add the pine nuts with just a couple of strokes. Spoon into the prepared muffin tin.

5. Bake until the edges are golden brown and the caps are high and rounded, 15 to 20 minutes. Serve hot.

Wholesome Ginger-Pear Muffins with a Lemon Glaze

MAKES 16 MUFFINS

This wondrous fresh ginger muffin rises from my long-held conviction that pear and ginger are a perfect pairing (whether in sorbet or pear butter), as are ginger and lemon, and lemon and pear. All three together—wow! The pears can be on the verge of overripe. You could add a few tablespoons of chopped toasted walnuts or almonds to these as well.

As always when using grated citrus fruit zest, try to use organic, since the nonorganic are heavily sprayed (the theory being that people don't eat the rind and therefore stuff not suited for human consumption can be used with impunity).

Vegetable oil cooking spray

4 ounces fresh gingerroot, unpeeled, cut into chunks

1/2 cup sugar

1 teaspoon corn syrup (optional)

1 cup unbleached white flour

1 cup stone-ground yellow cornmeal

2 teaspoons baking powder

3/4 teaspoon baking soda

1/2 teaspoon salt

1/4 cup oatmeal (rolled oats)

1/4 cup (1/2 stick) butter, melted and cooled slightly

2 eggs

1 1/2 teaspoons grated lemon zest, preferably organic

1 cup buttermilk

2 ripe, flavorful pears, Bartlett, Bosc, or Anjou, cored but peel left on, in 1/4-inch dice

1 batch Lemon Glaze (recipe follows)

It was upon a Lammas night,
When corn rigs are bonny,
Beneath the moon's unclouded light,
I held awhile to Annie;
The time flew by, with tentless heed,
Till, 'tween the late and early,
With small persuasion she agreed
To see me through the barley.

Corn rigs, an' barley rigs,
An' corn rigs are bonny:
I'll ne'er forget that happy night,
Among the rigs with Annie.

—ROBERT BURNS,
"CORN RIGS AN' BARLEY RIGS," 1783

I. Preheat the oven to 375°F. Spray 16 muffin-tin cups with oil.

2. Prepare the ginger by pulse-chopping it very fine in a food processor, pausing to scrape down the sides of the work bowl. Place it in a small skillet, adding ¼ cup of the sugar and the teaspoon of corn syrup, if using. Put the skillet over medium heat and, keeping a close eye on it and giving the pan an occasional shake, cook just until the sugar has melted, about 6 minutes. The mixture will be quite hot. Remove from the heat and let it cool.

3. Sift the flour, cornmeal, baking powder, baking soda, salt, and the remaining ¼ cup sugar into a large bowl. Stir in the oatmeal.

4. Whisk together the butter, eggs, lemon zest, and buttermilk in a small bowl.

5. Combine the wet and dry mixtures with a few preliminary strokes, then add the prepared ginger and the diced pears. Stir just a few more times, until the ingredients are barely combined.

6. Spoon the batter into the prepared muffin cups and bake until golden and crusty, 15 minutes. Let the muffins cool briefly, then pour the lemon glaze over them (it is quite thin and sticky and will be well absorbed by the muffins, making for extra-moist, very lemony muffins that will have you licking your fingers).

LEMON GLAZE

ENOUGH FOR 16 MUFFINS

Finely grated zest of 1 lemon, preferably organic
⅓ cup fresh lemon juice
⅓ cup sugar

Combine all ingredients in a small pan and bring to a boil, stirring to dissolve the sugar. Lower the heat and simmer the glaze until slightly thickened, 4 to 5 minutes. Let cool slightly, and use as directed above.

BLUE, BLUE BLUEBERRY CORN MUFFINS

MAKES 18 STANDARD MUFFINS OR
12 LARGE MUFFINS

Almost everyone's first and favorite muffin is blueberry. Here are a few twists. Cornmeal adds its ever-pleasing gritty crunchiness, and what cornmeal-loving cook could resist blue cornmeal with blueberries? You can make these with frozen blues (unthawed), but I recommend fresh—to me, blueberry muffins are one of the best wait-for-the-season foods. Since they're so very juicy, you might use muffin papers in the tins instead of oiling the tins. Your call (and cleanup).

Blue cornmeal is available at natural foods stores, or online. If you want to take these over the top, serve them with the Blueberry–Cream Cheese–Honey Butter that follows.

**Vegetable oil cooking spray or
    muffin papers**
1⅔ cups unbleached white flour, divided
**⅓ cup stone-ground blue cornmeal
    (see Pantry, page 350)**
½ teaspoon salt
1 tablespoon baking powder
½ teaspoon baking soda
⅓ cup butter, at room temperature
½ cup sugar
1 egg
½ teaspoon pure vanilla extract
¼ teaspoon freshly grated nutmeg
**1 cup low-fat milk, plain or vanilla
    soy milk, or a combination
    (see Note)**
1 cup blueberries
**½ cup chopped toasted walnuts
    (optional)**
**Blueberry–Cream Cheese–Honey Butter,
    for serving (optional; recipe follows)**

1. Preheat the oven to 425°F. Spray 18 standard-size or 12 large muffin-tin cups with oil, or line the cups with papers.

2. Stir together the flour, blue cornmeal, salt, baking powder, and baking soda into a large bowl. Set aside.

3. Cream together the butter and sugar in a small bowl, then beat in the egg, vanilla, and nutmeg.

4. Stir the creamed mixture into the dry mixture along with the milk, until not quite blended. Then add the blueberries and the walnuts, if using, with just a couple of strokes, so the mixture is just barely combined. Spoon into the prepared muffin cups.

5. Bake until the edges of the muffins are golden brown and the caps are rounded and also golden, 22 to 27 minutes. Let cool for just a few minutes, then remove from the cups. Serve warm (or rewarm before eating them), with blueberry–cream cheese–honey butter if you like.

NOTE: Why the suggestion of combining low-fat dairy milk and soy milk? Because soy milk has a genuinely rich, cream-like texture. Combine it with low-fat milk for dairy flavor with cream texture. The combination was the preference of my tasters.

VARIATION: BLUEBERRY-WALNUT STREUSEL MUFFINS

Substitute brown sugar for white in the muffin batter; pass on the optional walnuts. Make the streusel topping: Cut together 2 tablespoons butter, 3 tablespoons brown sugar, 2 tablespoons unbleached white flour, and 1 tablespoon oatmeal until crumbly. Toss in 1/3 cup chopped toasted walnuts. Divide this mixture among the tops of the unbaked muffins. Bake as directed.

BLUEBERRY-CREAM CHEESE-HONEY BUTTER

ABOUT 1¹/₂ CUPS

If you used frozen blueberries for the muffin recipe, you'll have some left over in the bag. Use them to make this luscious spread for the muffins.

> **About 1 cup frozen blueberries (more or less is fine), thawed**
> **¹/₂ cup (1 stick) butter, at room temperature**
> **8 ounces Neufchâtel or low-fat cream cheese**
> **¹/₄ cup honey**
> **2 teaspoons crème de cassis, Chambord, or Grand Marnier (optional)**

Combine all ingredients (including any blueberry juice) in a food processor. Buzz until smooth, and transfer to a serving dish. Pop in the freezer for a few minutes as the muffins bake, so the butter will firm up just a bit. Serve with the warm blueberry muffins and you almost won't miss the fresh blueberries. *Almost.*

VARIATION: FRESH BLUEBERRY-CREAM CHEESE-HONEY BUTTER

Use ¹/₂ cup fresh blueberries in place of the thawed to raise the swoon factor. Serve on pancakes, waffles, or toast, or in crepes with whole fresh blueberries.

THE DAILY GRIND

In recipe after recipe, I call for stone-ground cornmeal. Let's cozy up to the what and why.

Cornmeal is simply dried, ground-up, whole-kernel field corn, usually of the variety called flint or dent. It is "sweet" only in contrast to nixtamalized corn kernels (which have been soaked in an alkaline solution to make them easier to grind—as a bonus, this process also makes the corn easier to digest); the sweet corn grown for cornmeal is not sweet in the high-sugar, eat-it-fresh-off-the-cob sense.

How this "sweet" corn is ground to meal has everything to do with its nutritive value, flavor, and texture. Corn has a larger percentage of oil than wheat and many other grains; because oil easily turns rancid, corn needs greater care than wheat in grinding and milling to stay at its best.

Corn is ground in one of two ways: between slowly moving stones, to create stone-ground whole-grain cornmeal (sometimes called "water-ground," because the grinding stones are often powered by water), or between mammoth steel rollers, the industrial milling method. These steel rollers get extremely hot, destroying much of the corn's flavor and nutritive value by partially cooking it. The meal created by this method has its germ and hull removed, thus becoming the pitiful commercial product known as "enriched-degerminated cornmeal." Dry, uniform in texture, it's virtually flavorless.

Does this mass-produced cornmeal have anything going for it? Sure. It's cheap, you can buy it almost anywhere, and it almost never spoils. Its shelf life is indefinite; due to the processing, there's nothing left in it to spoil.

Stone-grinding in a small, usually

water-powered mill produces a better, tastier, and more nutritious meal, with unmistakable, wonderful texture. Because it is a precise and painstaking process, the corn is necessarily ground in small quantities, under the watchful eye of a miller (or "milleress," as Zoë Caywood, doyenne of the famous War Eagle Mill in Rogers, Arkansas, proudly refers to herself). The miller(ess) shapes the final result at every step, from the corn varieties purchased, to the grinding method, to how, where, and to whom the meal is marketed.

Such mills steward whole-grain meal: the flavorful germ is left in, as is the healthful and wonderfully textured outer part, the bran. Then there's a tiny dark dot at the heart of whole-grain corn's germ, sometimes called the speckle or freckle. When the germ is ground, the result is sometimes called "speckle-heart" cornmeal. Some aficionados claim the freckle holds most of the flavor.

Unlike steel rollers, stone grinding wheels do not heat up. Barely warm even at peak use, they ensure that the cornmeal loses neither taste nor nutritive value. The result: flavorful, textural cornmeal, full of the tastes that the spectrum of nutritional elements have given it; and of slightly irregularly sized particles, some floury, some the size of fine sand, some a full yellow, some a creamier yellow, with tiny freckles visible if you hold a bit in your hand. This grainy texture gives cornbread and other baked goods made from whole-grain, stone-ground corn their magical, distinctive, toothsome crunch and grit.

Drawbacks? Well, in some parts of America stone-ground cornmeal is hard to find, other than by mail order. Because it's more labor-intensive, it's more expensive. Too, stone-ground cornmeal doesn't keep for long and it's more prone to insect infestation. To those who love good food, these drawbacks are trifling.

CRUMBLE-BUMBLE LEMON BLUEBERRY BABYCAKES

MAKES 12 BABYCAKES

These are rich, sweet, and very cake-like. Hence, "babycakes"— what else would you call the ultimate in a conventional-but-with-a-twist muffin that is a simply scrumptious, not-for-every-day treat? Save these for fresh blueberries. If you add the optional streusel topping, you are at serious risk of lily-gilding. Sweet enough to be dessert, the batter would be excellent baked in a cake pan, served warm and sprinkled with a little confectioners' sugar, and a scoop of vanilla ice cream or frozen yogurt.

Note that these rise a good bit, making an extra-crunchy, larger-than-normal top that flows onto the upper surface of the muffin tin. So, be sure to oil that surface as well.

Vegetable oil cooking spray

⅓ cup butter, at room temperature

¾ cup sugar, preferably unrefined (see Pantry, page 356)

2 eggs

1 teaspoon pure vanilla extract

Finely grated zest of 1 to 2 lemons, preferably organic

1¼ cups unbleached white flour

¼ cup whole wheat pastry flour

¼ cup stone-ground yellow cornmeal

½ teaspoon salt

1 tablespoon baking powder

½ cup milk (I prefer vanilla soy milk here)

1½ to 2 cups fresh blueberries

½ cup chopped walnuts, toasted or not

Rich Cinnamon-Nut Crumble-Bumble Streusel (optional; recipe follows)

1. Preheat the oven to 400°F. Spray a 12-cup muffin tin with oil or line the cups with papers. In either case, be sure to spray the top surface of the muffin tin.

2. Cream the butter and sugar in a medium bowl until thoroughly incorporated, then beat in the eggs, one at a time. Add the vanilla and lemon zest.

3. Stir together the flours, cornmeal, salt, and baking powder in a large bowl (you may sift these if you want an even lighter muffin). Set aside.

4. Stir the creamed mixture into the flour mixture, alternating with the milk. Don't overbeat. The moment the mixtures are mostly combined, stir in the blueberries and nuts with a few quick strokes.

5. Fill the muffin cups; this amount of batter will make them fuller than usual. If you like, sprinkle them with the streusel.

6. Bake until the kitchen is fragrant and the edges and tops of the muffins are golden brown and a little crunchy looking, about 25 minutes. Let cool just a few minutes, then remove from the pan. Serve warm.

RICH CINNAMON-NUT CRUMBLE-BUMBLE STREUSEL

ENOUGH FOR 12 BABYCAKES

This streusel has lots and lots of nuts, and is spiced lightly with cinnamon. How can you go wrong?

2 tablespoons cold butter, finely diced

3 tablespoons sugar, preferably unrefined (see Pantry, page 356)

1 tablespoon unbleached white flour

½ teaspoon ground cinnamon

1 cup untoasted walnut pieces

·M·E·N·U·

BREAK-OF-DAY BLUEBERRIES

Blueberries, Raspberries, and Finely Diced Early Fall Apples

*

Crustless Fresh Tomato Quiche with Gruyère and Freshly Grated Parmesan

*

Crisped Sausage or Soysage Patties Brushed with a little Jalapeño Jelly

*

Blue, Blue Blueberry Corn Muffins (page 132)

*

Crumble-Bumble Lemon Blueberry Babycakes

*

Butter * Blueberry Jam

*

Colombian Coffee * Ceylon Breakfast Tea

Using your fingers, combine the butter, sugar, flour, and cinnamon in a bowl until crumbly. Toss in the walnuts. Divide this mixture among the unbaked muffins, sprinkling it evenly over their tops. Bake as directed.

DK's Banana-Ginger Corn Muffins

MAKES 12 MUFFINS

Cornmeal adds its characteristic toothsomeness to this simply wonderful cake-textured muffin, giving it a beautiful yellow color. These were devised for David Koff, aka Davio (due to a trip we took to Italy together in years past). He's fond of ripe bananas, and adores crystallized ginger, and with this muffin, he got them both . . . Out of this world, these muffins, with a smattering of almonds, and just a bit of crunchy topping—an edible valentine for my then-new sweetheart on a gray, rainy February morning in 2003.

I hope you have an equivalent occasion on which to bring them forth, but if you don't, try taking them sometime to an early morning meeting. Their effect could be remarkably persuasive.

The optional Aphrodite Butter can be made the night before.

Vegetable oil cooking spray

DRY INGREDIENTS
1 cup unbleached white flour

¾ cup stone-ground yellow cornmeal

½ cup brown sugar or unrefined sugar (see Pantry, page 356)

2½ teaspoons baking powder

¼ teaspoon salt

A vigorous grating of nutmeg

STREUSEL TOPPING
2 tablespoons butter, melted or very soft

3 tablespoons brown sugar

3 tablespoons unbleached white flour

½ teaspoon ground cinnamon

WET INGREDIENTS
⅔ cup milk

¼ cup (½ stick) butter, melted and cooled slightly

1 large egg

ADD-INS
2 to 3 tablespoons diced crystallized ginger, or 1 to 2 tablespoons finely grated peeled fresh gingerroot

2 very ripe bananas, mashed

½ cup sliced almonds, preferably toasted

FOR SERVING (OPTIONAL)
Aphrodite Butter (recipe follows)

1. Preheat the oven to 400°F. Spray a 12-cup muffin tin with oil.

2. Combine all the dry ingredients in a large bowl, stirring well. Set aside.

3. Moving on to the streusel topping, cream the butter and brown sugar together in a small bowl, then add the flour and cinnamon. Using your fingers, blend to form a crumbly mixture. Set it aside, too.

4. You guessed it: Combine and beat together the wet ingredients. (If you measure the milk into a 2-cup measure and add the butter and egg, beating with a fork, it's one less dish to wash.)

5. Pour the wet ingredients into the dry, and stir until the mixture is not quite blended. Stir in the add-ins, with just a couple of strokes, so the mixture is just barely combined.

6. Spoon the batter into the prepared muffin tin, and divide the streusel crumbs evenly among the muffins, sprinkling a bit atop each. Bake until golden brown, 15 to 20 minutes. Serve hot, with Aphrodite Butter if you like.

APHRODITE BUTTER

MAKES ABOUT 1 CUP

Totally indulgent, pale pink, impossibly good, this pretty spread is romanced with rosewater. Thin it slightly and add more confectioners' sugar, and you could use it to ice butter cookies: perhaps heart-shaped ones.

¼ cup (½ stick) butter, cut into quarters, at room temperature

4 or 5 fresh strawberries, stemmed and quartered

·M·E·N·U·

MY FUNNY VALENTINE

Fruit Coupe: Cut-up Strawberries, Pineapple, Apple, and Navel Oranges

*

Hashed Brown Potatoes with a Mix of Sautéed Vegetables, topped with a Poached Egg and a Sprinkle of Grated Vermont Cheddar

*

DK's Banana-Ginger Corn Muffins, served warm

*

Aphrodite Butter

*

Darjeeling Tea with Hot Milk

---

1 package (8 ounces) cream cheese, at room temperature

¼ cup sifted confectioners' sugar

1 tablespoon honey

2 or 3 drops rosewater

Place all the ingredients in a food processor and pulse until well combined, pausing occasionally to scrape down the sides of the work bowl. Transfer to a serving dish. Chill for at least an hour to firm up.

DRIED CRANBERRY-BLACK WALNUT CORN MUFFINS

MAKES 12 MUFFINS

Don't let another Thanksgiving weekend go by without these muffins. On their own, they're an excellent not-too-sweet addition to the breadbasket at the feast proper. But served with the luscious make-ahead cranberry-maple-bourbon butter, they're perfect for brunch, or as a simple tide-over continental breakfast.

The ingredients of both the muffin and the butter offer a nod to the first Thanksgiving via corn: one contains cornmeal and the other, slyly, bourbon, also made from corn. It pays homage, too, to other native American ingredients: cranberries (both fresh and dried), maple syrup, and black walnuts.

Vegetable oil cooking spray
1 cup stone-ground yellow cornmeal
1 cup unbleached white flour
1/3 cup brown sugar
2 tablespoons white sugar
2 teaspoons baking powder
1 teaspoon baking soda
1/2 teaspoon salt
1/2 to 3/4 cup dried cranberries
1/2 cup black walnuts (or English walnuts or pecans), toasted and chopped
1 egg
1 1/2 cups buttermilk
1/3 cup mild vegetable oil
Cranberry-Maple-Bourbon Butter for serving (optional; recipe follows)

1. Preheat the oven to 400°F. Spray a 12-cup muffin tin with oil. Set aside.

2. Combine the cornmeal, flour, sugars, baking powder, baking soda, and salt in a medium bowl. Toss them together well, breaking up any lumps of brown sugar with your fingers. Set aside.

3. Combine the dried cranberries and walnuts in a small bowl. Sprinkle 1 tablespoon of the dry cornmeal mixture over them and toss well. Set aside.

4. Whisk together the egg, buttermilk, and oil in a small bowl or large glass measuring cup.

5. Pour the egg mixture into the cornmeal mixture and, working with as few strokes as possible, combine the two. When they are moistened but not quite incorporated and the batter is still far from smooth, stir in the meal-dusted cranberries and nuts.

6. Scoop the batter into the prepared tin and bake until the muffins are golden brown, slightly crusty around the edges, and test clean with a toothpick, 15 to 20 minutes. Serve, hot, straight from the oven, with the flavored butter, if desired.

VARIATION: ORANGE-GLAZED CRANBERRY CORN MUFFINS

Cranberry and orange, a time-honored holiday combination, appear in cranberry relishes and quick breads galore. But see if their goodness in this sweet muffin with its exquisitely sticky glaze doesn't just knock you out. Follow the above recipe, but add the grated zest of 2 oranges, preferably organic, when you add the cranberries and nuts. After the muffins are in the oven, juice the 2 naked oranges. Place the juice in a small saucepan, add ¼ cup sugar, and boil quickly until syrupy, no more than 5 minutes. When the muffins come out of the oven, brush them, while hot, with this sweet, sticky glaze. Yum!

> "Take your partner,
> Pat her on the head;
> If she don't like biscuits,
> feed her cornbread."
>
> —TRADITIONAL OZARK
> SQUARE DANCE CALL

CRANBERRY-MAPLE-BOURBON BUTTER

MAKES ABOUT 1⅓ CUPS

This butter is all parts festive. It can be made several days in advance and left to firm up in the fridge. Or, it can be quickly done while the muffins bake—though its texture will be much softer, bordering on drippy. That is not necessarily a drawback . . . the better to soak into you, my little muffin.

The maple extract intensifies the flavor, but it is not strictly necessary. Use a natural extract, not an artificial one; the latter will taint the whole thing.

½ cup pure maple syrup
2 tablespoons brown sugar
⅔ cup fresh cranberries
2 teaspoons bourbon
1 teaspoon natural maple extract (optional)
½ cup (1 stick) butter, at room temperature

Combine all ingredients in a food processor. Buzz until all is well combined, pausing to scrape down the sides of the work bowl. Transfer the butter to a 2-cup container (preferably glass, to show off the color) from which you will serve it with the muffins. Refrigerate it for a bit, just to firm it up slightly.

Neighborly Sweet Potato Muffins

MAKES 12 MUFFINS

I made these for my neighbor Carroll, who loves the combination of sweet potato and corn. They are luscious, with a cinnamon-spice-and-everything-nice caress and small hidden treasures of medjool date pieces and pecans. Picture-perfect for a fall brunch; dreamy served with really good coffee. Next time you bake or steam sweet potatoes, remember this recipe and fix an extra sweet potato. Because the sweet potato keeps them so moist, I once FedExed a dozen, carefully wrapped, to a friend for his birthday.

Vegetable oil cooking spray

DRY INGREDIENTS

½ cup whole wheat pastry flour
½ cup unbleached white flour
¾ cup stone-ground yellow cornmeal
¼ teaspoon salt
1 tablespoon baking powder
½ teaspoon baking soda

WET INGREDIENTS

1 egg
1 cup buttermilk
⅓ cup dark brown sugar
3 tablespoons butter, melted and cooled slightly, or mild vegetable oil
1⅓ cups cooked mashed sweet potato (about 1 medium-large sweet potato)

STREUSEL TOPPING

2 tablespoons butter, at room temperature
3 tablespoons brown sugar
¼ cup unbleached white flour
2 tablespoons oatmeal (rolled oats)
½ teaspoon ground cinnamon
Freshly grated nutmeg

ADD-INS

½ cup pitted, chopped dates, preferably medjool
⅓ cup chopped toasted pecans or walnuts

1. Preheat the oven to 400°F. Spray a 12-cup muffin tin with oil.

2. Combine all the dry ingredients in a large bowl, stirring well. Set aside.

3. Now combine the wet ingredients in a medium bowl, whisking everything together.

4. Moving on to the streusel topping, cream the butter and brown sugar together in a small bowl, then add the flour, oatmeal, cinnamon, and nutmeg to taste. Blend with your fingers to form a crumbly mixture. Set it aside, too.

5. Combine the add-ins in a small bowl with 2 tablespoons of the dry mixture and toss well.

6. Stir the wet mixture into the dry mixture until not quite blended, then add the dates and pecans, with just a couple of strokes, so the mixture is just barely combined. Spoon into the prepared muffin tin. Divide the streusel evenly, sprinkling over the tops of the muffins.

7. Bake until golden brown, 15 to 20 minutes. Let cool slightly on a rack, then serve, warm.

"All the wide world is narrowed down
to the walls of corn, now sere and brown."

—ELLEN P. ALLERTON, FROM "WALLS OF CORN," ANTHOLOGIZED IN *Sunflowers: A Book of Kansas Poetry*

SWEET-HOT AZTEC TWO-STEPS

MAKES 12 MUFFINS

66 Aztec two-step" refers to three things: first, Lawrence Ferlinghetti's phrase from an untitled poem in *A Coney Island of the Mind;* second, the name of a dynamic and much-loved New York City folk-rock duo; and third, these muffins.

Step one: traditional Aztec flavorings and native foodstuffs: chocolate, cayenne, blue cornmeal, and mesquite meal. Step two: contemporary ingredients and cooking methods. Put them together, and what a delectable dance these exquisite, hauntingly piquant muffins do! Not too sweet, these have several mysterious, delicious backbeats of flavor.

Please note the range on the cayenne. A quarter teaspoon gives you just the faintest whisper of heat, a full teaspoon turns up the volume considerably. Tone it down, if you must, but please don't omit this ingredient.

Vegetable oil cooking spray

3 tablespoons butter

1 ounce semisweet chocolate

¾ cup plus 2 tablespoons whole wheat pastry flour

¾ cup stone-ground blue cornmeal (see Pantry, page 350)

½ cup mesquite meal, preferably Peruvian (see Pantry, page 355)

¼ cup unsweetened cocoa

1 tablespoon baking powder

½ teaspoon baking soda

½ teaspoon salt

½ teaspoon freshly grated nutmeg

½ teaspoon ground cinnamon

¼ to 1 teaspoon ground cayenne

2 eggs

⅓ cup dark brown sugar

½ teaspoon pure vanilla extract

1 cup milk

½ cup raisins or dried cherries

¼ to ½ cup semisweet chocolate chips (optional)

1. Preheat the oven to 400°F. Spray a 12-cup muffin tin with oil.

2. Melt the butter and 1 ounce semisweet chocolate together in a small saucepan set over low heat, stirring occasionally. When the chocolate has melted, set the saucepan aside to cool slightly.

3. As the chocolate cools, combine, in a medium-large bowl, the whole wheat flour, cornmeal, mesquite meal, cocoa, baking powder, baking soda, salt, nutmeg, cinnamon, and cayenne. Stir it all together very well (you don't want to run into a clump of unmitigated cayenne).

4. Beat the eggs, brown sugar, and vanilla into the cooled chocolate.

5. Combine the chocolate mixture, the flour mixture, and the milk, stirring together until just blended. Then quickly stir in the raisins or dried cherries and chocolate chips, if using. Spoon the batter into the prepared muffin tin and bake until crusty and firm on top, about 20 minutes. Mmm, what a fragrance as they bake!

WILD RICE-CORN SLIPPERDOWNS

MAKES 12 SLIPPERDOWNS

Muffins made with leftover cornmeal mush in Colonial days were called "slipperdowns," possibly because they were initially made fireside on a hanging griddle, a process that sounds as if it would involve a great deal of the batter slipping down. But, baked in an oven, muffins incorporating leftover cooked cereal grains are much neater. And they're excellent: moist, grainy, satisfying. I love these gems, in which the earthy flavor of wild rice combines with cornmeal's characteristic texture. However, you could use almost any leftover cooked grain: oatmeal, brown rice, any of the numerous multigrain porridges (you know, that bit leftover from breakfast). The more moist the cooked grain, the moister, though heavier, the finished slipperdown will be.

⅔ cup buttermilk or plain yogurt

3 tablespoons butter or mild vegetable oil

½ cup stone-ground white or yellow cornmeal

½ cup very well-cooked wild rice (the kernels should be split open), well-drained and tightly packed, or any other cooked grain

3 tablespoons brown sugar or unrefined sugar (see Pantry, page 356)

½ teaspoon salt

2 eggs, separated

½ cup unbleached white or whole wheat pastry flour

Vegetable oil cooking spray

2½ teaspoons baking powder

¼ teaspoon baking soda

I. Preheat the oven to 400°F.

2. Combine the buttermilk or yogurt and butter in a small saucepan. Place over medium heat until scalding hot (the butter will melt).

3. Meanwhile, place the cornmeal, wild rice, sugar, and salt in the work bowl of a food processor or a blender. Pour the scalded dairy mixture over it and buzz quickly (and carefully—hot liquid!) to make a thinnish but textured porridge-like mixture, leaving the grains of wild rice cut but not puréed. Let stand for about 10 minutes. When the mixture has cooled to lukewarm, pulse in the 2 egg yolks.

4. Transfer the cornmeal-rice mixture to a large bowl. Stir in the flour.

5. Spray a 12-cup muffin tin with oil, and place the tin, unfilled, into the oven to get good and hot.

6. Place the 2 egg whites in a small, high-sided, very clean bowl. Beat the egg whites until they're stiff but not dry (see Beating Egg Whites, pages 186–187).

7. Sprinkle the baking powder and baking soda over the batter and stir it in thoroughly. Add a little of the egg whites, stirring them in, too. Then, gently fold the remaining egg whites into the batter.

8. Remove the heated muffin tin from the oven and divide the batter among the oiled, hot muffin cups (it should sizzle slightly as it goes in). Don't worry; the batter for these gems is a little thinner and somewhat differently textured than the usual muffin batter.

9. Bake until the tops are rounded, golden brown, and crusty, 15 to 20 minutes. Remove the tin and let it cool slightly before running a knife around the edge of each muffin and turning them out.

VARIATION:
SLIPPERDOWNS WITH TOASTED PECANS OR WALNUTS

The flavor of the wild rice is highly compatible with that of toasted nuts, especially walnuts or pecans. Add an extra tablespoon of brown sugar to the batter, and stir ⅓ cup coarsely chopped toasted nuts in with the last few folds of egg white.

SIPPIN' CORN

In old age, after a lifetime of making corn likker and shooting at the revenuers, an apocryphal Ozark moonshine-runner got religion. Saving such a notorious long-time reprobate was naturally a great catch for the church that had succeeded where many had failed. The new convert was deluged with invitations to dine from the congregation. The first was Sunday dinner at the preacher's.

The table was spread with an abundance of summer vegetables, fresh from the garden. Politely the preacher's wife asked the moonshiner, "Now, will ye take some corn?" Accustomed to a life where this vegetable was used in a different fashion, he responded with equal politeness, "Oh, yes, m'am, and I thank ye"—and passed her his glass.

COUNTRYSIDE CORNSTICKS

MAKES 16 TO 18 CORNSTICKS

This delectable, rich, almost cake-like farmhouse recipe using milk, sour cream, eggs, and butter, dates from the days when caloric intake was irrelevant because labor was physical. The ingredients came from right there on the farm, and when you had them, you had them in abundance.

As with skillet-baked cornbread and the gems that follow, to get the ultimate delicious crustiness, the cornstick molds must be well seasoned (see How to Season a Cast-Iron Skillet, pages 16–17), well greased, and heated to smokingly, sizzlingly hot before the batter is poured in.

⅓ cup butter

1¼ cups stone-ground yellow cornmeal

¾ cup unbleached white flour

2 to 3 tablespoons sugar

¾ teaspoon baking soda

2 teaspoons baking powder

½ teaspoon salt

¼ cup milk

¾ cup full-fat sour cream or plain yogurt

2 eggs

Vegetable oil cooking spray

1. Preheat the oven to 425°F. Place an ungreased cornstick pan (or pans) in the oven to preheat.

2. Melt ¼ cup (4 tablespoons) of the butter.

3. Combine the cornmeal, flour, sugar, baking soda, baking powder, and salt in a large bowl. In a smaller bowl, beat together the milk, sour cream or yogurt, and eggs. Whisk in the melted butter.

4. Quickly combine the wet and dry mixtures, being careful, as always in cornbreadland, not to overbeat.

5. Carefully remove the hot cornstick pan or pans from the oven. First spray them very, very well with the cooking spray, then divide the remaining butter, placing a little chip of it in each cornstick mold. It will sizzle a bit as it goes in. Shake the pan a little to distribute the now-melted butter in the bottom of each mold.

6. Divide the batter among the hot molds of the cornstick pan(s), filling no more than two thirds of the way. Bake until the cornsticks are golden, crusty, and fragrant, 12 to 15 minutes. Let rest for a few moments, then turn the sticks out of the pans, nudging each along with the tip of a knife. (If you only have one cornstick pan with just a few molds, you may have to repeat this a few times.) Serve hot, from a basket lined with a calico napkin, to the great delight of everyone at your table.

CHEDDAR-SCALLION-BLACK PEPPER CORNSTICKS

MAKES 14 TO 16 CORNSTICKS

Want to make a simple bowl of lentil soup and a salad into a special meal? Try a basket of these rich, flavorful cornsticks. They're not much more elaborate than a typical cornbread or muffin, but they are just jazzy enough to make you say "Wow!" with each bite. You want the sharpest Cheddar cheese you can find: aged Vermont, English Cheshire, or Canadian Black Diamond are all good choices. The scallion–black pepper mix is better than it has any right to be.

Also, make sure your cornstick pan is well seasoned (see How to Season a Cast-Iron Skillet, pages 16–17) and grease it very well, just to be sure; the cheese might want to stick otherwise. Depending on the number of molds your cornstick pan has, you might need to bake a couple of batches.

"Farinaceous and milk food: such dishes as cornmeal mush and milk, or cornbread or corn muffins and milk or buttermilk, or bread, butter, fruit, and buttermilk, are the specialties of some lunch houses. These fine bakery lunches are all cheap and healthful dishes and many customers avail themselves of the opportunity to avoid meat eating altogether."

—JESSUP WHITEHEAD, *Cooking for Profit: A New American Cookbook Adapted for the Use of All Who Serve Meals for a Price, 1893*

1½ cups unbleached white flour
1¼ cups stone-ground yellow cornmeal
2 tablespoons sugar
2 teaspoons baking powder
½ teaspoon baking soda
½ teaspoon salt
1 to 1½ teaspoons coarse freshly ground black pepper, to taste
2 cups (8 ounces) very finely grated extra-sharp Cheddar cheese
2 eggs
1¼ cups buttermilk
¼ cup (½ stick) butter, melted
3 scallions, chopped very, very fine
Vegetable oil cooking spray

1. Preheat the oven to 350°F.

2. Combine the flour, cornmeal, sugar, baking powder, baking soda, salt, and black pepper in a large bowl, stirring very well. Remove 2 tablespoons of this mixture and toss it in a small bowl with the finely grated cheese. Set aside.

3. Beat the eggs and buttermilk together in a medium bowl, then beat in the melted butter. Stir this into the flour-cornmeal mix with just a few strokes—it shouldn't be fully incorporated yet. Sprinkle with the scallions and cheese and stir a few more times, just until combined.

4. Spray the cornstick pan very liberally with oil, and spoon the batter into the molds. You want the molds about three quarters of the way full.

5. Bake until the cornsticks are crusty and golden, 18 to 20 minutes. Cool briefly in the pans, then turn out onto a rack to cool a little more. Serve warm.

White Cornmeal Gems

MAKES 12 LARGE GEMS

Hauntingly delicious, with clear, simple flavors: The good graininess of the white cornmeal comes through wonderfully. As with cornsticks, make sure the pan— in this case a muffin tin—is very hot when you add the batter. This batter is much more liquid than your typical cornbread or muffin. And as with soufflés, don't open the oven during the early phases of baking, or you will deflate the gems' puffiness. They'll still be delicious, but their tops will be much flatter.

> **1 cup milk**
> **2 tablespoons butter**
> **1¼ cups stone-ground white cornmeal**
> **2 tablespoons brown sugar**
> **½ teaspoon salt**
> **2 eggs, separated**
> **Vegetable oil cooking spray**
> **2½ teaspoons baking powder**

1. Preheat the oven to 400°F.

2. Combine ½ cup water with the milk and butter in a small saucepan. Place over medium heat until the liquid is scalding hot and the butter melts.

3. Meanwhile, place the cornmeal, brown sugar, and salt in a heat-proof bowl. Pour the scalded milk-butter mixture over it, stir or mix well, and let stand for 10 minutes to cool.

4. Beat the egg yolks into the cooled cornmeal mixture and place the whites in a small, high-sided, very clean bowl (you'll be beating them shortly, so get out your hand-held beater now, too, and set it up near them). Spray a 12-cup muffin tin with oil and place the tin, unfilled, into the oven to get nice and hot.

5. Beat the egg whites until they are stiff but not dry (see Beating Egg Whites, pages 186–187). Sprinkle the baking powder over the cornmeal mixture and add about one third of the egg whites, stirring both in well. Then, gently fold the remaining egg whites into the batter.

6. Remove the heated muffin tin from the oven and divide the batter among the oil-sprayed, hot muffin cups (it should sizzle slightly as it goes in). The batter is thin enough so that your dividing will be somewhere between pouring and spooning: Don't worry!

7. Bake until the tops are rounded, golden brown, and crusty, 15 to 20 minutes. Remove, and let cool slightly before running a knife around the edge of each muffin and turning them out.

·M·E·N·U·

December I'll-Make-Breakfast-While-You-Shovel-the-Walk

Sections of California Navel Orange and Texas Ruby Red Grapefruit, from the Holiday Gift Boxes, with a Splash of Campari

*

Omelets of Sautéed Onion, Red Bell Pepper, and Extra-Sharp Vermont Cheddar

*

White Cornmeal Gems * **Butter** * **Strawberry Jam**

*

Sautéed Sausage or Soysage

*

Lapsang Souchong Tea with Warm Milk and Honey

CHARLISA-STYLED SESAME DROP BISCUIT-MUFFINS

MAKES ABOUT 48 MINIATURE
BISCUIT-MUFFINS

Charlisa Cato, my dear long-time friend, had an ace up her sleeve in this, an almost instant, incredibly tasty quick drop bread, somewhere between muffin and biscuit. These wonderful morsels are addictive: rich as sin, savory, and laced with toasted sesame seeds. She shared the recipe with me and countless grateful readers in *Dairy Hollow House Soup & Bread.* How, I wondered, would the formula fare with self-rising cornmeal instead of flour?

I don't use self-rising cornmeal often, as you may have noticed; once you have it on hand for these, you'll want to try it in Patsy Bruce's Tennessee Cornbread, page 23.

Vegetable oil cooking spray
**2 cups self-rising cornmeal
(see Pantry, page 350)**

**1 cup (2 sticks) butter, at room
temperature**
**1 cup full-fat or reduced-fat sour
cream (not fat-free)**
1/2 cup lightly toasted sesame seeds
**1 tablespoon paprika, preferably
Hungarian sweet**

1. Preheat the oven to 425°F. Spray either 2 mini-muffin tins or 2 baking sheets with oil.

2. Combine the self-rising cornmeal and butter with a fork in a mixing bowl, stirring until barely blended. Add the sour cream, sesame seeds, and paprika, and mix again, very briefly.

3. Drop the dough by teaspoonfuls either into the muffin tin or onto the baking sheet. Pop the biscuit-muffins into the oven and bake until brown around the edges and deliciously fragrant, about 10 minutes. Watch closely; they burn easily, and they're so good you wouldn't want to lose even one to excess browning.

> "Small loaves are better than large, and make less waste."
>
> —MRS. FRANCES E. OWENS,
> *Mrs. Owens' Cook Book and Useful
> Household Hints, 1883*

SAVORY ALMOND HERB BISCUITS

MAKES 12 LARGE BISCUITS

This toothsome biscuit is based on one I developed for the California Almond Board. Filled with layers of texture and flavor, the outside is crunchy, the inside soft and savory. Serve with a good salad and a tomato soup—a hot one in winter, a gazpacho in summer—for a dinner that will have everyone asking for seconds. (On that tomato soup: If you get really pressed for time, try one of the tomato soups made by Pacific or Imagine Foods. Jazz it up with a little cognac if you wish or make it more hearty with a can of well-drained chickpeas or kidney beans.) Then, assuming you have salad dressing on hand, the only thing you need to fool with are these biscuits.

By the way, these are drop biscuits, ultraeasy in both creation and cleanup: no patting out, no rolling or rolling pin, no floured bread board, no biscuit cutter.

Vegetable oil cooking spray
½ cup slivered almonds

1 tablespoon plus ⅓ cup cold butter or vegetable shortening such as Crisco, or a combination
1 small onion, finely chopped
2 garlic cloves, pressed or finely chopped
½ cup stone-ground cornmeal, preferably yellow
½ cup whole wheat pastry flour
1 cup unbleached white flour
1 tablespoon baking powder
½ teaspoon baking soda
1 teaspoon salt
1¼ cups buttermilk
2 tablespoons finely minced fresh flat-leaf parsley
1 tablespoon assorted fresh, finely minced herbs (a combination of rosemary, sage, thyme, and just a bit of dill is excellent here)
Additional butter, for serving

1. Preheat the oven to 450°F. Spray a baking sheet with oil and set aside.

2. Over medium-high heat, heat a heavy cast-iron skillet. When it's good and hot, lower the heat slightly and add the almonds. Stirring almost constantly, toast the almonds until they become fragrant and turn golden, then immediately transfer them to a cutting board to cool slightly.

3. Without bothering to wash it, spray the hot skillet with oil and return it to medium-high

heat, adding 1 tablespoon of the butter or shortening. When it melts, add the onion and sauté, stirring often, until the onion is limp, golden, and fragrant, about 5 minutes. Remove from the heat and stir in the garlic. Let the onion and garlic remain in the skillet, but off the stove.

4. As the skillet cools, combine the cornmeal, flours, baking powder, baking soda, and salt in a large bowl. Cut in the remaining ⅓ cup butter or shortening until the mixture has the consistency of fine crumbs.

5. Return to the almonds you toasted earlier, and coarsely chop them on the cutting board.

6. After the skillet has cooled slightly, pour the buttermilk into it, scraping to get up any little flavorsome bits of onion or garlic that have stuck to the bottom of the pan. Pour this into the cornmeal mixture, stirring with as few strokes as possible to just barely combine the wet and dry, stopping while there are still some dry clumps. Add the reserved almonds and the herbs and give a few more stirs.

7. Drop the batter by rounded tablespoonfuls onto the prepared baking sheet. Bake until golden, 10 to 15 minutes. Serve with additional butter.

VARIATION: SESAME-COCONUT CORNMEAL BISCUITS FOR KWANZAA

Omit the almonds, onion, garlic, and herbs from the above recipe, and cut the buttermilk back by 2 tablespoons. Beat 1 egg and 2 to 3 tablespoons of sugar and a touch of vanilla into the buttermilk *before* adding it to the dough. At the time when you would have added the onions, instead stir in 2 tablespoons toasted sesame seeds and ½ cup moist, sweetened coconut flakes. Bake as directed, and serve with butter and honey. (For more on Kwanzaa, see pages 32–33.)

"Two happy lovers make one bread."
—PABLO NERUDA

Sweet Maple-Glazed Almond Drop Scones

MAKES 12 LARGE SCONES

These rich, flavorful scones are perfect rainy-day food, and they are easy to make because they are dropped from a spoon, not rolled. As for the maple glaze: As a child, when asked if I wanted powdered sugar or maple syrup with my French toast, I always replied "Both," and, with a fork, mashed them into a sweet paste with butter on my plate. This glaze is a grown-up version. Try to get Grade B maple syrup. It's darker, stronger, and more maple-y than Grade A.

Vegetable oil cooking spray

1/2 cup slivered almonds

1/2 cup stone-ground cornmeal, preferably yellow

1/2 cup whole wheat pastry flour

1 cup unbleached white flour

3 tablespoons sugar

1 tablespoon baking powder

1/2 teaspoon baking soda

1 teaspoon salt

1/3 cup plus 1 tablespoon cold butter or vegetable shortening such as Crisco

1/2 cup buttermilk

1/2 cup reduced-fat (not fat-free) sour cream

1 egg

1 teaspoon pure vanilla extract

1/4 teaspoon pure almond extract

Maple Glaze (recipe follows)

I. Preheat the oven to 450°F. Spray a baking sheet with oil and set aside.

2. Over medium-high heat, heat a cast-iron skillet for 2 to 3 minutes. When it is good and hot, lower the heat slightly and add the almonds. Stirring almost constantly, toast the almonds until they become fragrant and turn golden, then immediately transfer them to a cutting board to cool slightly. Coarsely chop them.

3. Sift together into a large bowl the cornmeal, flours, sugar, baking powder, baking soda, and salt. Cut in the butter or shortening until the mixture has the consistency of fine crumbs.

4. Whisk together the buttermilk, sour cream, egg, and vanilla and almond extracts in a medium bowl until smooth. Pour this into the dry mixture, stirring with as few strokes as possible to just barely combine the wet and dry; stop while there are still some dry clumps. Add the reserved almonds and give a few more stirs.

5. Drop the batter by rounded tablespoonfuls onto the prepared baking sheet. Bake until golden, 10 to 15 minutes (you can make the glaze as the scones bake). Remove the scones from the oven and let cool, briefly, on a rack set over a rimmed baking sheet. Drizzle the glaze over each scone, allowing the excess to drip onto the baking sheet. Serve, warm. No butter is needed—these are rich enough.

MAPLE GLAZE

ENOUGH FOR I BATCH OF DROP SCONES, WITH A BIT LEFT OVER

1⅓ **cups confectioners' sugar, sifted**
1½ **teaspoons pure vanilla extract**
¼ **teaspoon pure almond extract**
**About ⅓ cup pure maple syrup,
   preferably grade B**

Combine the sugar and extracts in a small bowl. Gradually begin stirring in the maple syrup; you want a consistency thin enough to be drizzled onto the scones and drip a little, but not so thin it all rolls away or is just absorbed by the scones.

GETTING FRESH

How do you know if your cornmeal is fresh? It will taste ever so slightly sweet, and have a definite corn flavor. It will barely have a scent at all. Cornmeal that is past its prime, however, will have an off, slightly rancid odor and a bitter taste. Unless it's really very rancid, you won't get that taste until a beat after putting the cornmeal on your tongue; it's more an aftertaste, and an unpleasant one.

Use freshly stone-ground cornmeal within two or three weeks (a little longer in cold weather) or refrigerate it or freeze it for use within six months. For the best meal, purchase it from a mill, reputable mail-order source, or natural foods store or supermarket that has a high turnover.

Why go out of your way to get fresh stone-ground meal? Because cornbreads, polentas, grits, and mushes are *so* good made with the real, true, right stuff.

ROSEMARY CORN CRACKERS

MAKES ABOUT FIFTY 1-INCH
DIAMOND-SHAPED CRACKERS

A crisp version of your favorite focaccia: Olive oil and rosemary are an unbeatable combination, and when you add cornmeal's faint sweetness and crunch, and the savor of Parmesan cheese, you get way into the triple digits of pleasure. These are addictive.

For the rolling-out technique to work, you need rimless baking sheets (a double-insulated type is ideal).

Be sure to serve these in a basket with a large sprig of fresh rosemary tucked in beside them.

$\frac{1}{2}$ **cup buttermilk, or more as needed**

1 tablespoon fresh rosemary leaves, finely minced

$\frac{1}{2}$ **cup whole wheat pastry flour**

1 cup stone-ground yellow cornmeal

$\frac{1}{2}$ **teaspoon salt**

$\frac{1}{4}$ **teaspoon baking soda**

2 tablespoons very finely grated fresh Parmesan cheese

2 tablespoons plus 1 teaspoon extra-virgin olive oil

1 tablespoon butter, melted

Olive oil cooking spray

1. Combine the buttermilk and rosemary in a small bowl. Let stand for 1 hour.

2. Preheat the oven to 375°F.

3. Sift together the flour, cornmeal, salt, and baking soda into a medium bowl. Stir in the Parmesan, olive oil, and butter, then the buttermilk-rosemary mixture, making a dough that is tender and moist but not wet (it has to be roll-out-able). If necessary, add an extra teaspoon or two or three of buttermilk to achieve this texture.

4. Portion the dough into 2 large balls. Spray two rimless 12-by-18-inch baking sheets with the oil. Allow the dough balls to rest for a few moments (this relaxes the gluten and makes them slightly easier to roll out).

5. Working with one ball of dough at a time, place it on one of the oiled sheets and press down to flatten it into a thickish oval or circle. Then cover the sheet, and the dough, with wax paper, and start rolling the dough out gently, making an effort to keep the dough of even thickness all over, between $\frac{1}{8}$ and $\frac{1}{16}$ of an inch. Remove the wax paper and repeat with the second roll of dough.

6. Score the rolled-out dough, on its sheet, into crackers. I like small diamond shapes, and I use a pizza wheel for cutting, but any shape and sharp cutting implement will do. (Just don't press and draw the knife so hard that you cut through the dough completely or scar the baking sheet.)

7. Bake the first sheet on the middle rack until firmed up but not quite done, 5 to 10 minutes; if colored at all it should be only slightly, around the edges. Remove the sheet from the oven, and replace it with the second sheet. Let the first batch cool on its sheet while the second batch is baking, and just before it's due to come out of the oven, carefully break apart the crackers of the first batch along the score lines, pulling the crackers apart but leaving them on the sheet.

8. Return batch one—the crackers separated now—to the oven and bake for another 5 minutes or so, hovering around the kitchen, for at this point they can burn easily. You'll know they're done when they're golden— not dark—brown, and the air is suddenly intoxicatingly fragrant.

9. Repeat the procedure with the second sheet. Let the crackers cool on the baking sheet, and serve, warm or not. If you're doing them ahead of time, let them cool completely on a rack before wrapping them up tightly in foil.

VARIATION: Omit the rosemary for a plain cracker, or stir a couple of tablespoons toasted sesame seeds into the dough, using sesame oil instead of olive.

> "Love my wife, love my baby,
> Love my biscuits sopped in gravy."
> —"BLACK-EYED SUSIE," AMERICAN FOLKSONG

RICH SOUTHERN-STYLE CORNMEAL CHEESE COINS

MAKES ABOUT 100 CHEESE COINS

I don't think I have ever been to a wedding in the South where some variation of these wasn't served. They are always very rich ("short," as the parlance goes, meaning with a lot of shortening), crispy-flaky, and truly addictive.

In some versions the dough is rolled out like a crust and cut, in others it's formed into a cylinder like refrigerator cookie dough, and the coins are sliced off in rounds. Those who care to fuss with cookie presses sometimes squeeze the dough out into little curled ribbons. This cornmeal variation adds a new dimension to the genre, providing extra crunch and extra savor. It also has a little kick, thanks to the cayenne, which you can amp up or turn down as you wish.

> **3 cups unbleached white flour**
>
> **$\frac{1}{2}$ cup stone-ground yellow cornmeal**
>
> **$\frac{1}{4}$ teaspoon salt**
>
> **1 to $2\frac{1}{2}$ teaspoons cayenne pepper (How hot do you want 'em?)**
>
> **$1\frac{1}{2}$ cups (3 sticks) cold butter, cut into small cubes or grated**
>
> **4 cups (1 pound) finely grated extra-sharp Cheddar cheese**
>
> **Ice water**

1. Stir the flour, cornmeal, salt, and cayenne together very well in a large bowl.

2. Then, cut in the butter, as for pie crust, either by hand, using a pastry cutter, or pulsing quickly in a food processor.

3. Mix in the cheese likewise and, working with your hands, form into a dough that just barely holds together, drizzling in a little ice water if you need to. The texture will be somewhat crumbly, but the dough should hold together when pressed. Form the dough into three cylindrical logs, wrap tightly in plastic wrap, and refrigerate overnight, or until very firm.

4. Preheat the oven to 375°F, and remove the first cylinder of dough from the fridge. Using a very sharp knife, slice the dough into coins, $\frac{1}{8}$ inch thick or so. Place the coins, not touching each other, on an ungreased baking sheet.

5. Bake, staying in the kitchen (probably preparing the next batch on a second baking sheet). Check at 8 or 9 minutes, although it will likely take more like 10 to 11 minutes per batch; they do burn easily. When done, the coins should just barely have begun to color on their bottoms, and will still be delicate though firmed up. Let the cheese coins cool on the baking sheet for 5 minutes, then transfer them to a rack to cool completely. This can be done several days in advance of when you need them, if you let the crackers cool completely and pack them very carefully into tightly covered containers.

6. Repeat with the remaining dough logs.

Chapter 6

YEASTED CORNBREADS
Getting a Rise out of 'Em

There is perhaps one point of agreement defining most of the cornbreads in previous chapters—whether from north, south, east, west, or somewhere in between: They are either quick breads, raised with baking powder or baking soda, or altogether unleavened (such as tortillas, pones, and arepas). So what are we to make of *yeast*-risen cornbread, a seeming oxymoron? Wheat, not corn, is the near-universal flour grain for yeast-risen breads, and there's a good reason for that: gluten. This is the elastic, springy substance created

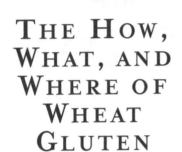

THE HOW, WHAT, AND WHERE OF WHEAT GLUTEN

To get a respectable rise on any yeast dough that contains up to one-third part cornmeal (or other non-gluten-containing grain flour or meal), you'll need to add about two tablespoons of wheat gluten per single loaf. Gluten is usually sold in powdered form as vital wheat gluten or gluten flour, and it's most likely stocked at your nearest natural foods store, either boxed or in bulk. If not, never fear—you can also purchase it by mail through King Arthur Flour (see Pantry, page 353).

when two wheat proteins are activated by the addition of liquid and developed by the action of kneading or stirring. It is gluten, which traps the air bubbles created as the dough is made, that provides the structural support and classic texture for yeast-risen bread. Since corn doesn't have any gluten, a 100-percent cornmeal cornbread cannot be leavened with yeast.

Corn is not alone in its gluten-less-ness: rice, quinoa, and millet are also without this stretchy stuff. And while gluten-less grains can make wonderful breads, they are most often used in quick breads, so called because they are leavened by rapid-acting baking powder or baking soda, as opposed to the more time-consuming yeast. Countless much-loved cornbreads demonstrate the merit of this approach.

So, can one make a good yeast-risen cornbread? Yes. How? First of all, expand your definition of cornbread. Know that a yeasted cornbread will not be "cornbread" as such—not the quick, corn-dominant breads to which most of this book is devoted. Rather, *yeast-raised cornbreads are multigrain breads containing cornmeal.* Once yeast enters the picture, wheat or spelt flour, unbleached or whole, must *always* be added to cornmeal if you want any kind of rise. And sometimes a little extra gluten is needed, too, in the form of a fine, slightly granular powder called gluten flour or vital wheat gluten; it helps give the yeast an additional structural boost.

So why use cornmeal in a yeast-raised bread in the first place? Why not just let cornbreads be quick and wheat breads be yeasty? Because the addition of cornmeal to a yeast bread dough does something wonderful. That characteristic toothsome, pleasing, irresistible grit makes you feel, to paraphrase Gertrude Stein, that there's a *there* there when you bite into a slice. No one wants a yeast bread that is leaden. But substantial, even dense, may be another matter. Not everyone feels that "light" is the be-all and end-all of bread. I love hearty, hefty, soulful multigrain breads, whether I purchase them or make them myself; it is the rare white bread that really does it for me.

There is another factor, too, in cornmeal-containing yeast breads: You miss out on some great traditional breads if you stick with straight wheat, however high-rising it may be. There are historic breads, like New England Rye'n'Injun (page 162); regional breads, like the famous anadama (page 165); and ethnic breads, like the pure and unadorned Portuguese broa, which we already encountered in the Global Cornbreads chapter, on page 103. A bread lover's life would be lacking without the experience of such loaves. In some breads, like the aforementioned broa, heaviness and density are inherent to the pleasure and personality of the bread.

That's why cornmeal in yeast-risen breads can be so surprisingly delicious. It makes for breads that are rich and diverse in flavor and texture: a wholesome cornucopia in every bite.

NEW ENGLAND RYE'N'INJUN

MAKES TWO 8¹/₂-BY-3¹/₄-INCH LOAVES

Rye'n'Injun is a favored early New England–style yeasted bread. It combined the Old World grains of rye and wheat with the New World's corn, the latter often called "Indian meal" or just "injun." So popular was this combination that the run-together names of its two dominant ingredients became shorthand for the bread itself. These early breads were dense, simple, often raised with sourdough; little more than the "mixture of rye and Indian meal most convenient and agreeable" that Henry David Thoreau baked "before [his] fire outdoors on a shingle" at Walden Pond.

This contemporary version is a bit more highfalutin, enriched with eggs, milk, and fat—precious, once seasonal ingredients, rarely used in early American breads, other than on very special occasions (and then only if the cows were fresh and the chickens laying).

2 cups milk

2 cups stone-ground yellow cornmeal

¼ cup brown sugar

1 tablespoon blackstrap molasses

2 teaspoons salt

2 tablespoons butter

½ cup lukewarm water

2 tablespoons active dry yeast

1 teaspoon white sugar

1 egg, beaten

1½ cups rye flour

1¾ cups whole wheat flour

2 tablespoons gluten flour (see Pantry, page 353)

About 2½ cups unbleached white flour, plus extra for kneading

Vegetable oil cooking spray

1. Place the milk in a small saucepan over medium heat. Meanwhile, combine the cornmeal, brown sugar, molasses, salt, and butter in a large heat-proof bowl.

2. When the milk is scalding hot (almost but not quite boiling), pour it over the cornmeal mixture, and stir well. Let stand until lukewarm, about 10 minutes.

3. During the last few minutes of this cooling time, combine the lukewarm water, yeast, and white sugar in a small cup (I usually do this right in the glass measuring cup). Set aside until bubbly, about 10 minutes.

4. Stir the yeast mixture with the egg into the cooled cornmeal mixture, and stir in the rye flour. Add the whole wheat flour, then the gluten flour, then the unbleached flour, a cup at a time, to make a fairly stiff dough. Turn the dough out onto a floured board and let it rest for a few minutes while you wash, dry, and oil the bowl in which it was mixed. Also spray two 8½-by-3¼-inch loaf pans with oil.

5. Knead the dough until it is somewhat springy and elastic and much less sticky, 5 or 6 minutes. Return the dough to the oiled bowl, cover with a clean cloth, and let rise in a warm spot until doubled in bulk, about 1 hour. Then punch it down, divide the dough in half, and shape it into 2 loaves, placing one in each of the prepared bread pans. Cover again, and let rise until doubled again. This second rise will be about 35 to 45 minutes. When about 30 minutes have passed, preheat the oven to 400°F.

6. Bake the risen loaves for 15 minutes, then lower the heat to 350°F and bake until the crust is firm and warmly brown, 30 minutes more. Let cool in the pans for 5 minutes, then on racks for at least 10 minutes more before tearing into them.

HOW WARM IS LUKEWARM?

The optimum temperature for dissolving and activating dry yeast is 105° to 115°F, or lukewarm. If you've ever tested warmed milk for a baby's bottle, lukewarm is about that warm. If the liquid is a little colder, the yeast will still work, it'll just take longer. If, however, it's too hot, you could kill the yeast altogether. So err on the side of cool . . . but lukewarm is best, and not difficult to achieve. After your first success, you'll never wonder again.

GAP MOUNTAIN
BAKERY AND CAFE,
KEENE, NEW HAMPSHIRE

In a yellow house just off the commons of Troy, New Hampshire, the tiny, casual Gap Mountain Bakery and Cafe was the place for gossip, news, socializing, and good bread for more than 20 years. Established in 1980, it's been owned by presiding bread-and-cookie goddess Diane Kellner since 1999. (In recent years, the bakery moved to the larger city of Keene.)

In addition to the fourteen bread varieties baked weekly (which include the anadama bread, right), other favorites appear periodically. During the holidays, Dresden stollen and apple spice bread show up, along with three kinds of partially prebaked rolls. Fridays bring golden, eggy challah. And add-ons simply appear as the spirit moves Diane: Irish soda bread, Swedish limpa, Parmesan-garlic bread . . . Though she has invented or developed countless recipes, the anadama bread is one that Diane inherited when she bought the bakery.

In 1988, Diane and her partner, Peter Knieste, left New York City to head north. "He wanted to go where there were no people, just caribou—like, the Arctic Circle," says Diane. "I need a little more social and cultural stimulation." They compromised on Troy, New Hampshire, after a week's trip around the state. Later, they took over Gap Mountain Bakery. Destiny, karma, kismet, besherte? Diane says, "Maybe it was meant to be. My last name, Kellner, is German for 'waiter.'" Peter adds, "Yeah. And mine, Knieste, means 'potato.'"

DIANE'S GAP MOUNTAIN ANADAMA BREAD

MAKES TWO 9-BY-5-INCH LOAVES

I've tasted many an anadama, the molasses-sweetened, single most famous yeast-raised cornbread. Whatever the word anadama's origins (see What's in the Name?, page 167), I've never met one I didn't like. But when I tasted the Gap Mountain version, honey, with one bite I knew I was in anadama heaven. Lighter-textured than most, it had a mysterious, delicious *je ne sais quoi*. As in the John Collier short story "The Touch of Nutmeg Makes It," it turned out to be that very spice that made the bread so over the top, although you don't detect it as such. Unlike many anadamas, in this recipe the cornmeal is not presoftened in boiling water, so be sure to use relatively fine-ground cornmeal, not corn grits.

The recipe is courtesy of Diane Kellner, owner of Gap Mountain Bakery and Cafe, once the social and culinary center of the tiny town of Troy, New Hampshire, now located in larger Keene. I scaled down the fourteen loaves to a manageable home-size batch of two.

·M·E·N·U·

BRIGHT BITE BROWN BAG

Egg Salad Sandwich on Toasted Diane's Gap Mountain Anadama Bread with Leaf Lettuce and Farmers' Market Tomatoes

*

Carrot and Celery Sticks

*

Orchard Apples

*

A bittersweet Chocolate Mouse, from L.A. Burdick Chocolate (www.burdickchocolate.com)

---

2 packages active dry yeast

2 cups lukewarm water

2 tablespoons canola oil

3 tablespoons blackstrap molasses

1 cup fine stone-ground cornmeal, any color (Diane uses yellow)

¾ teaspoon nutmeg, preferably freshly grated

3½ to 4 cups unbleached white flour, plus extra for kneading

1¾ to 2 cups whole wheat flour

2 teaspoons salt

Vegetable oil cooking spray

1. Combine the yeast and lukewarm water in a large bowl. Let stand until the yeast dissolves and gets a bit bubbly, about 10 minutes. Stir in the canola oil and molasses and let stand 1 minute longer.

2. Stir in the remaining ingredients (except the cooking spray!) in the order given, starting with 3¼ cups of the white flour and 1½ cups of the whole wheat flour, "making sure to add the salt last so it does not come in contact with the yeast," as Diane warns.

3. Mix thoroughly, beating with a wooden spoon, until the dough reaches the desirable texture: moist but not sticky, and kneadable. The exact amount of flour required will vary with the humidity; add more as needed, using two parts white to one part whole wheat.

4. Knead the dough thoroughly for about 5 minutes, adding a little more flour as you need to, but not too much; this is, again, a somewhat moist dough.

5. Place the dough in an oiled bowl, covered with a clean cloth, and let rise in a warm place until doubled in bulk, 1 to 1½ hours. Punch down, cover again, and allow the dough to rise a second time, again until doubled; this second rise will run 45 to 50 minutes. Meanwhile, spray two 9-by-5-inch loaf pans with oil.

6. Punch the dough down again and divide it in half. Form into loaves, and place the loaves in the prepared loaf pans. Let rise a third time, again covered, this time until not quite doubled in bulk, 30 to 35 minutes. Toward the end of this rising, preheat the oven to 350°F.

7. Bake the loaves until nicely browned, and crusty on both tops and bottoms, 45 to 55 minutes. (How to tell on the bottoms? Grasp a pan in one pot-holdered hand; flip the loaf out onto a second pot-holdered hand, and check. The bottom should be lightly browned and firm. If the loaf is not fully done, return it to the pan and give it a few minutes more.)

8. Remove the baked loaves from the pans immediately, and let cool on a rack. Don't cut the bread for at least 30 minutes.

Herb-Scented Corn-Whole Wheat Bread

Makes one 8½-by-4½-inch loaf

The herbal flavor in this dense and close-grained bread is neither subtle nor overwhelming: Like Baby Bear's porridge, it's just right. It works alongside stews, makes wonderful toast (especially with Jarlsberg cheese melted on top), and always perks up a simple egg salad or a ham-and-cheese sandwich. And, it's just about perfect with the occasional soft-boiled breakfast egg. The cornmeal is not recognizable as such; you will merely celebrate its presence in the characteristic crunch of pleasant texture it leaves behind.

- **¾ cup stone-ground yellow or white cornmeal, plus extra for kneading**
- **1 tablespoon butter, at room temperature**
- **2 tablespoons plus 1 teaspoon honey**
- **2 tablespoons sorghum or molasses (see Note)**
- **1 teaspoon dried oregano leaves**
- **1½ teaspoons dried sage leaves**
- **1½ teaspoons salt**
- **½ teaspoon ground ginger**
- **¾ cup very hot milk (brought to a boil and turned off)**
- **½ cup warm water**
- **1 tablespoon active dry yeast**
- **2 teaspoons minced fresh dill**
- **¼ cup minced fresh flat-leaf parsley**
- **1 cup whole wheat flour**
- **1¼ cups unbleached white flour, plus extra for kneading**
- **2 tablespoons gluten flour (see Pantry, page 353)**
- **Vegetable oil cooking spray**

WHAT'S IN THE NAME?

When a disgruntled farmer's slatternly wife, Anna, was nowhere to be found, he mixed up a bunch of whatever was on hand and said, "Take this to Anna, damn her, and tell her to bake it." So goes the legend of anadama bread. His name, and where and when the unhappy couple lived, is never stated, nor is there any plausible explanation of how the story got handed down. No wonder it is distrusted by as many people as believe it. I lean toward the disbelievers, as does the kind, erudite food historian Sandy Oliver: "I'd caution you off 'Anna, damn her'—it smells like a myth to me." The three authors of the *Laurel's Kitchen Bread Book* also dispute the story: "This fine combination could never have been born of anger; it is just too good." I agree!

1. Place the cornmeal, butter, the 2 tablespoons honey, the sorghum, dried herbs, salt, and ginger in a medium-large heat-proof bowl. Pour the very hot milk over them and stir well. Let stand for 10 minutes, or until lukewarm.

2. Meanwhile, combine the warm water, yeast, and the 1 teaspoon honey in a small bowl or measuring cup. Let stand until bubbly, about 10 minutes.

3. When the cornmeal mixture is lukewarm, stir in the yeast, mixing thoroughly. Then add the fresh herbs and the whole wheat, white, and gluten flours. Turn the dough out on a floured board; it will still be on the sticky side. Let it stand for a few minutes while you wash and dry the mixing bowl. Then, begin to knead the dough, adding more flour or meal a tablespoon at a time until the proper texture is reached. Total kneading time: 5 to 7 minutes.

4. Spray the washed-and-dried bowl with oil, and transfer the dough to it. Cover with a clean towel, and set in a warm place. Let it rise until high and rounded and doubled in bulk, about an hour and 10 minutes. Then, turn the dough back out onto the floured board, give it a couple of kneads, and shape it into a loaf. Oil an 8½-by-4½-inch loaf pan, and place the dough in it.

5. Cover the bread loosely with a clean towel and let it rise in a warm place until doubled in bulk a second time, 45 minutes to 1 hour. In the last 15 minutes of rising time, preheat the oven to 400°F.

6. Bake the bread for 15 minutes, then turn down the heat to 350°F and bake until the loaf is deep brown and crusty, 35 to 45 minutes more. Remove the finished loaf from the pan, and let it cool on a rack.

NOTE: Sorghum is a sweet, sticky, dark, flavorful syrup made from pressed sorghum cane, and it is common in the South. Although its taste is distinctive and delicious, if you can't get sorghum, molasses is an adequate substitute.

CORNFLAKE MAPLE MOLASSES BREAD

MAKES ONE 8½-BY-4½-INCH LOAF

You typically do not want your cornflakes to get soggy, but in this delectable, homey brown bread you do. It's a new take on a pleasing regional oddity found in most contemporary New England community cookbooks: Shredded Wheat Bread. (Perhaps the only thing odder or more incomprehensible to non–New Englanders is Grape-Nuts Pudding . . . like rice pudding, but made with Grape-Nuts cereal.) In the original, this pleasing hearty bread is an all-white-flour loaf, the only whole wheat coming from $2\frac{1}{2}$ ounces of Shredded Wheat; not so here.

Gluten flour is optional but good, giving the loaf a better, higher rise. The recipe doubles easily; why not make two loaves, and freeze the second?

1 cup milk, scalded
$2\frac{1}{2}$ teaspoons active dry yeast
$2\frac{1}{2}$ ounces (approximately $1\frac{3}{4}$ cups)
cornflakes, slightly crushed
1 tablespoon butter, at room
temperature
1 tablespoon mild vegetable oil
2 tablespoons molasses
$\frac{1}{4}$ cup pure maple syrup,
preferably Grade B
$1\frac{1}{2}$ teaspoons salt
$\frac{1}{8}$ teaspoon ground cinnamon
$\frac{1}{4}$ teaspoon freshly grated nutmeg
About 2 cups whole wheat flour
About $\frac{1}{4}$ cup stone-ground
yellow cornmeal
1 tablespoon gluten flour
(see Pantry, page 353; optional)
About $\frac{3}{4}$ cup unbleached white flour
Vegetable oil cooking spray

1. Place the hot milk in a 2-cup or larger measuring cup to cool. When it is lukewarm, add the yeast and let it proof until bubbly, about 10 minutes.

2. Place the cornflakes in a large, heat-proof bowl and pour the milk mixture over them. Give a stir and let it stand for another 10 minutes, then stir in the butter, oil, molasses, maple syrup, salt, cinnamon, and nutmeg. Combine thoroughly, then add the whole wheat flour, cornmeal, and gluten, starting with the amounts given.

3. Stir in the unbleached flour until you have a nice shaggy dough of good kneading consistency, and start kneading on a very well-floured board. It's a quite sticky dough, so add more whole wheat or white flour if you need to. It will take about 10 minutes to knead by hand, 4 to 5 minutes to knead with a heavy-duty stand mixer with a dough-hook attachment.

4. Let the dough rest while you wash, dry, and oil-spray the bowl you mixed the dough up in. Then place the resting dough back in the bowl, cover with a clean cloth, and let rise until almost but not quite doubled in bulk, $1\frac{1}{2}$ to 2 hours.

5. Punch the dough down, and let it rise a second time in the bowl, covered, again until just about doubled, about 1 hour and 15 minutes.

6. Punch the dough down yet again, and transfer it back to the floured board. Shape it into a loaf, placing it in an oil-sprayed $8\frac{1}{2}$-by-$4\frac{1}{2}$-inch loaf pan. Use the oil spray one more time, to coat one side of a piece of plastic wrap, and cover the loaf with it, oiled side down. This allows the loaf to get a good rise, up to or, when the yeast gods smile, well above the rim of the loaf pan, without danger of the plastic sticking to it.

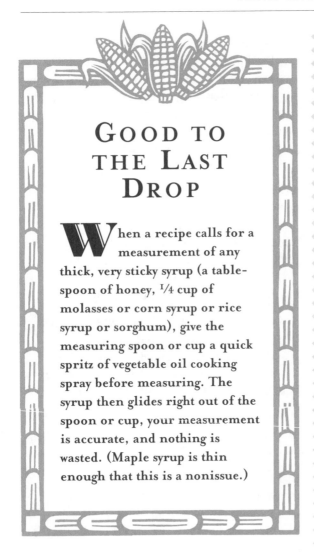

GOOD TO THE LAST DROP

When a recipe calls for a measurement of any thick, very sticky syrup (a tablespoon of honey, 1/4 cup of molasses or corn syrup or rice syrup or sorghum), give the measuring spoon or cup a quick spritz of vegetable oil cooking spray before measuring. The syrup then glides right out of the spoon or cup, your measurement is accurate, and nothing is wasted. (Maple syrup is thin enough that this is a nonissue.)

7. About 45 minutes into this third rise, preheat the oven to 350°F. Let the dough continue this final rise about 15 minutes more, then uncover it and pop it in the preheated oven.

8. Let bake for about 25 minutes, then check and see how brown it's getting (because of the relatively high amount of sweetener, it might brown a bit excessively before it's fully done). If it seems to be getting too dark, cover it loosely with aluminum foil. Continue baking until the bottom of the loaf is brown and crusty, another 12 to 18 minutes. (Turn the loaf out of its pan to test—if the bread bottom is soft and not brown and crusty yet, put it back in and bake it just a little longer, 5 to 10 minutes.) Remove the loaf and place it on a rack. Let the loaf cool, really—the loaf tears easily if you slice it when hot, but slices beautifully once it cools.

MASA BREAD

MAKES ONE 8 1/2 - BY - 4 1/2 - INCH LOAF

Once I'd tried this moist yeast bread with its distinctive corn tortilla taste and aroma, I just couldn't stop making it. The recipe comes from my Minneapolis pan pal, cookbook author Beth Hensperger, and I have probably made it every other week since first experimenting with it. It's that good, and it goes with everything.

Although the dough contains only a cup of masa harina (see Pantry, page 354), that cup is magic. Masa harina is cornmeal that has been soaked in an alkaline solution, making it easier to grind and to digest. It is *the* focal point of corn tortillas, and the minute you open the masa harina bag, you will sniff the one-of-a-kind aroma typical of tortillas, quite different from that of regular cornmeal. That aroma calls hauntingly as the bread bakes. The masa adds moistness, too; the bread's just as good the second day. It's excellent plain or toasted, or treated with butter and good honey or cinnamon-sugar, or with any bowl of Southwestern-style beans or soup.

About 2½ cups whole wheat flour
1½ cups unbleached white flour
1 cup masa, preferably white masa
  para tortillas
1 tablespoon salt
1 package active dry yeast
2 cups warm water
¼ cup dark brown sugar
2 tablespoons butter, at room
  temperature
Vegetable oil cooking spray
About 3 tablespoons stone-ground
  white cornmeal

I. Combine the whole wheat flour (start with the 2½ cups), unbleached flour, masa, and salt in a large bowl. In a second, smaller bowl combine the yeast and ½ cup of the warm water, and let stand until bubbly, about 10 minutes.

2. Add the yeast mixture to the flours with the remaining 1½ cups warm water, the brown sugar, and butter. Stir to incorporate.

3. Begin kneading. While this is a moist dough, a bit sticky, you don't want it too wet. (If you own a bread machine, this is a nice recipe to use it for, on the "dough" cycle.) Add more whole wheat flour as needed, somewhere between 2 tablespoons and ⅓ cup, to achieve this sticky, barely kneadable dough. Transfer the dough to an oil-sprayed bowl and set, covered, in a warm place.

4. Let the dough rise until doubled in bulk, 1 hour. Punch it down, and let it rise a second time until it is again high and full of itself, 45 minutes to an hour. Punch down a second time.

5. Spray an 8½-by-4½-inch loaf pan with the oil, then sprinkle the cornmeal inside and shake it around (you're flouring the pan, except with cornmeal instead of flour). Tap out any excess cornmeal onto a paper plate, flexible cutting surface, or piece of wax paper.

6. After the dough's second rise is complete, turn it out into the loaf pan. As mentioned, it will be a bit sticky; you won't really form it into a loaf as such, rather it will spread out into the pan somewhat. Sprinkle the excess cornmeal over the top of the loaf and cover it with a sheet of wax paper and then a towel, so the bread can rise a third and final time. (The cornmeal keeps the wax paper from sticking to the dough.)

7. When the dough is 15 to 20 minutes into this third rise, preheat the oven to 400°F. Let the dough continue to rise until it is rounding up against the wax paper, another 20 minutes or so. Carefully remove the wax paper, trying not to deflate the dough. (If it does sag just a bit, let it rise uncovered for a few more minutes.)

8. Put the loaf in the oven. Bake for 15 minutes, then lower the heat to 325°F and continue baking until the loaf is a deep, earthy brown, speckled with its white dusting of cornmeal, about 20 minutes longer.

9. Let the loaf cool in its pan on a rack for about 10 minutes, then turn it out of the pan to continue cooling. Try to wait until it's warm, not hot, before cutting into it, because the slices will tear otherwise.

·M·E·N·U·

BLUSTER ON, FEBRUARY

Bowl of Black Bean Soup

*

**Masa Bread Toast
Topped with Pimento Cheese,
Lettuce, and Tomato**

*

**Green Salad with Apple Cider
Syrup Vinaigrette (page 299)**

*

**Sliced Ginger-Gold Apples
and Peanut Butter Cookies**

NATIVE HARVEST BREAD

MAKES 5 MINI-LOAVES

I like to make this sweet, fruit-and-nut-laden yeast bread in small loaves to be cut into thin slices for a snack or sandwich bread. It is quite wonderful toasted lightly and spread with a little cream cheese, served with hot, milky English Breakfast tea. It is packed to overflowing with native ingredients, including mesquite meal. It's not as over-the-top sweet and rich as typical baking powder–leavened fruit and nut bread is, but it is still a nice indulgence.

2 packages active dry yeast

1 cup lukewarm water

1 tablespoon salt

½ cup stone-ground cornmeal, preferably blue (see Pantry, page 349)

½ cup mesquite meal (see Pantry, page 355)

2½ to 2¾ cups whole wheat flour

2½ to 3 cups unbleached white flour

⅓ cup brown sugar

1 egg, at room temperature

2 tablespoons butter, at room temperature

1½ cups pumpkin or winter squash purée (preferably fresh but canned is alright in a pinch), warm or at room temperature

Vegetable oil cooking spray

⅔ cup chopped hickory nuts, black walnuts, or roasted, salted pumpkin seeds

⅔ cup dried cranberries or blueberries, or chopped dates

1. Proof the yeast in the warm water in a large bowl until lively and bubbly, about 10 minutes.

2. While waiting for the yeast to proof, combine the salt, cornmeal, mesquite meal, and the lesser amounts of both the whole wheat and unbleached white flours in a large bowl.

3. After the yeast has done its thing, whisk into it the brown sugar, egg, butter, and pumpkin purée. Next beat in 2 cups of the flour-mesquite mix. Cover tightly with plastic wrap and set aside to rise for 45 minutes to an hour. (This wet dough is called a sponge.)

4. Stir down the sponge, and incorporate the remaining flour-mesquite mixture into it. At some point you will be able to turn the dough out on a floured bread board and knead it, using additional whole wheat and white flours as needed, until smooth and not too sticky. Let the kneaded dough rest on the bread board for a moment while you wash and dry the dough bowl. (If you use hot water and leave the bowl a little warm, so much the better for the yeast.) Spray the bowl with oil.

5. Now, come back to the dough. Knead in the nuts and dried fruit. This will take a bit of time and effort. Transfer the fruited, kneaded dough to the prepared bowl and let rise, covered, in a warm place until rounded and doubled in bulk (or nearly so), 1½ hours.

6. Spray 5 small loaf pans with oil. Punch down the risen dough and divide it into 5 equal portions, shaping each into a loaf and putting it in the bread pan. Let rise again, covered, until doubled in bulk, about 1 hour this time around.

7. In the final 15 minutes of the bread's last rise, preheat the oven to 425°F. Then, just before you put the loaves in, lower the heat to 350°F. Let the mini-loaves bake until nicely browned and firm of crust, about 25 minutes. Let cool on a rack before slicing into them.

VARIATION: Hazelnut Native Harvest Bread

Substitute hazelnut oil for the butter and the vegetable oil cooking spray, and use chopped, toasted hazelnuts instead of the nuts or seeds called for.

GLORIOUS YEAST-RISEN SAMBUCA CORNBREAD À LA CAROL FIELD

MAKES 1 ROUNDED LOAF

This eggy, sweet cornmeal bread—scented with anise—is adapted from a recipe by Carol Field, a wonderful baker and an authority on Italian cuisine. I've added some aniseeds and golden raisins. The result is purely wonderful, ideal for breakfast—or even for dessert, with vanilla ice cream.

1 package active dry yeast
¼ cup warm water
2 tablespoons milk
1 cup unbleached white flour, plus extra for kneading
¼ cup Sambuca (anise liqueur)
⅓ cup golden raisins
1 cup stone-ground yellow cornmeal
¾ cup sugar
1 to 2 teaspoons aniseeds
¾ teaspoon salt
3 eggs
⅓ cup butter, at room temperature
Vegetable oil cooking spray

"LET RISE IN A WARM PLACE"

This is among the coziest phrases commonly used in bread-baking directions (the other, to my mind, would be, "Cover with a clean tea towel"). I thought, one recent day as I was baking bread, about all the "warm places" I have known and loved and in which I have set bread to rise.

Most often, I've probably used a turned-off gas oven, assuming the warmth from the pilot light is adequate. But if the oven has no pilot light or is in use, part of the fun is figuring out your alternative warm place. On warm, sunny days, I put many a dough to rise on the little twig table that used to be on my front porch back in Arkansas (out of direct sun, but still quite cozy). In the winter in frigid Vermont, however, I often set doughs over the floor heat register, either directly on the floor or on a small stool or chair (this often involves moving the cat, who does not appreciate having her role as Heat Hog and register-blocker altered). Come fall, in Vermont or Arkansas, a sunny window, open, is a good place if the day is warm and not breezy. And occasionally, when I'm not sure if I've let the yeast develop enough before mixing up the dough, or I just want to hurry the rise, I set the covered bowl in a sink full of very warm water. That always does the trick . . . but it's a good idea to put a Post-it note explaining what that covered bowl bobbing along there is, in case someone else should come along and helpfully try to do the dishes. . . . Ask me how I know this!

I. Combine the yeast, warm water, and milk in a medium bowl, and proof it until nice and foamy, 5 to 8 minutes. Then beat in the unbleached white flour, making a thick sponge. Cover the bowl tightly with plastic wrap and let the dough rise in a warm place for about 2 hours.

2. Meanwhile, combine 3 tablespoons of the Sambuca with the raisins in a small bowl and let the raisins plump in the liqueur. Stir once in a while to distribute everything.

3. After the sponge's 2-hour rise, beat in the cornmeal and sugar. Drain the raisins and add any residual liquid from the raisins to the sponge, along with the aniseeds, salt, and eggs. Work in the butter, and finally the drained soaked raisins.

4. On a floured board, using as much additional flour as you need to get the dough just unsticky enough to be kneadable, knead the dough until it is satiny smooth, 6 to 8 minutes. Like most eggy doughs, it's a pleasure to work with, smooth and voluptuous.

5. Spray a deep, rounded 6-to-8-cup casserole dish with oil. Transfer the dough into it, cover with a clean cloth, and let rise in a cozy warm place until doubled in bulk, 2 to 3 hours.

6. Toward the end of the rise, preheat the oven to 375°F. When the oven has reached temperature and the bread has risen, brush the bread gently with the remaining tablespoon of Sambuca, and pop it in the oven. Let this fragrant rounded moon of a bread bake for 50 minutes to an hour. Set it, in its baking dish, on a rack to cool for about 30 minutes, then turn it out onto the rack to finish cooling.

GLAZED MAPLE CORNMEAL ROLLS

MAKES 3 TO 4 DOZEN ROLLS

I make only one cornmeal-based roll dough, featured here. Why just the one? Because (she says modestly), it's perfect.

There's a second reason: The dough is lovely to work with—silky, sensuous, with a most satisfactory rise—and accommodatingly variable (part of its perfection). You can make simple round rolls, the method for which I've given here. But truth be told, I like the elaborations even more: the darling Maple Cornmeal Butterhorns (shaped like small croissants, but with pleasing heft and texture; page 182) and the most exquisite Cinnamon Walnut Sticky Buns (page 180). In fact, almost any shape or type of slightly sweet rich roll—Parker House, cloverleaf—can be made from this basic recipe, which can itself be varied quite a bit (for more on this, see "Triple Crowning" the Rolls, page 179).

When these whole-grainy and light, sweet and hearty rolls are tucked while still warm into a napkin-lined basket and partnered with a soup or salad, they're hard to beat. The sweet-salty oatmeal-sprinkled glaze is not strictly necessary, but it is very tasty, and it gives the finished rolls a certain rustic charm.

You can partially make these ahead of time, finishing them at the last minute (see page 180)—a good idea if you are planning to serve them for a big-deal meal, such as Thanksgiving.

2 cups buttermilk
1/2 cup pure maple syrup
2 teaspoons salt
1/4 cup (1/2 stick) butter, at room temperature
1 1/3 cups stone-ground yellow or white cornmeal
4 to 5 tablespoons oatmeal (rolled oats)
1 egg
2 egg yolks
2 packages active dry yeast
1/2 cup lukewarm water
1 teaspoon sugar
2 1/2 to 3 cups unbleached white flour
2 1/2 to 3 cups whole wheat flour
Vegetable oil cooking spray
Sweet-Salty Glaze (recipe follows)

1. Bring the buttermilk almost to a boil in a small pot. It will curdle, but that doesn't matter. As it's heating, combine, in a large heat-proof bowl, the maple syrup, salt, butter, cornmeal, and 2 tablespoons of the oatmeal (reserve the rest for sprinkling on the rolls after they're glazed). When the buttermilk is good and hot, pour it over this mixture. Stir it well, so that the butter melts and all is well combined. Cover and let cool until softened and lukewarm, about 15 minutes. Beat in the egg and egg yolks.

2. Meanwhile, combine the yeast, lukewarm water, and sugar in a large measuring cup. Let stand until the cornmeal mixture has cooled, by which time the yeast will soften, then dissolve, then start to bubble. Add this to the now-lukewarm cornmeal mixture, along with 1 cup of the white flour and 1 cup of the whole wheat.

3. Using a wooden spoon, beat the dough with vigor for about 2 minutes, then gradually add more of the flours, 1/2 cup or so at a time, alternating white and wheat. Keep adding, stirring hard after each addition, until the dough begins to pull away from the sides of the bowl, becoming almost kneadable (by the time you have added about 4 cups total flour). Transfer the dough to a floured work surface.

4. Begin to knead, again adding the flours alternately a little at a time, until the dough is smooth and elastic, more tender than many doughs, 5 to 6 minutes.

5. Spray a bowl with oil and place the dough in it. Cover the bowl with a towel and let it rise in a warm place until doubled in bulk, about 1 hour. Go ahead and clean your kneading surface, getting all the flour off it, drying it well, and lightly oiling it.

6. Spray two 12-inch round pans with 2-inch-deep sides, three 9-inch round pans with 2-inch sides, or three 12-cup muffin tins with the oil. Punch down the risen dough and turn it out onto the kneading surface. Divide the dough into about 3 dozen equal pieces (or to finish the dough in three different ways, see "Triple Crowning" the Rolls, page 179). Roll each piece into a ball about 1½ inches in diameter and place it in the oiled pans or muffin cups. Cover with towels, and let rise again in a warm place until almost doubled, about 45 minutes.

7. In the last 15 minutes of this period, preheat the oven to 375°F. When the rolls are ready, bake them for about 15 minutes, preparing the glaze as they bake.

8. Remove the partially baked rolls from the oven and brush the glaze over them. Then sprinkle with the remaining 2 or 3 tablespoons of oatmeal. Return the rolls to the oven and bake until the glaze is shiny and deeply brown, 5 to 8 minutes.

9. Take the rolls from the oven and remove them from the pans. Let cool on wire racks until warm, then transfer them to a napkin-lined basket and serve.

Sweet-Salty Glaze

ABOUT ²/₃ CUP, ENOUGH FOR 1 FULL BATCH OF GLAZED MAPLE CORNMEAL ROLLS

> **3 tablespoons butter**
> **1¼ teaspoons salt**
> **2 tablespoons brown sugar**
> **2 tablespoons pure maple syrup**
> **1 egg**

Combine ¼ cup water with the butter, salt, sugar, and maple syrup in a small saucepan. Bring to a boil, then quickly remove from the heat and beat in the egg. Use to glaze rolls.

Variations:
Land of Milk and Honey Rolls

Substitute milk for the buttermilk and honey for the maple syrup.

Citrus-Sparked Hot Cross Buns

Add, along with the maple syrup, 1 teaspoon pure vanilla extract, 1 teaspoon ground cardamom, and the grated zest of 1 lemon or orange, preferably organic. When you punch the dough down, knead into it a small handful each of currants and chopped walnuts, pecans, or almonds. Bake as directed for the basic rolls, but omit the salt from the glaze. After the rolls have been brushed with the glaze and are out of the oven, make an icing of sifted confectioners' sugar mixed with just enough lemon or orange juice to allow it to drizzle from a spoon. Drizzle a cross over each slightly cooled bun. Have the Easter bunny bring you a basket of these.

Pumpkin Maple Cornmeal Rolls

Cut the buttermilk back to ¾ cup, heating, with it, 1½ cups canned unsweetened pumpkin or leftover fresh butternut squash purée. Cut the lukewarm water in which the yeast softens back to ¼ cup. Leave as is for a subtly pumpkin flavor, or make it sweet with classic pumpkin pie flavors: Add 1¾ teaspoons pumpkin pie spice (or ¾ teaspoon ground cinnamon, ½ teaspoon ground ginger, ½ teaspoon freshly grated nutmeg, and a few dashes of ground cloves) when you add the pumpkin. Another option: Knead in ½ cup or so of chopped toasted pecans toward the end of kneading in the flour. Then, as these gems of the fall bake, instead of the sweet-salty glaze, make up the quick but voluptuous maple glaze on page 155. Let the rolls cool slightly before drizzling this amply over them.

"Triple Crowning" the Rolls

There is enough dough in the Glazed Maple Cornmeal Rolls recipe on page 176 to make three delicious and slightly different types of rolls from a single batch. In step 6, divide the dough into thirds. Form and flavor each third slightly differently:

Form the first third into the round Glazed Maple Cornmeal Rolls or one of its variations.

Make the second third into Maple Cornmeal Butterhorns (page 182).

Use the final third to create the toothsome Cinnamon Walnut Sticky Buns on page 180.

PREP, FREEZE, AND FINISH LATER

To partially prepare, freeze, and finish these rolls, make the basic recipe through most of step 6, to the point where the rolls have been formed and placed in their pans for the final rise. Instead of letting them rise, however, cover them very tightly with plastic wrap and freeze them.

The night before you want to serve the rolls, remove them to the refrigerator to thaw overnight. Bring them to room temperature in the morning, and let them rise (this will take about 1½ hours). Then bake and glaze as directed.

Bread dough that has been frozen as above seems to have a slightly more pronounced bready, yeasty taste—quite good.

CINNAMON WALNUT STICKY BUNS

MAKES ABOUT 12 BUNS

If you are a devotee of sticky buns and/or cinnamon rolls, with or without nuts, you will be thrilled with these—perhaps the best version of either you may have come across.

The brown sugar and butter are used twice—you'll be using part in the sticky topping and part in the filling. The sweet-salty glaze that accompanies the Glazed Maple Cornmeal Rolls on page 176 and the Maple Cornmeal Butterhorns on page 182 is not needed here.

⅓ of the dough from a recipe of Glazed Maple Cornmeal Rolls (page 176)

Vegetable oil cooking spray

6 tablespoons butter, at room temperature

6 tablespoons brown sugar

2 to 3 tablespoons pure maple syrup

½ to ⅔ cup chopped walnuts or pecan halves

1 teaspoon to 1 tablespoon cinnamon

1. On a lightly floured bread board, roll the dough out into a rectangle about 12 inches by 16 to 18 inches.

2. Let the dough rest for a moment while you make the topping for the rolls: Spray a 10- to 12-inch round pan (or iron skillet) with oil. Then smear 2 to 3 tablespoons of the butter over the bottom of the pan, and sprinkle 2 tablespoons of the brown sugar over that. Next, drizzle the maple syrup over that. Sprinkle the nuts of choice over the syrup.

3. Now return to your dough rectangle. Smear the remaining butter over the rectangle and sprinkle it with the remaining brown sugar. Last, shake some cinnamon liberally (to your taste) over the whole dough. Roll up the cinnamon dough from the long bottom edge up (rather than from short side to short side).

4. With a sharp knife, cut the cylinder of rolled dough into circles (which will squish down a bit into ovals) about ⅓ to ½ inch thick. Place the slices spiral-side up in the pan, on top of the nutted maple-sugar mixture, leaving about 2 inches of room around each roll. Cover the pan, place in a warm spot, and let rise until the rolls have risen to where there is not much space between them, 35 to 40 minutes.

5. In the last 15 minutes of this period, preheat the oven to 375°F. When the buns are ready, bake them until they are brown and crusty on top and have expanded to the point that the filling is invisible, 20 to 22 minutes.

·M·E·N·U·

DEEP WINTER LET'S-HAVE-BREAKFAST-FOR-DINNER DINNER

**Platter of Sliced Navel Oranges,
Blood Oranges,
and Ruby Red Grapefruit**

*

**Omelets with Sautéed Mushrooms,
Spinach, and Gruyère Cheese**

*

Sautéed Sausage or Soysage

*

**Diane's Gap Mountain Anadama
(page 165) or Masa Bread (page 170)**

*

**Warm Cinnamon Walnut Sticky Buns
with Vanilla Ice Cream**

*

Decaf coffee

6. Have ready a plate of slightly larger diameter than the pan in which you've baked the buns. Within 5 minutes of removing the buns from the oven, reverse them out onto the plate (wait any longer and the sticky mixture will harden, and you won't be able to get them out). Let cool for at least 15 minutes before eating them. The sticky, walnut-studded syrup hardens slightly, making an almost-but-not-quite-crunchy topping. Just unbeatable.

MAPLE CORNMEAL BUTTERHORNS

MAKES 16 BUTTERHORNS

⅓ of the dough from a recipe of Glazed Maple Cornmeal Rolls (page 176)

Vegetable oil cooking spray

Unbleached white flour, for kneading the dough

About ⅓ cup butter, at room temperature

1 recipe of Sweet-Salty Glaze (page 179)

1. Form the dough into 2 large balls. Spray a baking sheet with oil.

2. Lightly flour a bread board and roll each ball out into a circle about 12 to 14 inches across and about ¼ inch thick. Smear each circle lightly with butter. Cut each circle into 8 wedges.

3. Roll up each wedge starting at the wide end and working toward the point, forming a sort of miniature croissant. Curve each roll slightly, making a crescent shape, and place it on the oil-sprayed baking sheet.

4. Let the rolls rise until not quite doubled in bulk, 30 to 40 minutes.

5. About 15 minutes before the end of this period, preheat the oven to 375°F. When the rolls are ready, bake them until deeply golden brown, about 15 minutes. Glaze them with the Sweet-Salty Glaze, and return them to the oven until the glaze is shiny and browned, another 5 to 8 minutes.

> **"I had rather munch a crust of brown bread and an onion in a corner, without any more ado or ceremony, than feed upon turkey at another man's table."**
>
> —CERVANTES, *Don Quixote*

Chapter 7

SOULFUL SPOONBREADS
Soaring Soufflés and Pleasing Puddings

Rich with eggs, butter, and milk, spoonbread is considered by many to be the ne plus ultra of cornbread. It's "the apotheosis of cornbread," according to Southern culturist Redding Sugg (in a famous 1974 article that appeared in *Southern Voices*). And, to John Edgerton, author of the definitive *Southern Food*, it's "the lightest, richest, and most delicious of all cornmeal dishes, a veritable cornbread soufflé."

Spoonbread, essentially a cooked mush of either white

or yellow cornmeal, is lightened with eggs, either whole or separated, and baked in the oven. It proves, again, the generous versatility of corn-based breadstuffs in meeting the full spectrum of human needs, from survival to celebration.

I was first introduced to spoonbread by Miss Helen Kay, a much-loved neighbor and adopted grandmother with whom I spent many happy childhood afternoons cooking in Hastings-on-Hudson, New York. As I recall, the casserole dish had just come out of the oven when I conveniently dropped in around supper-time. She told me what was in it, and that it was so named because it was a bread you spooned out of the casserole onto the plate. (As it turns out, she may have been mistaken about that: Some scholars say that the bread's name derives from *suppawn*, the Native American word for "porridge," not from the utensil. But there's no proof either way.)

I eyed the casserole with the skepticism of childhood: *spoon* bread? Bread was something you baked and sliced, held and made sandwiches of, toasted and buttered, not something moist and fragile you ate with a spoon. But, because I loved Miss Kay and had had many happy food adventures with her, I politely nibbled a dollop of spoonbread. I liked it from the first bite, though it was subtle for my taste, and too *not-bread*. But then, I couldn't stop eating it; I had one bite, then another, then another. By the last, I loved it. This is a problem for spoonbread fans generally: We don't know when to stop.

In the South, spoonbread is often served as part of a special meal—a Sunday or holiday dinner, say. Or, it might be the centerpiece of an otherwise unpretentious supper. The late Craig Claiborne, former *New York Times* food columnist and a native of Sunflower, Mississippi, noted, "In my house, [it] was always served with sliced, home-cured ham or with butter to be added according to taste," while a WPA-era recipe collected by folklorist-historian Kate C. Hubbard recommends it with smoked sausage.

PULCHRITUDINOUS POSSIBILITIES

As a vegetarian, I like spoonbread for an occasional special-friends-are-here-for-the-weekend brunch, as is, or with butter and jam, or, occasionally, with crisp soysage patties and a poached egg, the egg's pellucid golden yolk awaiting only the poke of a fork to become a sauce for the spoon-bread. Or with a drizzle of heated-up, good-quality jarred green or red chile sauce (I'm partial to those made by 505 Southwestern, see www.505chile.com).

Alternatively, it's a fine centerpiece for a vegetable dinner, surrounded by a necklace of summer vegetables: a garlicky sauté of bitter greens, some sliced carrots slicked in a sweet glaze, maybe green beans or okra slowly cooked with tomato and more garlic. It's also extremely tasty with cheese, especially Parmesan or Cheddar, sprinkled atop it while still hot. And I have used it as the most elegant possible bed for a dark and aromatically gravied ragout of mixed wild fall mushrooms.

There are fewer variations in traditional spoonbread recipes than in other varieties of cornbread, and the variations that do exist are less hotly contested. The main hot button is whether the eggs should be separated or not. Unseparated eggs yield a simple-to-make, very moist spoonbread, a little heavy but delicious, somewhere between pudding, custard, and less-eggy quiche. Separated eggs give a still-moist but drier, and far lighter, finished spoonbread; in fact, this variety of spoonbread is a soufflé: puffed, golden brown, and ethereal. But, you do have the extra bowl and beaters to wash, as in any recipe calling for separated eggs. I have divided the spoonbread recipes here into soufflé style and pudding style.

What other spoonbread variables will you find? Whether yellow or white cornmeal should be used; whether, in the soufflé-style spoonbreads, baking powder (which supplies additional lift) should be employed; whether or not a touch of sugar is appropriate (very few spoonbreads use it). How much and which liquid or liquids should be used is another variable, and an important one structurally. Sometimes the preliminary mush is cooked in water, more frequently in milk. Sometimes the liquid is divided; only a portion goes to cooking the meal, and the rest is stirred in later. This makes another variation possible: The meal can be cooked in sweet milk or water, and then have buttermilk added later on.

Though I'm a skillet-sizzled cornbread type of girl as a rule, sometimes nothing else will do but that subtle puff of elevated cornmeal, grainy yet delicate, quiveringly moist and pale within, crisped and golden without. In its humble origins and sophisticated trans-mogrification, spoonbread is, like all of us, made from common stuff yet capable of transcendence.

BEATING EGG WHITES

First, know that even a trace of fat inhibits the structure and formation of the egg-white foam. Not only must you always use a scrupulously clean bowl and beaters, free of any trace of oil or fat, but also the eggs must be separated perfectly, with not a speck of the fatty yolk in the whites. Foaming is slightly enhanced if the whites are at room temperature when you begin.

Second, know your egg-white beating bowls. Do *not* use a plastic bowl to beat egg whites. (Odd as it may seem, plastics have an inherent trace of fatty matter on their surfaces, which means that the egg-white foam's structure will be compromised.) Choose a stainless-steel, glass, ceramic, or, best of all, copper bowl; these will not affect the foaming stability one way or the other except for the last, which actually assists in the process. A copper bowl, or a tiny pinch of cream of tartar added to the whites, slightly alters the whites' pH and protein molecules to the benefit of the final result. In addition to using the right type of bowl, choose one that is large enough. Egg whites expand in volume eight to nine times in the course of beating.

The third trick is proper beating, which lies primarily in knowing when to stop.

Place the yolk-free whites, ideally at room temperature, in a very clean bowl. Add the cream of tartar, if using (no need for it if you are using a copper bowl). Making sure the beaters are also very clean, use either a hand-held or fixed mixer, or, if your wrists and forearms are sturdy indeed, a whisk, and begin beating the whites at medium speed. You will rapidly see the whites move from a viscous, transparent liquid to a slightly foamy consistency, at which point you should amp up the speed to as high as it can get. When using a hand-held mixer, keep moving the beaters around the bowl, up and around and through the whites, thus incorporating more air.

How do you know when you've beaten enough? As you approach this point, you'll begin to notice the beater leaves waves or ridges of white that hold their shape in its wake. Turn off the mixer and lift the beaters from the foam. The foam should remain in stiff, upstanding glossy peaks, which do not flop back down, and the foam itself should have a smooth, uniform look to it. Stop here.

Last, bear in mind that even when beaten to perfection, egg whites' stiff status is delicate. Unless otherwise instructed, all other ingredients in a recipe should be mixed and incorporated *before* you beat the whites, and the oven should be preheated, so that all that remains is the gentle folding in of the whites. Folding is always done by hand, never with a mixer, and always in a bowl large enough to accommodate both batter and whites. Start by blobbing about one third of the beaten whites atop the batter and then, working with a curved rubber spatula (sometimes called a "spoonula"), begin scooping batter from the bottom of the bowl up over the egg whites and down around, toward you, rotating the bowl as you do so, and cutting in through the largest visible patch of whites. When this first third is incorporated, add the remaining two thirds and repeat, always delicately, until the whites are incorporated. The exception to the one third–two thirds rule: If the recipe calls for two eggs or fewer, as is the case with Dixie Spoonbread, on page 191, just put the beaten whites in all at once.

In either case, there should be no large blobs visible post-folding, and the mixture as a whole should be far airier and lighter than in its previous batter stage.

If you have followed the directions, all that will remain is to transfer the batter into the prepared baking pan, ready for an instant pop into the hot waiting oven.

CRAIG CLAIBORNE'S SUNFLOWER, MISSISSIPPI, SPOONBREAD

SERVES 4 AS AN ENTRÉE,
6 AS A SIDE DISH

"In countless interviews for *The New York Times* over the past thirty years, I have learned that nothing can equal the universal appeal of the food of one's childhood and early youth," wrote Craig Claiborne in the introduction to his 1987 book, *Southern Cooking.* For him, that was the food prepared by his mother ("a magnificent cook") and the family's servants, first in Sunflower, Mississippi, and then later in Indianola, where his mother ran a boarding house.

I have adapted Claiborne's recipe for a delicious, basic soufflé-style spoonbread. See the Sunflower Supper menu, right, for ideas on how it might star at your table.

Vegetable oil cooking spray
3 cups milk
1½ cups sifted stone-ground yellow
cornmeal
3 tablespoons butter

·M·E·N·U·

SUNFLOWER SUPPER

Fresh Tomato Slices, with
Minced Parsley and Chervil
(or Celery Leaves), Salt, and Pepper
*
Craig Claiborne's Sunflower,
Mississippi, Spoonbread
*
Thin-Sliced Home-Style Ham,
and/or Beans, Old South Style
(page 303)
or Beans Dragon-in-the-New-South
Style (page 305)
*
Greens, Old South Style (page 290)
or Greens, New South Style
(page 293)
*
Peach Ice Cream
Benne Seed Cookies

1 teaspoon salt
4 eggs, separated
2 teaspoons baking powder

1. Preheat the oven to 350°F. Spray a deep 1½- to 2-quart baking dish with oil.

2. Bring the milk to a boil in a medium saucepan, preferably nonstick. Gradually pour in the cornmeal with one hand, whisking with the other, creating a very thick mixture. Lower the heat and add the butter and salt. Continue cooking over low heat, stirring almost constantly, for 10 minutes.

3. Remove the cooked mush from the stove and transfer it into a medium-size heat-proof bowl. Let the mush cool to lukewarm, about 20 minutes.

4. Meanwhile, place the egg yolks in a small bowl and the whites in a large, high-sided, non-plastic bowl. When the mush is lukewarm, beat the yolks vigorously with a fork, then whip the baking powder into them and quickly mix the yolks into the mush. Make sure the yolk mixture is thoroughly and evenly incorporated.

5. Beat the egg whites until stiff and glossy (see Beating Egg Whites, pages 186–187). Gently fold them into the mush and transfer this thick batter to the prepared dish.

6. Bake until a knife inserted into the center comes out barely clean, 40 minutes. The spoonbread will have risen slightly, and its top will be irregular, with little patches that are deeply golden brown. Serve at once, hot from the oven.

CLASSIC SOUFFLÉED SPOONBREAD

SERVES 4 AS AN ENTRÉE, 6 TO 8 AS A SIDE DISH

The texture of this finished spoonbread is smooth and tender, its flavor pure. This is the kind of spoonbread I remember eating at Miss Kay's (see page 341), and you will find its close cousins in virtually all Southern community cookbooks. I prefer it made with white cornmeal, but it will work with yellow just fine.

Vegetable oil cooking spray
4 cups milk
1 cup sifted stone-ground white or yellow cornmeal
2 tablespoons butter
1½ teaspoons salt
4 eggs, separated

1. Preheat the oven to 375°F. Spray a deep 1½- to 2-quart baking dish with oil.

2. Bring the milk to a boil in a medium saucepan, preferably nonstick. Gradually pour in the cornmeal with one hand, whisking with the other, creating a very thick mixture. Lower the heat and add the butter and salt. Continue cooking over low heat, stirring almost constantly, for 10 minutes.

3. Remove the cooked mush from the stove and transfer it to a medium-size heat-proof bowl. Let the mush cool to lukewarm, about 20 minutes.

4. Meanwhile, place the egg yolks in a small bowl and the whites in a large, high-sided, non-plastic bowl. When the mush is lukewarm, beat the yolks vigorously with a fork, then mix the yolks into the mush, making sure they are thoroughly and evenly incorporated.

5. Beat the egg whites until stiff and glossy (see Beating Egg Whites, pages 186–187). Gently fold them into the batter as much as you can (the batter will be fairly liquid) and pour this into the prepared dish.

6. Bake until a knife inserted into the center comes out barely clean and the top is deeply golden brown, 40 to 45 minutes. Serve at once, straight from the dish and hot from the oven.

OLD-TIME SOUTHERN SPOONBREAD

**SERVES 4 AS AN ENTRÉE,
6 TO 8 AS A SIDE DISH**

This spoonbread's got three eggs rather than the usual four, and water replaces part of the milk. But plenty of butter and the stone-ground grainy goodness shine through, making it exceptional. And it's still fancier than regular cornbread; a company's-coming dish, as are all spoonbreads.

> **Vegetable oil cooking spray**
> **1 cup sifted stone-ground white cornmeal**
> **¼ cup (½ stick) butter**
> **1 cup boiling water**
> **3 eggs, separated**
> **1½ teaspoons salt**
> **1 tablespoon baking powder**
> **1¾ cups milk**

1. Preheat the oven to 375°F. Spray a deep 1½- to 2-quart baking dish with oil.

2. Place the cornmeal and butter in a heat-proof bowl and gradually pour the boiling water over it with one hand, whisking, then

"It was such a satisfaction not to have to fix party food for people more interested in the bar: thin sliced beef, shrimp on beds of ice, vegetables presented as works of art. Just a skillet of stew, some spoon bread, and washed salad greens . . . What a feast."

—SHELBY HEARON,
Life Estates

stirring, with the other, to create a very, very thick paste-like mixture. Set aside.

3. Beat together the egg yolks, salt, baking powder, and milk in a separate bowl. Add the liquid mixture gradually to the cornmeal mixture, working it in first with a spoon, then a whisk, until it is smooth.

4. Place the egg whites in a large, high-sided, non-plastic bowl. Beat them until stiff and glossy (see Beating Egg Whites, pages 186–187). Gently fold them into the batter and transfer the batter to the prepared dish.

5. Bake until a knife inserted into the center comes out barely clean and the top is deeply golden brown, 30 to 35 minutes. Serve at once, straight from the dish and hot from the oven.

DIXIE SPOONBREAD

SERVES 4 AS AN ENTRÉE,
6 AS A SIDE DISH

This is one of my all-time favorite spoonbreads. It has an especially tender interior with a nice, even consistency, and a beautifully crusty top. It has an extra depth of flavor, perhaps because it uses all buttermilk and white cornmeal. Because it contains only two eggs and a tablespoon of butter, it is also a relatively low-fat spoonbread.

Vegetable oil cooking spray
2 cups stone-ground white cornmeal
1½ teaspoons salt
2 cups boiling water
1 tablespoon melted butter
2 eggs, separated
1 teaspoon baking soda
2 cups buttermilk

1. Preheat the oven to 400°F. Spray a 2-quart baking dish with oil and set aside.

2. Sift the cornmeal and salt into a large heat-proof bowl. Pour the boiling water and melted butter over the cornmeal and salt, stirring it in to make a thick, smooth, porridge-like mixture. Let cool to lukewarm, 15 to 20 minutes. Then beat in the egg yolks, incorporating them thoroughly.

·M·E·N·U·

I Wish I Was in Dixie

Chicken-Fried Steak or
Chicken-Fried Tofu, with Gravy
*
Dixie Spoonbread
*
Slow-Cooked Greens with
Garlic and Tomato
*
Chow-Chow or Piccalili
Pickled Beets
*
Pecan Pie

3. Combine the baking soda and buttermilk in a small bowl or large measuring cup, stirring to dissolve the soda (it will bubble). Gradually stir this into the cornmeal mixture, beating until smooth. (You will think it is too liquid at this point. It's not.)

4. Place the egg whites in a large, high-sided, non-plastic bowl and beat them until stiff and glossy (see Beating Egg Whites, pages 186–187). Gently fold them all at once (instead of in two batches) into the batter, a bit of a challenge because the batter is fairly liquid. Pour the batter into the prepared dish.

5. Bake until proudly puffed and deeply golden, 40 to 45 minutes.

Rich Virginia-Style Plantation Spoonbread

SERVES 4 AS AN ENTRÉE,
6 AS A SIDE DISH

Three eggs, heavy cream, butter—this is a definite fat-of-the-land spoonbread, for state occasions. It uses ingredients similar to those in a recipe by Bill Neal, which appears in his *Biscuits, Spoonbread, and Sweet Potato Pie,* one of the great canonical texts of Southern cooking.

Vegetable oil cooking spray
1 cup stone-ground yellow cornmeal
1/4 cup extra-coarse stone-ground yellow cornmeal (grits)
1 teaspoon salt
3 eggs, separated
1/4 cup (1/2 stick) butter, at room temperature
1 cup heavy cream
Extra butter, for serving

1. Spray a medium-large, heavy pot with oil, add 1 cup water, and bring to a boil. As you are waiting for it to boil, combine the two cornmeals in a large bowl and stir in 1½ cups water. Add the moistened cornmeals to the boiling water with the salt, stirring in very slowly and carefully. Bring the whole thing back to a boil, then lower the heat almost as far as it will go. Cook the mixture very, very slowly, stirring often, until it's good and thick and smooth, about 30 minutes. About halfway into the cooking period, preheat the oven to 375°F.

2. Remove the cooked meal from the heat and let it cool for about 15 minutes. Meanwhile, beat the egg yolks in a small bowl with a fork, setting the whites aside in a larger, high-sided, non-plastic bowl for later whipping.

3. When the corn mixture has cooled, beat in the butter, cream, and egg yolks. Spray an 8-inch square pan with oil and set aside. Then, using clean beaters, whip the egg whites until soft peaks form (see Beating Egg Whites, pages 186–187). Fold them gently into the corn-cream mixture.

4. Transfer the batter into the prepared pan. Bake until puffed and lightly golden brown, about 30 minutes. Serve immediately—of course, with extra butter.

> **"Grits may be substituted for cornmeal. There are few morning parties where one or the other is not present. And whoever heard of chicken hash without spoon bread. It is nice for serving under creamed chicken or turkey for a luncheon, and for late suppers a must."**
>
> —HELEN CORBITT,
> *Helen Corbitt's Cookbook*

FRESH CORN SPOONBREAD

SERVES 4 AS AN ENTRÉE, 6 TO 8 AS A SIDE DISH

Somewhere between soufflé and fresh corn pudding, this incorporates fresh corn cut off the cob. It's ideal toward summer's end, when there's just a bit of cool in the air but the gardens are still producing and the roadside stands and farmers' markets are still abundant with produce. This is an excellent spoonbread to choose as the centerpiece for a vegetable dinner. Start with a bright green salad (prepare and eat it as the spoonbread bakes), then follow with the spoonbread, serving it hot from the oven with sliced fresh tomatoes and a scallion or two to nibble on. Dessert: height-of-the-season ripe cantaloupe or sliced fresh dead-ripe peaches with a scoop of vanilla ice cream.

> **Vegetable oil cooking spray**
> **3½ cups milk**
> **⅔ cup sifted stone-ground yellow cornmeal**
> **1 tablespoon honey**
> **2 tablespoons butter**
> **1½ teaspoons salt**
> **½ cup buttermilk**
> **3 cups fresh corn kernels (cut from about 6 ears of corn; see Shuck and Jive, page 49)**
> **4 eggs, separated**
> **1 teaspoon baking powder**
> **¼ teaspoon baking soda**

1. Preheat the oven to 375°F. Spray a deep 1½- to 2-quart baking dish with oil.

2. Bring the milk to a boil in a medium saucepan, preferably nonstick. Gradually pour in the cornmeal with one hand, whisking with the other, creating a very thick mixture. Lower the heat and add the honey, butter, and salt. Continue cooking over low heat, stirring almost constantly, for 10 minutes.

3. Remove the cooked mush from the stove and transfer it into a medium-size, heat-proof bowl.

4. Place the buttermilk in a food processor with the fresh corn. Pulse-chop to cut the corn into fine pieces, but don't purée it. Stir the corn mixture into the cornmeal mush, which will bring the temperature down to the requisite lukewarm.

5. Place the egg yolks in a small bowl and the whites in a large, high-sided, non-plastic bowl; set the whites aside. Beat the yolks vigorously with a fork, then beat in the baking powder and baking soda. Mix the yolks into the mush, making sure they are thoroughly and evenly incorporated.

6. Beat the egg whites until stiff and glossy (see Beating Egg Whites, pages 186–187). Gently fold them into the batter and transfer the batter to the prepared dish.

7. Bake until a knife inserted into the center comes out barely clean and the top is deeply golden brown, 40 to 45 minutes. Serve at once, hot from the oven and straight from the dish.

> "Get up, old man,
> Day is breaking
> Fire's in the stove
> Hoe-cakes a-baking."
>
> —TRADITIONAL OZARK
> MOUNTAIN FOLKSONG

SOUTHERN FOOD:
SOME DELICIOUS READING

Are you interested in Southern food? Lord knows, you should be by now. Here are my very favorite Southern cookbooks—I browse amongst them like a bee, dizzied by the choice of flowers.

Biscuits, Spoonbread, and Sweet Potato Pie by Bill Neal (University of North Carolina Press, 2003)

Butter Beans to Blackberries: Recipes from the Southern Garden by Ronni Lundy (Northpoint Press, 1999)

Frank Stitt's Southern Table by Frank Stitt (Artisan, 2004)

The Gift of Southern Cooking by Edna Lewis and Scott Peacock (Knopf, 2003)

Shuck Beans, Stack Cakes, and Honest Fried Chicken by Ronni Lundy (Atlantic Monthly Press, 1991)

Southern Food by John Edgerton (University of North Carolina Press, 1993)

Spoonbread and Strawberry Wine by Norma Jean and Carole Darden (Main Street Books, 1994)

Also, there's a fine annual anthology of writing put out by the Southern Foodways Alliance (a nonprofit group of which Ned, my late husband, and I were charter members). Published by the University of North Carolina Press, it's edited by Ronni Lundy and called— what else?—*Cornbread Nation*!

Corn-Rice Spoonbread

SERVES 4 TO 6

This spoonbread's roots are old and unpretentious: Leftover cooked rice (either plain or "Spanish") is required. With plain rice, this becomes a pleasing neutral starch dish, nice anywhere you'd serve potatoes or cooked grains. If you use a leftover seasoned rice, it anchors a Mexican, Tex-Mex, or South American–style meal perfectly. Try it with chili or any pot of spicy beans ladled over it. Add a dab of sour cream, a sprinkle of cilantro, a spoonful of salsa, sliced avocado, and you are good to go. Flan for dessert, of course.

Vegetable oil cooking spray
¼ cup stone-ground yellow cornmeal
1 teaspoon salt
½ teaspoon baking soda
2 tablespoons butter, melted and cooled
2 eggs
2 cups buttermilk
1 cup cooked leftover rice, either plain white, Spanish, or brown

1. Preheat the oven to 325°F. Spray an 8-inch square baking pan, preferably glass, with oil, and set aside.

· M · E · N · U ·

Guilford Garden Spoon Swoon

Sautéed Broccoli Rabe
with Garlic and Olive Oil
*
Fresh Corn Spoonbread (page 193)
*
Butternut Squash Chunks with
Maple Syrup and a Squidge of Butter
*
Tomatoes Stuffed
with Spinach and Parmesan
*
Ben & Jerry's Coffee
Heath Bar Crunch Ice Cream
*
Brownies

2. Combine the cornmeal, salt, and baking soda in a small bowl. Set aside.

3. Combine the melted butter, eggs, and buttermilk in a larger bowl and whisk them together well.

4. Pour the dry mixture into the wet, and stir all together. Stir in the cooked rice and transfer the mixture to the prepared baking dish.

5. Bake until firmed, puffy, and nicely browned, 50 to 55 minutes.

IN PRAISE OF PORRIDGE

As we think about corn and the way it has taken root the world over, we must pay our dues to another widespread way—beside cornbread—the primal ingredients of cornmeal, water, salt come together the world over. When not being cooked by dry heat (that is, being baked, whether on a griddle or in an oven), these same three ingredients are usually becoming porridge.

Depending on who's doing the eating, the porridges—the thicker ones similar in texture to spoonbreads—are known by different names. Native Americans called them *sagamite, samp, nassasump,* and *suppawn.* (Thinner versions were *sofkee,* known in the Southwest as *atole* or *pinole.*) These were among the main corn dishes that the eastern colonists found Indians cooking and eating when they arrived. The colonists quickly imitated these thicker porridges, which became "mush" or, if sweetened, "hasty pudding" or "Indian pudding."

Next corn began its triumphal journey around the world, often in the form of this porridge. The North Italian's polenta; the Romanian's mamaliga; the East African's *ugali;* the South African's mealie, *nshima,* or *sadza;* the West African's *fufu* (which was usually composed of yam, manioc, and/or plantain, mixed with corn) or *putu*—all are the same, cornmeal cooked in water until as thick, in most cases, as mashed potatoes.

Everywhere corn mush took root, it served as a filling backdrop for whatever one might ladle upon it. This was often stews (across cultures, these stews usually contained greens and/or beans) and sauces (often either spicy-hot or tomato-based). The recipes in Great Go-Withs, pages 287–326, pay homage to these universal pairings. Top your spoonbread—porridge's close cousin—with a mess of greens or a heap of beans, and dig in.

RONNI'S KENTUCKY SPOONBREAD

SERVES 4 AS AN ENTRÉE, 6 AS A
SIDE DISH

My friend Ronni Lundy, to whom I've referred throughout this book, makes a simple, classic pudding-style spoonbread: "just company cornbread all gussied up and in its Sunday best," as she says. Her recipe is unusual because the batter gets a long (ten-minute!) beating just before it goes into the pan. Here's my adaptation.

> Vegetable oil cooking spray
> 3 cups low-fat milk
> 1¼ cups stone-ground yellow or white
>   cornmeal
> 1 teaspoon salt
> 3 eggs
> 2 tablespoons butter
> 1¾ teaspoons baking powder

1. Preheat the oven to 400°F. Spray a 10-inch cast-iron skillet with oil and set aside.

2. Bring the milk to a boil in a medium saucepan, preferably nonstick. Gradually pour in the cornmeal with one hand, whisking with the other, creating a very thick mixture. Lower the heat and add the salt. Continue cooking over low heat, stirring almost constantly, for about 2 minutes. The mush will be very thick. Let cool for 10 to 15 minutes.

3. Toward the end of the mush-cooling time, beat the eggs in a large bowl on high speed until well blended, foamy, and paler, 2 minutes. Place the butter in the prepared skillet and put the skillet in the oven to melt the butter.

4. Transfer the cooled mush to the bowl containing the beaten eggs, and sprinkle in the baking powder. Remove the skillet from the oven and carefully pour the melted butter into the batter, leaving just a bit in the skillet. Now begins the long beating: 10 minutes at medium speed, pausing to scrape the sides of the bowl. The batter will be thick and creamy.

5. Transfer the batter to the buttered skillet. Bake until golden brown, 25 to 30 minutes. Serve at once, hot from the oven.

> "I ladled out the stew, which gave off steam as it reached our plates, and scooped up mounds of spoon bread swimming in butter. . . . I'd tossed dandelion greens, arugula, Boston lettuce, and endive with a buttermilk dressing."
>
> —SHELBY HEARON,
> *Life Estates*

Chapter 8

BOTH SIDES NOW

Pancakes and Other Griddled Cornbreads

Cornbreads began on a griddle, for open fire came long before the oven. Although that griddle might have been a flat, hot stone or the side of a long-handled hoe held over an open fire, these flat breads—tortillas, hoecakes, jonnycakes, and a host of other mostly unleavened griddled cakes—were the ancestors of today's light, leavened pancakes. Americans have enjoyed the latter over the last 200 years, since the invention of quick leaveners like baking powder (prior to this, pancakes were leavened with either yeast or beaten egg whites).

But plain or embellished, simple or complex, thick or thin, a crepe or a pocketed waffle: all are griddled, distinctive, and worthy of a place at the table.

A place, perhaps, especially at the family table. Is there a child alive who doesn't adore pancakes? They're special, not-for-every-day food. They're excellent absorbent carriers for syrup. They're fun to eat, stacked (and you can watch the butter melt between the layers), and they're round. Round, that is, unless you're an exceptionally lucky child whose mother, father, big brother or sister, even babysitter might have dripped the batter carefully into bunnies or initials . . . yours. In a time and place where the loss of shared mealtime is epidemic, family pancake-making is as much about creating relationship and ritual as it is about making food. An inherently lingered-over breakfast item, pancakes mean that someone is standing there dipping and flipping, asking those at the table, "How many more do you think you want?"

Some forms of griddled cakes certainly do find their ways into other meals, occasions, and relationships. The elegant crepe, represented on page 234 as Wanda's Soft Corn Crepes, is lovely dinner fare, filled with anything from a stir-fry of chile-laced vegetables to shredded, well-seasoned chicken and mushrooms, then sauced appropriately. Want to impress at a first-home-cooked-meal-for-new-boyfriend-or-girlfriend? For dessert, fill these same tender crepes (batter made in advance) with sautéed bananas or sliced fresh strawberries, and flame with a little rum or brandy.

The conversational intercourse of daily life, the way that, starting in childhood, continuing through friendship, dating, mating, and aging wisely and well, we begin and continue weaving together our participation in the human race, is subtle, ongoing, full of color and variety . . . as are griddled cakes themselves, round as life.

As we Americans learn our way into the healthy, delicious world of whole grains, griddled cakes are a terrific place to experiment with the flavors and textures of different, new-to-us flours . . . you know, the ones we're always being advised to eat but rarely do or even know how to. Griddled cakes reach new heights of interest, flavor, and texture when they incorporate corn. Whether it appears as meal (white, yellow, blue) as in White Cornmeal Griddle Cakes Old Alabam' (page 209), as kernels (fresh off the cob, frozen, even hominy) as in "Last Rows of Summer" Waffles (page 223), or as masa harina (again see Wanda's Soft Corn Crepes), corn, in its many forms, adds dimension.

STACKED OR WRAPPED, DAY OR NIGHT

Griddled cakes' interest quotient expands on several other counts. We've mentioned crepes, wrapped around an infinite number of sweet or savory fillings. But, less highfalutin traditional American-style pancakes can also have an amazing nightlife: Add chopped vegetables to the batter and stack the cakes, sometimes with a little grated cheese between them, and serve not with syrup but with . . . soy sauce. Fast! Amazing! Healthful! Yeah, it sounds improbable, but try it once, and you'll be a convert.

Then there are the infinitely versatile lacy-thin Newport-style jonnycakes (page 224), which can do triple duty as a starter (topped with chopped heirloom tomatoes, fresh basil, and coarse salt), as a side (cozying up to a bowl of spicy corn chowder), and as a dessert (with sliced seasonal lightly sweetened strawberries and real whipped cream—in my view, better than traditional strawberry shortcake any day). And if ever there was a Sunday-night supper dish to look forward to, wouldn't waffles stake the claim? Try the sesame-embellished ones from your own homemade mix (page 212); you'll be glad the mix is copious, because you'll go through it *fast*.

Breakfast, dinner; sweet, savory; embellished, plain: there is a place and time, on the palate, menu, and table, for the simple and the elaborate, in corn-centered griddled cakes as in

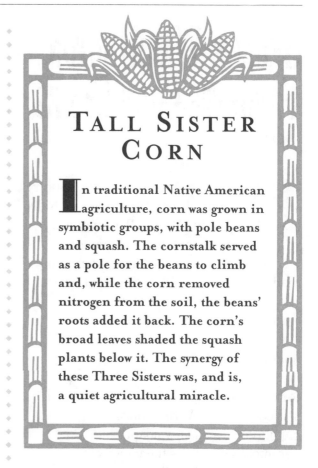

TALL SISTER CORN

In traditional Native American agriculture, corn was grown in symbiotic groups, with pole beans and squash. The cornstalk served as a pole for the beans to climb and, while the corn removed nitrogen from the soil, the beans' roots added it back. The corn's broad leaves shaded the squash plants below it. The synergy of these Three Sisters was, and is, a quiet agricultural miracle.

everything else. To everything, as Ecclesiastes reminds us, there is a season. And as Joni Mitchell wrote and sang, it's "Both Sides Now." Anything griddled has two sides, a front and a back, and a certain amount of flipping over is involved. Which, I think, applies not only to what we eat, but to who we are and were and will become. Life and griddle cakes: circular.

Come; let's circumambulate the round world of griddle cakes together.

George Washington's Favorite Corn Cakes

SERVES 4

How did the father of our country start his day? According to Nelly Custis, Martha Washington's youngest granddaughter, Washington ". . . rose before sunrise, always wrote or read until seven in summer or half past seven in winter. His breakfast was then ready—he ate three small mush cakes (Indian meal) swimming in butter and honey, drank three cups of tea without cream. . . ." She followed with a recipe for corn cakes, presumably like the ones served at Mount Vernon during her childhood. This is my adaptation. The cornmeal's grit gives the pancakes heartiness, but their thin, not-quite-lacy texture is delicate. If you serve them "swimming in butter and honey," you might, unlike George, find it hard to stop at three small ones.

Start these the night before.

2 cups stone-ground white cornmeal

1½ to 2 cups lukewarm water

1 package active dry yeast

½ teaspoon salt

1 large egg

Mild vegetable oil, for greasing the griddle

Optional accompaniments: honey and butter

1. The evening before you plan on breakfasting on these, combine 1 cup of the cornmeal, 1½ cups of the lukewarm water, and the yeast in a medium-size nonreactive bowl. Whisk well; the mixture will be thin. Cover the bowl tightly and let sit out overnight in a warm place.

2. The next morning, whisk in the remaining 1 cup cornmeal, the salt, and the egg. Re-cover the bowl and let it stand for 15 to 20 minutes (this allows the just-added cornmeal to absorb some of the liquid and soften somewhat).

3. Check the consistency; you want it similar to a thin pancake batter, neither nearly liquid, nor as thick as heavy cream. You might need to add a little more lukewarm water to achieve this.

4. Start heating a well-seasoned cast-iron skillet or griddle (see pages 16–17) over medium-high heat. Moisten a paper towel with vegetable oil. Once the skillet is good and hot, rub its interior quickly but thoroughly using the oiled paper towel.

5. Give the batter a good stir and, using a ladle, pour 3 or 4 thin, 3-inch pancakes onto the hot skillet. The batter will spread out fairly thin, and if it doesn't sizzle a little as you pour it out, the skillet isn't hot enough. If it sizzles a lot,

WELL, THEY *ARE* CALLED HOTCAKES

Pancakes are almost, but not quite, a no-brainer. The trick is that your skillet or griddle must be hot enough, but not too hot. How do you know if it's there? Drop enough batter for 1 pancake onto the heated surface and listen closely; it should hiss just a little as the batter makes contact with the pan. If it's not hot enough yet, wait a little longer and try again. Even experienced pancake makers will tell you they often have to throw out the first couple of cakes (or nibble these slightly underdone or overdone but still pretty good imperfect ones) to get the heat just right. But when you follow the general guidelines above, as well as follow the visual and time cues given in each recipe, you'll get it down pretty quickly. Also, each batter is slightly different. When the cakes are done—again, look to individual recipes for clues—flip them over. Flip one over to start, taking note of its degree of doneness (brown, firm), under-doneness (pale, drippy, hard to turn), or overdoneness (too dark) and adjust the heat and time accordingly. The second side is never as pretty as the first, but it cooks more quickly.

however, you may need to lower the heat just a little.

6. Watch closely. Almost immediately you'll see little bubbles appear throughout. When the top surface is completely dry and the edges are curling, flip one cake. It should be pleasantly golden brown, nicely mottled, neither pale nor too dark. Allow 50 to 70 seconds for the first side (once you've got your skillet at the right temp) and 30 to 50 on the second side. Repeat with the remaining cakes and batter. (You'll want to stir the batter occasionally, as it tends to separate.) Serve with honey and butter, if you wish.

VARIATION: GEORGE WASHINGTON'S FAVORITE CORN CAKES WITH SOURDOUGH

If you happen to have some sourdough starter around, omit the instant dry yeast and use 3 tablespoons of starter, stirring it in the night before at the point at which you would have used the yeast.

"The bread business is as follows—if you wish to make $2\frac{1}{2}$ quarts of flour up—take at night one quart of flour, five table spoonfuls of yeast & as much lukewarm water as will make it the consistency of pancake batter, mix it in a large stone pot & set it near a warm hearth (or a moderate fire) make it at candlelight & let it remain until the next morning then add the remaining quart & a half by degrees with a spoon—when well mixed let it stand 15 or 20 minutes & then bake it—of this dough in the morning, beat up a white & half of the yolk of an egg—add as much lukewarm water as will make it like pancake batter, drop a spoonful at a time on a hoe or griddle (as we say in the South)—When done on one side turn the other—the griddle must be rubbed in the first instance with a piece of beef suet or the fat of cold corned beef."

—NELLY CUSTIS LEWIS,
Martha Washington's granddaughter, in a letter to her friend, Elizabeth Bordley Gibson, January 7, 1821 (note that "flour" refers to cornmeal)

NED AND CRESCENT'S FAVORITE MULTIGRAIN PANCAKES

SERVES 2 TO 4

George Washington and Edmund George Shank, aka Ned, my late and beloved husband—pancake guys both. This simple, basic whole-grain and buttermilk pancake, unembellished and straightforward, was one stop on Ned's Search for the Perfect Pancake. They were our joint favorite for the last five or six years of our shared journey. These days, when I eat them alone I try to enjoy them doubly, on Ned's behalf, and when I eat them with others, I think about loving and being loved and all the forms this takes over a lifetime. I appreciate those I love now all the more, knowing the temporal nature of all life's shared feasts. And in either case, or sometimes when I'm not thinking about anything in particular, I just plain enjoy these fine cakes.

If you don't have all the flours listed, feel free to substitute. The cornmeal is essential, but the 1/2 cup whole wheat pastry flour plus 1/4 cup each unbleached white and buckwheat flours (adding up to 1 cup total) can be almost any flour combination. You may certainly use all unbleached or all whole wheat for the flour, or mix and match like crazy: I have substituted spelt flour, wild rice flour, barley flour, and rye flour for all or part of the suggested flours, and all were very good.

Serve these with Warm Maple-Apple Sauté (recipe follows), or virtually any other fruit sauce or topping you like.

1/2 cup stone-ground yellow cornmeal
1/2 cup whole wheat pastry flour
1/4 cup unbleached white flour
1/4 cup buckwheat flour
1 teaspoon salt
2 teaspoons baking soda
2 eggs
2 cups buttermilk
2 tablespoons butter, melted
Vegetable oil cooking spray (optional)
Warm Maple-Apple Sauté (recipe follows; optional), for serving

1. Stirring well, combine the cornmeal, flours, salt, and baking soda in a medium bowl.

2. Beat the eggs in another medium bowl, then whisk in the buttermilk and melted butter.

3. Stir the two mixtures together, just enough to combine the wet and dry (be careful not to overbeat). Don't worry about a few lumps, as long as there are no patches of unmoistened flour.

4. Over medium-high heat, heat a skillet or griddle. If it is nonstick, you need add no oil (though I often use just a bit); if it is conventional, give it a good spray of vegetable oil. When the skillet is good and hot, lower the heat slightly to medium and spoon the batter onto it, using 2 to 3 tablespoonfuls batter per pancake. If the skillet is hot enough, the pancake batter will sizzle slightly as it makes contact with the pan surface. Cook the pancakes until bubbles that remain intact appear around the edges, just over 1 minute. Flip the pancakes and cook the second side for about 50 seconds. Serve, hot, from the griddle, or keep warm in a low (250°F) oven for a few minutes until ready to serve.

VARIATION: EVENING MULTIGRAIN PANCAKES
Try these cakes at supper, as supper—with stir-fried tamari'd vegetables and a little grated cheese between each pancake

> "Time passing and corn growing cannot be seen; one can notice only that the moon has become so much older, the corn so much higher."
> —OLIVER LA FARGE,
> *Laughing Boy*

in the stack. Sounds weird, but it's a great Sunday-evening-at-home kind of dinner, exuding down-home comfort.

WARM MAPLE-APPLE SAUTE
MAKES ABOUT 2 TO 2¹/₂ CUPS

This apple sauté would make any slightly sweet corn cake happy. Try it piled on Ned and Crescent's Favorite Multigrain Pancakes or any of the pancakes in this chapter; finish it with a dollop of really good plain yogurt.

This is a great place to try some of the splendidly flavored heirloom apples now coming into most farmers' markets. Look for one that is spicy-sweet-tart, juicy, and crisp without being hard. In almost all cases, this crispness turns meltingly soft when cooked. (Granny Smiths, the exception to the rule, do not soften; don't use them here.) McIntoshes are one premier New England apple; they don't keep well, though, so be sure to get new-crop local fall Macs. Query the sellers at your local farmstand about the qualities of whichever varieties are offered. Greenings are superb, as are Ginger-Golds, Sheep's Nose, and Cortlands. Make your choice, then make your sauté.

MY GRIDDLING,
FIDDLING OLD SWEETHEART

I spent twenty-three years with a pancake aficionado (and yes, he did play the violin/fiddle, too). My late husband's way of evaluating a cookbook was, for years before I met him, to simply flip to the index and see how many pancake recipes it had. The usual childhood pancake-joy had been extra-large for Ned; he never outgrew it. The perfect pancake was a holy grail for him. Yet, since he liked all types of pancakes, there was no such thing as pancake perfection; so the search was, for him, happily endless. He loved both thin pancakes in the crepe line, which he described as "noodle-y," and the thick, more porous type, which he called "bread-y." Either description was a compliment coming from him.

All my life I will remember tall Ned, leaning in the door-frame of the tiny studio apartment I was then renting from Starr Mitchell, on Scott Street in Little Rock, Arkansas. This couldn't have been more than two weeks after we met. I, unaware of his pancake history, had mixed up pancake batter and was standing by the stove, flipping as he watched me. It was an overcast fall day. And he said, out of nowhere, out of everywhere and everything that was happening, "I love you." The first time either of us had said it.

As often as Ned and I would make pancakes over the years, a hundred thousand times more frequently than that, we said those words to each other.

Vegetable oil cooking spray

1 tablespoon butter

5 to 6 apples, peeled, cored,
and thinly sliced

½ teaspoon ground cinnamon

2 tablespoons brown sugar

3 tablespoons pure maple syrup

1 tablespoon Calvados
(apple brandy; optional)

1. Spray a large skillet with oil. Place over medium heat and add the butter.

2. When the butter melts and sizzles, add the sliced apples, tossing at once to coat the apples with the fat. Raise the heat slightly and continue to cook, stirring often, until the apples begin to grow translucent and tender, 4 to 5 minutes (if some of the apples brown slightly, so much the better). Sprinkle the cinnamon over them, and stir for about 30 seconds more.

3. Add the brown sugar, maple syrup, and Calvados if using. Heat through, and serve.

LYNN LARSON'S CRISP CORN FLAPJACKS

SERVES 2

My friend Lynn Larson makes neat, small pancakes that are crisped around the edges. They are made without eggs, without sweetener, and with just a touch of flour: mostly the time-honored cornmeal-buttermilk combo takes center stage. Since most children tend to view pancakes as essentially sponge-like carriers for as much syrup as possible, it is worth noting that Lynn says, "My kids loved these with just a bit of butter, or plain: no syrup or jelly."

⅔ cup stone-ground yellow cornmeal

½ teaspoon salt

¼ teaspoon baking soda

2 tablespoons unbleached white flour

2 tablespoons butter, cold, cut into
small pieces

Vegetable oil cooking spray

1 cup buttermilk

1. Combine the cornmeal, salt, baking soda, and flour in a medium bowl. Using two knives or a pastry blender, cut in the butter.

·M·E·N·U·

SOUTHERN CALIFORNIA SUNDAY SUPPER THAT COULD BE BREAKFAST

Eggs Scrambled with
Green and Red Bell Peppers,
Onions, Garlic, and Tomatoes

❊

Sautéed Sausage or Soysage Patties

❊

Lynn Larson's Crisp Corn Flapjacks

❊

Fresh Limeade spiked
with Ginger Ale

2. Spray a heavy cast-iron skillet with oil and place it over medium heat. Give it a few minutes to heat. When it's fairly hot, quickly add the buttermilk to the dry mixture, stirring just long enough to combine everything and no longer.

3. By now the skillet should be good and hot. Pour the batter onto the hot skillet in small spoonfuls; you want cakes between 2 and 3 inches in diameter, no larger. The batter should sizzle a bit when it hits the pan. Let the cakes cook for 50 to 70 seconds on one side (test one

to see if it's browned nicely), then turn once. The second side will be quicker.

4. Serve, hot from the griddle, plain or with your favorite accompaniments.

WHITE CORNMEAL GRIDDLE CAKES OLD ALABAM'

SERVES 4 TO 6

A version of this unusually appealing pancake recipe was sent to me by a reader from Birmingham, Alabama. I've adapted it slightly, keeping, however, the presoftened meal that is its secret. Try these with sorghum or molasses and plenty of butter and a sautéed patty of your favorite sausage or soysage for a substantial breakfast.

About 1¼ cups water or milk
½ cup stone-ground white cornmeal
½ teaspoon salt
½ cup unbleached white flour
1¼ teaspoons baking powder
1 egg
Vegetable oil cooking spray

I. Place 1¼ cups of water or milk in a small saucepan and bring to a boil. Meanwhile, place the cornmeal and salt in a heat-proof bowl. When the liquid has come to a boil, pour it over the meal and salt, whisking well. Let stand for 10 to 15 minutes.

2. Combine the flour and baking powder, and sift them over the soaked mixture. Stir a few times, then stir in the egg. Beat well. If the batter seems too thick, add a few more tablespoons water or milk, which need not be heated this go-round.

3. Spray a good heavy cast-iron skillet with oil and place it over medium-high heat for a few minutes. When the pan's good and hot, lower the heat to medium and begin dropping the batter by tablespoonfuls into it (it should sizzle a bit when it hits the pan). Wait until you know the underside is cooked before flipping: You'll see the air bubbles on the top side form, then burst, then start to look dryish; that is the moment when you know they're ready to flip, about 3 minutes. Turn them, cooking the other side slightly more briefly. Serve, hot from the griddle.

·M·E·N·U·

Franconia Notch Pre-Cross-Country Ski Breakfast

Fresh Orange Juice

＊

**Clove-Studded Baked Apples
Glazed with Maple Syrup**

＊

**White Cornmeal Griddle Cakes
Old Alabam', with Butter,
Sorghum or Molasses,
and/or Ribbon Cane Syrup**

＊

**Blueberry Preserves
from Last Summer** ＊
Plain or Vanilla Yogurt

＊

**Sautéed Sausage
or Soysage Patties**

＊

**Mugs of Mocha
(Hot Chocolate and Coffee,
mixed with Half and Half),
Whipped Cream Optional**

THE TOLERS' SOUTHERN CORNMEAL PANCAKES

SERVES 4

I first knew the Tolers as guests at Dairy Hollow House, the inn my late husband, Ned, and I owned and ran for eighteen years. Later, when they moved to Eureka Springs, Arkansas, where we and the inn were, they became neighbors: active participants at almost every cultural event, quietly sassy, well-read, thoughtful, smart, kind—altogether their own persons, always up to something interesting.

Perhaps one secret of their zest is that the Tolers are powered by delicious and healthful dishes like these pancakes, which they serve with maple syrup, bananas, strawberries, and pecans.

¾ cup stone-ground cornmeal
¼ cup stone-ground whole wheat flour
¼ cup toasted wheat germ
2 teaspoons brown sugar
1 teaspoon baking powder
½ teaspoon baking soda
½ teaspoon salt
1 egg
1¼ cups buttermilk
2 tablespoons mild vegetable oil
Vegetable oil cooking spray (optional)
Optional accompaniments: butter, pure maple syrup, sliced bananas, sliced strawberries, and/or chopped toasted pecans

1. Combine the cornmeal, flour, wheat germ, brown sugar, baking powder, baking soda, and salt in a medium bowl.

2. Separately, in a smaller bowl, beat the egg, then stir in the buttermilk. Add the oil.

3. Pour the liquid mixture into the dry mixture and whisk quickly to blend the ingredients thoroughly. Do not overbeat.

4. Heat a skillet or griddle over medium-high heat. If it is nonstick, as the Tolers prefer, you need not spray it with oil; if it is conventional, give it a thorough spray. When the skillet is good and hot, lower the heat slightly to medium and spoon the batter onto it, using about 2 tablespoons of batter per pancake. If the skillet is hot enough, the pancake batter will sizzle slightly as it makes contact with the pan surface.

5. Let the pancakes cook until bubbles that remain intact appear around the edges, 70 to 80 seconds. Flip the pancakes and cook the second side for about 50 seconds. Serve, hot, from the griddle, with any or all of the accompaniments.

Toasted Sesame Multigrain Pancake Mix

MAKES ABOUT 4 QUARTS, OR EIGHT
1-CUP BATCHES WHEN RECONSTITUTED,
EACH BATCH SERVING 2 TO 4 PEOPLE

This is a very lovable recipe. I know: Pancake batters are easily made from scratch, *and* there are count-less pancake mixtures of every description out there. But I guarantee you there's no mix either this delicious or this healthy on the market. The griddle cakes and waffles it makes are both tender and pleasingly textured, full of delightful grainy flavors yet not at all health-foody. The slightly sweet batter has the mildest possible tang of buttermilk (in powdered form: you'll find it in either the baking section of the supermarket, or next to the other dried milks), and it contains the hearty goodness of four whole grains, including cornmeal. But it's the toasted sesame seeds that take it over the top.

If you are a gifts-from-the-kitchen type of person, divide the finished mix into zip-top bags or 1-pint Mason jars; print out a copy of the recipe for reconstituting the mix; line a pretty gift bag with tissue paper; throw in the recipe, a container of the mix, a bottle of pure maple syrup (or perhaps a jar of homemade preserves), and a small bottle of sesame oil; and give it to a friend. But don't give too much away, because you and your family are going to love this.

Important: Because of the toasted sesame seeds, this mix really keeps best when frozen or refrigerated. (Be sure to note this on any bags or containers you may give as gifts.)

1 cup hulled sesame seeds
  (available at natural foods markets)
1 cup oatmeal (rolled oats)
3 cups whole wheat pastry flour
2 ¾ cups unbleached white flour
1½ cups buckwheat flour
2 ¾ cups stone-ground yellow or white
  cornmeal
1 cup raw or unrefined sugar (see
  Pantry, page 356)
1 container (12 ounces) buttermilk
  powder
5 tablespoons baking powder
2 tablespoons baking soda
2 tablespoons salt

1. Toast the sesame seeds: Place them in a large cast-iron skillet over medium-high heat. Stir constantly until the sesame seeds become fragrant and start to brown, about 4 minutes; don't turn your back for a second. Then immediately remove them from the stove. Turn them into a bowl and let them cool slightly.

2. Buzz the oatmeal in a food processor until it is powdery. Add the sesame seeds and pulse them with the oatmeal to grind them somewhat: The mixture should be mostly powdery with a few whole seeds here and there (don't overgrind, or you'll end up releasing too much oil).

3. Transfer the sesame-oatmeal mixture to a large bowl. Add all the flours, the cornmeal, sugar, and buttermilk powder. Stir together very thoroughly.

4. Sift the baking powder, baking soda, and salt a little at a time over the flour mixture, stopping periodically to stir. You want to make sure the salt and leavenings are thoroughly and evenly mixed into the whole.

5. Transfer the mix into gallon-size zip-top freezer bags. Label and date each bag. To prevent rancidity, both from the whole-grain flours, and especially from the toasted ground sesame, store the bags of mix in the freezer.

6. Use the mix as needed, straight from the freezer, making pancakes or waffles with the recipes on pages 214 and 220, and be glad you did this.

BUTTERMILK IS BETTER

You may have noticed that the liquid in the pancake recipes here is all or part buttermilk. To me, nothing makes a more tender pancake, and buttermilk's tang adds a depth of flavor not otherwise found.

If you don't have buttermilk on hand, you can use a good-quality plain, unsweetened yogurt, diluted 50-50 with water, for an effect that's almost as good. And, a pretty decent dried buttermilk powder is available these days in most supermarkets, near the other powdered milks. (You'll see I call for it in the multigrain pancake mix, left.) Your other alternative: Use 1 cup regular milk with 1 teaspoon vinegar or lemon juice added. For vegan (nondairy) buttermilk, add the vinegar or lemon juice to plain, unsweetened soy milk.

"Breakfast, July 12, 1893

Happily for us all this little company of visitors this week contains no distressful hypochondriacs nor people with special aversions. But some of them have intimated that it is essential to their happiness to have corn bread for breakfast constantly, both baked and griddled. Menu: Fresh black cap raspberries (1 qt, 10 cents); Oatmeal (3 cents); Fish plain fried, lard for frying (12 cents); Liver breaded (12 cents); Beefsteak (20 cents); Potatoes (7 cents); Corn bread and corn batter cakes (16 cents); Cream and milk, syrup, butter, coffee, tea (65 cents); Total, $1.65; 6½ cents a plate. The deuce take this troublesome business of boarding people for profit!"

—JESSUP WHITEHEAD,
Eight Weeks at a Summer Resort:
Our Daily Bill of Fare
and What It Cost, 1893

TOASTED SESAME MULTIGRAIN PANCAKES

SERVES 2 AS THE MAIN ITEM,
4 AS PART OF A MORE SUBSTANTIAL
BREAKFAST

I just marvel at how good these are, and how long they keep me going energy-wise. I think you will also be very pleased.

It's the double hit of sesame that takes these over the top.

- 1 egg
- 1½ cups water, preferably spring or filtered (or, for extra-light pancakes, use club soda or a naturally carbonated water, such as San Pellegrino)
- 1 cup Toasted Sesame Multigrain Pancake Mix (page 212)
- 1 teaspoon mild vegetable oil
- 1½ teaspoons toasted sesame oil
- Optional accompaniments: butter or Better (see Pantry, page 346), pure maple syrup, fresh sliced fruit, and/or sautéed fruit

1. In a medium bowl, beat together the egg and water.

2. Whisk in the pancake mix, the vegetable oil, and the sesame oil, being careful to combine thoroughly but not overbeat.

3. Heat a heavy nonstick or well-seasoned cast-iron skillet over medium-high heat. When the skillet is good and hot, ladle on the batter—it should make the telltale hiss as it hits the skillet's surface if you have it hot enough. Make the cakes as large or small as your family likes. Lower the heat to medium. When the pancakes have risen and have a few bubbles around the edges, about 2 to 3 minutes, flip them. The second side usually takes 1 to 2 minutes.

4. Serve hot from the griddle, with whatever accompaniments you like.

GOLDEN APPLES OF THE SUN PANCAKES

SERVES 4 TO 6

Faintly sweet, so lightly cinnamon'd that you don't even identify the spice as much more than a fragrance, these are substantial. Cornmeal gives grittiness, buttermilk provides a tender cake, and apple pieces stud each bite. These cakes make a good fall brunch or breakfast, with applesauce, apple butter, or the Warm Maple-Apple Sauté on page 206. Top with butter, a dab of cottage cheese or sour cream, or a drizzle of honey.

Choose a not-too-crisp yet full-flavored variety of apple: a McIntosh, Macoun, or Golden Delicious. Be sure to dice the apple *very fine;* large chunks leave sections of the pancakes undercooked, but grating them makes the cakes overly moist.

1¼ cups stone-ground yellow cornmeal

1¼ cups unbleached white flour

¼ cup sugar

1 tablespoon baking powder

1 teaspoon baking soda

½ teaspoon salt

½ teaspoon ground cinnamon

2 eggs

1 cup milk

1 cup plus 2 tablespoons buttermilk

1 teaspoon mild vegetable oil

2 apples, peeled, cored, and finely diced into ⅛-inch pieces

Vegetable oil cooking spray (optional)

Optional accompaniments: Warm Maple-Apple Sauté, applesauce, apple butter, butter, cottage cheese, sour cream, and/or honey

1. Combine the cornmeal, flour, sugar, baking powder, baking soda, salt, and cinnamon in a medium bowl.

2. Separately, in a smaller bowl, beat the eggs, then stir in the milk and buttermilk. Add the oil.

3. Pour the liquid mixture into the dry and whisk quickly to blend the ingredients thoroughly. Do not overbeat. Stir in the diced apple.

4. Heat a skillet or griddle over medium-high heat. If it is nonstick, you need not spray it with oil; if it is conventional, give it a good spray. When the skillet is nice and hot, lower the heat slightly to medium and spoon the batter onto it, using about 2 tablespoons of batter per pancake. If the skillet is hot enough, the pancake batter will sizzle slightly as it makes contact with the pan surface.

5. Let the pancakes cook until bubbles that do not burst appear around the edges, 70 to 80 seconds. Flip the pancakes and cook the second side for about 50 seconds. Serve, hot, from the griddle, with the accompaniments of your choice.

VARIATION: SOUFFLÉED GOLDEN APPLES OF THE SUN PANCAKES

This is a much lighter, airier version. Separate the eggs. Beat the yolks in with the liquids, as above. In a small, deep bowl, beat the whites until stiff (see Beating Egg Whites, pages 186–187). After adding the apple in step 3, gently fold in the beaten whites. Griddle the pancakes as directed.

"The people had a responsibility to this world, as the world had a responsibility to them. The physical environment of the Iroquois was infused with religious and spiritual meaning. . . . The corn does not just grow by itself; the Iroquois believed plants think and feel and know the way we do. The Corn Mother watches over the crop, the people perform the rituals, the fields flourish."

—HAZEL W. HERTZBERG,
The Great Tree and the Longhouse

Orange-Blueberry Cornmeal Pancakes

Serves 4 to 6

These are wonderful pancakes, and they are surprisingly delicate considering the whole grains. The citrus adds a subtle, almost floral sweetness. Make them at the height of fresh blueberry time, and luxuriate. Or try them on a gray winter Sunday, using frozen berries—and remember summer fondly with each bite. Either will satisfy.

If you do use frozen berries, *don't thaw them first*, or your batter will turn a less-than-appetizing blue-gray. Another tip: Since the batter is a bit more fragile than that of some pancakes, cook the cakes in a nonstick pan, for a slightly longer time, at a slightly lower heat. This compensates for this delicacy, firming the cakes up nicely.

These are so good that you might eat them perfectly plain, or with just a touch of butter and the traditional maple syrup.

1 cup stone-ground yellow cornmeal
½ cup unbleached white flour
½ cup whole wheat flour, preferably pastry flour
1 tablespoon sugar
1 tablespoon baking powder
1¼ teaspoons baking soda
½ teaspoon salt
1 egg
Finely grated zest of 1 orange, preferably organic
1 cup orange juice, preferably freshly squeezed (about 2 large oranges)
1 cup plus 2 tablespoons buttermilk
2 teaspoons melted butter or mild vegetable oil
1 cup blueberries, fresh or frozen (unthawed)
Vegetable oil cooking spray (optional)

1. Combine the cornmeal, white and whole wheat flours, sugar, baking powder, baking soda, and salt in a medium bowl.

2. In a smaller bowl, beat the egg, then stir in the orange zest, orange juice, and buttermilk. Stir in the butter or oil.

3. Pour the liquid mixture into the dry mixture and whisk quickly to blend the ingredients thoroughly. Do not overbeat. Stir in the berries.

4. Heat a skillet or griddle over medium-high heat. If it is nonstick, you need add no oil; if it is conventional, give it a good spray of vegetable oil. When the skillet is nice and hot, lower the heat slightly to medium and spoon the batter onto it, using about 2 tablespoons batter per pancake. (If the skillet is hot enough, the pancake batter will sizzle slightly as it makes contact with the pan.) Cook the pancakes until bubbles that do not burst appear around the edges, about 1½ minutes. Flip the pancakes and cook the second side for about 50 seconds. Serve, hot, from the griddle, or keep warm in a low (250°F) oven for a few minutes until ready to serve.

·M·E·N·U·

"I Only Have Eyes for You" Birthday Breakfast

Sectioned Ruby Red Grapefruit Halves with Granulated Maple Sugar

*

Orange-Blueberry Cornmeal Pancakes

*

Butter * Cottage Cheese * Maple Syrup from the Family Trees (and a Birthday Candle on the Top of the Birthday Girl/Boy's Pancake Stack)

*

Sautéed Bacon or Smoked Tempeh Strips

*

Hot Ceylon Tea with Milk

Double-Corn Cottage Pancakes

SERVES 4

The "double" in this recipe's title refers to both the yellow corn-meal in the batter and the corn kernels stirred into it. To me, these pancakes are superb dinner fare, whether with something old-fashioned (meatloaf) or new-fashioned (baked tempeh with gravy). But they certainly fit the breakfast bill also, especially in the sweeter variation that follows.

3 eggs

1 cup cottage cheese (see Choosing Good Cottage Cheese, page 221)

1 tablespoon mild vegetable oil

⅓ cup stone-ground yellow cornmeal

2 tablespoons unbleached white flour

½ teaspoon baking soda

⅛ teaspoon salt

¾ cup corn kernels, cut from 1 or 2 ears of fresh corn (see Shuck and Jive, page 49), or frozen corn kernels, measured and thawed

Vegetable oil cooking spray

**Optional accompaniments: butter
or Better (see Pantry, page 346),
pure maple syrup, and/or
unsweetened applesauce**

1. Buzz the eggs, cottage cheese, and oil or
butter in a food processor until well combined.

2. Add the cornmeal, flour, baking soda, and
salt and pulse a few times, just to combine
well. Add the corn kernels, giving one or two
pulses only.

3. Spray your largest nonstick skillet well,
and place it over medium-high heat for a few
minutes. Let it get good and hot, then begin
dropping the pancake batter by rounded
tablespoonfuls onto the skillet (the batter
should sizzle a bit when it hits the pan).

4. Allowing about 70 seconds for the first side,
watch the pancakes closely (the cottage cheese
makes the batter's texture atypical, so there are
fewer telltale bubbles). When they are ready to
be flipped, you will notice the top sides have
firmed up a little (not as much as you might
think) and have a slightly dulled finish. Flip one
cake gently; if it's a nice, even golden brown,
your timing was impeccable. Allow about 30
seconds for side two and continue flipping the
other pancakes.

5. Serve immediately, hot from the griddle, with
any or all of the accompaniments, if desired.

NOTE: Leftover batter for these cakes thickens
more than usual when refrigerated overnight.

Simply add buttermilk, or yogurt thinned with
water, to the batter, stirring until it is of about the
same consistency as the original batter. Don't be
surprised if it takes quite a bit of additional liquid
to get it just right. The buttermilked déjà batter
is, if anything, even better than the first day's
batch—and for some reason you do get more of
the indicative flip-me-now pancake holes.

VARIATIONS:

BLUEBERRY BLINTZ-STYLE CORN COTTAGE
CAKES
This is the same wonderful cottage
cheese–based pancake batter given above,
but minus the corn kernels and seasoned like
the filling of a cheese blintz. To make them,
add the following seasonings to the batter,
along with the eggs and cottage cheese: finely
grated zest of 1 lemon, preferably organic;
$\frac{1}{8}$ teaspoon ground cinnamon; several gratings
of whole nutmeg; 2 tablespoons sugar, preferably unrefined (see Pantry, page 356), or brown
sugar; and $\frac{1}{2}$ teaspoon pure vanilla extract.
Then, when it comes time to add the corn, stir
in $\frac{1}{2}$ to $\frac{3}{4}$ cup blueberries instead. There you
have it; and invite me to breakfast!

APPLE-GINGER CORN COTTAGE CAKES
Follow the basic recipe, but omit the corn
kernels. Use, instead, 1 flavorful, crisp but not
too hard apple—a Fuji, Braeburn, Pink Lady,
or even Golden Delicious, for instance—peeled,
cored, and finely diced. Stir this in along with

2 to 3 teaspoons very, very finely minced or grated fresh gingerroot (you need not peel it). Although a little cinnamon and a tablespoon of sugar are classic additions here and certainly are tasty, I like the freshness of the straight apple-ginger combo. Excellent served with applesauce or apple butter, butter, and plain yogurt.

Toasted Sesame Multigrain Waffles

SERVES 4 TO 6, DEPENDING ON ACCOMPANIMENTS

So very, very good. The sesame makes for an extra bit of crunch, which enhances the pocketed waffle surface. I like separating the eggs for the light, airy quality it gives, but if that's too fussy for you, just leave them whole.

Please note the Waffle World menu that follows; it is suitable for a big congenial holiday or family reunion or for breakfast after a weekend party. Almost everything can be made in advance. All you do is put the waffle batter together and cook it, as guests and family wait eagerly.

2 eggs, separated

1 cup water (or for extra-light waffles, use club soda or a naturally carbonated water, such as San Pellegrino)

2 cups Toasted Sesame Multigrain Pancake Mix (page 212)

1 tablespoon mild vegetable oil

2 tablespoons toasted sesame oil

Optional accompaniments: butter or Better (see Pantry, page 346), pure maple syrup, fresh fruit, and/or sautéed fruit

CHOOSING GOOD COTTAGE CHEESE

The Double-Corn Cottage Pancakes on page 218 are only as good as the cottage cheese that forms their base, and finding a good cottage cheese might take a little doing. But it's worthwhile, for, like the girl with the curl in the middle of her forehead, when cottage cheese is good, it's very, very good (clean, fresh- and light-tasting, with a bouncy texture), and when it's bad, it's horrid (as if it had been sitting around too long, and a bit chemical-y).

Start with the label. Read it. Avoid any cottage cheese with a long list of ingredients; basically, you want milk, cream, salt; perhaps dry milk, perhaps acidophilus and/or bifidus cultures, perhaps lactic acid. Steer clear of gums, stabilizers, and preservatives. You want certified organic milk that is free of bovine growth hormone; that

is, produced by cows that have been raised without antibiotics or hormones added to their feed, which in turn is without pesticides. (As a vegetarian, I also try to avoid rennet on the ingredient list, sometimes listed as simply "enzymes." Rennet, one substance used to coagulate milk into cheese, is derived from an enzyme in calves' stomachs. However, it is not needed to make cottage cheese, and brands without it are available.)

My favorite nationally distributed brand is Nancy's, simply delicious rennetless organic low-fat cottage cheese. It is so good, it could make you entirely rethink your views of cottage cheese. A second good nation- ally distributed brand is Alta-Dena, and sometimes you can find excellent regional brands. Experiment until you find the ones you like best.

1. Whisk together the egg yolks and water in a large bowl, then whisk in the mix and the oils just until well combined. Heat up your waffle iron.

2. Using clean beaters and a high-sided bowl, beat the egg whites until stiff (see Beating Egg Whites, pages 186–187), then gently fold them into the batter.

3. When the iron is good and hot and ready to waffle, pour in the batter, following your waffle maker's directions. Let the waffles bake in the griddle until done, 4 to 6 minutes. How can you tell when they're done? Less steam is emitted from the waffle iron and they will smell done. Some waffle irons have an indicator light, gauge, or even a beeper that tips you off.

4. Serve, hot from the waffle iron, with any or all of the accompaniments, if you like.

·M·E·N·U·

WAFFLE WORLD EXTRAVAGANZA

AT THE BUFFET:
Quartered Ripe Strawberries Tossed with Blueberries

∗

Mixture of $1/3$ Unsweetened Yogurt, $1/3$ Cottage Cheese & $1/3$ Sour Cream

∗

Lightly Sweetened Whipped Cream

∗

Platter of Oven-Baked Crisp Bacon and Sausage or Soysage

FRESH FROM THE WAFFLE IRON:
Toasted Sesame Multigrain Waffles

AT THE BEVERAGE TABLE:
Pitcher of Freshly Squeezed Juice

∗

Hot Colombian Coffee, Regular and/or Decaf

∗

Basket of Tea Bags: Herbal, Black, and Green ∗ **Thermos of Very Hot Water**

∗

Honey, Sugar, Milk, Soy Milk

"Last Rows of Summer" Waffles

SERVES 4 TO 6, DEPENDING ON
ACCOMPANIMENTS

These are so good that two people can polish off one recipe's worth—yep, two people, twelve waffles. Don't ask me how I know this, but it has been done.

When made with frozen corn in the winter, this is a terrific Sunday morning breakfast. Try it with a compote of cranberries, cooked just until they pop, with diced pears and brown sugar or an alternative sweetener to taste, and good-quality plain yogurt on the side. *Major* yum. But the waffles are at their best when you are scarfing up the very last of the late-summer local corn, knowing you won't see it again until the next July.

½ to 1 cup corn kernels, cut from 1 or 2 ears of fresh corn (see Shuck and Jive, page 49), frozen corn kernels, measured and thawed, or well-drained canned corn

2 eggs

2 cups plain yogurt or buttermilk, or a combination

1 teaspoon sugar

1 tablespoon melted butter

¾ cup whole-grain yellow corn flour (see Pantry, page 353)

¾ cup whole wheat pastry flour

1 teaspoon baking powder

¼ teaspoon baking soda

¼ teaspoon salt

Optional accompaniments: butter or Better (see Pantry, page 346), pure maple syrup, and/or plain yogurt

1. In a food processor, combine the corn kernels, eggs, yogurt and/or buttermilk, sugar, and butter. Buzz until the corn is a fine purée and the ingredients are thoroughly blended.

2. Combine the corn flour, whole wheat pastry flour, baking powder, baking soda, and salt in a medium-large bowl. Stir well.

3. Heat up your waffle iron.

4. When the iron is good and hot and waffle-ready, pour in the batter according to the waffle maker's directions. Let the waffles bake in the griddle until done, 4 to 6 minutes. How can you tell when they're done? Less steam is emitted from the waffle iron, and they will smell done. Some waffle irons have an indicator light, gauge, or even a beeper that tips you off.

5. Remove, preferably to warmed plates, and serve with your favorite accompaniments, if desired.

NEWPORT COUNTY-STYLE THIN AND LACY JONNYCAKES

SERVES 2 AS AN ENTRÉE,
4 AS AN APPETIZER

These thin, crisp, lacy, shatteringly elegant, utterly addictive jonnycakes were, to me, *the* surprise hit of the book. Wholly unlike any other pancake or corn cake I have ever tasted, these are in a class by themselves. A bit on the buttery side, they are so perfect as is that serving them with additional butter would subtract from their delicacy.

I came to them late in life, but I guarantee you, I will be making this style of jonnycake for the rest of my life. Look at all the possibilities that follow in One Cake, Many Uses (opposite): These can serve as the base for a starter, accompany an entrée, or act as the beginning for dessert. The numbers of suggestions I've offered are but a small measure of my huge regard for these crisp cakes.

Vegetable oil cooking spray
1½ cups cold 2% milk or water
1 cup finely ground white cornmeal, preferably whitecap flint (see Pantry, page 350)
½ teaspoon salt
3 tablespoons butter, melted

1. Spray your largest cast-iron skillet with the oil, and set it over medium-low heat to preheat it.

2. Put the cold milk into a medium bowl and pour in the cornmeal and salt, whisking vigorously. Add the butter. The batter will be suspiciously thin, but don't worry.

3. Raise the heat under the skillet. You want that skillet good and hot, enough so that the batter will sizzle when you drop it in. When it is ready, drop the batter onto the skillet, using a tablespoon to make 3-inch-wide jonnycakes, or a teaspoon to make adorable petite ones, and tilting the skillet as needed to make them round. Each and *every* time you spoon up batter, *always* stir or whisk it like the dickens, otherwise the cornmeal will settle on the bottom. Please note: At first the cakes will look so filled with holes that they will appear impossible to flip, and you'll think something's wrong. It isn't.

4. These cakes take a little longer to cook than usual—4 to 5 minutes for the first side. It's time to flip when all the little holes except those at the edge have filled in, and the top is almost dry. Turn one cake, using the thinnest spatula you own, and if it holds together neatly and is nicely golden brown, you're there. Allow 3 to 4 minutes for side two.

One Cake, Many Uses

Use Newport County–Style Thin and Lacy Jonnycakes as follows:

For hors d'oeuvres (in small size):

- With low-fat sour cream or tofu sour cream and chives (optional caviar for those who like it)

- With a spoonful of peeled, seeded, chopped tomatoes (preferably a mix of red, yellow, and green assorted heirlooms, at high summer) with a little shredded basil and a grinding of coarse salt

- With a dab of not-too-oily basil pesto

- With finely minced pitted kalamata olives, a small cube or crumble of feta cheese, and a dill sprig

With a main course (in larger size):

- Chili of any kind, or any spicy bean ragout

- Corn chowder, particularly a spicy one

- Chilled red pepper soup or Golden Gazpacho (page 266)

- Large mesclun salad with avocado, fresh corn kernels, scallions, crumbled goat cheese or tofu, fresh tomatoes, well-drained black-eyed peas, a cilantro vinaigrette

- Pork loin or tempeh glazed with apple cider and maple syrup, with steamed green beans and baked winter squash

For dessert:

- With height-of-season, fresh, local strawberries and a drizzle of lavender honey (this, to me, beats strawberry shortcake—no whipped cream needed)

- With peach ice cream topped with raspberries and puréed fresh peaches

- With bananas sautéed in butter and brown sugar, flamed with rum, served with pineapple-coconut sorbet

LESLIE'S NARRAGANSETT BAY-STYLE THICK AND HEARTY JONNYCAKES

SERVES 2 AS THE MAIN ITEM,
4 AS PART OF A SUBSTANTIAL BREAKFAST

A few changes in proportion and technique, and you end up with a wholly different jonnycake: thick, hearty cakes, perfect for starting a cold morning. Just ask Leslie Shaw, who grew up eating them every Sunday. Leslie is a Narragansett Bay native whose family tree is rooted in the soil of 1630s Rhode Island.

Sometimes Leslie's family served the Sunday morning jonnycakes loaded with maple syrup. Sometimes they accompanied them with sausage, bacon, or fried eggs. Leslie's favorite memory: summertime, at the family camp at Lake Champlain. "There, we had jonnycakes with fresh-water perch, breaded in cornmeal and fried."

Leslie's grandfather also had his preferences. "See, he had this trick: He would warm the cornmeal, and brown it just a little, in a skillet on the stove, before he added the boiling water." That, and frying the jonnycakes in bacon drippings, she said, were the secrets (although these days she usually uses oil). "Oh, and you have to get the consistency just right. You don't want the batter so thick you could shape it into patties."

Kenyon's Grist Mill's Johnny Cake Corn Meal is preferred for this recipe. To order, go to www.kenyonsgristmill.com.

1½ cups stone-ground white cornmeal

1 teaspoon salt, or to taste

3 cups boiling water

1 egg

Milk as needed

Bacon drippings and/or oil as needed, enough to reach a depth of ¼ inch in the skillet

Optional accompaniments: fried eggs, bacon or tempeh bacon, sausage or soysage, or perch; pure maple syrup and/or hot milk and butter (in which case the jonnycakes are served in a bowl, the hot milk poured over them)

1. Place the cornmeal in a large saucepan or a deep skillet, setting the pan over medium heat. Toast the dry cornmeal, stirring, until it just starts to brown and smells like popcorn, 3 to 4 minutes. Add the salt.

2. Transfer the cornmeal, in its pan, to the sink. Slowly pour in the boiling water, and use a wooden spoon to stir it in a little at a time, until the meal is moistened. (Working in the sink prevents cornmeal from spraying here and there during this procedure.) Transfer the soaked cornmeal to a bowl, and wash the skillet.

3. Make a well in the cornmeal and drop in the egg. Beat it into the cornmeal mixture with the wooden spoon.

4. Begin adding milk, 1 to 2 tablespoons at a time, until the right consistency is achieved: The batter should be like very soft cookie dough and slump a little when dropped into the hot fat.

5. Place the bacon drippings or oil in a skillet to reach a depth of ¼ inch. Now, begin to heat the skillet over a medium flame.

6. When the fat is good and hot, but not smoking, drop spoonfuls of batter about the size of a biscuit or smaller, and about ¼ inch thick, into it. These thick cakes cook slowly; they will need at least 10 minutes per side. You want both sides to be golden brown and the interior to remain moist and soft.

7. As the cakes are done, set them on paper towels to drain. Serve with the accompaniments of your choice.

VARIATION: SOUTH COUNTY JONNYCAKES

Try this South County version. It is not the same as Leslie's with its extra-crispy exterior, but it's also an almost-classic and mighty good (makes about 18 browned-but-not-fried cakes): Combine 1½ cups stone-ground white cornmeal, pretoasted in a skillet as above; 1½ cups boiling water; ½ teaspoon salt; 3 tablespoons butter; and 2 tablespoons milk. Let the dough stand for 15 minutes, then shape into cakes about 2½ inches round and ¾ inch or so thick. Brown them on a well-oiled skillet over medium heat, allowing about 10 minutes per side (check to make sure they are browning right), and adding a little oil as needed.

RHODE ISLAND SANGFROID

Besides its direct claim to cornbread fame, the small state of Rhode Island, 1,200 square miles of territory, boasts more than 350 miles of coastline. Much of it is rocky and treacherous to sailors, but because of the area's convenience to coastal traffic routes, mariners have always used it anyway, relying on lighthouses to warn them of especially dangerous spots. There were plenty of shipwrecks, even so.

In 1875, a freak March snowmelt moved enormous chunks of ice down the Providence River, destroying the small lighthouse keepers' home and the pier on which it stood at the treacherous Conimicut Point on Narragansett Bay. The lighthouse keeper and his son barely escaped with their lives. The lighthouse itself still stood; but without a keeper, who would tend the light? Who would risk his life, even if to possibly save other lives out at sea?

The intrepid Captain John Weeden, that's who. Former keeper of another lighthouse, he volunteered to row out to Conimicut Light (which, since its pier was now gone, could only be reached by boat). But, as Weeden began tending the light, making repairs, and so on, more upriver ice chunks moved down and destroyed his boat, leaving him trapped.

Then a blizzard set in.

What did Weeden do? Somehow, he built a fire, and he is said to have "calmly prepared himself a breakfast of tea and jonnycakes." Only then did he ring the fog bell, alerting those on the mainland to his plight.

That evening, he was finally rescued.

BLOCK ISLAND JONNYCAKES

SERVES 2 AS THE MAIN ITEM, 4 AS PART OF A MORE SUBSTANTIAL MEAL

Block Island jonnycakes are similar to my friend Leslie's (see page 226): thick and with a touch of sugar as well as egg. If you like, you can toast the cornmeal before adding it to the batter (see step 1 of the aforementioned recipe).

1 cup fine stone-ground white cornmeal, preferably whitecap flint (see Pantry, page 350)

½ teaspoon salt

1 tablespoon sugar

1 cup boiling water

1 egg

2 tablespoons milk

3 to 4 tablespoons butter, melted

1. Combine the cornmeal, salt, and sugar in a medium-size, heat-proof bowl. Pour in the boiling water and stir well with a fork. There will be just enough water to moisten the ingredients. Let stand for 10 minutes.

2. Beat together the egg and milk with a fork in a small bowl, then stir this into the moistened cornmeal along with 1 tablespoon of the butter. This will make a thick dough-like batter; knead it if you like.

3. Heat a cast-iron skillet over medium-high heat with another tablespoon or so of the butter. When it is good and hot, drop the batter by rounded tablespoonfuls and flatten slightly with the back of the spoon onto the skillet, so that you end up with cakes about 2½ inches in diameter and about ¾ inch thick.

4. Reduce the heat. Brown the cakes slowly, patiently allowing 8 to 10 minutes per side. You want them brown and crispy but cooked through, and this takes time. Repeat with the remaining batter and butter, remembering to begin each round with the skillet good and hot, then lowering the heat for the long, slow browning.

"Lovely! See the cloud, the cloud appear!
Lovely! See the rain, the rain draw near!
Who spoke? What talk?
It was the little corn ear
High on the tip of the stalk."

—TRADITIONAL ZUNI CORN GRINDING SONG

JONNYCAKES:
PURELY RHODE ISLAND

For sheer hard-headed contentiousness in matters of cornbread, no one—not even Southerners—matches Rhode Islanders. This tiny state has no fewer than three distinct versions of their form of cornbread, the jonnycake, *and* there is actually a state regulation, passed in 1937 and still on the books, stating that anything known as a *jonnycake* must be made from whitecap flint corn that has been grown and ground within the borders of Rhode Island. And it turns out that H, not A, is the scarlet letter in this case: Any corn cake in the state that does *not* meet these stringent requirements must be spelled with a telltale "h," making it a mere *johnnycake.*

When did all this hoopla begin? A bread very similar to a jonnycake was made by the Narragansett Indians, who shared the recipe with early European settlers. Legend has it that the settlers called the bread "journey-cake" because it kept well and could be carried while traveling. The jonnycake has been enjoyed as an authentic, if argued-about, Rhode Island recipe ever since.

But there is agreement about one thing: the use of whitecap flint corn. Like all corn, it is a great-great-great grandchild of the wild grass first crossed and domesticated by indigenous people in central Mexico. Native Americans developed and bred varieties of corn appropriate to differing climates and microclimates. The Narragansetts' whitecap flint variety, some 500 years old, is particularly well suited to Rhode Island's soil, long winters, and coastal weather.

Today whitecap flint is considered notoriously difficult to raise. It cannot be grown near any other variety of corn. It's a purebred, a corn strain that reproduces by open-air pollination. This means it mutates, losing its unique qualities, on contact with any other strains of corn. And even when grown in contented isolation, whitecap flint corn produces yields that are only half to three quarters that of most corn breeds. Nor does its finickiness end at harvest. Although all flint corns are hard, the whitecap is one of the very hardest varieties, and is thus difficult to grind.

Yet, Rhode Islanders insist that the only true jonnycake meal is made from Rhode Island-grown whitecap flint corn. Over and over you'll hear it: Any other kind of cornmeal *will not do.* (My local real estate appraiser, Leslie Shaw, who was born and raised in Narragansett Bay and whose jonnycake recipe appears on page 226, has hers shipped to Vermont.)

P.S. In HBO's *The Sopranos,* season six offers a plot line where a closeted gay Mafia guy tries to escape his world and hides out in a small New England town. There, he falls in love with a handsome volunteer fireman/short-order cook. This character's specialty? "Jonnycakes," also the episode's title.

SAVORY ONION-SCALLION CORN CAKES

MAKES 12 CAKES; SERVES 2 AS AN
ENTRÉE, 4 AS A SIDE DISH

Almost fritter-like, but not fried, these are an excellent supper side dish and an off-the-charts entrée when served as a Mexi-Stack (see the variation that follows). If you like, substitute ¼ cup masa harina (see Pantry, page 354) for ¼ cup of the cornmeal, to give the cakes a bit of corn tortilla-like flavor and a smoother texture.

- **1 cup unbleached white flour**
- **½ cup stone-ground yellow cornmeal (or ¼ cup each stone-ground yellow cornmeal and masa harina)**
- **1 teaspoon baking powder**
- **½ teaspoon baking soda**
- **½ teaspoon salt**
- **1½ cups buttermilk**
- **1 large egg**
- **1 teaspoon sugar**
- **½ onion, finely chopped**
- **3 scallions, trimmed, white and green portions thinly sliced**
- **Kernels cut from 3 ears of fresh corn (about 1½ cups; see Shuck and Jive, page 49)**
- **½ to 1 green chile, finely minced (with seeds for heat, without for mildness)**
- **Vegetable oil cooking spray**

1. Combine the flour, cornmeal or cornmeal and masa harina, baking powder, baking soda, and salt in a large bowl, stirring well. Set aside.

2. Combine the buttermilk, egg, and sugar in a second, smaller bowl, whisking together. Set aside.

3. Combine the onion, scallion, corn, and chile in a third bowl. Set aside.

4. Using as few strokes as possible, stir the buttermilk mixture into the flour mixture until the two are barely smoothed out. Then stir in all the vegetables.

5. Spray a heavy nonstick skillet with oil, then place over medium-high heat. When it's hot, ladle on the batter; using a ¼-cup ladle will yield about 12 good-size pancakes, which will make 4 Mexi-Stacks, see right (a slightly smaller size is good for these when you're using them as a side dish). Flip the cakes when the tops have plenty of bubbles and the sides look done, 2½ to 3½ minutes. The second side takes 1½ to 2 minutes.

6. Serve hot from the griddle.

VARIATION: MEXI-STACKS

Make the masa variation of the cakes. Open a can (15 ounces) of black beans and pour the contents, juice and all, into a small saucepan. Heat the beans through while you assemble the following on a tray:

- 1 cup grated sharp Cheddar or Monterey Jack cheese
- 2 or 3 ripe Hass avocados, peeled, pitted, and coarsely mashed in a small bowl with the juice of 1/2 lemon and a little salt
- Homemade or bottled salsa
- Dairy or tofu sour cream (optional)
- Chopped fresh cilantro (optional)

Have 4 heated plates ready. As the cakes come off the skillet, lay 1 in the center of each plate. Spoon the hot black beans over them, dividing equally. Sprinkle the grated cheese over the beans, and top with a second cake. Quickly spread the mashed avocado over the second cake layers, and top with a third cake. Spoon the salsa on top, add a dab of sour cream and a snowfall of cilantro, if using, and serve immediately—to many wows.

·M·E·N·U·

CASA DE CORAZON CONFABULATION

**Chicken Soup
with a Splash of Lime**

*

Mexi-Stacks

*

**Corn on the Cob
with Jalapeño Butter**

*

Sliced Brandywine Tomatoes

*

**Salad of Mixed Greens,
Scallions, and Slivered Cabbage,
Dressed with Oil, Fresh Lemon
and Orange Juice, Salt, and
Cracked Black Pepper**

*

**CopperWynd Chocolate
Bread Pudding
(page 332)**

WANDA'S SOFT CORN CREPES

MAKES ABOUT 8 CREPES

In 1982, long before I became Cornbread Cupcake of Concupiscence (I began signing e-mails this way to a select few during the late phases of writing this book), I was introduced to this lovely, delicate crepe by my dear friend and longtime pan pal Jan Brown. She in turn learned it from *her* friend Wanda Ross. The recipe's secret? Masa harina. It makes a crepe that is exceptionally tender and flavorful.

Crepes may be the little black dress of the food world: They can wrap almost anything and make it look and taste good; and they can serve as appetizer, main course, or dessert; for breakfast, lunch, dinner, or a snack, depending on filling and presentation. Wanda's soft corn crepes are divine with anything, but the flavor of the masa harina makes them especially good with Southwestern tastes: A black-bean-and-corn filling with cilantro, the filled crepes dabbed with guacamole on top, is hard to beat. A sauté of onion, summer squash, and chile and bell peppers is another possibility, as is shredded chicken with sautéed mushrooms, a poblano-accented white sauce, green chile sauce, and a little grated cheese.

> 1 egg
> 1 cup milk
> $\frac{1}{2}$ cup masa harina (see Pantry, page 354)
> 1 heaping tablespoon unbleached white flour or 1 level tablespoon cornstarch
> $\frac{1}{2}$ teaspoon salt
> Vegetable oil cooking spray and butter, for the pan

1. Place the egg, milk, masa harina, flour or cornstarch, and salt in a large bowl. Either whisk the dickens out of the batter or pour it into a food processor and buzz until thoroughly combined. Let stand for an hour.

2. Heat a crepe pan—that is, any $5\frac{1}{2}$- to 6-inch skillet with rounded sides, nonstick or cast aluminum or stainless steel. Spray it with oil and place it over medium heat. When the pan is nice and hot, brush it with a bit of butter.

3. Once the butter sizzles and then stops sizzling, pour in just enough batter to coat the pan thinly. Shake the pan to distribute the batter evenly, and cook the crepe until the top side has a slightly duller, drier finish, 30 seconds to 1 minute. Flip the crepe and let it cook for another 30 seconds, then slide the finished crepe onto a plate to await whatever filling you might wish to give it, placing wax paper between crepes. Please note, the second side of a crepe never browns as prettily as the first.

Chapter 9

CRISPED CORNBREADS

Fritters, Hush Puppies, and Other Fried Cakes

Let it be stated, unequivocally and up front, that I am not now and never will be a member of any Frequent Fryers club. But, assuming that you, like me, want to try at least occasional fried cornbread sojourns, I am about to present both the objections to this cooking method *and* strategies for how to overcome them.

Are you ready to take the "Who's Frying Now?" Challenge? Yes? Good. Let's begin.

True or False: Fried foods are high in fat, hence high in calories, hence fattening.
True—if eaten to excess.
Strategy: Eat them only occasionally. Fry at the proper temperature, which is between 360° and 370°F, 365°F being ideal. Use enough oil at this temperature, and the fried foods will absorb comparatively little. Foods fried in oil that's too cool or in not enough oil will wind up absorbing more.

True or False: Fats are unhealthy.
True-ish. This is myth mixed with truth.
Strategy: It's as unhealthy to omit fat from the diet wholly as it is to eat too much of it. That said, there are healthier ways to ingest fat—such as olive oil on your salad or butter on your toast—than by deep-frying or pan-frying foods in fat. Still, you can minimize fried foods' deleterious effects by careful choice of fat and proper cooking method.

True or False: Heated fats are unhealthy.
True, unless you are extremely careful. Oxidation (when foodstuffs deteriorate on exposure to air) is almost unavoidable when oil is heated. Other kinds of deterioration also take place when moisture or escaped particles of food (from whatever's being fried) release into the oil. These changes collectively promote rancidity, whereby oil undergoes changes on the molecular level. Some of those changes have been implicated in heart disease. Finally, even light and heat—such as the heat in a hot kitchen—can cause oil to deteriorate.

Strategy: Again, think "occasional" and "proper heat, 365°F." Choose pure, fresh, refined (purified) vegetable oils with as high a smoke point as possible, preferably stored in the refrigerator after opening (some people even store oils there *before* opening).

The smoke point is the point above which the oil will burst into flame. You want oils with smoke points higher than the magic 365°F. Good choices: corn and peanut (450°), *untoasted* sesame (410°), canola and grapeseed (400°), and safflower (510°). You can combine these if you like; corn-canola and peanut-safflower are both good combinations. In addition, never, *ever* reuse the same fat for frying on two separate occasions, even if you strain and refrigerate the oil. Plus, eat all fried foods as soon as possible post-frying.

True or False: Frying leaves your kitchen curtains smelling like you've fried something for quite some time.
True—but corn fritters, hush puppies, and the like do not seem to linger as long as fried chicken, which hangs out for a month.
Strategy: Open the windows (if feasible). Turn on the exhaust fan (if you have one). And does your kitchen really *need* curtains, anyway? Also, if you use fresh refined oil and you use it only once, the linger factor is fairly minimal; not like when you walk past the funnel-cake stand at a fair and feel your pores and arteries seizing up from the heavy smell of hot, overused (rancid) fat.

True or False: Frying is one of the most dangerous of cooking methods, both because of handling all that hot, slippery fat and because fat easily catches fire. True.

Strategy: To prevent accidents with hot fat spilling, use a heavy skillet or pot or Dutch oven with a flat, absolutely non-tippy bottom, handle turned inward to avoid the risk of bumping into it and knocking the hot fat off the stove. Make sure children, pets, and anything or anyone else who might get underfoot are out of the way. And leave the pot of hot oil at the back of the stove until it cools before moving it.

To prevent fires from fat, keep the deep-fry temperature at 365°F (use a frying thermometer to monitor the temperature), and keep a heavy pot lid handy to clap on the frying pan in case the oil does catch; depriving the fire of oxygen is the most effective way to stop it. If you have salt or baking soda handy, either of those, also amply sprinkled, will douse the flames. But never, ever use water in any attempt to extinguish a fat-based fire; it only spreads it. Always make sure there are several inches of pan above the surface of the fat, too.

Finally, every kitchen should have a small, accessible all-purpose fire extinguisher.

Why, when there are so many drawbacks and hazards, would you *want* to become a member of even the Occasional Fryers club? Well, as the credit card people used to say, membership has its privileges. Straighten out and fry right, and you end up with foods that are moist and cooked (by the trapped internal steam) and light on the inside yet covered with an incomparable brown, crispy-crunchy exterior, rich but not greasy, whatever sugars are present having caramelized nicely. After the particular food undergoes its bubbling, transformative bath in the perfectly-hot-but-not-too-hot fresh oil, the resulting hush puppies, corn fritters, and other fried corn delights are quite addictive. Therein lies their problem as a treat: You inevitably want to eat too many of them.

But life would be less without fresh, height-of-summer corn fritters or spicy-crisp hush puppies, or other such oh-so-munchable fried delights. I say, eat them once in a great while, and then eat as many of them as you want to, with abandon.

FRESH CORN FRITTERS

SERVES 2 AS THE MAIN ITEM,
4 AS A SMALL SIDE DISH

Flat, almost pancake-like cakes made with fresh corn cut from the cob, these, fried in oil, are the type of fritter I grew up eating, only they taste even better now because of the super-sweet, very tender corn on the market today. Because contemporary corn is so sweet, these fritters no longer require even a squib of the maple syrup that used to be de rigueur. Hugely delicious, simple to make—and how convenient it is that at the height of fresh corn season, exactly when you don't want to be heating up the oven, they're cooked on the stovetop.

Caution: Occasionally a kernel of the fresh corn will make a loud pop during the cooking process, as the moisture in the kernel turns to steam on contact with the hot fat. Don't be startled, but do stand back a bit so as not to get splashed with hot oil.

2 eggs
¼ cup milk
Kernels cut from 2 ears of fresh corn, about 1 cup, plus any scrapings of liquid you can get by running a knife blade along the cob (see Shuck and Jive, page 49)

"I love corn fritters. On my birthday, the only day of the year when my mother consulted me about the dinner menu, I chose fritters, a simple concoction of flour, eggs, milk, and corn. She dropped heaping spoonfuls of batter into the deep fat fryer, where they turned golden brown and puffed up to the size of baseballs. . . . I still eat them once or twice a year, soft luxuries of dough and sweet corn . . ."
—SALLIE TISDALE,
The Best Thing I Ever Tasted

2 tablespoons stone-ground white or yellow cornmeal
¼ cup unbleached white flour
1 teaspoon sugar
¼ teaspoon salt
2¼ teaspoons baking powder
Mild vegetable oil, for frying

1. Whisk together the eggs and milk in a large bowl. Stir in the corn and any corn liquid.

2. Combine the cornmeal, flour, sugar, salt, and baking powder in a medium bowl. Sift this dry mixture into the wet mixture and stir together to make a batter that is thick but still can be dropped from a spoon.

3. Pour oil into a heavy cast-iron skillet to reach a depth of ½ inch. Place the skillet over medium-high heat and bring the oil to 365°F, using a thermometer to gauge the temperature (you can also use an electric skillet, which will tell you exactly when you've reached this temp). When the oil has reached 365°, lower the heat slightly to keep the temperature stabilized, and drop the batter by tablespoon-fuls onto the skillet. It will sizzle as it goes into the oil. If the first fritter doesn't sizzle, wait and let the oil get a little hotter before adding more fritters. Don't crowd the skillet, because crowding will bring down the heat; no more than 4 to 6 fritters, not touching, at a time.

4. Let the corn fritters cook until they are golden and crispy on the underneath side, about 3 minutes. When it's time to flip them, the edges will be colored just slightly and will be noticeably firmer, and the top of the fritter will no longer be moist. Reverse the fritters. Allow about 3 minutes more on side two. As they cook, line a tray with paper towels or torn-open brown paper grocery sacks.

5. Place the cooked fritters on the paper towels or brown paper and blot them quickly with another piece of paper. Serve immediately, nice and hot.

·M·E·N·U·

END OF SUMMER SPREAD

Chilled Cucumber-Yogurt Soup with Grapes and Fresh Mint

*

Salad of Mixed Greens with Blanched, Chilled Green Beans, Scallions, Tomatoes, and Mustard Vinaigrette

*

Steamed Fresh Edamame Served in the Pod

*

Fresh Corn Fritters

*

Butternut Squash Purée

*

Fresh Plum Cake, Dusted with Powdered Sugar

*

Decaf Café au Lait

VARIATION: ETHEREAL SOUFFLÉED FRESH CORN FRITTERS

Separate the eggs, adding the yolk in step 1 and the beaten-stiff egg whites (see Beating Egg Whites, pages 186–187) at the end of step 2, folding them in ever so gently.

CORN FRITTER STORY #1

Okay, this story goes way, way back. I was eighteen, living in Eureka Springs, Arkansas, sharing a tiny house with my then best friend Maren, also eighteen. I was a high-school dropout, she a college dropout, and we both thought we were reasonably grown-up. *As if.*

Each week we walked the mile or so into town to take a Wednesday night yoga class with a sweet guy named Toby. Very serious, very . . . self-consciously spiritual.

The class was vigorous, and long, so we would usually wind up eating a very early dinner before we walked in. One particular summer night our pre-yoga feast was a supper of corn fritters.

Wouldn't you know that was the evening poor Toby, explaining why it was necessary to really focus on your poses while you were in class, used the unfortunate phrase, "After all, you don't want to fritter away your time here."

Maren and I, friends since the fourth grade, looked at each other from our respective mats and simultaneously burst into a storm of giggles, which became laughs, which became gigantic snorting guffaws, disrupting the entire class. Had we still been in school, it would have gotten us sent to the principal's office or at the very least merited a curt "Would you two mind sharing what's so funny with the rest of the class?"

Toby was too kind to expel us. We explained, apologetically, but still wiping away the tears of laughter. The class (everyone else was a good five or ten years older than Maren and me) laughed politely, but didn't really get it. We all went back to our asanas, Maren and I scrupulously avoiding eye contact, like the sophisticated, mature eighteen-year-olds we were.

Indonesian-Style Corn and Eggplant Fritters

SERVES 6 TO 8 AS AN APPETIZER
OR SIDE DISH

I've tinkered over the years with this luscious recipe adapted from *Indonesian Food and Cookery*, a much reincarnated cookbook first published in 1976 by Sri Owen, one of the world's most indefatigable, knowledgeable, but gentle authorities on Asian cooking. I remember copying Sri's version onto a card from a library long ago—a card I managed to keep, much-splattered, all these years. If you like eggplant, spicy flavors, and sweet corn, and can imagine how good they might be together, you'll know why I copied it out. Sweet, savory, chile-hot, semi-crisp from the frying . . . just addictive. To me, they are made to serve with an icy lemon or lime drink, alcoholic or not, and a sweet-hot salsa, like the one that follows.

**1 medium eggplant, peeled and cut
   in ¹⁄₂-inch dice**

Salt

2 teaspoons toasted sesame oil

**2 tablespoons peanut oil, plus extra
   for frying**

3 to 4 shallots, finely chopped

**¹⁄₂ to 1 teaspoon cayenne or other
   red chile powder, to taste**

**4 large garlic cloves, halved lengthwise
   and sliced**

1 teaspoon ground coriander

**Kernels cut from 4 ears of fresh corn,
   about 2 cups (see Shuck and Jive,
   page 49)**

1 tablespoon cornstarch

**1 tablespoon stone-ground yellow
   cornmeal**

1 egg

3 tablespoons unbleached white flour

1 teaspoon baking powder

¹⁄₂ teaspoon salt

**1 bunch of scallions, white and
   2 inches of green, finely minced**

Chopped fresh cilantro, for serving

**Pineapple-Ginger Salsa (recipe
   follows) or Thai sweet chile sauce,
   for serving (optional)**

1. Toss the eggplant with about 1 tablespoon salt and set aside in a colander for about 1 hour. Then, quickly rinse the salted eggplant with cold water and drain thoroughly. Squeeze the eggplant firmly with your hands to get as much liquid out of it as possible; you want it as dry as you can get it.

2. Select a large, heavy skillet with a tight-fitting cover. Set the skillet over medium-high heat with the toasted sesame oil and 2 tablespoons of the peanut oil. When the oil and skillet are good and hot, lower the heat slightly and add the shallots and cayenne, stirring nonstop for about a minute. Add the garlic and stir-fry for another minute. Add the reserved eggplant, stir-fry for another minute, then stir in the coriander, lower the heat a bit more, and cover the pot tightly. Let the eggplant steam in its own juices until tender, 3 to 4 minutes.

3. Remove the skillet from the heat and scrape the eggplant into a large dish, the better to cool quickly. (Wash the skillet while you're at it— you'll need it again shortly.)

4. As the eggplant cools, prepare the corn batter by placing the fresh corn, cornstarch, cornmeal, and egg in a food processor. Pulse-chop quickly to combine the ingredients and make a very textured semi-purée of the corn. Turn this mixture into a bowl. Sift the flour, baking powder, and salt over it.

5. Stir in the cooled eggplant and the scallions.

6. Pour peanut oil into the skillet to reach a depth of ½ inch. Set the skillet over medium-high heat. When the oil is hot enough to fry in (365°F on a thermometer, or test with a little drop of the batter, which should sizzle immediately and start to brown), drop the batter in by tablespoonfuls, flattening the fritters slightly with a spatula. Don't overfill the

skillet; no more than 4 to 6 fritters, not touching, at a time. Lower the heat to medium and let the fritters cook until golden brown, about 3 minutes for the first side and slightly less for the second side. Drain well on paper towels and serve, hot or at room temperature, with a scatter of chopped cilantro over the fritters and pineapple-ginger salsa or Thai sweet chile sauce on the side, if desired.

·M·E·N·U·

COOL-BY-THE-POOL AUGUST EVENING

Margaritas or Fresh Limeade with Ginger

✳

Indonesian-Style Corn and Eggplant Fritters

✳

Pineapple-Ginger Salsa and Thai Sweet Chile Sauce

✳

Chilled Short-Grain Brown Rice Salad with Roasted Tofu, Scallions, Tamari, and Minced Peanuts

✳

Coconut Sorbet with Chilled Canned Lychee Nuts, Drizzled with Lychee Syrup

Pineapple-Ginger Salsa

MAKES 2 TO 2½ CUPS, DEPENDING ON THE SIZE OF THE PINEAPPLE

An intriguing, refreshing salsa, just perfect with the corn-eggplant fritters. Find the ripest, sweetest fresh pineapple you can. There's an easy way to tell: Just sniff the pineapples, looking for one that's intoxicatingly fragrant.

P.S. This recipe calls for half a pineapple. Save the other half for a fresh pineapple upside-down cake.

Double P.S. When peaches are at their height, substitute 2 or 3 of them, ripe and preferably peeled, for the pineapple in this recipe.

Another pleasant variation is to use fresh spearmint either instead of, or in addition to, the cilantro.

- ½ medium-size fresh, very ripe pineapple, top and skin removed and eyes dug out, finely chopped
- ½ onion, very finely chopped
- 1 red bell pepper, cored, seeded, and finely diced
- 1 to 2 jalapeños, chopped (with seeds for heat, without for mildness)
- ½ teaspoon salt

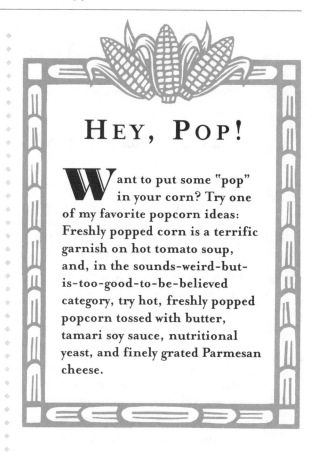

HEY, POP!

Want to put some "pop" in your corn? Try one of my favorite popcorn ideas: Freshly popped corn is a terrific garnish on hot tomato soup, and, in the sounds-weird-but-is-too-good-to-be-believed category, try hot, freshly popped popcorn tossed with butter, tamari soy sauce, nutritional yeast, and finely grated Parmesan cheese.

- Juice of 1 lime
- 1 to 2 teaspoons honey
- 2 teaspoons finely minced peeled fresh, tender gingerroot
- 1 to 2 tablespoons finely chopped fresh cilantro and/or spearmint

Toss all the ingredients in a large bowl, adding the jalapeños to taste. Serve, or refrigerate, covered, for up to 2 days.

How Extremely Sweet It Is

If you're old enough, you might recall the mythology surrounding fresh corn: that the pot of water must be boiling before you run to the garden, pluck the corn, run back to the kitchen, shuck it, and fling it into the pot—quickly, while it was still very sweet. This modus operandi was necessary, and did truly work, with the corn varieties of yesteryear. That just-picked, immediately boiled corn *was* extraordinarily sweet, on another order entirely from the regular supermarket or even the farmstand corn of that era.

Why did this procedure make such a shocking flavor difference to the corn of yesterday, but not today? Well, back then, the sugar in traditional fresh corn began to convert to starch almost instantly after picking. This traditional sweet corn has about 14 percent sugar, more or less what an apple or pear has. But it quickly—within a couple of hours of picking—becomes barely sweet at all.

This is no longer the case. Agriculturalists have tinkered with corn (which is, by the way, probably the single plant food most tinkered with by humans, sometimes lovingly and respectfully, as the natives of North and South America did it, and at other times more sinisterly, as with the large commercial breeders of closed hybrid corn or corn with its own built-in pesticides). By breeding a recessive gene that blocks the natural sugar-to-starch transition, seed developers have now made available "super-sweet" corn varieties, in which the sugars change only very slowly, if at all, to starch. These weigh in at 36 percent sucrose, more than double the traditional types.

If you buy fresh corn on the cob nowadays, the odds are very good that you are buying one of the super-sweets.

CHILE-CORN FRITTERS

SERVES 4

Chile-hot flavors move from Southeast Asia back home to the Southwest. Serve this delish fritter alongside black beans cooked in beer, with salsa or pico de gallo, sliced avocado, and a green salad with cilantro dressing; coffee ice cream with Kahlúa for dessert.

Mild vegetable oil

½ red bell pepper, cored, seeded, and diced

½ yellow bell pepper, cored, seeded, and diced

1 poblano pepper, diced (with seeds for a little heat, without for more mildness)

½ onion, minced

1 tablespoon mild red chile powder

2 cups corn kernels, cut from about 4 ears of fresh corn (see Shuck and Jive, page 49)

2 tablespoons vegetable stock, plus extra as needed

¾ cup unbleached white flour

¼ cup yellow or white masa harina (see Pantry, page 354)

½ teaspoon baking powder

¼ teaspoon salt

1 teaspoon sugar

1 egg

½ cup milk, plus extra as needed

1 tablespoon butter, melted

1. First, precook the vegetables: Add 1 tablespoon of the vegetable oil to a large skillet and heat over medium-high heat. Add the peppers and onion and sauté, stirring, until the vegetables soften slightly, 3 to 4 minutes. Sprinkle with the chile powder and sauté, stirring, for 1 minute more. Stir in the corn, then scrape the corn mixture into a small bowl to cool. Deglaze the skillet with the 2 tablespoons of vegetable stock and add it, too, to the corn mixture.

2. Now, prepare the batter. Combine the flour, masa harina, baking powder, salt, and sugar in a large bowl, stirring all together well. Mix together the egg, milk, and butter in a separate bowl. Blend the egg mixture into the flour mixture with a few strokes, then stir in the vegetable mixture until it is just combined and the flour is thoroughly moistened; add a tablespoon or 2 more milk or vegetable stock if needed to achieve this.

3. Pour vegetable oil into the skillet to reach a depth of ½ inch. Place the skillet over medium-high heat. When the oil is hot enough to fry in (365°F on thermometer, or test with a little drop of batter, which should sizzle immediately and start to brown), drop the batter in by tablespoonfuls. Don't overfill the skillet; no

CORN FRITTER STORY #2

At age nineteen, I worked for a season at the kitchen of the Crescent (no relation) Hotel, a venerable if unlikely castle of stone built in the 1880s atop East Mountain in Eureka Springs, Arkansas. In those days, before its restoration, the hotel catered to bus tours: We might have fifty people walk in at one time for lunch, sometimes without reservations. We fed them at a buffet line, and developed strategies to keep pretty good food fresh and hot and coming out, no matter what.

One of the best pull-it-out-of-a-hat dishes for the buffet line was corn fritters. We had a huge commercial griddle. I'd skim it with oil, get it very hot, and throw together essentially a pancake batter with a lot of thawed frozen corn tossed in. I'd ladle out row upon row of evenly spaced fritters, and by the time I ladled out the last,

the first would be ready to be flipped over. By the time they were all turned, I was ready to go back to the first, blot them with paper towels, and take them out to the buffet. I must have done forty or fifty at a time, maybe more. They were cute little things, tasty and well received.

One day I was transferring a fresh batch from tray to buffet table when a just-past-middle-aged lady, on a bus tour from I think Ohio, asked me, "Excuse me, dear, but what are those?"

"Corn fritters, m'am," I replied (having lived in the South long enough to have my m'ams down pat). "Freshly made."

"Oh, how *nice*!" exclaimed the lady. With an expression of wonderment she turned to her husband and said, "Look, Henry, *corn critters*!"

more than 4 to 6 fritters at a time, and they shouldn't touch. Lower the heat slightly and cook the fritters until golden brown, about 3 minutes on the first side and slightly less for the second side. Drain well on paper towels and serve, hot or at room temperature.

BASIC DOWN-HOME HUSH PUPPIES

MAKES 15 TO 20 (SERVES 4 TO 5)

This is the traditional hush puppy, the one most people who grew up eating hush puppies recall happily. Some grandmas grated the onion, some minced it; some, these days, pulse-chop it in the processor. Some wouldn't think of eating hush puppies without ketchup, while others enjoy them sprinkled with a bit of coarse salt and malt vinegar (à la British fish-and-chips). Still others are partisans of butter and honey—yes, even with the onions.

1²⁄₃ cups stone-ground cornmeal, preferably white
¼ cup unbleached white flour
2 teaspoons baking powder
½ teaspoon baking soda
½ to 1½ teaspoons sugar
½ teaspoon freshly ground black pepper (optional, but good)
2 eggs
1 cup buttermilk
½ medium onion, very finely minced
Mild vegetable oil, for frying

1. If you don't intend to serve the hush puppies virtually straight from the stove, preheat the oven to 200°F.

2. Combine the dry ingredients thoroughly in a medium bowl.

3. Beat together the eggs and buttermilk in a small bowl. Stir this into the dry ingredients to make a batter thick enough to mound on the end of a teaspoon. Stir in the onion. As is almost always the case with cornbreads, don't overbeat the batter or you'll toughen the hush puppies.

4. Pour the oil into a large skillet to reach a depth of 1 to 1½ inches, depending on the depth of your skillet. Place the skillet over medium-high heat. When the oil is hot enough to fry in (365°F on a thermometer, or test with a drop of batter, which should sizzle immediately and start to brown), drop the batter in by small rounded teaspoonfuls, using a second teaspoon to scrape off the batter into the fat. Working in batches, fry 5 or 6 hush puppies at a time, making sure not to overcrowd the skillet. Fry until the balls are golden brown on their underneath sides, 45 seconds to 1 minute. Then turn them with a slotted spoon and continue cooking until the other side is nice and golden, too, 30 to 40 seconds more.

5. Either transfer to a serving dish, blot with paper towels, and serve posthaste, or line a baking sheet with paper towels (or, traditionally, torn-open brown paper grocery sacks) and scoop the finished hush puppies from the fat onto the paper-lined sheet. Transfer them to the preheated oven to keep them warm, and begin frying the next batch.

VARIATIONS:
SWEET MILK HUSH PUPPIES

A milk batter has slightly less tang and tenderness than one made with buttermilk. Use milk to replace the buttermilk, omit the baking soda, and use 1 level tablespoon of baking powder to leaven the batter.

TEXAS HUSH PUPPIES

Use stone-ground yellow cornmeal instead of white. Add a teaspoon of garlic powder or (infinitely better in my view) 3 or 4 pressed garlic cloves. Omit the black pepper, but add 1 to 2 finely minced fresh or pickled jalapeño peppers (leaving in the seeds, if you wish, for extra kick). If you like, add a little minced parsley or cilantro. And—I am told this is the secret—fry the hush puppies in the same oil used for frying the fish you're serving them with.

QUICKIE GARDEN HUSH PUPPIES

Substitute 2 cups minus 2 tablespoons of self-rising cornmeal (White Lily is the preferred brand) for the flour, cornmeal, baking powder, baking soda, and salt. Use milk or water in place of the buttermilk, adding a few tablespoons of finely minced tomatoes to the liquid, to equal the 1 cup total. Use 2 or 3 finely chopped scallions instead of the regular onion.

PEDIGREED HUSH PUPPIES

As history has it, the little rounds of fried cornbread now known as hush puppies originated southwest of Tallahassee, Florida, in the fishing village of Apalachicola (the bay of which is famed for its oysters). The tale (tail?) goes that a dough made up with what was at hand (including the seasoned cornmeal-flour mix in which the just-caught fish had been breaded) was tossed in a skillet full of fat over the campfire, fried, and then tossed to the yapping dogs to quiet them. Hence the name. Although this explanation is only a little more plausible than the legend behind anadama bread (see page 165), hush puppies are now an accepted accompaniment to fried fish all over the South, and are also popular at barbecues.

The moistening liquid in the batter is most commonly buttermilk. But it's often swapped out for other, sometimes surprising, agents, such as beer, ketchup, tomato juice, sweet milk, or salsa—any or all of which may be mixed with a little mayonnaise. And, as America's taste for all things *caliente* has increased, jalapeños and other green chiles, cayenne and Tabasco or similar hot sauces, garlic, and ever more freshly ground black pepper have found their way into the hush puppies. Onions, finely chopped, are almost universally used in hush puppies, but they may be scallions, especially the green part (especially in Louisiana); yellow onions (most common); red onions (occasionally); or even onion powder (not in my kitchen, ever, however).

And back in apocryphal Apalachicola? It hosts an annual Florida Seafood Festival, at which hundreds of pounds of mullet, shrimp, oysters, scallops, and other fish and seafood are fried in enormous vats—right alongside the hush puppies.

South Louisiana-Style Hush Puppies

MAKES 12 TO 15 (SERVES 4 TO 5)

This repeats several of the elements of the Basic Down-Home Hush Puppies (page 247) but combines them in a method just different enough to warrant its own recipe. If you've done any Cajun cooking, you'll recognize the trinity of onion, celery, and green bell pepper that is a backbone of this region's cuisine, but any native will tell you it's the green onion tops that make this distinctly South Louisianan. You'll find some variation on this theme in every community cookbook of the area.

1 cup stone-ground cornmeal, preferably yellow
1 teaspoon baking powder
¾ teaspoon salt
1 teaspoon sugar
1 cup unbleached white flour
1 egg
¾ cup milk
⅛ teaspoon cayenne pepper
¼ to ½ cup finely chopped scallions, green tops only
1 tablespoon grated white onion
1 tablespoon very finely minced celery
1 tablespoon very finely minced green bell pepper
2 teaspoons very finely minced fresh flat-leaf parsley
Mild vegetable oil, for frying

1. Sift the cornmeal, baking powder, salt, sugar, and flour into a large bowl.

2. Separately, beat the egg and milk together in a small bowl, and add this to the cornmeal mixture, stirring until just combined. With a few more stirs add, all at once, the cayenne, scallions, white onion, celery, green pepper, and parsley, stirring until just blended.

3. Pour the oil into a large skillet to reach a depth of 1 to 1½ inches, depending on the depth of your skillet. Place the skillet over medium-high heat. When the oil is hot enough to fry in (365°F on a thermometer, or test with a drop of batter, which should sizzle immediately and start to brown), drop the batter in by rounded teaspoonfuls, using a second teaspoon to scrape off the batter into the fat. Fry 5 or 6 hush puppies at a time, but don't overcrowd the pan. Work in batches. Fry until the balls are golden brown underneath, 45 seconds to 1 minute. Turn them with a slotted spoon and continue cooking until the second side is also golden, in 40 to 50 seconds more.

4. Remove the puppies from the skillet, blot well with paper towels, and serve as soon as possible.

Howlin' Hush Puppies

MAKES 15 TO 18 (SERVES 5 TO 6)

At the National Cornbread Festival, held annually in South Pittsburg, Tennessee, you can taste a plateful of different cornbreads at Cornbread Alley, each type made by a different local church, youth group, or nonprofit organization. When I saw these at the festival in 2003, I didn't expect to like them—*ketchup* in the batter?—but I did. In fact, they are probably my favorite hush puppies. Here's my version.

2 cups stone-ground white cornmeal

1 tablespoon sugar

¾ teaspoon baking soda

**2 teaspoons hot sauce,
    such as Tabasco**

1 tablespoon finely minced onion

¼ cup ketchup

**½ cup pickled jalapeño slices,
    well drained and finely chopped**

1 cup buttermilk

About ¼ cup cold water

Mild vegetable oil, for frying

1. Combine the cornmeal, sugar, and baking soda in a medium bowl (sift in the baking soda if it's at all lumpy). Whisk together well.

2. Whisk together the hot sauce, onion, ketchup, jalapeño, and buttermilk in a separate bowl, beating until frothy.

3. Add the hot sauce mixture to the flour mixture all at once with a couple of stirs, and then drizzle in the water, a tablespoon or so at a time, until the batter is thick enough to scrape from one teaspoon with another, but not too wet.

4. Pour the oil into a large skillet to reach a depth of 1 to 1½ inches, depending on the depth of your skillet. Place the skillet over medium-high heat. When the oil is hot enough to fry in (365°F on a thermometer, or test with a drop of batter, which should sizzle immediately and start to brown), drop the batter in by teaspoonfuls, frying several at a time, not overcrowding the pan. Fry until the balls are golden brown underneath, 45 seconds to 1 minute. Then turn them with a slotted spoon, and continue cooking until the second side is golden, too, 40 to 50 seconds more.

5. Remove from the skillet, blot well with paper towels, and serve right away.

ONCE A PONE A TIME

Corn pone is an Anglicization of two Native American words: the Narragansett *suppawn* and the Algonquian *appone*. It is the somewhat bulkier East Coast equivalent of Southwestern tortillas. Cornmeal was mixed with water and salt, making a local staple bread in the areas where the British colonists first decamped, now called New England. Northeastern tribes did also employ the magic of the alkalinizing process called nixtamalization (see page 355), but the resulting soaked and hulled kernels, which we call hominy and which in that neck of the woods was called samp, was mostly water-cooked (hot cereal–style), not baked as bread. Pone quickly spread south once the colonists arrived, and it became the primary foodstuff for feeding slaves because corn grew so well and had so abundant a yield, while wheat had to be imported and

hence was an expensive luxury food. In *The African-American Kitchen*, Angela Shelf Medearis cites a recipe she identifies as "from a slave narrative."

> *Light a fire from whatever brush or twigs there may be. On the greased blade of your hoe, mix meal and water until it is thick enough to fry. Add salt, if you remembered to bring any. Lean the hoe into the fire until the top side of the bread bubbles. Flip it and brown the other side.*

Now you know why one of the many names for these flat breads made from cornmeal is hoecakes.

These cornbreads were also known as ash cakes (some Native Americans and slaves baked them directly in the fire's ashes, sometimes wrapped in leaves before-hand, sometimes not). The possible cooking methods for them were many; they were sometimes, if one is to believe the old recipes, baked on a board which was "put . . . before the fire."

Easier said than done, according to corn documentarian Betty Fussell, who attempted to recreate such bread from the directions in the 1847 *Carolina Housewife* (authored by "A Lady of Charleston"). After a series of unsuccessful tries left her "choked with smoke, front red with heat and back blue with cold and stiff from bending," Fussell says she had "new respect for [her] ancestral grandmothers."

If only Fussell had been able to hang out with Phillis, the Senegambian cook of Thomas J. Hazard's grandfather, whom the younger Hazard described in *The Jonny-Cake Letters I-XII* (1880). Hazard describes how Phillis sifted the cornmeal, scalded it with boiling water, kneaded it in a wooden tray, at last placing the cake on a board and setting it "upright on the hearth before a bright, hard-green-wood fire." She then used a heart-shaped flatiron to hold the board perpendicular to the fire "until the main part of the cake was sufficiently baked."

Could this much hassle possibly have been worth it? According to Hazard, yes. For "Such . . . was the process of making and baking the best article of farinaceous food that was ever partaken of by mortal man."

Jonnycake, ash cake, hoecake, pone—as my late father used to say, "No matter how you slice it, it's still baloney." Let us apply the same logic here: No matter how you bake it, it's still pone.

Today we get to a far more delicious cornbread far more simply by baking it in an oven instead of using ashes, a hoe, or an open fire. But a look back shows how easy we have it, and breeds respect for those who thrived, and baked, and fed themselves under much harsher conditions.

Ronni's Fried Hot Water Pan Cornbread

MAKES ABOUT 12 CORN PONES
(SERVES 4 TO 6)

This is from my friend Ronni Lundy, who, as I noted on page 21, once told me that she could write a cornbread book, too, but it would only be one page long. Come on now, Ronni, with these fried pones, wouldn't it be at least *two* pages?

Like Ronni's skillet cornbread, this has a pure, unadulterated goodness. Unlike her cornbread, it does contain some flour—all of 4 teaspoons. No sugar, though. As Ronni explains, "The boiling water steams the meal in the corn pones, giving them a delicious creamy texture but a fresh, popcorn-like taste. They should be eaten while hot, but it's a good idea to break the first ones open and let the steam escape before taking a bite."

2 cups stone-ground white cornmeal

1 teaspoon salt

1 tablespoon plus 1 teaspoon unbleached white flour

About 2 cups boiling water

Mild vegetable oil, for frying

1. Whisk the cornmeal, salt, and flour together in a large heat-proof bowl. Then whisk in the boiling water, mixing completely. Ronni notes, "The 2-cup measure is approximate. Some meal may require more, some a little less. You want the mixture to be thoroughly moistened and firm enough to hold together, but you don't want it soupy like a batter."

2. Pour the oil into a large skillet to reach a depth of 1 to 1½ inches, depending on the depth of your skillet. Place the skillet over medium-high heat and let the oil heat to 365°F (test with a thermometer, or drop in a bit of pone mixture, which should sizzle immediately and start to brown).

3. Working in batches, heap a spoonful of the pone mixture into your hand and form it into a cake about 3½ inches long, 2 inches wide, and ¾ inch thick in the middle. The batter will be hot, so you might want to chill your hands in ice water beforehand (be sure to dry them thoroughly because any drops that get in the hot oil can splatter back at you). Carefully lay each pone into the hot oil with your fingers or with a spatula (safer, but messier). Make enough pones to fill the pan without crowding. If the pones touch, they're likely to fall apart.

4. Fry until golden on the bottom, 2 to 3 minutes, then flip them over and cook until the other side is golden, 1 minute more. Lift them out of the oil with a slotted spatula and put them on paper towels to drain, blotting well. Repeat with remaining pone mixture.

Chapter 10

DÉJÀ FOOD

or Why You Should Always Make a Double Batch

Leftover cornbread? Today most people make this once-daily American staple from scratch so rarely (if at all) that when they do, they devour it ravenously and joyfully, down to the last crumb, so that the very idea of cornbread leftovers is sacrilegious, an oxymoron, or both. But listen up. As you ought to know by this stage in our culinary travels, I think being mostly cornbread-less is a sad state of affairs, one I am personally out to change. If you agree, the day will come when you'll have leftover cornbread . . . and you will be glad you do.

> **"You've got to continue to grow, or you're just like last night's cornbread—stale and dry."**
>
> —Loretta Lynn

I am a big proponent of the cook-once-for-several-meals school. Intentional cornbread planned-overs allow you to use time-sparing strategies (which not only gets you better meals on the table more quickly and healthfully than you might imagine possible, but leaves you with a quietly smug, money-in-the-bank, I'm-prepared-for-anything feeling). I hope this chapter gives you many reasons why, if you're baking one skillet or pan's worth of cornbread, you might as well make two, in anticipation of its possible rebirths. These reincarnations cover every meal, and just about every course in every meal.

I am an expert on the uses of leftover cornbread. For six of the eighteen years my late husband, Ned, and I owned and ran Dairy Hollow House, our inn in Eureka Springs, Arkansas, we also ran the inn's restaurant, where cornbread occupied a prominent place in our breadbaskets (it's the one on page 12). It also occupied a prominent place in the hearts of our guests and, indeed, in our own lives and identities. At the restaurant we prided

ourselves on never running out of cornbread (freshly baked that evening just before serving time, of course). And if it ever looked like there was the faintest possibility that we might run out—if, let us say, a particular family was in such ecstasies over it that they kept sending their breadbasket back for more, and more—why, cornbread is so quick to put together, I could always whomp another skillet or two's worth into the oven, and have hot, fresh-baked cornbread out to the guests by the time they had finished their starter and/or salad and were ready for soup and bread.

But this abundance inevitably meant leftovers. What to do with them?

Once Made, Twice Blessed

Canny, thrifty, close-to-the-edge people have often made wise and delicious use of leftover breadstuffs, even (sometimes especially) stale breadstuffs. I've always admired this spirit, not just because waste bothers me but because it's a creative and transformative response. Stale bread? Whoosh! French toast! "Use it up, wear it out; make it do, or do without" is a phrase an Arkansas native once quoted to me, and to me, this is an act not just of thrift, but of imagination and invention. And the use of bread, staff of life, sacred in some contexts, might serve as a textbook illustration of the heights to which human beings soar, sometimes just because they have to.

Stale bread is an ingredient in many of the world's great home-style dishes. Much of Western Europe—Spain, Italy, France—makes glorious soup of little more than bread, garlic, olive oil, and water. Other soups—vegetable or bean or meat or poultry—are thickened by crumbs of stale bread, or are served over or under thick slices of it. Think of fragrant gratinéed onion soup, its hot darkness floating and softening the raft of once-hard cheese-covered bread atop it, or *pappa al pomodoro*, bread-based soup in which tomatoes, olive oil, and other fresh and good things transmute stale to succulent. Then there's the surprising deliciousness of *panzanella* salad, in which tomatoes and olive oil meet again, along with garlic, sweet onion, and a sparkle of vinegar, to reincarnate days-old bread. Jews the world over transform stale matzo into delectable matzo brei, while Germans, Hungarians, and Czechs all have bread-based dumplings. Indeed every bread-eating culture on our bright spinning globe "extends" expensive ground-meat dishes with bread, uses bread-crumb toppings on casseroles, and makes stuffings or dressings of stale bread, whether it be perfumed with sage and stuffed inside a Thanksgiving turkey or cunningly lodged in a mushroom cap, artichoke half, or tomato.

Can we do less with America's native bread? Back in the days when zip-top bag after zip-top bag was filled with the odd wedge or two or three remaining even after inn guests and then staff had partaken, I would look at that bounty and be filled with a sense of challenge. For I thought then, as I do now, that cornbread itself is a national treasure, to be respected, enjoyed, savored, appreciated . . . and that leftover cornbread, too, could and should be held in high esteem and put to good use.

In this chapter you'll find soups, salads, stuffings, dressings, and many more ways to do just that. And don't forget to see chapter 12, on Sweet Somethings, for an extra helping.

CORNBREAD AND BUTTERMILK

SERVES 1

This simplest of leftover cornbread preparations is served in a tall glass or a bowl and is eaten with a spoon. It's a traditional light supper in the American South that is oh so much more satisfying than it sounds. Please note that for this simple preparation to work you *must*, I repeat *must*, use an all-cornmeal cornbread, either wholly unsweetened or just barely sweet. Many of the Southern cornbreads (pages 7–33) fit the bill. But pass on using sweet cornbreads or cornbreads that contain flour, otherwise you will not understand the magic of this dish nor grasp why it has pleased generations of Southerners, including my friend George West's late father, who now eats, always, at the table of George's memory.

1 slice stale cornbread
1 to 2 cups buttermilk
1 scallion, trimmed (optional)

1. Crumble the stale cornbread into a single-serving bowl or a glass.

2. Pour the buttermilk to taste over the cornbread. Let it sit, for a minute or two, no more.

3. Eat, using a spoon (an iced-tea spoon if using a tall glass), with the scallion on the side. Take little nibbles of scallion, bite by bite, along with your cornbread.

> "And he gave it for his opinion, that whoever could make two ears of corn, or two blades of grass, to grow upon a spot of ground where only one grew before, would deserve better of mankind, and do more essential service to his country, than the whole race of politicians put together."
>
> —JONATHAN SWIFT, *Gulliver's Travels*

KENTUCKY CORN DODGERS

SERVES 2 AS THE MAIN DISH,
4 AS PART OF A SUBSTANTIAL BREAKFAST

Nothing went to waste in the thrifty mountain kitchens of the Ozarks and the Appalachians, least of all perfectly good cornbread crumbs. These would often find their way into some form of pan-fried cakes, usually called corn dodgers. To my Missouri-born friend Blake Clark, who recalls his childhood as one of "adventuring in woods that were a mixture of Twain's woods and Burroughs's jungles," these were even better than the original cornbread. Since you needed "a good amount of cornbread left over from the night before," Blake remembers, "everyone ate as little cornbread as they could, well knowing that the less they ate now, the more for dodgers in the morning."

Blake's Missouri mama's dodgers were simple: cornbread crumbs soaked in milk and fried in patties. But my friend Ronni's mama's Kentucky dodgers were a bit more elaborate, more of a pancake batter with cornbread crumbs stirred in. Here's my adaptation of Ronni's version.

The best cornbreads to use here are simple, unsweetened Southern cornbreads, such as Ronni's Appalachian (page 21), Truman Capote's Family's (page 13), or White River (page 25).

1 cup fine, dry cornbread crumbs

1 cup milk

1 cup unbleached white flour

1 teaspoon salt

¾ teaspoon baking powder

¼ teaspoon baking soda

1 to 2 tablespoons brown sugar

2 teaspoons mild vegetable oil, plus extra as needed

1 cup buttermilk

2 eggs

Vegetable oil cooking spray (optional)

Optional accompaniments: butter or Better (page 346), pure maple syrup, sliced fruit, and/or Warm Maple-Apple Sauté (page 206)

1. Combine the cornbread crumbs and milk in a small bowl. Cover and let soak, refrigerated, for at least 1 hour or as long as overnight.

2. When ready to fix your dodgers, sift together the flour, salt, baking powder, and baking soda in a medium bowl.

3. Whisk together the brown sugar, 2 teaspoons oil, buttermilk, and eggs in a medium bowl. Stir in the flour mixture and the soaked cornbread crumbs.

4. Heat a large skillet over medium heat. If it's a well-seasoned cast-iron skillet, all you need by way of greasing it is a good spritz of cooking oil spray or a few drops of oil. If it's nonstick, you can do without any fat at all. When the skillet is good and hot, drop in small spoonfuls of batter, about 3 inches in diameter. Cook, turning once when bubbles appear around the dodgers' edges. Serve them straight from the griddle, with the accompaniments of your choice.

CORNBREAD FRITTATA-PANCAKE

SERVES 2 AS THE MAIN ITEM, 4 AS A SIDE DISH

This makes one large, thick cake—something like a substantial, open-face, flipped-over omelet, nice and brown on both sides. It's delicious finished with or without cheese and any of a variety of sauces. If you choose to prepare one of the variations that follow, have the fixings ready before you begin the frittata. Hearty enough for lunch (with salad) or supper (with soup and salad, cooked greens, or a mixed vegetable stir-fry), it's also very quick, assuming you have leftover cornbread.

> **4 eggs**
> **¼ cup milk**
> **Salt and freshly ground black pepper**
> **1 to 1½ cups any style crumbled cornbread, preferably quite stale**
> **Vegetable oil cooking spray**
> **About 1 tablespoon butter or olive oil**
> **½ to ¾ cup (2 to 3 ounces) grated cheese of your choice (optional)**

1. Whisk together the eggs, milk, and salt and pepper to taste in a medium bowl. Stir in the cornbread crumbs.

2. Spray a large, heavy pan, preferably a sauté pan with curved sides, with oil and place the pan over medium-high heat. When the pan is good and hot, add the butter or olive oil.

3. When the butter melts, sizzles, and then stops sizzling, or when the olive oil thins, scrape in the egg-cornbread mixture. It should sizzle as it goes in. Lower the heat to medium.

4. Let the frittata cook uncovered, without stirring, for 5 to 8 minutes. When it's partially set but still wet on top, you may lift the edges with a spatula and tip the pan slightly to allow any uncooked egg to flow in that direction, as you would with an omelet. You'll also want to peek underneath to see how well it's browning.

5. When the frittata is golden brown underneath and slightly moist but no longer wet on top, and is fairly solid, screw up your courage, take your spatula, and flip the whole thing over, so the other side can get nice and brown, too, again 5 to 8 minutes. There! Was that so hard?

6. If you are using the optional cheese, sprinkle it on the golden side you've just placed on top, so it can melt as you let the second side cook.

7. Serve hot, at room temperature, or even cold, cut into wedges.

VARIATIONS:

FRITTATA MEXICANA

Cook the frittata in olive oil, then sprinkle on Monterey Jack cheese in step 6. Once finished, top the frittata with salsa, warmed verde or enchilada sauce, a scatter of fresh cilantro, and/or a slice of avocado for garnish.

GARLICKY GREENS FRITTATA

In step 6, use Parmesan, sharp Cheddar, or a combination of the two. Top the finished frittata with fresh broccoli, broccoli rabe, kale, Swiss chard, or a combo of greens, blanched and sautéed in olive oil with lots of garlic and a broken-up dried red chile or two.

GOOD EARTH FRITTATA

Use Swiss, Gruyère, or Jarlsberg cheese in step 6. Top the finished frittata with big fat slices of portobello mushrooms, sautéed with lots of garlic in oil and a little butter, and a sprinkle of minced fresh parsley.

FRITTATA NAPOLETANA

Cook the frittata in olive oil, and use Parmesan in step 6. Dollop with your favorite marinara sauce, homemade or commercial, well heated. And could a scattering of good black olives and some shreds of fresh basil atop the marinara sauce be amiss? You can also make a much more substantial meal of this variation by adding sliced sautéed Italian-style sausage or soysage to the tomato sauce.

Garden Variety Frittata

Use butter to cook the frittata, and Swiss, Gruyère, or Jarlsberg cheese, or a crumble of a nice creamy chèvre (Goat cheese) in step 6. Then, sauté in butter 1 onion sliced vertically into crescents, adding 2 julienned carrots after the onion has cooked for a few minutes. Sauté the onion-carrot mixture for 5 minutes more, then toss in two handfuls of chopped spinach. Stir till the spinach wilts, and shower the finished frittata with this bright mix.

Greek Frittata

Layer on top of the frittata some fresh sliced tomatoes, a little finely diced raw red onion, a scattering of fresh dill, a few strips of roasted red or green pepper, plus some coarsely chopped kalamata olives. The cheese for step 6? Crumbles of feta.

A Variation to Any of the Above

Add a sliced scallion or two and/or ½ to 1 cup corn kernels cut from 1 to 2 ears of fresh (raw) corn (see Shuck and Jive, page 49) to the frittata batter.

Featherbed Eggs

SERVES 6 TO 8 AS AN ENTRÉE

Layered, strata-type savory bread pudding is a standby at many inns, for it tastes very, very good, yet is easy to make ahead and has countless variations. The Dairy Hollow House version was stuffed with a bit of cream cheese and green chiles, and was made with cornbread crumbs rather than conventional bread: the inspiration of my late husband, Ned. Thus a good dish became great, and there was a large uptick in how often visitors requested the recipe.

Use canned green chiles or fresh; if you like heat, amp up the amount of chiles.

Vegetable oil cooking spray

1 batch Dairy Hollow House Skillet-Sizzled Cornbread (page 12), crumbled into large chunks and left to dry out overnight

Salt and freshly ground black pepper

1 to 3 tablespoons minced green chiles (canned, or fresh fire-roasted poblano, peeled and seeded)

4 ounces Neufchâtel or cream cheese, at room temperature

1½ cups (6 ounces) shredded sharp
  Cheddar or Monterey Jack cheese,
  or a combination of the two

8 large eggs

2 cups milk (or a combination
  of milk and heavy cream or
  half-and-half)

Dash of hot pepper sauce, such as
  Tabasco

Dash of Pickapeppa or Worcestershire
  sauce

1. Preheat the oven to 350°F. Spray eight to ten
1- to 1½-cup ramekins or a single 14-by-11-inch
shallow baking dish with oil. If using ramekins,
place them on a cookie sheet.

2. Scatter the cornbread crumbs over the
baking dish, or divide among the ramekins.
Salt and pepper the crumbs to taste, scatter
the green chiles to taste on top, then place a
teaspoon or so of Neufchâtel or cream cheese
in the center of each ramekin or dab here and
there throughout the baking dish. Last, divide
the Cheddar or Monterey Jack cheese over all,
pressing it down lightly.

3. Whisk together the eggs, milk, hot sauce,
and Pickapeppa or Worcestershire in a large
bowl, then pour this over the mixture in
the prepared ramekins or dish. You can do
everything up to this point ahead of time,
(except preheat the oven), even the night
before (do keep the ramekins or dish tightly
covered and refrigerated, however, if you
do that).

·M·E·N·U·

BREAKFAST IN THE ROSE ROOM, REMEMBERED

Fresh-Squeezed Orange Juice
Blended with Peach Nectar

*

Fresh Fruit Plate with Green Grapes,
Sliced Kiwi, Green Apple,
and Spearmint

*

Featherbed Eggs
in Individual Ramekins with Salsa

*

Sautéed Bacon or
Smoked Tempeh Strips

*

Breadbasket: Wholesome Ginger-Pear
Muffins with a Lemon Glaze
(page 130)

*

Butter * Assorted Jams and Jellies

4. Bake until the eggs are set and slightly
puffed (enjoy this showy puff, but know that
it will sink), with a golden brown top and a
scrumptious aroma, 20 minutes for individual
ramekins, about 30 for the larger baking dish,
a little more if you've prepped and refrigerated
everything the night before. Don't overbake.

Eggs Eureka

Serves 8

Though too rich by far for every day, these are an enormous hit at Sunday brunch. A poached egg sits astride a crisply toasted wedge of the previous night's cornbread, with a slice of garden tomato beneath it, along with strips of either traditional bacon or tempeh bacon. Over the whole, a drizzle of sharp, flavorful Mornay sauce, made with a good organic Cheddar that has some real bite to it. You really can't go wrong.

> **1 batch Dairy Hollow House Skillet-Sizzled Cornbread (page 12), cut into 8 wedges**
> **8 small pats of butter**
> **8 slices crisp-cooked bacon or smoked tempeh strips**
> **8 thick slices of summer tomatoes**
> **8 poached eggs**
> **3 cups Mornay Sauce (recipe follows), heated**

I. Split the cornbread wedges in half horizontally, as you would an English muffin. Lightly toast the cut sides under the broiler, keeping the matching sets of upper and lower pieces adjacent. Place a small pat of butter on each of the lower pieces.

2. Place these buttered, toasted wedges on warmed plates. Top the bottom half of each buttered cornbread wedge with a slice of bacon or tempeh bacon, a slice of tomato, and a poached egg.

3. Ladle on the good hot Mornay sauce, then place the top half of each cornbread wedge on its side, next to the egg-topped piece. (This allows diners to top the bottom wedge with the second piece, or eat it as bread, or crumble it into the sauce . . . all good options.) Serve very hot, as soon as possible.

Mornay Sauce

Makes about 2¹/4 cups

A good cheese sauce—which is what Mornay is—is a basic that belongs in every good cook's repertoire. It's an essential component of Eggs Eureka, but that's just one of the countless ways you'll find use for it. Toss it with steamed cauliflower, and you've got cauliflower au gratin. Toss it with cooked macaroni, run it under the broiler, and you've got a macaroni and cheese that will make the kids (and their adults) quite happy. Thin it with vegetable stock and stir in cooked potatoes and broccoli: voilà, potato and broccoli cheese soup.

Some people use white pepper in this so as not to mar the Mornay's pristine pale creaminess with little black flecks, but frankly, I'm not that persnickety. I am, however, particular about seasoning my cheese sauce: It just wouldn't taste right to me without a bit of nutmeg, a little dried mustard, and a small drizzle of Pickapeppa. Sometimes I also add a dash of cayenne and a teaspoon of nutritional yeast (which, oddly, heightens the cheese flavor beautifully).

2½ tablespoons butter

3 tablespoons all-purpose flour

2 cups hot milk

½ to ¾ cup (2 to 3 ounces) grated extra-sharp aged Cheddar, such as a Vermont or Canadian Black Diamond

A few gratings of nutmeg

¼ teaspoon mustard powder

½ teaspoon Pickapeppa or Worcestershire sauce

Salt and freshly ground black pepper

Dash of cayenne pepper (optional)

1 teaspoon nutritional yeast (optional)

1. Melt the butter in a medium-size saucepan over medium-high heat. Add the flour and cook, stirring constantly, until the mixture is a pale parchment yellow, 1 to 1½ minutes. This thickening paste is your roux and, in this recipe, you do *not* want it to cook until brown.

2. Slowly whisk the hot milk into the roux. Keep on whisking until the sauce thickens and comes to a boil, 2 to 3 minutes. Lower the heat to a simmer and stir in the cheese. Whisk again and simmer for 1 to 2 minutes more.

3. Then whisk in the nutmeg, mustard powder, Pickapeppa or Worcestershire, salt and pepper to taste (go easy on the salt at first; the cheese is salty), and the cayenne and nutritional yeast, if using. If you want to make it ahead, do so: Refrigerate it, then reheat it gently in the top of a double boiler when ready to serve.

VARIATION:
Of course you can substitute just about any cheese, or combination of cheeses, you like. Try it with ½ cup grated Gruyère or Jarlsberg cheese instead of the Cheddar, along with a tablespoon of finely grated Parmesan. Lose the dry mustard and Pickapeppa with this variation, but keep the nutmeg.

GOLDEN GAZPACHO

SERVES 6, GENEROUSLY

Inspired by a hot spell that had me making cold soup almost nightly, I one night set out to make a not-atypical gazpacho: a tomato-cucumber number, though I wanted to give it some heft by adding a little stale bread in with the vegetables. And I thought . . . why not cornbread? Why not . . . yellow tomatoes? And yellow peppers? Suddenly: not typical at all.

Make this the next time summer rolls around—preferably after a visit to the farmers' market. Since one element is cooked, make it in the afternoon so it will be icy by dinnertime. To me this is at least twenty times more interesting and refreshing than standard-issue gazpacho. It's amazing how many good, golden, fresh things there are, and how well they merge and blend.

Vegetable oil cooking spray

1 tablespoon mild vegetable oil

1 large onion, chopped

2 cups mild vegetable stock

3 medium-size yellow summer crookneck squash (about 1 pound), stem ends removed, cut into large chunks

4 cups diced, perfectly ripe, sweet yellow summer tomatoes (about 2 pounds)

About 3 cups corn kernels, cut from about 6 ears fresh corn (see Shuck and Jive, page 49)

1 cup carrot juice (optional; if hard to find or if you don't like the sweetness this will add, substitute buttermilk or stock)

1½ cups buttermilk

1 to 2 large yellow bell peppers, roasted, peeled, cored, and seeded (or ⅓ cup chopped commercial roasted yellow peppers)

1 large wedge of stale cornbread (any kind will do)

Salt

Reduced-fat sour cream or plain yogurt, for garnish (optional)

Finely diced red bell pepper, for garnish (optional)

1. Spray a large skillet, one that has a lid, with oil, then add the tablespoon of oil. Place over medium-high heat and add the onions. Sauté, stirring often, until the onions are translucent and start to color, about 4 minutes. Turn the heat to medium and continue cooking until they are golden, but not overly brown, around the edges, another 10 minutes or so.

2. Add the 2 cups vegetable stock to the skillet, along with the squash. Bring to a boil, turn down to a simmer, cover, and let cook until the squash are quite soft, 12 to 15 minutes.

3. Meanwhile, place half of the diced tomatoes and half of the corn in a large bowl with the carrot juice (or liquid equivalent) and about a third of the buttermilk. Place the remaining tomatoes and corn in a food processor along with the roasted bell peppers. Purée the mixture and transfer it to the bowl with the unprocessed ingredients, stirring well. Don't clean the processor just yet.

4. At this point the squash should be just about done. Add the stale cornbread to it, breaking it into the hot liquid to soften a bit. It doesn't matter if the cornbread actually cooks in the liquid for a few minutes, or just sits in it. In either case, let the skillet sit for a few moments to cool down somewhat. Then, transfer the cool or lukewarm contents of the skillet to the processor with the remaining buttermilk and buzz it to as close to smoothness as you can. Stir this, too, into the bowl. Taste the mixture and add salt to taste—this soup really requires salt to bring out all the vegetable nuances.

5. Cover and refrigerate the soup. Chill deeply and serve, very cold, in chilled cups, with or without the garnishes: a rounded teaspoon of the sour cream plus a scatter of red bell pepper atop each chilled cup or bowl.

· M · E · N · U ·

SCREENED PORCH SUMMER RAIN SUPPER

Golden Gazpacho

*

Wanda's Soft Corn Crepes (page 234), filled with Sautéed Fresh Spinach and Mushrooms and Fresh Corn Cut from the Cob, Topped with Mornay Sauce (Gruyère Variation; page 264)

*

Sliced Green Zebra Tomatoes

*

Grapefruit Sorbet

VARIATION: CRUNCHILY RED-PEPPERED GOLDEN GAZPACHO

If you like a more textured soup, a little more similar to conventional gazpacho (not a copycat, however, by any means), omit the roasted peppers and instead stir in ⅓ cup finely minced raw red and yellow peppers and one cucumber, peeled, seeded, and diced, into the finished soup (do not purée them).

CORN-TROVERSY: MARITAL DIALOGUE, WITH CORNBREAD

She's Stephanie. He's LeBron. They're both Colvins, married to each other. They live in South Pittsburg, Tennessee. The Colvins are part of the one third of South Pittsburg's population that works all year long to pull off the annual National Cornbread Festival.

I met the Colvins as follows: I'd inquired of a Festival volunteer where I might find a drugstore open on Sunday. She'd said, "Why, what do you need, honey?" "Sunblock," I told her. "Oh, just go on to the Information / First Aid / Lost and Found booth, you can get you some there."

And the Information / First Aid / Lost and Found booth is where I met the Colvins. Gratis sunscreen was just one of the items they were dispensing: Evidently I was not the first visitor to get a little crispy around the edges. In the shade of a green awning, by the map where visitors could place a pin

showing how far they'd come to attend the festival, I smeared every uncovered millimeter of my skin with sunblock, and the Colvins and I fell into the only kind of conversation likely under the circumstances: cornbread-related.

There was not cornbread accord in the Colvin household.

STEPHANIE: See, I'm from Virginia.

LEBRON: And I'm from right here in Tennessee.

STEPHANIE: My mother's cornbread wasn't baked in a skillet. It was baked in a little square Corning Ware dish. That's just how you did it. Skillet? No skillet. Whoever heard of cornbread in a skillet? And it was sweet—well, of course, we put sugar in it, that's what you did. It was kind of cakey. It was *supposed* to be cakey.

LEBRON (simultaneously shaking his head and moaning softly): No, no, no, no. No, no, unh-unh, no.

STEPHANIE: I just couldn't relate to their cornbread down here at first. You put *bacon* fat in it? My mother would have flipped out. And you do *what?* You break it up into little pieces and stir it into your pinto beans? I couldn't, could *not,* relate. I have kind of got with the program by now; his mother gave me some skillets, seasoned, and that was a big thing, 'cause you *know* down here they guard their old skillets. But still, to get the kind of cornbread he really likes, he has to go to Mama's. I know my place. I keep my mom-in-law happy.

LEBRON (earnestly): See, cornbread like it's meant to be is *grainy.* It's *coarse.* It's definitely *not* sweet. It is *not* like a . . . (a disgusted look crosses his face) . . . cake.

STEPHANIE: I do know this much. And I bet a whole lot of people down here have already told you this: To get the kind of cornbread they eat here, you've got to get that skillet hot, I mean we're talking hot-hot, before you add the batter.

LEBRON: With cornbread, a lot of what you're experiencing is the texture. You lose that if you start messing it up with flour. And let's don't even *talk* about sugar. You want cornbread grainy. You do *not* want cornbread sweet. You know, my granddad used to crumble his into buttermilk.

STEPHANIE (simultaneously shaking her head and moaning): No, umm-um, no.

LEBRON: Yes he did, and he ate it with a spoon. Now, see, you couldn't do that with *her* type of cornbread. You could, I guess, but the texture would be all wrong. It would disintegrate. It would dissolve—it would just be . . . (He can't find words for the horror, and gives a small involuntary shiver: even the thought of it seems to give him the all-overs.) It would *not* be good.

STEPHANIE: That was another "You do *what?*" thing for me when I came down here. Crumble cornbread, of any kind, into *buttermilk?* Unh-unh, no way, *no* way. No way.

LEBRON (smiling): *Way.*

ROMANIAN-STYLE SWEET AND SOUR CABBAGE SOUP

SERVES 6 TO 8

66 I never met a stuffed cabbage I didn't like," proclaims Elizabeth Rozin in her 1999 book, *Crossroads Cooking: The Meeting and Mating of Ethnic Cuisines—From Burma to Texas in 200 Recipes.* This brilliant food historian was one of the first to codify the ways in which almost all dishes on the world's tables are the result of ethnic crosscurrents. She describes an "eccentric" sweet and sour stuffed cabbage recipe that uses as a base not the common rice, ground meat, or bread crumbs, but mamaliga, Romanian cornmeal mush. (Can't you just tell how much they love it by that word, mamaliga?)

Elizabeth's comments put me in mind of one of my own personal cabbage favorites, the rich Russian soup called *s'chi.* S'chi is sweet and sour, utterly delicious, and deeply, satisfyingly warming on a bitter day.

·M·E·N·U·

JUST STARTING TO WARM UP SUPPER

Romanian-Style Sweet and Sour Cabbage Soup

✳

Boiled Fingerling Potatoes with Butter and Fresh Dill

✳

Raisin-Studded Pumpernickel Rye with Butter

✳

Elderflower Cordial

What would happen if I slightly thickened s'chi with a little leftover cornbread, instead of serving it with potatoes or kasha as the starchy component? I did, and . . . wow. The recipe bears grafts of all I've mentioned and more, a fine, sturdy hybrid of cuisines. Set a steaming tureen down on your table and taste this lovely, substantial intersection.

Use the darkest, richest vegetable stock you can find for this. As for your sauerkraut, get a natural foods brand in a jar or bag, never a can. Sauerkraut from cans always has a noticeable metallic taste. But any unembellished cornbread, sweet or not, will work just fine.

Vegetable oil cooking spray

2 tablespoons butter

1 large or 2 medium onions, chopped

1 carrot, scrubbed and diced

4 to 5 garlic cloves, chopped

1½ teaspoons tamari or soy sauce

2 quarts (8 cups) rich, dark vegetable stock

1½ cups fine ribbon-cut green cabbage

1½ cups sauerkraut

1½ cups canned diced tomatoes with their juice

½ cup raisins or diced pitted prunes

1 to 2 tablespoons honey

1 to 2 tablespoons cider vinegar

1 bay leaf

Salt and freshly cracked black pepper

2 wedges cornbread, preferably stale

Sour cream, for garnish (optional)

Fresh sprigs of dill, for garnish (optional)

1. Spray a 10-inch skillet with oil and set on medium-high heat. Add the butter, and when it melts, add the onions. Sauté over high heat for 5 minutes, then add the carrots, lower the heat, and sauté until the onions are very soft and starting to turn golden, another 5 to 8 minutes. Lower the heat again and add the garlic and tamari. Stirring often, cook for another 5 minutes. Remove from the heat and set aside to cool slightly.

2. Meanwhile, spray a large, heavy soup pot with oil and add the stock, cabbage, sauerkraut, tomatoes with their juice, raisins or prunes, 1 tablespoon of the honey, 1 tablespoon of the vinegar, the bay leaf, and salt and pepper to taste. Ladle out a little of the stock into the skillet used for the onion mixture and stir and scrape to deglaze the pan. Add the sautéed vegetables and the deglazing liquid to the soup pot. Bring to a boil, turn down the heat to medium low, and gently simmer the soup, half covered, for about 45 minutes. Taste for seasonings, correcting with salt, pepper, honey, and vinegar to get the requisite sweet-sourness, which should be noticeable but not sharp. The dried fruits should have just about melted into the broth by now.

3. Crumble in the cornbread pieces. Stir very, very well. Cover the soup, turn the heat down even lower, and let the soup gently simmer for another 30 minutes, stirring occasionally.

4. When the soup has thickened and you've tasted it yet again to achieve the perfect balance of sweet and sour, remove the bay leaf and serve the soup very hot. Dollop each bowlful with sour cream and a sprig of dill, if desired, and sigh with pleasure.

Patsy's Cornbread Salad

Serves **8** to **10**

❝I really think it's the dressing that does it," says Patsy Barker, seriously and thoughtfully. "It is the dressing that is so important." She knows: She is the Patsy of Patsy's Cornbread Salad, one of the annual, much-anticipated culinary highlights of the National Cornbread Festival in South Pittsburg, Tennessee. There, literal *tons* of it have been dished out, a scoop at a time, to countless grateful cornbread enthusiasts. There is always a line in front of the booth that serves Patsy's cornbread salad. (Incidentally, that booth is sponsored by Citizen's Tri-County Bank, where Patsy's husband, H. Glenn Barker, is chairman. Profits from the booth go directly to the Cornbread Festival itself, creating seed money for the following year's festival.)

Patsy has never given out her recipe before, and she was reluctant to do it this time, but finally, thankfully, she gave in. She's not exactly sure of the salad's origins— "It was one my daughter made that she got from somewhere," she told me, "and I've tinkered with it a little." She gave it to me anecdotally, beginning "First you make up a skillet of cornbread . . ." and continuing from there. I've put it in conventional recipe format, but I kept some of her tips, comments, and ingredients.

Use any crusty nonsweet all-cornmeal Southern cornbread, such as Truman Capote's Family's (page 13), Sylvia's Ozark (page 18), or Ronni's Appalachian (page 21).

1 skillet of cornbread

¾ pound bacon

1 cup mayonnaise ("I use Kraft")

½ cup sweet pickle relish ("I just use Heinz")

¼ cup juice from sweet pickle relish

1 tablespoon sugar

2 Vidalia or other sweet onions, finely chopped

2 green bell peppers, cored, seeded, and finely chopped

4 to 5 juicy, ripe tomatoes, cut into medium-size chunks

1. Coarsely crumble the cornbread "into a good big bowl" and let it dry out for a few hours.

2. Cook the bacon, draining off all excess fat. "You want it cooked real brown and crispy," Patsy says. When the bacon has cooled, crumble it coarsely and set it aside.

3. Stir or whisk together the mayo, relish, relish juice, and sugar. That's your dressing. Set it aside.

4. When the crumbled cornbread has dried slightly, toss in the onions, peppers, tomatoes, and crumbled bacon. Toss well, so that everything is well distributed.

5. Spoon the dressing over the top and stir thoroughly. Cover tightly and refrigerate until ready to serve. It can be made up to 24 hours in advance.

VARIATIONS:

CD's Version

I substitute crumbled crisp sautéed smoked tempeh strips for the bacon, and add a teaspoon of hot sauce to the dressing.

Elayne's Version

My friend Elayne Ross's version of cornbread salad is semi-Southwestern and mighty good: Substitute 1 can (15 ounces) well-drained pinto beans for the bacon and 1 bunch scallions, chopped, for the Vidalia. Add 2 cups (8 ounces) grated sharp Cheddar cheese and 1 or 2 finely minced jalapeños in addition to the green bell peppers. Her dressing: ½ cup each mayonnaise and yogurt or sour cream, ½ cup sweet pickle relish plus 2 tablespoons juice, and 2 tablespoons smoky barbecue sauce, ideally chipotle barbecue sauce. Sprinkle minced cilantro over the top.

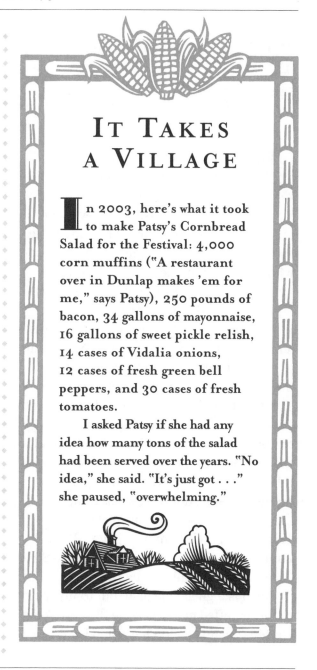

IT TAKES A VILLAGE

In 2003, here's what it took to make Patsy's Cornbread Salad for the Festival: 4,000 corn muffins ("A restaurant over in Dunlap makes 'em for me," says Patsy), 250 pounds of bacon, 34 gallons of mayonnaise, 16 gallons of sweet pickle relish, 14 cases of Vidalia onions, 12 cases of fresh green bell peppers, and 30 cases of fresh tomatoes.

I asked Patsy if she had any idea how many tons of the salad had been served over the years. "No idea," she said. "It's just got . . .," she paused, "overwhelming."

KUSH

SERVES 4 TO 6 AS A HEARTY SIDE DISH,
4 AS STUFFING FOR A VEGETABLE

A guarantee: A few bites of kush will introduce a whole new comfort food to your repertoire. It is not the prettiest dish you'll ever see, but everyone who's sampled it at my table has asked for the recipe, and two of those who did took it home, tried it on their families, and promptly saw it elevated to "Mama, make that kush again" status.

So what is kush? Imagine a thick, moist almost-porridge, with the flavors of stuffing or dressing and a consistency similar to that of polenta or mashed potatoes, with savory bits and bites of sautéed vegetables stirred in—a kind of delicious precursor to commercial "stuffing" that can be made atop the stove, to which it is a distant relative. The ideal cornbread here is one on the dry side, not too sweet, rich, or eggy. Ronni's Appalachian (page 21), Truman Capote's Family's (page 13), or Pam Anderson's "Perfect" New South–Style (page 14) would all do nicely.

Kush is a great side dish, but to my mind it's best stuffed in a vegetable. I've offered a stuffed tomato version here, and have been known to serve it in a pumpkin . . . though semantic play demands I also suggest Kush in Cushaw (a sweet winter squash stuffed with kush).

Vegetable oil cooking spray

1 tablespoon mild vegetable oil

½ large onion, chopped

1 celery rib, chopped

4 medium mushrooms, chopped

3 cups crumbled leftover cornbread, ideally stale

1 cup leftover stale coarse bread or biscuit crumbs, preferably whole-grain

2½ cups vegetable or chicken stock, or, if need be, water

3 hard-cooked eggs, peeled and coarsely chopped (optional)

1 teaspoon dried leaf sage (not ground), crumbled, or 1 tablespoon finely minced fresh sage leaf (optional)

Salt and freshly ground black pepper

1. Spray a 9- to 10-inch skillet with oil and place over medium-high heat. Add the tablespoon of oil and, when it's hot, the onions. Sauté for 4 or 5 minutes, stirring, then add the celery and mushrooms, and sauté until the vegetables soften a little, about 4 minutes more. Lower the heat slightly.

2. Add the cornbread, bread or biscuit crumbs, and the stock or water. Add the stock gradually, as the crumbs absorb it, mashing it into the crumbs with the back of a spoon. Bring the kush to a slow boil, raising the heat slightly as needed.

3. Keep stirring. After about 5 minutes, add the eggs, if using. Continue cooking and stirring until the bread absorbs the liquid evenly, softening to a kind of porridge, but with little texture-y nubbins of crumb remaining, another 5 to 7 minutes.

4. Remove the kush from the stove. Stir in the sage, if using, and salt and pepper to taste.

VARIATIONS:

TOMATOES STUFFED WITH KUSH

Preheat the oven to 400°F. Cut the tops off 4 large tomatoes and, using a spoon, scoop out the tomato innards, reserving them for another purpose. Fill the tomatoes with kush, rounding up over the top. Place the stuffed tomatoes in an oil-sprayed baking dish and bake until the kush is crusty on top, 20 minutes. Serve as a hearty dinner, with a beany vegetable soup to start and garlic-sautéed broccoli as an accompaniment.

DOUBLE-CORN KUSH

Stir in the kernels of 2 ears of fresh corn (see Shuck and Jive, page 49) along with the seasonings at the last. This enhances the corn taste and texture.

·M·E·N·U·

MID-SOUTH SUMMER DINNER FROM THE GARDEN

**Platter of Assorted
Sliced Heirloom Tomatoes**

*

Kush

*

**Green Beans, Slow Cooked
with Tomatoes and Garlic**

*

**Beans, Old South Style
(page 303) or
Beans,
Dragon-in-the-New-South Style
(page 305)**

*

Bread and Butter Pickles

*

Peach Ice Cream

*

Iced Tea

WHEN KUSH COMES TO LOVE

Kush, sometimes spelled with a C, is a make-do, thrifty dish built around stale cornbread. Today about the only place where it is commonly eaten and much-loved is among the Oklahoma Cherokee. The Cherokee like it with any meat dish, especially pork, but it's also eaten with roast chicken or turkey, like a moist stuffing/dressing. Vegetarians like kush on its own or stuffed in a vegetable.

Kush has a long, uneven history. Its original incarnation was probably Native American "soft bread": cooked cornmeal with meat fat and pounded sunflower seeds or nuts. When European settlers arrived and began using cornmeal to make breads of the type they were most familiar with, the "soft bread" idea transmuted: crumbled leftovers were re-cooked in the Native American style, in a skillet with some form of fat and savory liquid.

Kush can be elaborate, as is mine and most contemporary versions. But it can also be straightforward, to the point of being barely edible survival food—as in the Civil War. Then, when the staple corn pone of Confederate rations was too hard to eat (most of the time), soldiers broke the pone up into an iron skillet with as much bacon grease as was available, some liquid, and, in the springtime, possibly some ramps (wild garlic grass) or wild greens. This when-push-comes-to-shove dish, cooked over an open fire with much stirring wherever the regiment had set up camp, eventually became edible. But, in the unappetizing words of historian William C. David, it was "a thick glutinous mess."

Kush in good times is entirely different. Every time you're in the cornbread groove, make some extra, so thus, kush can come to love.

SAVORY CORNBREAD DRESSING

MAKES II TO I3 CUPS DRESSING,
ENOUGH TO STUFF AN I8- TO 20-POUND
TURKEY OR A LARGE PUMPKIN

Although I prefer a not-too-sweet cornbread made with both flour and cornmeal for this recipe, such as the Dairy Hollow House Skillet-Sizzled Cornbread on page 12, I am honor-bound to say that many opt for the plainest of cornmeal-only cornbreads for their dressing—and such dressings are mighty pleasing, too. In this latter category, try Ronni's Appalachian Cornbread (page 21), Sylvia's Ozark Cornbread (page 18), or Truman Capote's Family's Cornbread (page 13).

In my view, a stuffing of this type just isn't tasty if you make it ultra-low-fat, so my advice is, don't even try. And also, like all dressings it is an accompaniment, designed to be served with a main dish and some sort of gravy. I have offered a vegetarian alternative for the sausage in this dressing, so vegetarians can think outside the bird by baking it in a pumpkin and serving it with lentil croquettes or breaded, oven-crisped tempeh or tofu, and a wonderful mushroom sauce.

Vegetable oil cooking spray

11 to 12 cups coarsely crumbled cornbread (about 2 skillets' worth)

12 to 16 ounces bulk sausage, or about 13 ounces any good vegetarian soysage (such as Gimme Lean Sausage Style, Lightlife Smart Links, or Boca Breakfast Patties)

2 tablespoons mild vegetable oil (optional)

1 large onion, chopped

2 to 3 celery ribs with leaves, split lengthwise twice, then chopped

2 garlic cloves, finely chopped

1 tablespoon dried leaf sage (not ground), crumbled, or more as needed

2 teaspoons dried leaf thyme, crumbled, or more as needed

½ bunch of flat-leaf parsley, leaves only, finely chopped

1 cup dried cherries, raisins, apricots, or cranberries (optional)

Salt and freshly ground black pepper

2 to 2½ cups vegetable, chicken, or turkey stock

3 tablespoons to ¼ cup (½ stick) butter

I. Preheat the oven to 400°F for 20 minutes. Then turn the heat down to 300°F. Spray 2 rimmed baking sheets or jelly-roll pans with oil.

2. Spread the crumbled cornbread in a single layer on each baking sheet. You will have to do this in several batches. Checking every 10 minutes or so and shaking the pans to redistribute the crumbs, bake the crumbs until they are quite dry but not browned, 30 to 35 minutes. Transfer the dry cornbread to a large bowl.

3. As the cornbread toasts, prepare the sausage. *For the meat version*, brown the sausage in a large skillet over medium heat, breaking up the pieces with a spatula. Remove the browned sausage with a slotted spoon, and add it to the dry cornbread in the bowl along with 1 or 2 tablespoons of the sausage grease (discard any remaining grease). *For the vegetarian version:* Place the oil in a large pan over medium heat. When the pan is hot, add the soysage and sauté according to package directions, keeping any leftover fat in the pan. Dice the cooked soysage as necessary into bite-size pieces, and add it, along with the cooking oil, to the cornbread in the bowl.

4. Add the onion, celery, garlic, sage, thyme, parsley, dried fruit, and salt and freshly ground black pepper to taste to the bowl. (Note: You can prepare the dressing in advance up to this point. Let it cool, stash it in zip-top bags, and store, refrigerated, until ready to complete the recipe.)

5. Heat 2 cups of the stock and 3 tablespoons of the butter in a small saucepan. When the butter melts, pour the liquid over the crumb mixture and toss well, using your hands. Taste,

and if you like, add the extra ½ cup stock and adjust the seasonings. Use to stuff the bird or vegetable of choice, according to your favorite roast turkey or pumpkin recipe. Or bake as is as an accompaniment (see step 6).

6. To bake the dressing on its own, place it in a deep oil-sprayed baking dish with a 4-quart capacity. Dot the top with the reserved tablespoon of butter and bake at 325°F, tightly covered, for 1 hour. Uncover, raise the heat to 375°F, and bake for another 10 minutes.

VARIATIONS:
SAVORY CORNBREAD DRESSING WITH BACON
Substitute 1 pound crumbled crisp-cooked bacon for the sausage.

VEGETARIAN SAVORY CORNBREAD DRESSING WITH TEMPEH BACON
Substitute 1 pound smoked tempeh, cooked until crisp in ¼ cup oil or butter, then diced, for the sausage. You may use the fat the tempeh was cooked in instead of the butter in step 5.

SAVORY CORNBREAD DRESSING WITH EGGS
To some, a savory dressing without hard-cooked eggs is a sham and a mockery. If you are one of these people, simply add 4 to 6 hard-cooked eggs, coarsely chopped, to the dressing along with the vegetables and herbs.

Sweet-Savory Cornbread Dressing

MAKES 11 TO 13 CUPS DRESSING,
ENOUGH TO STUFF AN 18- TO 20-POUND
TURKEY OR A LARGE PUMPKIN

This is close to the kind of dressing I grew up with, and which I made for many years at the inn. It is studded with dried and fresh fruits as well as herbs and onions, and it is irresistibly delicious. Children and adults alike love it.

Either a nonsweet or slightly sweet cornbread works fine here, as does a mixture of cornbread and wheat bread (when using wheat, I choose a whole-grain, and I toast the cubed pieces of bread alongside the cornbread). Almost any cornbread would work here as a base, except the jalapeño varieties and the Yankee "Spider" Cornbread with a Custard Layer. I'm partial to Dairy Hollow House Skillet-Sizzled Cornbread (page 12), myself.

For a richer dressing, double or even triple the amount of butter called for.

Vegetable oil cooking spray
½ pound dried apricots
½ pound dried pitted prunes
1 cup apple cider, heated to boiling
10 to 12 cups coarsely crumbled cornbread (about 2 skillets' worth)
1 large onion, chopped
2 celery ribs with leaves, split lengthwise, then chopped
1½ teaspoons dried leaf basil, crumbled, or more as needed
1 tablespoon dried leaf sage (not ground), crumbled, or more as needed
2 teaspoons dried leaf thyme, crumbled, or more as needed
2 tart apples, such as McIntosh, Cortland, or Greening (not Granny Smith), peeled, cored, and coarsely chopped
Salt and freshly ground black pepper
1¾ to 2¼ cups vegetable, chicken, or turkey stock, as needed
3 tablespoons butter

What's Wrong with Granny?

Why are Granny Smith apples, the most widely available crisp, tart apple and arguably the tastiest of the mainstream apple varieties, specifically excluded from the list of apple varieties given in the recipe for Sweet-Savory Cornbread Dressing? Because Grannys, while excellent for eating out of hand or for use raw, as in salads or as an accompaniment for fine cheese, resist cooking. They just won't move from firmness to that melting softness that is essential not only in this dressing, but in baked apples, apple brown betty, apple pie, even simple sautéed apple slices—all dishes that require this softening to reach perfection.

Individual ingredients, even so seemingly minor as particular apple varieties, always have secrets to tell. You can learn them, but only if you listen closely.

I. Preheat the oven to 400°F for 20 minutes. Then turn the heat down to 300°F. Spray 2 rimmed baking sheets or jelly-roll pans with oil.

2. Place the apricots and prunes in a small, heat-proof bowl. Pour the boiling cider over them, and let them soak.

3. Spread the crumbled cornbread in a single layer on each baking sheet. Depending on your oven size and the number of sheets you have,

you may have to do several batches. Bake the cornbread until it is quite dry but not browned, 20 to 25 minutes. Transfer it to a large bowl.

4. Add the onion, celery, basil, sage, thyme, apples, and salt and pepper to taste to the cornbread bowl.

5. Drain the dried fruit, reserving the cider. Coarsely chop the prunes and apricots and add them to the cornbread bowl.

6. Add 1¾ cups of the stock to the reserved apple cider to equal 2½ cups total (hold back the remaining stock just in case you need it). In a small saucepan, heat this with the butter over medium heat. When the butter melts, pour the liquid over the cornbread mixture and toss well, using your hands. Taste and adjust the seasonings, adding the remaining ½ cup stock if needed to get it nice and moist. Use to stuff a bird or vegetable of your choice.

VARIATION: MIDWEST HARVEST SWEET-SAVORY DRESSING

Substitute 1 cup cooked wild rice for 1 cup of the cornbread, and add ½ to 1 cup dried tart cherries to the dressing, along with ½ cup chopped toasted walnuts or hickory nuts. This is a delicious dressing. Meat eaters love it with roasted chicken, while vegetarians are thrilled with it side by side with a platter of roasted vegetables and any savory tofu or tempeh and gravy.

SOUTHWESTERN-STYLE CORNBREAD CASSEROLE WITH CHORIZO

SERVES 4 TO 6 AMPLY AS AN ENTRÉE

I know it's rare to have leftovers of any of the always-popular chile-and corn-studded Southwestern-style cornbreads (see Chapter 4), but it's worth squirreling some away for this stuffing. In addition to the Border Cuisine notes the cornbread itself adds to the finished dish, such native American foodstuffs as squash and tomatoes find their way into this succulent baked casserole. They moisten the dressing while adding flavor that riffs wonderfully off the cumin, coriander, and chorizo. (And speaking of chorizo, I've offered an alternative to the pork chorizo so this recipe can be enjoyed by vegetarians and meatists alike.)

This is a dish that has "take me to a potluck" written all over it. Serve it with a pot of black or refried beans, a favorite slaw, some watermelon and/or maybe ice cream or frozen yogurt and some home-made oatmeal cookies for dessert, and you have a down-home not-quite-but-almost Tex-Mex meal that is, oh, so satisfying.

Vegetable oil cooking spray

2 tablespoons olive oil

6 ounces traditional pork chorizo or vegetarian chorizo soysage, such as Soyrizo

3½ to 4 cups crumbled stale Southwestern-style cornbread

1 large onion, chopped

2 garlic cloves, minced

2 teaspoons cumin seeds

1 teaspoon ground coriander

2 teaspoons ground red chile powder (powdered chiles, not the blended chili powder spices)

1 cup peeled, diced raw butternut squash

¾ cup vegetable stock, plus extra as needed

2 eggs

2 large or 3 small to medium tomatoes, coarsely chopped (you can peel and seed them, but truthfully, I never bother)

Salt and freshly ground black pepper

1. Preheat the oven to 350°F. Spray a deep casserole, 9 inches square or thereabouts, with oil, and set aside.

2. Spray a large skillet with oil and place it over medium-high heat. Heat 1 tablespoon of the olive oil in it. Add the pork or vegetarian

> **"Where the corn is full of kernels and the colonels full of corn."**
> —WILLIAM JAMES LAMPTON (1859–1917), FROM "KENTUCKY"

chorizo. If using the pork chorizo, sauté until firm and cooked through, then drain off the excess fat; if using the vegetarian chorizo, just brown it slightly. Place the cooked chorizo in a large bowl and add 3½ cups of the crumbled cornbread. Set aside.

3. Add the remaining tablespoon of oil to the hot skillet (don't bother to wash it) along with the onion. Sauté, stirring, until the onion has started to soften and is fragrant, about 4 minutes. Lower the heat slightly and add the garlic, cumin, coriander, and chile powder. Continue sautéing for another 4 minutes, then add the squash and ¼ cup of the stock. Cover, and let the squash and spices steam together or until the squash has softened, about 4 minutes more. Remove from the heat and let cool for a few minutes.

4. Meanwhile, whisk together the eggs with the remaining ½ cup stock in a small bowl. Add the egg mixture to the cornbread mixture, and toss well. Add the tomatoes and the sautéed vegetables and toss again. You want to achieve

DRESSING VS. STUFFING: THE GREAT DEBATE

At some mysterious point that does not directly correspond with the Mason-Dixon line, the toothsome Thanksgiving mixture of herbed and enriched bread crumbs changes from "stuffing" to "dressing" or "dressing" to "stuffing." Whatever you call it, it goes inside a turkey or chicken or, for vegetarians, a large pumpkin or other vegetable, and gets baked to moist perfection. Although some cooks use white or whole wheat bread as the base, many would agree that the superlatives of the dressing/stuffing world have a cornbread base.

To make the dressings/stuffings I've offered here—as well as the one almost-dressing Southwestern-spiced casserole on the opposite page, which can serve as either entrée or side-dish—save odds and ends of any leftover cornbreads for the few months previous to dressing day. Well wrapped in zip-top bags and stored in the freezer, they keep well and are perfect for just this purpose. But remember, the cornbread *must* be stale. Remove from the freezer, crumble it, and leave the crumbles out, uncovered, overnight. You want your cornbread dried out here, the better to absorb whatever goodness is coming its way.

the consistency of a moist stuffing; add a little more cornbread or stock if you need it to get there. Season to taste with salt and pepper.

5. Transfer the mixture to the prepared pan and cover tightly with foil. Bake until heated through and slightly set (due to the egg), 25 to 30 minutes. Uncover and bake just long enough to dry the top out slightly, not make it really crusty, an additional 5 to 10 minutes. Serve warm or hot.

VARIATION: CHEESE-CRUSTED SOUTHWESTERN-STYLE CORNBREAD CASSEROLE WITH CHORIZO AND BLACK BEANS

The addition of black beans makes this dish even heartier. Add, along with the tomatoes, 1 can (15 ounces) black beans, drained very well and rinsed. Bake as directed, but when you uncover the casserole, top it with 1 to 1½ cups (4 to 6 ounces) grated sharp Cheddar or Monterey Jack cheese, or a combination of the two, and raise the heat (or run the dish under a broiler) until the cheese is browned and bubbly. Serve generous scoops of the casserole hot from the oven, dolloped with reduced-fat sour cream and a generous shower of chopped fresh cilantro.

·M·E·N·U·

SUNLIGHT-ON-SNOW SOUTHWESTERN-STYLE WINTER LUNCH

Avocado, Orange, and Scallion Salad
with a Slightly Sweet–Slightly Spicy
Dressing

*

Cheese-Crusted Southwestern-Style
Cornbread Casserole
with Chorizo and Black Beans

*

Chocolate Sorbet and
Dulce de Leche Ice Cream
with Toasted Pine Nuts

New Day Connecticut-Style Cornbread Pudding

SERVES 6 TO 8 AS AN ENTRÉE

This is my vegetarian and cornbread-based update of a New England–style corn pudding, a favorite of community cookbooks in the Northeast. It can happily and deliciously serve as a vegetarian entrée, either in itself or side by side with another vegetable (I like it as part of a component dinner, alongside a tomato stuffed with spinach and Parmesan). Start with a fresh green salad with a vinaigrette so sharp and bright and mustardy it talks back to you; conclude with a slice of ripe cantaloupe, a ball of lemon sorbet resting in its curve and a smattering of fresh raspberries: a flat-out wonderful late-summer meal.

The original calls for conventional bacon, but smoked tempeh is every bit as delicious. Although I like using fresh raw corn cut off the cob, you can also use kernels cut off leftover cooked corn (in the unlikely event that you have some) or, if need be, thawed frozen kernel corn. Also, although you can use dairy milk, the creaminess of soy milk is a plus here; original New England recipes typically used half heavy cream, half light cream (which, of course, you can use if you like). Soy comes closer, but more healthfully, to that texture than does low-fat dairy milk.

Any type of cornbread will do here, but the sweetened Yankee cornbreads are particularly good (see chapter 2).

Vegetable oil cooking spray

2 tablespoons mild vegetable oil

1 package smoked tempeh strips, such as Lightlife brand

1 medium onion, chopped

1 red bell pepper, cored, seeded, and finely diced

2 eggs

Kernels cut from 4 ears of fresh corn, about 2 cups (see Shuck and Jive, page 49)

½ cup soft, very well crumbled cornbread

2 cups plain soy milk or 1 cup each heavy (whipping) cream and half-and-half

½ teaspoon salt

½ cup fine crisp bread crumbs, preferably whole wheat

1 to 2 teaspoons butter

I. Preheat the oven to 350°F. Spray a deep 1½-quart baking dish with oil and set aside. Also spray a large, heavy skillet with oil.

2. Place the skillet, with 1 tablespoon of the oil, over medium heat. When it's good and hot, add the tempeh strips and cook them until nicely browned, about 3 minutes per side. Remove the strips and place them on a cutting board.

3. Add the remaining oil to the hot skillet (don't bother to wash it). Add the onions, and sauté until the onions are softening slightly and growing translucent, about 4 minutes. Then add the bell pepper and continue sautéing for another 3 minutes. Remove from the heat, and let cool slightly.

4. Between stirs of the sauté, coarsely chop the tempeh strips into large chunks.

5. Break the eggs into a large bowl and whisk them. Then stir in the corn, crumbled cornbread, soy milk or heavy cream–half-and-half combination, and salt. Add the chopped tempeh strips and sautéed onions and bell pepper. Stir well again, and transfer to the baking dish.

6. Sprinkle the top of the pudding with the bread crumbs and dot with the butter to taste. Bake, uncovered, until the edges have firmed up nicely and the center is a bit wobbly, but not wet, 1 hour (40 minutes if your casserole dish is on the shallow side). Serve hot or warm or at room temperature.

Chapter 11

GREAT CORNBREAD GO-WITHS

Greens, Beans, and So Much More

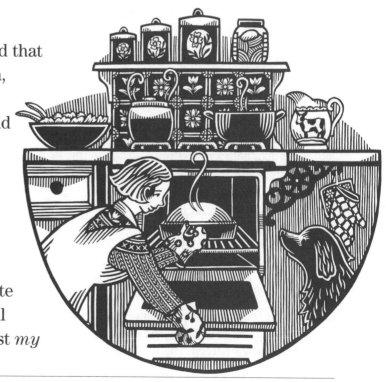

In Deuteronomy we're told that man (presumably woman, too) cannot live by bread alone. Cornbread-eaters the world over agree: You cannot live on bread, *even cornbread*, alone.

You need something to go with it.

Leaving aside that Something that is spiritual sustenance, this chapter offers some of my favorite ways to turn cornbread into a full repast. Of course, these aren't just *my* favorite ways. People of all places and times have responded to the question "What goes with cornbread?" with remarkably similar answers: universal in the basics, infinitely varied in the particulars.

Most cornbread-eating human beings have relied on the same three partners for the culinary sleight-of-hand that turns maize bread into the not-so-slight of dinner. Two of these partners are ingredients: greens and beans. The third is a type of dish, thick soups or stews. These soulful mélanges, in addition to meat and/or vegetables and seasonings, often *contain* one or both of the two ingredient partners, beans and greens.

Monotonous? Not so, as the numberless and varied ways of stews, beans, and greens worldwide prove.

Take greens. They might be slow-cooked collards with salt pork in the American South (see page 290) or their vegetarian counterpart (see page 293), served up with scallions, hot sauce, and vinegar on the side—and of course, skillet-sizzled, nonsweet cornbread. But in the north of India you'll find mustard greens, also simmered slowly, aromatic with ginger and garlic and chile and spices (see Mr. Panseer's version on page 294), which is served with Makki Ki Roti (page 109). Back in the United States, the greens might be plain old unassuming cabbage, quickly sautéed, tender-crisp, a little sweet, browned around the edges, served with just-as-simple white cornmeal "plain bread" (see page 297). The contemporary take? A panoply of greens (spinach, arugula,

cress, butterhead, romaine, and red oak leaf lettuces) raw, not cooked at all, but gloriously fresh, in a gigantic salad. A scatter of golden sundrop tomatoes, lightly blanched green beans, or whatever garden or market offers; homemade dressing, simple or exotic; maybe crumbled feta or blue cheese or nuts; and, with a basket of hot cornbread, you have a summer supper that's perfection. (For salad suggestions, see page 298.)

Beans, also appearing over and over, are equally variable. Think frijoles (see page 306) and fresh tortillas; chili and corn muffins—one bite of any of these and you know why beans and cornbread were meant to be together. Cornbread often accompanies bean-rich soups, like Lentil Soup with Garlic and Greens (page 315), or Portuguese Caldo Verde (page 318). And Boston Brown Bread (page 62), though only partly based on cornmeal, is universally served in New England with slowly baked beans, in their spicy-sweet, perfect familiar bath (see page 310).

Perhaps it ought to go without saying that given these cornbread companions' consistent appearance around the world, across culture, and throughout time, these combinations are all very good to eat, soul-satisfying in the *I-think-I'll-have-just-a-little-more* manner. But these cornbreads *with* their companions are also highly nourishing. Beans and corn (or other whole grains) form an amiably peppy nutritional symbiosis, on which masses of human beings have relied as a dietary mainstay, and thrived. Such pairings offer complete and heart-healthy protein, a spectrum of B-vitamins, "good" carbohydrates, almost no fat, and particularly beneficial forms of fiber. Filling, inexpensive, far easier on the environment than animal protein: corn and beans together are as good for you as they are pleasing to eat.

Greens and cornbread also do a distinctive nutritional tandem march. Leading the parade, greens are packed with vitamins, minerals, and phyto-chemicals (the healthful *je ne sais quoi* components most edible plants contain). The baton twirlers? Vitamin A (as beta-carotene), several B vitamins, and vitamin C, plus iron, calcium, and magnesium. But lutein and zeaxanthin, compounds present in many greens, clinically proven for their protective effect on vision, are bugling proudly not far behind. And all greens in the Cruciferae (cabbage) family, which includes kale, broccoli rabe, turnip, collard greens, and mustard greens, form the rearguard, banging triumphantly on their indole glucosinates, linked to a lowered incidence of several cancers.

The beneficial procession of humanity and foodstuffs snakes back through time, never-ending, triumphant. Did hungry minds and tongues find their way to cornbread's boon companions because these foods taste so good together? Or because our earth's earlier inhabitants discovered that these pairings made for strength, growth, keen eyesight? Because corn and beans grow well together? We'll never know. But that breadstuffs of maize and their timeless go-withs nourish us body and soul is answer, celebration, and gift enough.

CORNBREAD AND GREENS-EATING PROTOCOL

Whether using the classic greens recipe here or the New South recipe (page 293), serve the greens in a wide bowl, with plenty of the pot likker and cornbread on the side. Each bite should include the greens, a little cornbread, and a nibble of onion. The hot sauce and vinegar are optional; pass them around at the table for those who like to doctor their greens with these piquancies. When you get down to just pot likker, crumble some cornbread into it, and have at it with a spoon.

GREENS, OLD SOUTH STYLE

SERVES 4 TO 6

This is the classic, slow-cooked Southern way with greens. After a lengthy simmer with a hunk of pork, the greens cook down to melting softness, imbued with the smoky flavor and rich fattiness of the meat. Naturally, the greens are a perfect accompaniment to Southern-style cornbread. The pot "liquor" or "likker"—the deliciously savory green cooking juice—is a highly prized part of the finished greens; many sop their cornbread right in it.

1/4 pound salt pork (sometimes sold as "white bacon")

1 1/2 pounds greens (turnip greens, mustard greens, beet greens, collard greens, kale, chard, or a combination)

Salt and freshly cracked black pepper

Any nonsweet cornbread, such as Ronni's Appalachian (page 21), Truman Capote's Family's (page 13), or Sylvia's Ozark (page 18), for serving

Washed and trimmed scallions or sliced raw onion, for serving

Hot sauce, such as Tabasco, or cider vinegar in a cruet, for serving (optional)

1. Combine 1 quart water and the salt pork in a large, heavy pot with a tight-fitting lid (a Dutch oven is ideal) and bring to a boil. Lower the heat and simmer, half-covered, for about 30 minutes.

2. Meanwhile, wash the greens thoroughly in several changes of water and with a couple of rinses; greens are notorious concealers of dirt and grit. Using a sharp knife, cut out any especially thick or tough stems, then tear or cut the greens into bite-size pieces.

3. Stir the greens down into the simmering salt pork and water. Greens are bulky, but they cook down quickly; you might have to do this in several batches. When you have as many greens as possible in the pot, pop the cover on it and let them cook until you can add more. Once all the greens are in, lower the heat to a low simmer, cover, and let cook slowly for at least 1 hour; some folks will tell you an hour and a half or even two or three.

4. Taste, adding salt and pepper as needed. Serve with the cornbread and a side of scallions or sliced onions, as well as the hot sauce or vinegar, if using.

VARIATIONS:
CRAIG CLAIBORNE'S MAMA'S GREENS

Like cornbread itself, the way you think your old-fashioned greens ought to be cooked, and with what, varies from person to person and has a lot to do with what your mama fed you when you were growing up. Some serve the finished greens with chopped or sliced raw onion, not scallion. Some use ham hock instead of or in addition to salt pork, or conventional breakfast-style bacon instead of salt pork. Some add a few more seasonings or throw in some additional vegetables.

For example, take Craig Claiborne's variation (Claiborne, the late redoubtable *New York Times* food editor, was born in Mississippi): Start by placing the slab of salt pork in the bottom of the hot Dutch oven, and when it has rendered out the fat, lower the heat slightly and sauté the following in the fat for about 5 minutes: 1 onion, chopped; 1 stalk celery, chopped; and 1 green bell pepper, cored, seeded, and chopped. Then stir in the greens, prepared as in step 2, plus 1 ham hock and 1 dried hot red pepper, broken in half. Cover, cook for about 15 minutes, then add 2 cups of water. Continue cooking over very low heat for about 1½ hours more.

NOMINALLY HEALTH-CONSCIOUS SLOW-COOKED GREENS

Substitute a smoked turkey wing for the salt pork.

UNIVERSAL COMPANIONS: GREENS AND CORNBREAD

The soul-deep pleasure in eating greens and cornbread together goes beyond taste, nutrition, custom, or tradition. Greens and cornbread just *belong* together, and after a few bites, your very cells will be saying "Yes! Yes! Yes!"

What kind of greens? First off, cooked, not raw: We are not talking salad here (though salad is a good pairing, in a different way). And we are talking about pot likker, too—the delectable, soul-satisfying green juice left from cooking the greens. Cornbread is perfect for sopping up pot likker. The greens can be delicate and domesticated, young, tender, a little sweet (think baby spinach). But more often they're not. They can be wild, and gathering them in the early spring is a seasonal rite for many of us: dandelion, poke, dock, lamb's quarter, plantain, sorrel, nettle, cress. But any old time, they can be made with turnip greens or mustard greens, kale or chard, or a combination of same. These are the greens that are classic, though fixing cabbage with cornbread is also not unknown to some. (My friend Wenonah Fay grew up eating her pone with skillet-fried cabbage; the recipe is on page 297.)

Though American Southerners claim this greens-cornbread combo as their own, it isn't so. Native Americans were eating gathered wild spring greens to go with their samps and pones and tortillas long, long before there was a place called "The South." And, when corn traveled the world and took hold elsewhere, without any prompting, the locals took to it with greens (see the North Indian *sarson* recipe on page 294). If you explore this serendipitous pairing further—and I urge you to do so with the greens recipes here—you'll take to it, too.

GREENS, NEW SOUTH STYLE

SERVES 4 TO 6

What's a dragon to do? I ate, and enjoyed, Old South–style greens from the time I was about age sixteen until I was twenty-two, when I began to cut back on meat, eventually quitting it altogether. Though I often simply stir-fry my greens quickly with garlic and oil, here's what I do when I want them cooked slowly, soulfully, and semi-Southernly. The improbable-sounding Asian and Southwestern ingredients give them meaty, smoky notes, yet keep them vegetarian and healthful. The finished greens are every bit as delectable as the classic.

4 tablespoons peanut oil or other mild vegetable oil

1 onion, chopped

1 celery rib, chopped

1 green bell pepper, cored, seeded, and chopped

5 garlic cloves, 3 chopped, 2 left whole

¼ to ½ dried chipotle pepper, broken in half

1½ pounds greens (turnip greens, mustard greens, beet greens, collard greens, kale, chard, or a combination)

1 heaping tablespoon dark miso

1 tablespoon toasted sesame oil

Salt and freshly cracked black pepper

Any nonsweet cornbread, for serving

Washed and trimmed scallions or sliced raw onion, for serving

Hot sauce such as Tabasco, or cider vinegar in a cruet, for serving (optional)

1. Heat the oil in a large, heavy pot with a tight-fitting lid (a Dutch oven is ideal). Add the onion, celery, and bell pepper and cook over medium-high heat for about 5 minutes, stirring often. Lower the heat slightly and add the chopped garlic. Sauté for 2 minutes more, then add 1 quart water and the chipotle pepper (to taste). Lower the heat and simmer, half-covered, for about 30 minutes.

2. Meanwhile, wash the greens thoroughly in several changes of water and with a couple of rinses; greens are notorious concealers of dirt and grit. Using a sharp knife, cut out any especially thick or tough stems, then tear or cut the greens into bite-size pieces.

3. Stir the greens down into the simmering vegetable liquid. Greens are bulky, but they cook down quickly; you'll do several batches. When as many greens as possible are in the pot, add the whole garlic cloves, cover the pot, and let the greens cook down until you can add more. Once all the greens are in, lower the heat to a low simmer, cover, and let cook slowly for 1 hour.

4. Lift the lid. Stir in the miso and sesame oil, smushing the miso in with a spoon. Cover; simmer for another 15 minutes. Remove the chipotle pepper.

5. Season to taste with salt and pepper. Serve in a bowl, with cornbread and scallions or sliced onions on the side, plus the hot sauce or vinegar, if using.

"How about some greens?" Patanni asked. "The other day, I seen pokeweed growing in the fencerows near the Tillman place. Since then I been hankering for a mess of greens," he said. "Pokeweed with spring onions on top, then doused with some of your grandma's hot sauce."

"Don't forget your cornbread," Matanni piped up.

"And a few slices of sweet tomatoes," I added.

"Yessir," Patanni said. . . . "Ain't no better eating in the world!"

—GWYN HYMAN RUBIO,
Icy Sparks

MR. PANSEER'S NORTH INDIAN-STYLE SARSON KA SAAG

SERVES 4

Nearly a decade ago I was picked up at Heathrow Airport by Mr. Panseer, a delightful North Indian limo driver, and we immediately fell into conversation about—what else?—food. I nearly fell over when he told me that Punjabis eat *cornbread and greens*. The cornbread? Makki Ki Roti (*makki* means corn, *roti* bread, see page 109). The greens? Slowly cooked mustard greens. As he gave me a precise verbal recipe, jet lag vanished and I started taking notes. One secret, he told me, was that "you must cut the *saag* [greens] small-small-small-small-small." *Small 5X*, I noted.

So listen up. These are exquisite: beyond good. If you don't have the time or inclination to prepare makki ki roti as a side, partner these flavorful greens with rice, chapatis, or tortillas—something to sop up the delicious liquid.

1 tablespoon clarified butter or
   mild vegetable oil

1 onion, finely diced

1 to 2 green chiles, such as serranos,
   diced (with seeds and membranes
   for heat, without for mildness)

1 tablespoon peeled, minced fresh
   gingerroot

1 tablespoon finely diced garlic

2 pounds fresh mustard greens, stems
   included, picked over, very well
   washed, very finely chopped

2 tablespoons water, preferably spring
   or filtered

1 teaspoon salt

½ teaspoon freshly ground black
   pepper

Makki ki roti, rice, chapatis,
   or corn or whole wheat tortillas,
   for serving

·M·E·N·U·

PUNJABI PUNCTUATION

Mr. Panseer's North Indian–Style
Sarson Ka Saag

*

Makki Ki Roti
(page 109)

*

Lime Pickle

*

Tamarind Chutney

*

Thick, Lightly Sweetened
Plain Yogurt with Rosewater,
Served over Sliced Mango,
topped with Chopped Pistachio Nuts

1. Heat 2 teaspoons of the clarified butter or oil in a large nonstick skillet with a tight-fitting lid. Add the onions and cook until they are starting to become translucent, about 2 minutes. Lower the heat slightly. Add half the chiles and half the gingerroot and sauté for 2 minutes. (Set the remaining gingerroot and chiles aside.) Add the garlic and sauté for 1 minute.

2. Begin heaping into the skillet the mustard greens, with the water still clinging to them. Jam in as much as you can, and cover the pan. As the mustard greens cook down, add another batch. Keep going until you've added all the mustard greens.

3. Add the water, salt, and pepper. Cover and cook, very slowly, over extremely low heat, until the mustard greens are entirely soft and velvety, at least 1 hour.

4. Just before the mustard greens are ready, heat the remaining clarified butter or oil in a small nonstick skillet. Add the remaining chiles and gingerroot and cook over medium-high heat until sizzling hot, about 45 seconds. Stir into the cooked mustard greens and serve at once. Serve with makki ki roti or the rice or bread of your choice.

WILD GREENS

In the days before transport made lettuce, spinach, and indeed all green vegetables available year round, by winter's end Southerners and Yankees alike were craving greens powerfully. When spring began to show its face, but before even the earliest garden could begin to yield, close-to-the-land people gathered young, tender wild greens and cooked them. And almost anywhere you live, if there's a patch of open ground, you can do the same, with the help of either a knowledgeable friend or a wild-foods identification guidebook.

Some choices: dandelion greens, young poke, young milkweed (before it gets milky), emerging fiddlehead ferns, lamb's quarters, nettles (wear gloves while picking them; they burn and sting the skin if you touch them raw, but ten seconds of heat transforms them to an edible spinach-like splendor), violet leaves, watercress, highland cress, sheep sorrel, chickweed, and many more. Don't have a knowledgeable friend? Check out any of the countless wild-foods guides out there, such as the Euell Gibbons classic *Stalking the Wild Asparagus.* Live in Gotham? Go on an expedition to gather wild plants in Central Park with wild-foods expert Steve Brill (www.wildmanstevebrill.com).

Wash wild greens very well (especially if you got them from Central Park!) and use any of the methods already given to cook them. Just cut the cooking time in half.

SKILLET-FRIED CABBAGE

SERVES 4, WITH CORNBREAD AND
ONE OTHER SIDE DISH

This sounds and is so simple—but it's also just extraordinarily good. Fresh cabbage contains a surprising amount of natural sugar, and when you slice and sauté it, some of the edges caramelize deliciously. Salt very, very lightly, if at all; you don't want to distract from the sweetness. You'll want your largest skillet for this, preferably a cast-iron one, for sure one with a tight-fitting lid.

Sometimes organic cabbages are smaller than conventional, but what they may lack in size, they usually make up for in flavor: they're much sweeter. Depending on the size of your cabbage, you may want to use three quarters of a head or even a whole one, rather than the half called for.

If you use the lesser amount of butter, spray the skillet with cooking oil first.

The "one other side dish" referred to above might be something as simple as a platter of sliced garden fresh-tomatoes, crisp bacon or tempeh bacon, or a big pot of stew beans.

½ large head of fresh green cabbage, tough outer leaves and core removed

1 to 3 tablespoons butter

Salt

Wenonah Fay's Mama's "Plain Bread" (page 29), for serving

A side dish of your choice, for serving

1. Slice the cabbage into strips no more than ½ inch wide.

2. Place a large skillet over high heat. When it's good and hot, add the butter to taste (use enough to prevent the cabbage from sticking). Lower the heat slightly and add the cabbage. There will be quite a lot of cabbage.

3. Let the cabbage sizzle a bit, then stir-fry it, cooking over medium to medium-high heat, until the shreds have gotten a bit limp, smaller in volume, and browned around the edges, 6 to 8 minutes.

4. Pop the cover on. Turn off the heat and let the cabbage steam in its own juices for a minute or two. Lift the cover and add the tiniest bit of salt. Then serve, hot, with the plain bread and one other side dish of your choice.

A Salad Green Gift Basket

Particularly in hot weather, nothing beats a huge salad for dinner. Splash it with home-made dressing; garnish it with assorted bits of this and that: cheese, shredded raw beet or sliced cooked beets, nuts, avocado, fruit or dried fruit (no, not all at once, for heaven's sake!). This adds substance, interest, protein, color, contrasting textures, and general deliciousness; arrange prettily; serve with additional dressing on the side, plus the cornbread of your choice; voilà!

A small plate of one of the more complex salads in this section also serves as a fine first course.

Across the board, *always, always* wash greens very well, and dry thoroughly. Enjoy your salad days!

October Orchard Idyll

SERVES 4

This salad is delicious with Quasi-Colonial Cornbread or its variation, Quasi-Colonial Cornbread with Apples (page 44 or 45). To make it a component of a larger meal for eight, divide the salad among eight dishes and follow with a creamy, comforting soup such as pumpkin soup or tomato bisque.

2 red beets, steamed tender-crisp, peeled, and thinly sliced

2 golden beets, steamed tender-crisp, peeled, and thinly sliced

About 6 cups well washed baby spinach leaves

1 cup slivered green cabbage

2 to 3 scallions, minced

2 tablespoons Apple Cider Syrup Vinaigrette (recipe follows), plus extra for serving

Salt and freshly cracked black pepper

2 tart, very crisp apples, cored and diced

¼ to ⅓ pound mild blue cheese, such as Bourse or Gorgonzola, crumbled

1 cup walnuts, toasted and chopped

1. Divide the beet slices among four plates, overlapping slices in alternate colors.

2. Toss the spinach, cabbage, and scallions with 2 tablespoons of the vinaigrette. Taste and season with salt and pepper as needed.

3. Pile one quarter of the dressed greens in the center of each plate, allowing the beets to show. Sprinkle each salad with the apples, cheese, and walnuts. Pass additional dressing at the table.

APPLE CIDER SYRUP VINAIGRETTE

ABOUT 1⅓ CUPS

No, you don't *have* to use the walnut oil called for in this recipe, since it's sometimes hard to find and always on the pricey side. But when salads include toasted walnuts, as in the October Orchard Idyll, it is heavenly.

> ¼ **cup apple cider vinegar**
>
> **4 to 5 circlets of dried apple**
>
> **3 tablespoons apple cider syrup (see Pantry, page 346)**
>
> **1 tablespoon Dijon mustard**
>
> ⅛ **teaspoon cayenne (optional)**
>
> **1 teaspoon salt**

Freshly ground black pepper

1 cup toasted walnut oil (or any mild vegetable oil)

1. Bring the apple cider vinegar to a boil in a small saucepan. Add the dried apples and set aside to cool, letting the apples soak in the vinegar for at least 1 hour.

2. Combine the remaining ingredients (using plenty of pepper) except the walnut oil in a food processor and turn the machine on. Buzz until the apples are puréed, then, with the motor running, drizzle the walnut oil in through the hole in the feed tube until the dressing has emulsified.

BOSPORUS BREEZES SALAD

SERVES 4

Serve this crunchy, colorful salad alongside Dairy Hollow House Skillet-Sizzled Cornbread (page 12) or Corn Thinbread with Olives, Walnuts, Feta, and Sun-dried Tomatoes (page 106). To make a more filling presentation, add a scoop of commercially prepared baba ganouj or some marinated eggplant atop the salad, or tuck in a couple of prepared stuffed grape leaves next to the tomatoes.

4 cups sliced romaine lettuce

1 cup slivered green cabbage

1 cup finely slivered red cabbage

2 carrots, grated

1 or 2 stalks celery, sliced on the diagonal

1 small bunch watercress, well washed, with tough stems removed

2 or 3 scallions, minced

3 to 4 tablespoons Lemon-Tahini-Tamari Dressing (recipe follows), plus extra for serving

Salt and freshly cracked black pepper

2 red-ripe garden tomatoes, in 8 slices

1 can (12.5 ounces) chickpeas, well drained

1/2 cup pitted, diced black olives (preferably Turkish Gemlik)

1/3 cup sesame seeds, toasted

1/2 pound flavorful feta cheese (preferably Lebanese) in 4 slices

4 to 8 very fresh red radishes with tops, well washed

I. In a large bowl, toss together the lettuce, cabbages, carrots, celery, watercress, scallions, and 3 to 4 tablespoons of the dressing. Taste and add salt, pepper, and additional dressing as needed.

2. Place 2 tomato slices on each of four plates, overlapping at the edges of each plate. Heap a quarter of the dressed greens mixture in the center of each plate, allowing the tomatoes to show. Divide the chickpeas, olives, and sesame seeds among the plates. Place a slice of feta cheese on each plate, and garnish with 1 or 2 whole radishes. Pass additional dressing at the table.

LEMON-TAHINI-TAMARI DRESSING

ABOUT 2 1/2 CUPS

I have remained loyal to the deliciousness of this dressing for twenty-five-plus years, ever since I first enjoyed it at a now-long-defunct Los Angeles natural foods restaurant. I swooned over it and the waiter relayed this to the chef, who came out, be-turbaned, and told me how to make it, while I scribbled notes on a paper napkin. Pretty memorable in itself, but the night also stands out because the actress Sally Field was dining at the same time as my father and I. (The ne plus ultra of accidental celebrity sightings of about this same period, though, was also with my late father: a very old, very ample, very blonde

Mae West seated in a booth with two very young, very buff men, one on either side of her, in a German restaurant on Sunset. But I digress.) This makes a good-sized batch, but will keep nicely for up to a month.

- **½ cup mild vegetable oil**
- **2 tablespoons toasted Asian sesame oil**
- **⅓ cup freshly squeezed lemon juice, plus extra as needed**
- **¼ cup tamari or naturally fermented soy sauce, plus extra as needed**
- **1 garlic clove**
- **1 celery rib chopped**
- **¾ cup sesame tahini (from toasted, not raw, sesame seeds)**

Combine all the ingredients in a food processor; whir until smooth and thick and wonderful, stopping to pulse-chop and scrape the sides of the work bowl as needed. Add extra lemon juice and/or tamari to taste.

·M·E·N·U·

DRAGON'S DELIGHT

Gigantic Salad of Greens
with Scallion, Red Cabbage,
and Sungold Tomatoes with
Lemon-Tahini-Tamari Dressing

*

Beans, Dragon-in-the-New-South Style
(page 305)

*

Dairy Hollow House Skillet-Sizzled
Cornbread (page 12)

*

Vanilla Ice Cream with
Warm Maple-Apple Sauté (page 206)
and a Shot of Brandy

POMEGRANATE-HAZELNUT SALAD

SERVES 4

This festive, gorgeous, delectable, and highly seasonal salad is perfect as a first course at any winter holiday meal. It's met with raves when I've started Thanksgiving, Christmas, and Hanukkah dinners with it. Serve it with Glazed Maple Cornmeal Rolls (page 176), or Simply Corn Muffins (page 119), and then move on to whatever your traditional meal is for the occasion.

About 8 cups well washed mesclun or spring mix baby lettuces

2 or 3 scallions, minced

2 to 3 tablespoons Pomegranate-Hazelnut Dressing (recipe follows), plus extra for serving

Salt and freshly cracked black pepper

2 perfectly ripe Hass avocados, pitted and coarsely diced

Juicy seeds of 2 pomegranates (remove and discard all rind and fiber)

1 cup hazelnuts, toasted, skinned, and chopped medium-fine

1. In a large bowl toss together the lettuces and scallions with 2 to 3 tablespoons of dressing. Taste and add salt, pepper, and additional dressing as needed.

2. Place a large heap of the dressed greens on each of four plates. Divide the avocados, pomegranate seeds, and chopped hazelnuts among the plates, topping each salad with a scattering of each. Pass additional dressing at the table.

POMEGRANATE-HAZELNUT DRESSING

ABOUT 1½ CUPS

This dressing has been one of my favorite combinations of the last few years. The nut flavor is carried through in both the toasted nut itself and the nut oil, and the fruit both in the salad and, in concentrated form, the dressing.

Pomegranate molasses, like apple cider syrup, is simply pomegranate juice that has been boiled down to a thick sweet-tart syrup. You can purchase it at a Middle Eastern market or on the Internet (www.thespicehouse.com), or make it yourself: Just boil down two 8-ounce bottles of unsweetened pomegranate juice to ½ cup.

⅓ cup raspberry or red wine vinegar

¼ cup pomegranate molasses

1 teaspoon salt

Freshly ground black pepper

1 cup hazelnut oil, preferably toasted
hazelnut oil

Combine all of the ingredients (use plenty of pepper) except the hazelnut oil in a food processor and turn the machine on. Then, with the motor running, drizzle the hazelnut oil in through the hole in the feed tube until the dressing has emulsified.

BEANS, OLD SOUTH STYLE

SERVES 6 TO 8

T his is the classic, slow-cooked Southern method with beans, sometimes called "soup beans." They are *always* served with cornbread. I haven't eaten meat since I was twenty-two, so it's been years since I've had them this way, but I enjoyed them when I did, and I enjoy my vegetarian alternative now, which follows on page 305.

·M·E·N·U·

THANKSGIVING ON THE HILL

Pomegranate-Hazelnut Salad
*
Pumpkin-Tomato Bisque
*
Turkey and/or Hubbard Squash
Filled with Sweet-Savory
Cornbread Dressing (page 279)
*
Yukon Gold Potatoes Mashed
with Celery Root and Mascarpone
*
Turkey Gravy and/or Shiitake
Mushroom Gravy
*
Broccoli Rabe
with Lemon and Garlic
*
Cranberry Sauce
*
Glazed Maple Cornmeal Rolls
(page 176)
*
Homemade Pies

Serve these with any nonsweet cornbread, such as Ronni's Appalachian (page 21), Truman Capote's Family's (page 13), or Sylvia's Ozark (page 18).

1 pound dried beans (black-eyed peas, pinto beans, navy beans, big dried butterbeans; almost any kind will do, but these are the classic Southern choices)

¼ pound salt pork (sometimes sold as "white bacon"), rinsed to remove excess salt; or a ham hock

1 medium onion, halved

1 garlic clove, quartered

1 dried hot red chile pepper pod (optional)

Salt and freshly cracked black pepper

Nonsweet (preferably crumbly) cornbread, for serving

1. Start the night before by picking over and rinsing the beans, then soaking them overnight in as much water as your biggest soaking-pot will hold. (Exception: Black-eyed peas do not need presoaking.)

2. The next day, drain the beans and rinse them well. Transfer the beans to a large, heavy pot with a tight-fitting lid (a Dutch oven is ideal), and add fresh water to cover the beans by 1½ to 2 inches. (Exception: Black-eyed peas, not having been soaked, need a little more water; cover them by 3 to 3½ inches.) Add the rinsed salt pork or the ham hock, the onion, garlic, and hot pepper, if using, and bring to a boil. Then lower the heat to a simmer and let the beans cook until very soft and starting to break open. This could be as little as 45 minutes to 1 hour for black-eyes if they're

this year's crop, but for all others, allow 1½ to 2 hours. Taste a bean (blow first) to be sure it's nice and soft (you should be able to squash it against the roof of your mouth with your tongue).

3. Once the beans have softened, scoop out the salt pork or ham hock, the chile pod if you used one, and the onion halves (the garlic will have pretty much dissolved into the beans). Let the meat cool enough that you can handle it.

4. Meanwhile, mash or process ¾ cup or so of the beans with the onion halves to a thick paste. Return this to the pot, stirring well. This thickens the soupy beans very nicely. Continue to simmer the beans, covered, but on even lower heat.

5. By now, the meat should be cool. Pull or cut away any little pieces of meat, discarding any gristle or fat (some of the fat will have dissolved into the beans already, however, adding flavor). If the pieces of ham on the hock are large, chop them. Add the meat back to the beans, and stir again.

6. Taste for salt and pepper at this point (adding salt earlier would have prevented the beans reaching full doneness, and might have been overkill since there's also salt in the pork). Season to your liking, stir well, and let simmer, uncovered, about 30 minutes longer. Serve right away, with a slab of cornbread alongside. Even better, let the beans cool, refrigerate them overnight, and reheat the next day.

BEANS, DRAGON-IN-THE-NEW-SOUTH STYLE

SERVES 6 TO 8

These beans riff on the traditional method and ingredients, much like Greens, New South Style on page 293. Adding salty miso and smoky-spicy chipotle makes for a very alluring not-quite-parallel salt-pork universe. You traditional-method devotees can laugh all you want, but I guarantee you, you'll ask for seconds. Omit the dried chipotle, or use just half, if you don't like your beans to dance along the pain-pleasure axis of heat.

Serve these with any nonsweet cornbread, such as Ronni's Appalachian (page 21), Truman Capote's Family's (page 13), or Sylvia's Ozark (page 18).

1 pound dried beans (black-eyed peas, pinto beans, navy beans, big dried butterbeans; almost any kind will do, but these are the classic Southern choices)

1/2 to 1 dried chipotle pepper, broken in half (optional)

2 large onions, 1 halved, 1 chopped

5 garlic cloves, 2 whole, 3 chopped

3 tablespoons mild vegetable oil

2 carrots, scrubbed and chopped

2 celery ribs, chopped

1 red bell pepper, cored, seeded, and chopped (optional)

1 tablespoon toasted sesame oil

1 to 2 heaping tablespoons dark or light miso

1 to 2 cups vegetable stock (optional)

Salt and freshly cracked black pepper

Nonsweet cornbread, for serving

1. Start the night before by picking over and rinsing the beans, then soaking them overnight in as much water as your biggest soaking-pot will hold. (Exception: Black-eyed peas do not need presoaking.)

2. The next day, drain the beans and rinse them well. Transfer the beans to a large, heavy pot with a tight-fitting lid (a Dutch oven is ideal), and add fresh water to cover the beans by 1½ to 2 inches. (Exception: Black-eyed peas, not having been soaked, will absorb more water, so cover them by 3 to 3½ inches.)

3. Add the dried chipotle, if using, the halved onion, and the whole garlic cloves. Bring to a boil, lower the heat to a simmer, and let the beans cook until they are very soft and starting to break open. This could be as little as 45 minutes to 1 hour for black-eyes if they're this year's crop, but for all others, allow 1½ to 2 hours. Taste a bean (blow first) to be sure it's nice and soft (you should be able to squash it against the roof of your mouth with your tongue).

4. As the beans near tenderness, place the vegetable oil in a separate skillet over medium heat. Add the chopped onions and sauté, stirring often, for about 8 minutes. Add the carrots and continue sautéing, stirring often, for another 3 to 4 minutes. Add the celery and bell pepper, if using, and sauté a few minutes longer. Finally, lower the heat, add the chopped garlic, and sauté 2 minutes more.

5. Once the beans have softened, stir in the vegetable sauté, sesame oil, and miso. By this time the halved onion and the garlic will have more or less dissolved into the beans' juice. Fish out the dried chipotle pieces (discard them, unless you want it so hot your hair will stand on end, in which case see the next step).

6. If you feel your beans should be thicker (there are partisans of both soupy beans and thick beans as cornbread accompaniments), scoop out ¾ cup or so of the beans (with, if desired, the chipotle pieces, minus their tough stem). Mash them together, either by hand or by buzzing in a food processor. Stir this back into the pot, thickening the soupy beans nicely. If, on the other hand, your beans seem *too* thick, add a cup or two of vegetable stock or water. Add salt (beans need quite a bit) and pepper as needed.

7. Continue to simmer the beans, covered, but on even lower heat, for another 15 minutes.

8. Taste for seasonings again. Serve in a bowl, with the cornbread.

BASIC FRIJOLES

SERVES 6 TO 8

Almost as much a staple to Mexican cuisine as the corn tortilla are these simply cooked Frijoles de la Olla, or Beans in a Soup Pot, an *olla* being the clay pot traditionally used. These are "basic" because they are the beginning of countless rustic Mexican dishes, a few of which are listed in the variations.

Serve these frijoles with Corn Tortillas (page 82), Chou-Chou's Original Dallas "Hot-Stuff" Cornbread (page 69), Jane's Texas-via-Vermont Mexican Cornbread (page 71), Budin de Elote (page 93), or Humitas (page 94).

1 pound dried pinto or pink beans

**2 large onions, 1 quartered,
  1 finely chopped**

1 to 1¾ teaspoons salt

**2 tablespoons olive or canola oil,
  bacon drippings, or lard**

4 garlic cloves, chopped

Tortillas or cornbread, for serving

UNIVERSAL COMPANIONS:
BEANS AND CORNBREAD

Cornbread loves company. Much like gently long-cooked greens, low- and slow-simmered beans make an ideal, and widely popular, cornbread companion, with almost the same soulful resonance as greens and cornbread: beyond taste, nutrition, or habit, though this duo is also rich in all three. In the Southwest, the beans might be in the form of chili and the cornbread might be tortillas or pan-style. In the Northeast the beans will be baked and sweetened and the cornbread will be Classic Boston Brown Bread (page 62). And in the South, the beans will be quite simple and straighforward, seasoned, as with the greens of this region, mostly by salt pork.

Whether layered with a spice market's complexity, or left relatively plain-Jane in a slightly savory soup-stew, beans bring out cornmeal's almost-sweet flavor, and round out every *cornbread* bite.

1. Start the night before by picking over and rinsing the beans, then soaking them overnight in as much water as your biggest soaking-pot will hold.

2. The next day, drain the beans and rinse them well. Transfer the beans to a large, heavy pot with a tight-fitting lid (a Dutch oven is ideal), and add fresh water to cover the beans by about 1½ inches. Add the quartered onion and bring to a boil. Then lower the heat to a simmer, cover, and let the beans cook until very soft and starting to break open. This could be as little as an hour, and you may need to add a little more boiling water if the level of liquid is getting low. Stir the beans occasionally. Taste

"When we arrived lentil soup was simmering on the wood stove, and there was buttery corn bread and a green salad with tahini dressing, and red wine. We scarfed up great hunks of bread, and plate after plate of soup, and . . . evening shrank the room into a little glowing bowl. . . . I knew . . . that I was one of the privileged of the earth."

—BONNIE FRIEDMAN,
Writing Past Dark

a bean (blow first) to be sure it's nice and soft (you should be able to squash it against the roof of your mouth with your tongue). When it's at this point, add the salt to taste.

3. As the beans near tenderness, place the oil, drippings, or lard in a separate skillet over medium heat. Add the chopped onion and sauté, stirring often, until slightly browned, about 6 minutes. Then, lower the heat, add the garlic, and sauté 2 minutes more. Stir the sauté into the salted, by-now-tender beans.

4. You can eat the beans right away, with tortillas or the cornbread of your choice, or prepare them ahead of time, refrigerate them overnight, and reheat them (which makes them more flavorful). Or, use them for any of the following variations.

VARIATIONS:
FRIJOLES BORRACHOS

This is my favorite Mexican way with beans, either as is or used in any of the variations that follow. Simply pour 1 bottle (12 ounces) of Mexican beer, such as Tecate or Dos Equis, over the soaked and drained beans in step 2, and then add water to cover by $1\frac{1}{2}$ inches. Continue as directed. Amazing how this small substitution deepens and enriches the beans' flavors.

FRIJOLES REFRITOS

Refritos means "well" fried, not "twice" fried, as you commonly hear it put in the U.S. Simply heat 3 or 4 tablespoons of the fat of your choice (choose the same as you did in the basic recipe) in a large, heavy skillet. Pour in 3 to 4 cups of the basic frijoles with their broth and raise the heat, stirring and mashing, either with the back of a spoon or with a potato masher. The object is to cook off most of the water, creating a nice, thick, texture-y purée, firm but moist; this will take 8 to 10 minutes.

FRIJOLES CON QUESO

Turn the oven to broil. Spread either the basic or refrito frijoles in a shallow, oiled baking dish, and top evenly with ½ to 1 cup (2 to 4 ounces) crumbled queso fresco, farmer's cheese, feta, or ricotta salata. Place under the broiler until the cheese is slightly melty and lightly browned.

FRIJOLES CHARROS

For these cowboy-style beans, heat a skillet and add 3 tablespoons of the fat of your choice. Add 6 ounces of Mexican chorizo (either traditional meat-style, or the soy type, like Soyrizo) and brown. Remove the browned chorizo from the pan with a slotted spoon or spatula, draining it on a paper towel or brown paper bag if very fatty. Add 1 large onion, finely chopped, and 1 to 2 fresh serrano chiles, finely chopped (with seeds for heat, without for mildness) to the fat remaining in the skillet and sauté until lightly browned, stirring often, 5 or 6 minutes. Add 2 or 3 fresh tomatoes, seeds and all, diced, and cook 2 or 3 minutes more. Stir this mixture into a

---

·M·E·N·U·

TEX-MEX IN THE GREEN MOUNTAINS

Guacamole

*

Frijoles Borrachos

*

Corn Tortillas (page 82)

*

Jane's Texas-via-Vermont
Mexican Cornbread (page 71)

*

Sizzling Hot Sauté of Onions,
Mushrooms, Red and Green Bell
Peppers, and Roasted Green Chile
Glazed with Soy and Honey

*

Sides of Salsa, Minced Cilantro,
and Grated Cheddar Cheese

*

Lime Sorbet with
Fresh Pineapple and Tequila

Dutch oven containing 5 or 6 cups of Basic Frijoles. Bring to a boil, lower the heat to simmer, and cook, stirring often, until the bean broth has reduced down and the flavors are nicely commingled, 20 to 25 minutes. Serve in bowls with a dab of sour cream and a sprinkle of fresh cilantro, if you like.

NEW ENGLAND BAKED BEANS

SERVES 6 TO 8

These are a must with Classic Boston Brown Bread (page 62). I first published this recipe in *The Bean Book* in 1972, and I still get requests for it from people who remember it fondly but lost their copy of the book along the way. (If you are one of those people, not to worry: Not only is the recipe here again below, but I'll be doing an updated reissue of my early leguminous tome one of these days.)

Vegetarians can omit the salt pork and add 2 or 3 tablespoons of butter or toasted sesame oil (plus a few cubes of firm tofu, for faux salt pork).

4 cups soldier beans, Maine yellow-eye beans, or white beans such as navy, Great Northern, or pea beans

Vegetable oil cooking spray

1 large onion, peeled and sliced

1 tablespoon salt

1/2 teaspoon freshly ground black pepper, plus extra as needed

1 1/2 teaspoons mustard powder

1/3 cup dark brown sugar

1/4 cup dark (but not blackstrap) molasses

4 whole cloves

2 medium onions, unpeeled

1/4 to 1/2 pound salt pork, rinsed, dried, and diced

Boiling water or bean stock, as needed

Classic Boston Brown Bread (page 62), for serving

1. Start the night before by picking over and rinsing the beans, then soaking them overnight in as much water as your biggest soaking-pot will hold.

2. The next day, drain the beans and rinse them well. Transfer the beans to a large, heavy pot with a tight-fitting lid (a Dutch oven is ideal), and add fresh water to cover the beans by about 1 1/2 inches. Bring to a boil. Then lower the heat to a simmer, cover, and let the beans cook until almost but not quite tender, 45 minutes to 1 1/4 hours. (Check the beans and give them a stir every once in a while; you may need to add a little more boiling water if the level of liquid is getting low.)

3. Remove the beans from the heat and let them cool. Preheat the oven to 250°F. Drain the beans, *reserving the bean liquid* (this is very important).

4. Spray a deep, lidded casserole, preferably an old-fashioned glazed pottery baked-bean pot, with oil. Spread the sliced onion over the bottom of the casserole, and spoon the beans, without their liquid, over the slices.

5. Now, take a quart of the reserved bean liquid and whisk into it the salt, ½ teaspoon pepper (or more to taste), mustard powder, brown sugar, and molasses. Pour this mixture over the beans.

6. Stick 2 cloves into each whole unpeeled onion, and bury both of these onions in the beans. Things are getting interesting now, aren't they? Also, go ahead and bury the diced salt pork in the beans.

7. Cover the pot, and bake the beans slowly for 7 to 8 hours, checking every so often and adding boiling water or bean stock as needed to keep the beans from drying out. During the last hour or so, uncover the beans so they have a chance to develop a nice crust. Remove the whole onions and serve with the Boston brown bread.

> **"Boston runs to brains as well as to beans and brown bread."**
> —WILLIAM COWPER BRANN,
> *The Iconoclast*

BRATTLEBORO BAKED BEANS BORRACHO

SERVES 6 TO 8, WITH ACCOMPANIMENTS (CORNBREAD PLUS A SALAD OR SLAW)

This fine, jazzed-up combination brings together New England–style baked beans with the Mexican touch of beer as part of the cooking liquid, making the beans *borracho* ("drunken"). The seasonings are also amped up: a deeply and interestingly tasty baked bean recipe, and vegetarian, too. Try this with Mary Baird's Johnny Cake (page 57), Quasi-Colonial Cornbread (page 44), any of the Southwestern cornbreads, Dairy Hollow House Skillet-Sizzled Cornbread (page 12), or, of course, Classic Boston Brown Bread (page 62).

Brattleboro Baked Beans Borracho are agreeable, as you can see.

1 pound dried soldier beans, Maine yellow-eye beans, or white beans such as navy, Great Northern, or pea beans

1 bottle (12 ounces) beer, ale, or stout

Vegetable oil cooking spray

1 large onion, chopped

3 garlic cloves, minced

⅓ cup tomato paste

⅔ cup pure maple syrup, preferably Grade B

⅓ cup brown sugar

1 tablespoon mustard powder

2 tablespoons finely minced peeled fresh gingerroot

1 canned chipotle pepper in adobo sauce, diced, with about 1 tablespoon of its sauce

1 tablespoon salt

1 teaspoon freshly cracked black pepper, plus extra as needed

Finely grated zest of 1 orange, preferably organic

2 tablespoons toasted sesame oil, or butter

6 whole cloves

2 small onions, unpeeled

6 ounces extra-firm tofu, well drained, diced (optional)

Boiling water or bean stock, as needed

Cornbread, for serving

1. Pick over and rinse the beans. Soak them overnight in enough water to cover them by 2 inches. Drain well the next morning, rinsing the beans several times.

2. Place the beans in a heavy pot or Dutch oven with a tight-fitting lid. Pour the bottle of beer over the beans, and then add enough fresh water to barely cover. Bring to a boil, lower the heat to a simmer, and let the beans cook, covered, until almost tender, about 1 hour. Give them the occasional stir, adding a little more water if you need to.

3. Preheat the oven to 250°F and spray a bean pot or any other deep, lidded casserole with oil. Scatter the chopped onion over the bottom.

4. Cool the almost-cooked beans, then drain them, reserving the liquid.

5. Place the drained beans in the prepared bean pot over the chopped onion.

6. Whisk together about 4 cups of the reserved bean liquid with the garlic, tomato paste, maple syrup, brown sugar, mustard powder, gingerroot, chipotle and adobo, salt, 1 teaspoon pepper (or more to taste), orange zest, and oil or butter. Whisk well, and add this to the beans. Give the beans a couple good stirs to distribute everything nicely.

7. Stick 3 cloves into each of the small onions and add to the pot along with the tofu (your faux salt pork), if desired. Pop the bean pot, covered, into the oven.

8. Bake the beans slowly for 7 to 8 hours, checking every so often and adding boiling water or bean stock as needed to keep the beans from drying out. During the last hour or so, uncover the beans so they have a chance to develop a nice crust. Serve, hot, with the cornbread of your choice.

SATISFYINGLY EFFECTIVE OVEN USE

When baking beans, capture a little of that extra oven space: Make a pan of baked apples alongside the beans (after their first hour of baking). This is a wise use of energy, and you can baste the apples (cored, studded with cloves, cavities filled with lemon, brown sugar, and half a cinnamon stick) with maple syrup or apple juice concentrate every time you stir the beans. While you're at it, bake a few sweet potatoes for tomorrow night's dinner. It's so satisfying to piggyback on fuel, warming and scenting your house meanwhile. I think a life built around such gentle economies and daily pleasures is "gaining on happiness," as my friend Pam Jones puts it.

A CHILI RECEPTION

I would be remiss if I didn't at least mention what many people think is the ultimate cornbread go-with soup-stew: chili. After nominal agonizing, I decided chili was just beyond the scope of this book. Why? Two reasons. First, because there are just too many chilies I love, and second, because chili itself is such a hotly (in both senses) debated subject . . . almost as much so as cornbread. A person could write a book on chili alone, and many have. So I refer you onward.

For the carnivorously inclined, check out Santa Fe cooking maven Jane Butel's classic book *Chili Madness* and the offering by Jane Stern of *Roadfood* fame, *Chili Nation,* which explores American chilies coast to coast and state by state. My favorite vegetarian chilies—seven of 'em—share pride of place in my last cookbook, *Passionate Vegetarian.*

One last chili note: Any chili can be made and frozen in advance, then thawed and held fabulously well in a slow-cooker set on low. When you have bunches of people arriving at different times for a long weekend, chili is just the ticket, because it is pleased to wait for and welcome each.

In fact, chili's become a night-before-Thanksgiving semi-tradition in my home. Make a big old batch of simple tortilla dough (see page 82) and as each guest arrives, swiftly press out and griddle a few fresh corn tortillas (an incredibly simple and fast process once you've done 'em a few times, I promise) and serve those and the chili. What reception could be warmer?

LENTIL SOUP WITH GARLIC AND GREENS

SERVES 4 TO 6, WITH CORNBREAD AND SALAD

L et's start our look at the third constant cornbread companion— soups and stews—with this luscious but simple soup. After all, it could have been placed under greens, beans, *or* stews. However you categorize it, you will love it with any slightly sweet cornbread, such as Dairy Hollow House Skillet-Sizzled Cornbread (page 12), Gold-and-White Tasty Cornbread (page 58), or Mary Baird's Johnny Cake (page 57).

If you are a wild-greens aficionado, this is one terrific place to use them. And don't miss the lemony Middle Eastern variation. Varying the seasonings makes it almost an entirely different soup.

1 pound lentils, picked over and rinsed

1 bay leaf, broken in half

About 2 quarts (8 cups) vegetable stock or water

Vegetable oil cooking spray

3 to 4 tablespoons olive oil

2 large onions, chopped

·M·E·N·U·

FIRST LIGHTING OF THE FIREPLACE, 2006

Mesclun Greens with Lemon-Tahini-Tamari Dressing (page 300)

*

Lentil Soup with Garlic and Greens

*

Dixie Spoonbread (page 191)

*

Dark, Extra-Gingery Gingerbread, with Darra's Hot Citrus Sauce (page 344)

---

1 head of garlic, peeled

2 carrots, sliced or diced (optional)

1 celery rib, halved lengthwise and diced (optional)

Salt and freshly ground black pepper

1 pound fresh spinach, well washed, stems finely chopped, leaves sliced

Cornbread, for serving

1. Place the lentils in a soup pot with the bay leaf, and cover with the stock or water. Bring to a boil, turn down to a simmer, and cook until the lentils are very soft, 45 to 60 minutes.

2. Meanwhile, spray a large cast-iron skillet with the oil and place it over medium heat. When it's hot, add 3 tablespoons of the olive oil, then the onions, lowering the heat slightly. Sauté, stirring often, for about 8 minutes. Between stirs, coarsely chop about half the garlic.

3. When the onions have reached the 8-minute point, add the carrots and celery, if using. (You may need the additional tablespoon of olive oil at this point.) Continue sautéing for another 2 minutes, then lower the heat, add the chopped garlic, and sauté, stirring, 2 to 3 minutes more. You want the onions very soft but not browned.

4. By this point, the lentils are probably about half-cooked. Scrape the vegetable sauté into them, deglazing the skillet with a little of the lentil cooking liquid. Let the lentils continue cooking until very soft, then add salt (you'll need quite a lot) and freshly ground pepper to taste.

5. When the lentils are soft, scoop out a good ladleful of them and transfer them to a food processor with the remaining (raw whole) garlic. Buzz to a purée and transfer this wonderfully heady purée back to the soup. Give a stir, add the spinach, and stir again.

6. Turn the heat down still lower, partially cover the pot, and simmer until the greens have softened and the flavors have blended, 10 to 15 minutes more. Taste again for salt and pepper, and serve, hot, with cornbread.

VARIATION: MIDDLE EASTERN-STYLE GARLICKY LENTIL SOUP WITH LEMON

The seasonings make all the difference here, and a delicious difference it is. Sometimes I like the plainer version of this soup, sometimes this one. Follow the original recipe, making the following changes: Omit the carrot and celery. Add, with the garlic in step 3, 2 teaspoons cumin seeds and 1½ teaspoons ground coriander seed. When you add the sauté to the simmering lentils in step 4, also add 1 teaspoon dried thyme leaves and 1 tablespoon tomato paste. When the soup is done, stir in the juice of 1 or 2 lemons. Serve, garnished with a scatter of chopped fresh parsley and cilantro mixed together, and a lemon slice, including rind, floating atop each bowl. This variation is just perfect with Corn Thinbread with Olives, Walnuts, Feta, and Sun-dried Tomatoes (page 106).

VEGETABLE MAFÉ

SERVES 8

A rich African vegetable stew, this is typically served over a starchy side dish—fufu or ugali (cornmeal mush), mashed plantains, rice, millet—but it's every bit as good with cornbread (see the Kwanzaa Karamu menu, page 47, for suggestions). Like many cornbread-friendly stews, it includes greens. Although I've given the main recipe using frozen spinach and fresh cabbage, the variation that follows, using robust fresh greens, is no doubt closer to the original.

You can turn the spiciness up (use 3 peppers, leave in their seeds and white fiber) or down (use just 1 or 2 peppers, seeds and fiber removed).

Vegetable oil cooking spray

2 tablespoons peanut or other mild vegetable oil

1 large onion, diced

1 tablespoon peeled, minced fresh gingerroot

2 garlic cloves, minced

2 to 3 hot chile peppers, such as serranos, finely chopped, to taste (with seeds and membranes for heat, without for mildness)

1 medium butternut squash, peeled and cut in ½-inch dice

1 medium rutabaga or turnip, cut in ½-inch dice

2 medium carrots, sliced in ½-inch rounds

2 to 3 small red potatoes, skin on, cut in ½-inch dice

¼ head of cabbage, thickly sliced

3 cups canned diced tomatoes in juice

½ cup vegetable stock or water

½ cup smooth peanut butter, preferably natural and unhydrogenated

2 teaspoons to 1 tablespoon honey

1 package (10 ounces) frozen chopped spinach, thawed (optional)

Salt and freshly ground black pepper

1. Spray a large, nonreactive pot or Dutch oven with oil, then add the peanut oil and place over medium heat. When it's good and hot, add the onion and cook, stirring frequently, until it starts to get limp and brown around the edges, 5 to 6 minutes. Add the gingerroot and sauté for 3 minutes longer. Add the garlic and chiles, and sauté for 1 minute longer. Lower the heat.

2. Add the butternut squash, rutabaga or turnip, carrots, potatoes, and cabbage. Stir well to coat them with the oil and the onion-gingerroot-chile sauté. Cook, stirring often, for 5 minutes longer. Then add the tomatoes and stock or water. Simmer, half-covered, until the vegetables are tender, 12 to 15 minutes.

3. Using a ladle, scoop out about ½ cup cooking liquid from the vegetables and place it in a medium heat-proof bowl. Stir or whisk in the peanut butter until the mixture is smooth. (You could also do this in a food processor.) Add this back to the pot along with the honey to taste, spinach, if using, and salt and pepper to taste. Cook just until heated through, about 5 minutes more.

VARIATION: VEGETABLE MAFÉ WITH A MESS OF FRESH GREENS

For the cabbage and frozen spinach, substitute 1 to 1½ pounds assorted hearty greens (collards, kale, and mustard), well washed and chopped. Follow the recipe through the point in step 2 where the vegetables cook with the onion-gingerroot-chile sauté for 5 minutes. Then add the greens, cover the pot, and turn the heat down just a bit; let the greens cook until they start to wilt. Give a stir or two, cover again, and let cook for a few minutes more. Add the tomatoes and stock, and cook for 10 minutes more. Continue through step 3.

CALDO VERDE

SERVES 6 TO 8

Healthy, hearty, and garlicky, a bowl of this stew with Portuguese broa (see page 103), is a meal that gets you through any literal or figurative stormy weather. I've heard caldo verde described as Portuguese soul food. *Caldo* means both "stew" and "stew pot" (like cauldron) and *verde*, "green." Here, I've combined a dozen different versions to come up with this one, rich and complex. Please note that this is one of those stews that uses both of cornbread's favorite partners: beans *and* greens; it is also a stew I used to eat with meat but now make vegetarian; both versions follow.

Garlic heads and individual garlic cloves vary greatly in size; you are probably looking at 3 to 4 heads of garlic to get the requisite cup. Although I am usually a stickler for peeling my own garlic right before use, caldo verde requires so very much garlic that you might be served well by buying one of the jars of prepeeled garlic available in many supermarket produce sections.

Vegetable oil cooking spray

2½ quarts (10 cups) vegetable,
beef, or chicken stock, or water

6 to 8 medium potatoes (about 2 pounds),
peeled and coarsely chopped

2 bay leaves

¼ teaspoon ground cloves

1 Golden Delicious or Gala apple, peeled,
cored, and halved

1 cup peeled garlic cloves (yes, you read
this right), chopped fine

3 to 4 tablespoons olive oil

2 onions, chopped

¾ pound chorizo sausage, removed
from its casing and crumbled

½ to 1½ teaspoons crushed red
pepper flakes

1 to 2 teaspoons Hungarian sweet
paprika, preferably smoked

1 pound kale, tough center ribs removed,
cut crosswise into thin ribbons

1 can (10 ounces) diced tomatoes in juice

2 cans (15 ounces each) white beans,
either navy or Great Northern

Salt and freshly ground black pepper

Broa, for serving (optional)

2 or 3 lemons, quartered lengthwise

I. Spray a large stockpot with the oil and add
the stock or water. Bring it to a boil, turn down
to a simmer, and drop in the potatoes, bay
leaves, ground cloves, apple, and about half the
garlic. Let simmer, half-covered, over medium

heat until the potatoes and apple are fairly soft,
about 20 minutes.

2. Meanwhile, heat 3 to 4 tablespoons of olive
oil in a skillet over medium heat. Add the
onions and sauté, stirring until softened, about
5 minutes. Add the chorizo, lower the heat
slightly, and continue sautéing for a few
minutes more, until the chorizo is browned and
has rendered most of its fat (which you may
then drain if you like). Add the remainder of
the garlic, the crushed red pepper, and paprika,
stirring and cooking 1 minute more, then turn
off the heat.

3. Back at the soup pot, once the potatoes are
done, scoop out about half of them along with
whatever apple pieces you can find (much of
the apple may simply have dissolved into the
soup). Mash these together in a bowl.

4. Scrape the onion-chorizo mixture into the
soup pot, deglazing the skillet with a little of
the potato broth and pouring the deglazed bits
into the soup pot as well. Then add the kale to
the soup pot and simmer, giving the occasional
stir, for another 15 minutes or so. When the kale
is nice and tender, stir in the mashed potato–
apple mixture, the tomatoes, and the beans.
Bring to a full boil, then turn back down to
medium low.

5. Let the soup simmer for another 15 minutes,
season with salt and pepper to taste (lots and
lots of black pepper, in my view the more the
better).

CALDO VERDE: PEEKING INTO THE MELTING POT

I first tasted the Portuguese cornbread called broa (see page 103) and caldo verde in Martha's Vineyard, where Portuguese fishing families go back generations (indeed, the largest single concentration of Portuguese Americans is in southern coastal Massachusetts; immigrants who weren't fishermen were usually farmers or millworkers). Some Portuguese were among the earliest American settlers; others came in the mid-twentieth century, when the dictator Salazar was in power.

My interest dates back to a tenth grade school trip to the Vineyard in January, to research tourism-based economies in the off-season. I got side-tracked: struck because I'd thought of early explorers of America as Spanish and British, and here were the Portuguese.

In the fifteenth century they were equally aggressive, colonizing parts of South America (Brazil), Africa (Angola, Mozambique), and India (Goa). Vigorous traders, they were the first Europeans to reach Japan, India, and China; the first to take New World corn and chiles to these places, and Africa.

The Portuguese were also spice traders. This is partly why caldo verde varies from family to family and village to village throughout Portugal and the Azores (as does *sancocho,* page 322, in Central America). One caldo verde may have chile, another black pepper, a third turmeric or cloves, a fourth paprika.

I didn't get a good grade on my off-season tourism paper. But from this remove I imagine the goodness of caldo verde has lasted me much longer, and served me much better.

6. Serve the soup with Broa, if you like, either right away, or cool it overnight and reheat it the next day—even better. Pass the lemons at the table.

VARIATION: VEGETARIAN CALDO VERDE

I can almost hear the Portuguese fishermen snorting, but this is great. Follow the recipe above, using vegetable stock or water as the cooking liquid, and substituting vegetarian chorizo, such as Soyrizo or Tofurky Chorizo, for the meat sausage.

UNCANNILY GOOD SANTA FE-STYLE QUICK GREEN CHILE SOUP-STEW

SERVES 4 TO 6 GENEROUSLY

I n an ever more time-pressured world, we all need the occasional quick-and-good fix. As fast as opening a few cans, this is uncannily good, even without the optional toppings. Begin

baking a batch of High Desert Blue Corn Muffins with Sage and Toasted Pine Nuts (page 129); this will be done by the time they emerge from the oven.

> Vegetable oil cooking spray
> 1 can (15 ounces) black beans
> 1 can (15 ounces) kidney beans
> 1 can (15 ounces) chickpeas
> 1 can (15 ounces) black-eyed peas
> 1 can (28 ounces) chopped tomatoes
> 2 cans (15 ounces each) New Mexico–style green chile enchilada sauce (mild, medium, or hot)
> 1 cup canned, unsweetened pumpkin purée
> Salt and freshly ground black pepper
> Grated Cheddar or Monterey Jack cheese, for serving (optional)
> Reduced-fat sour cream or tofu sour cream, for serving (optional)
> Minced cilantro, for serving (optional)

1. Spray a large, heavy soup pot with oil.

2. Place the beans, chickpeas, black-eyed peas, and tomatoes, including all their liquid, in the pot and heat together over medium-high heat, stirring often. When the mixture is good and hot, lower the heat to medium low and stir in the green enchilada sauce and pumpkin. Reheat, season with salt and pepper to taste, and, when piping hot, ladle it up into good thick soup bowls. Pass the optional accompaniments at the table. That's it! Can you believe how good it is?

Leyla's Chicken "Saturday Sancocho"

SERVES 4

Although this stew is prepared differently throughout Central and South America, cassava (or yuca) and green plantains are always key ingredients. Leyla Torres, author of the children's book *Saturday Sancocho*, says that the recipe below has been handed down in her family from one generation to the next. "When I researched it for my book I did call my Aunt Lola. She explained to me with great detail what I should put in this sancocho first and second and next, but when it came to amounts she never gave me anything with the precision I needed to write it and put it in print in a book. She assumed that I exactly understood how much she meant as she said 'Place THE plantains and THE corn in the pot before THE cassava.' When I pressed—'How much plantain, Lolita?' she said, 'You'll see, two or three, and if you feel like it, throw in a bit of squash.'"

There, Leyla and I agree, speaks a good cook. Leyla undertook the setting down of measurements.

Before beginning this, a trip to a Latino market or, in larger areas, the Latino produce section in the supermarket, will almost certainly be in order.

2 medium onions, chopped

2 garlic cloves, minced

1½ teaspoons salt

1 3-pound broiler-fryer chicken, cut into pieces

2 green plantains, peeled and cut crosswise into thirds

2 ears of fresh corn, shucked, cobs cut crosswise into fourths

2 small to medium yucca roots, peeled and cut into large pieces (see Note)

3 carrots, quartered

1 bunch of fresh cilantro, including stems, well rinsed and chopped, plus extra for garnish

2 tablespoons mild vegetable oil

4 small tomatoes, chopped

1 teaspoon ground cumin

Salt and freshly ground black pepper

Accompaniments (optional): Leyla's Arepas (page 99) and/or white rice

1. Combine 2 quarts water, half the onions, half the garlic, and the salt in a 6-quart soup pot. Bring to a gentle boil, and add the chicken. Cover the pot and reduce the heat; simmer for 10 minutes.

2. Add the plantains and corn; simmer for 5 more minutes. Add the yucca, carrots, and

cilantro. Let simmer until the vegetables are tender, about 40 minutes, over medium heat.

3. Toward the end of the 40 minutes, place the oil in a heavy skillet over medium heat. Add the remaining garlic and onions, and cook, stirring often, until the vegetables are soft but not brown, about 6 minutes. Add the tomatoes and cook for 2 to 3 minutes. Stir in the cumin, then add salt and pepper to taste.

4. Transfer the chicken to a large serving bowl and spoon the stew over it. Sprinkle with additional chopped cilantro and serve steaming hot, with arepas, and /or white rice, if you wish.

NOTE: Yucca, also known as manioc or cassava, is a white, starchy tropical root vegetable somewhat similar in flavor to a potato. Its cooking qualities are similar to that of potato as well, except that when it cooks in liquid, it has a clearer, more translucent quality than potato, and it tastes—well, yucca-y instead of potato-y.

To use yucca, peel away the thick brown skin with a sharp knife and cut the parchment-white flesh as needed. You might also need to cut away and discard the root's tough fibrous core.

DRAGON-STYLE SANCOCHO

SERVES 8

How does a New York–Arkansas–Vermont Jewish gringa have the temerity to come up with a sancocho when her own background has not the slightest Spanish inflection? Read and read and read, talk to people, compare recipes, combine recipes, take what I like best from any number of same, and tweak them to my personal taste and sensibilities. Though vegetarian and non-Latina I am, I stand by this intensely savory stew, with its layers of flavor and color, as proudly as I stood by my gumbo. With fresh hot arepas served alongside—it is just too good.

Besides, dragons are known for being *muy caliente*, right?

Despite the length of the ingredients list, this is simpler than it looks. You can make it the day before (which, if possible, makes the sancocho even more incredibly full-flavored); in some markets, you can even buy some of the vegetables, like the butternut squash, fresh but peeled and already diced. If you want a higher proportion of the savory liquid to solid components (my preference), use the lesser amount of all vegetables for which a range is given.

Many sancochos use the juice of *naranja agria*, or sour orange. A combination of orange, lemon or lime, and grapefruit juice works beautifully.

FOR THE MARINADE

Juice of 1 orange

Juice of 1/2 lime or lemon

Juice of 1/2 grapefruit

About 1/2 bunch of fresh flat-leaf parsley, stems included, rinsed and coarsely chopped

About 3/4 bunch of fresh cilantro, stems included, rinsed and coarsely chopped

About 1/4 bunch of fresh oregano, stems included, rinsed and coarsely chopped

1 bunch of scallions, discolored or dry stems removed, coarsely chopped

3 garlic cloves, smashed

2 teaspoons salt

Freshly ground black pepper

1 cake (4 ounces) tempeh, cut into chunky squares

FOR THE STEW

2 1/2 quarts (10 cups) good, flavorful vegetable stock

1 can (14 ounces) diced tomatoes in juice

1 to 2 ears of fresh corn, shucked, cut crosswise into 4 to 6 large rounds

1 green plaintain, peeled, cut in half lengthwise, then crosswise into 1/2-inch slices

1 ripe plaintain, peeled, cut in half lengthwise, then crosswise into 1/2-inch slices

1 small butternut squash, peeled, seeded, and cut into chunks (2 to 2 1/2 cups prepared chunks)

1 large sweet potato, peeled and cut into chunks (2 1/2 to 3 cups prepared chunks)

1 to 2 small yucca roots (see Note, page 323)

FOR THE FINISHING SAUTÉ

3 tablespoons mild vegetable oil

1 large onion, chopped

2 jalapeños or other hot green or red chiles, minced

2 large green bell peppers, cored, seeded, and chopped

1 package (12 to 14 ounces) soy chorizo (slice link sausages into 1-inch rounds; crumble bulk varieties)

Salt and freshly ground black pepper

Hot sauce, such as Tabasco, for serving

Chopped fresh cilantro, for serving

1. Combine all the marinade ingredients except the tempeh in a food processor and buzz well, stopping a few times to scrape down the sides.

Transfer this green and pungent combo to a large bowl. Add the tempeh, toss well, cover, and let marinate for 2 to 3 hours at room temperature, or refrigerate overnight.

2. In a large stockpot, combine 8 cups (2 quarts) of the stock and all the remaining ingredients in the stew component list. (Reserve the remaining stock for step 4 of the recipe.) Bring to a serious boil, then lower the heat to a simmer. Let simmer over medium heat, half-covered, for about 45 minutes.

3. Toward the end of this period, begin the sauté, either in a large, heavy Dutch oven or your largest skillet. Heat the oil in your chosen pan over medium heat. When it's good and hot, add the onion and sauté, stirring, until it has softened, about 6 minutes. Then add the jalapeño and bell peppers and sauté for 5 minutes more. Add the soy chorizo, either sliced or crumbled, and give it another minute or so. At this point, it may want to start sticking and will be developing a desirable browned crust on the bottom of the pan.

4. Remove the tempeh from the marinade, reserving the marinade. Shake off some of the marinade, but don't obsess over it. Add the tempeh to the contents of the skillet and, stirring constantly, sauté for 2 minutes more. Then pour in the marinade and the remaining 2 cups vegetable stock. Stir and scrape like crazy to get up those good browned bits; they're full of flavor.

5. Now, depending on which pot is larger, either transfer the sauté to the stew pot in which the vegetables are simmering, or the other way around. Give it all a good stir. Bring to a boil and turn down to a simmer. Let the contents simmer together, half-covered, for about 30 minutes. Enjoy the fragrance now permeating your kitchen.

6. You may serve the sancocho right away, after adjusting to taste with salt and pepper, or, better yet, let it sit off the heat for a while, which really helps the flavors to meld but prevents the vegetables from overcooking. You can also make it a day ahead, refrigerate it overnight, and reheat it before serving. In any case, serve it steaming hot, with Tabasco on the table and the fresh cilantro sprinkled over the top.

STORIED, SENSATIONAL SANCOCHO

In some Latin American countries —the Dominican Republic, Colombia, Venezuela, and El Salvador —sancocho is fabled in the way dishes like cassoulet or bouillabaisse or gumbo or paella are. And, like those dishes, each sancocho is prepared with its own particular twist in every region, every village, and every household. And, whichever way you grew up with it is the way sancocho is supposed to be.

Like a few other dishes beloved of particular ethnicities, sancocho has the honor of doing a kind of linguistic two-step (or perhaps rumba would be more like it). A word that starts out meaning a particular dish comes to refer also to a state of mind or being that reflects the qualities of that dish. A tzimmes, originally simply a Jewish side dish made of dried fruits and vegetables, thus sweet, savory, and a little confused as to its identity, came to mean as well a mixed-up state of affairs, a mess or messy situation. Similarly, *avial,* a South Indian stew that contains a little of almost everything, has come to mean mismatched; if someone says your outfit is avial, you are *not* receiving a compliment. In a similar vein, those who are said to be sancocho have been out working in the sun or otherwise breaking a sweat; they are stewing.

Want more proof of the iconic nature of this dish? Google "sancocho," and you'll find, besides dozens of recipes, a webzine by that name, a CD by that name which contains an eponymous cut (the group is Sol Y Canto), and an organization based in Holland (!) "for everyone with Latin spirit."

Chapter 12

SWEET SOMETHINGS

Cornbread- and Cornmeal-Based Desserts

"All's well that ends with a good meal." So the late children's book writer Arnold Lobel concluded one of the tales in *Fables*. I agree. And, to me a good meal, most of the time, ends with a good dessert. No, not every meal; no, not every night—but if you have a sweet tooth (I understand there are three or four human beings on the face of the planet who do not), satisfying it deeply and truly is one of the pleasures of a full life.

Now, though I am happy to finish many meals with fruit, sorbet, or something calorically reasonable, when I really want dessert, I want *dessert*. Not a sweet nothing, a definitive sweet *something*.

That is where cornmeal comes in. Its distinctive gritty texture adds a *something*-ness to many desserts. It fills out simple sweetness into more, giving complex texture to cakes like Very Lemony Cornmeal Pound Cake (page 339) and Miss Kay's Dark Secret Cornmeal Cake (page 341), a rich density to bread puddings like Bourbon-Banana Cornbread Pudding with Bourbon Sauce (page 334), and a warm hominess to fruit desserts like Apple Golden-Brown Betty (page 336).

So I'm pushing the envelope in this chapter. No, these aren't strictly cornbreads: Some are cakes that contain cornmeal, others are puddings that integrate stale cornbread thirsty for sweet, creamy custard. They are here because, well, just because . . . I like them, and I think you will too. We've almost ended our time together, and all's well that ends with a good dessert.

BUTTERMILK CORNBREAD PUDDING
WITH APRICOTS AND LEMON

SERVES 6

This is just-can't-stop-eating-it good. Buttermilk and cornbread are old Southern partners, but this dessert, with its almost cheesecake-like quality, takes these longtime friends to an entirely different, very seductive place.

Instead of the raisins found in many bread puddings, the apricots add little sudden bursts of flavor, sweetness, and texture, delightful to come across in the midst of that sweet, unctuous custard.

For the cornbread, use Dairy Hollow House Skillet-Sizzled (page 12), White River (page 25), Ronni's Appalachian (page 21), or Sylvia's Ozark (page 18).

Vegetable oil cooking spray

2 or 3 slices slightly stale not-too-sweet cornbread, in coarse crumbs (about 1 to 1½ cups, crumbled)

½ cup finely diced dried apricots
    (12 to 15 apricot halves), preferably
    unsulphured

2 tablespoons butter, at room
    temperature

¾ cup sugar

4 eggs

2 egg yolks

1 tablespoon unbleached white flour

2¾ cups buttermilk

½ cup sour cream or reduced-fat
    (not non-fat) sour cream

⅛ teaspoon salt

2 teaspoons pure vanilla extract

Finely grated zest of 2 lemons,
    preferably organic

½ to 1 teaspoon freshly grated nutmeg

½ cup finely chopped almonds
    (optional)

1. Spray an 8-inch square baking dish with oil. Preheat the oven to 350°F.

2. Scatter the cornbread crumbs and apricot pieces in the prepared baking dish.

3. In a food processor, combine the butter and sugar and buzz until smooth, pausing to scrape the sides of the bowl. Beat in the eggs, egg yolks, flour, buttermilk, sour cream, salt, vanilla, and lemon zest. Pour this mixture over the cornbread and let it stand, covered with plastic wrap, for 30 minutes.

4. Sprinkle the nutmeg over the entire

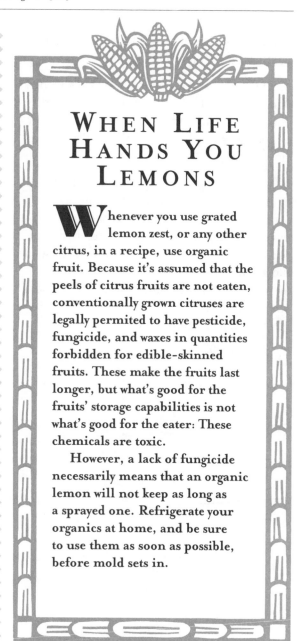

WHEN LIFE HANDS YOU LEMONS

Whenever you use grated lemon zest, or any other citrus, in a recipe, use organic fruit. Because it's assumed that the peels of citrus fruits are not eaten, conventionally grown citruses are legally permited to have pesticide, fungicide, and waxes in quantities forbidden for edible-skinned fruits. These make the fruits last longer, but what's good for the fruits' storage capabilities is not what's good for the eater: These chemicals are toxic.

However, a lack of fungicide necessarily means that an organic lemon will not keep as long as a sprayed one. Refrigerate your organics at home, and be sure to use them as soon as possible, before mold sets in.

pudding, using as much or as little as you like. Scatter the almonds atop that, if using.

5. Place the baking dish in a larger high-sided pan, and place both pans in the oven. Pour enough hot water into the larger pan to reach a little more than halfway up the sides of the smaller pan.

6. Bake until the pudding is almost but not quite set in the center, 40 to 45 minutes. It should still be a bit wiggly; you should wonder whether or not it is done (it is). Remove both pans from the oven (very carefully, because of the hot water bath), and then remove the pudding pan from the hot water. Cool to room temperature on a wire rack, then cover with plastic wrap and refrigerate.

7. Serve chilled.

CHERI'S CORNBREAD PUDDING WITH SWEET MEXICAN FLAVORS

SERVES 6 TO 8

Leftover cornbread always makes an excellent bread pudding, soaking up the custard thirstily and nearly dissolving into it, except for the lovely grainy texture of the cornmeal itself. Here, I've taken a classic formula for bread pudding, substituted cornbread, and altered it with the flavors of Colonial-era Mexico: the native corn and vanilla paired with Spanish custard, anise, almond, and canela cinnamon. Mexican vanilla is available at Latino groceries, or from Patricia Rain, the Vanilla Queen, at www.vanilla.com. This vanilla has a distinctive, delicious character and a scent that to me is both floral and hay-like.

This bread pudding, loved by my Arkansas friend, the writer Cheri White, is fondly dedicated to her. My favorite cornbread for this pudding is Truman Capote's Family's (page 13).

Vegetable oil cooking spray

4 to 6 slices leftover slightly stale
 nonsweet cornbread, in coarse crumbs
 (about 2 to 2½ cups, crumbled)

½ cup golden raisins

3 cups milk

½ cup heavy (whipping) cream
 or soy creamer

1 tablespoon butter

⅛ teaspoon salt

⅓ cup brown sugar

½ cup white sugar

5 eggs

2 egg yolks

1 tablespoon pure vanilla extract,
 preferably Mexican

½ teaspoon pure almond extract

1 teaspoon cinnamon, preferably
 canela (see Pantry, page 348)

1½ teaspoons aniseed

½ cup chopped unpeeled almonds,
 (optional)

Chilled heavy (whipping) cream,
 for serving (optional)

I. Preheat the oven to 375°F. Spray a shallow 2-quart baking dish with oil.

2. Scatter the cornbread crumbs in the prepared baking dish and the raisins evenly over the cornbread. (Let this sit out, the cornbread crumbs drying further, as you continue with the recipe.)

3. Heat the milk, cream or soy creamer, butter, salt, and sugars together in a large saucepan over medium heat, whisking a few times. Meanwhile, in a medium heat-proof bowl, whisk together the eggs, egg yolks, and vanilla and almond extracts.

4. When the butter melts and the milk is quite hot, remove it from the heat. Gradually pour it into the egg mixture, whisking like the dickens. Add the cinnamon and aniseed, whisk again, and ladle or pour this mixture over the cornbread crumbs and raisins. If you like, sprinkle the almonds atop the pudding. (Some like a crunch in puddings, trifles, et al—some don't.)

5. Place the baking dish in a larger high-sided pan, and place both pans in the oven. Pour enough hot water into the larger pan to reach a little more than halfway up the sides of the smaller pan.

6. Bake until the pudding is barely set in the center, about 45 minutes. It should still be wiggly in the center; you should wonder whether or not it is done. It *is* done (it will continue to set as it cools). Remove both pans from the oven (very carefully, because of the hot water bath), and remove the pudding pan from the hot water. Let cool to room temperature; then, if you're not eating it right away, cover tightly with plastic wrap and refrigerate.

7. Serve at room temperature or chilled. For extra decadence, serve with a pitcher of deeply chilled heavy cream, for guests to pour over their portion.

CopperWynd Chocolate Bread Pudding

SERVES 12 TO 15

At the CopperWynd Resort and Club in Scottsdale, Arizona, I enjoyed *the* most luscious souffléed chocolate bread pudding, with just a bit of smoky chipotle chile bite, created by their then-chef, Lisa Anne Smith. My adaptation, although unsouffléed, combines her bread pudding (including the *hot* hot chocolate sauce she served it with) with my own beloved Chocolate Bread Pudding Maurice. You say it makes quite a few servings? You think that's an accident? Something like this, you want to share: This is one primo party dessert.

Don't under any circumstances over-bake this. It should be quite wet when it comes out of the oven; it sets as it cools. That's one of its secrets. Another is to use really, really good-quality chocolate; my favorite, these days, is Scharffen Berger. Last of all, be sure you have a batch of

CopperWynd Chipotle Cornbread (page 80) made up the night before.

If a person believed a dessert could be "too rich," not that I do, this would probably be in that category. Get ready to swoon.

Vegetable oil cooking spray

1 batch CopperWynd Chipotle Cornbread, baked the night before, crumbled, and left to dry out overnight

2 cups heavy (whipping) cream

1⅓ cups half-and-half or whole milk

5 ounces semisweet chocolate, coarsely chopped

5 ounces unsweetened chocolate, coarsely chopped

3 egg yolks

5 eggs

1 tablespoon pure vanilla extract

1⅔ cups sugar

To serve

Hot Hot Tequila-Chocolate Sauce (recipe follows), heated

Vanilla ice cream

Accompaniments: strawberries, raspberries, kiwi slices, star fruit slices, and/or orange twists

1. Spray an 11-by-14-by-2-inch baking pan with oil, and sprinkle the dried cornbread crumbs over the bottom, spreading evenly. Set aside.

2. Combine the cream and half-and-half or

whole milk in a heavy-bottomed saucepan, and heat to scalding. Add the chopped chocolates to the hot cream mixture and whisk to melt the chocolate.

3. Place the eggs, egg yolks, vanilla, and sugar in a food processor; buzz to blend. Then add about half the chocolate mixture and buzz again until smooth and well combined. Pour this egg mixture back into the pot with the remaining chocolate mixture, whisking and stirring until very well combined.

4. Pour the chocolate-egg mixture over the bread crumbs in the baking pan. Let it sit, covered, at room temperature for 1 hour. Toward the end of the hour, preheat the oven to 325°F.

5. Set the filled pan in a larger high-sided pan. Pour enough hot water into the larger pan to reach a little more than halfway up the sides of the smaller pan. Bake until the top of the pudding is dark and glossy, about 35 minutes. Do *not* overbake; it should still be fairly liquid. The first time you make it you will be dubious that it will set up.

6. Remove both pans from the oven and remove the pudding pan from the hot water. Let cool slowly, at room temperature, then refrigerate. It will set up to the consistency of a soft, custard-like pudding as it cools; don't expect the brick-like mass you might have known in the past as bread pudding. This is scooped with a spoon, not cut into squares.

7. To serve: Place a scoop of bread pudding in a soup bowl. Have the tequila-chocolate sauce ready to go. Place a small scoop of vanilla ice cream upon the dense chocolate bread pudding, drizzle a little of the tequila-chocolate sauce over it, and serve, garnished with fresh fruit.

HOT HOT TEQUILA-CHOCOLATE SAUCE

MAKES ABOUT 2 CUPS

To make this ahead of time, prepare the recipe through step 1, chill the sauce, and then, just before serving, heat it up slowly in the top of a double boiler. Whisk every once in a while. When it's good and hot, and just before serving, follow step 2.

1 cup heavy (whipping) cream

½ teaspoon chili powder (yes, the spice blend you use for making chili)

½ teaspoon chipotle chile powder

Tiny pinch of salt

½ teaspoon canela cinnamon (see Pantry, page 348)

14 ounces semisweet chocolate, chopped

2 tablespoons tequila (preferably Patrón)

I. In a medium-size, heavy saucepan, slowly bring the cream to a full boil with the chili and chipotle powders, salt, and cinnamon. Once it reaches a boil, turn off the heat and stir in the chopped chocolate, whisking well until the chocolate is all smoothly melted into the hot cream.

2. Just before serving, add the tequila and whisk again.

·M·E·N·U·

A Prayer for New Orleans on the Anniversary of Katrina

Shrimp or Celery Root Rémoulade

*

Gumbo

*

Steamed White Rice

*

Classic Souffléed Spoonbread
(page 189)

*

Bourbon-Banana Cornbread Pudding
with Bourbon Sauce

Bourbon-Banana Cornbread Pudding with Bourbon Sauce

Serves 10 to 12

Classic New Orleans–style bread pudding was prepared and served at the Bon Ton on Magazine Street and many other restaurants in this once-great, now terribly beleaguered city. Though the bread pudding there is traditionally made from French bread, even so it involves corn because it is made with bourbon sauce, and by law, any American spirit labeled "bourbon" must be made from at least fifty-one percent corn mash (most bourbons use much more).

Quintessentially delicious as the original NOLA-style pudding is, I think this version—which uses cornbread instead of wheat bread and is enriched with both sweet and cultured dairy products—is even better. And the day the scent of some just-almost-too-ripe bananas crossed my nose as I was pouring in the bourbon and, on a whim, I added them—well, I knew this was impossible to beat.

Though ever so slightly less sweet and rich than the originals, it is plenty rich and sweet. And its unbelievable sauce, so alcohol-rich you could get drunk on it—well, one could label it sinful on many accounts.

This indulgence can be made ahead of time, and the yield is quite ample—all of which suggests its perfection as a company dessert, though a nonfancy one. Make the cornbread well in advance so you have time to let it cool, crumble it, and dry it out before you get started on the bread pudding proper. Use any unsweetened cornbread, such as White River (page 25), Sylvia's Ozark (page 18), Ronni's Appalachian (page 21), or Truman Capote's Family's (page 13).

1 cup raisins

¼ cup bourbon whiskey

1 can (12 ounces) evaporated milk

2 cups milk

⅔ cup mascarpone cheese

⅔ cup plain yogurt

¼ cup heavy (whipping) cream

3 eggs

6 egg yolks

1⅔ cups sugar

1 tablespoon pure vanilla extract

1 teaspoon ground cinnamon, preferably Saigon or canela (see Pantry, page 348)

Vigorous grating of nutmeg

Dash of salt

Vegetable oil cooking spray

1 batch any unsweetened cornbread, coarsely crumbled and slightly dry

2 very ripe bananas, peeled and coarsely mashed

1 recipe Bourbon Sauce (recipe follows)

I. In a small bowl, combine the raisins and bourbon. Let soak for at least 1 hour.

2. As the raisins soak, combine the evaporated milk, milk, mascarpone, yogurt, and cream in a large bowl. Whisk in the eggs, egg yolks, sugar, vanilla, cinnamon, nutmeg, and salt, beating thoroughly.

3. Spray a 9-by-14-inch baking pan, preferably one made of glass, with oil and sprinkle with an even layer of the dried-out cornbread crumbs. Next, scatter the soaked raisins on top (draining any accumulated bourbon into the milk-egg mixture). Now distribute bits of the mashed bananas over the crumbs. Finally, pour the egg-milk mixture over this and let it soak, covered, for about 30 minutes. Meanwhile preheat the oven to 350°F.

4. Set the pan inside a larger high-sided pan, and place the pans in the oven. Pour enough hot water into the larger pan to reach a little more than halfway up the sides of the smaller pan. Bake until the custard is barely firm in the middle but is nicely golden and crusty on top, about 40 minutes.

5. Carefully remove both pans from the oven and remove the pudding pan from the hot water bath. Cool the pudding slightly and serve it, in scoops, with the bourbon sauce over the top.

BOURBON SAUCE

MAKES A SCANT 2 CUPS

The original recipe used more butter and quite a bit more sugar. Lord knows, this version is rich enough. If any children are present and will be eating dessert, remove a little of the sauce and set it aside before adding the whiskey.

> **1 cup sugar**
> **¼ cup (½ stick) butter**
> **½ cup heavy (whipping) cream**
> **1 egg, beaten well**
> **¼ cup (2 ounces) bourbon whiskey (preferably Wild Turkey)**

I. Cream the sugar and butter together very well in a medium bowl. Then transfer to the top of a double boiler and cook slowly, whisking almost constantly, over simmering water, until the butter has melted and the sugar has dissolved. Add the cream and keep whisking for another couple of minutes, until all is very hot.

2. Whisk a little of the sugar-cream mixture into the beaten egg, and then return it all to the double boiler, whisking like the devil as you do so (this prevents curdling). When it's all whipped in and has cooked for a couple of minutes longer, the sauce will be a translucent ivory-gold color, slightly thickened. Remove from the heat, let cool slightly, and whisk in the bourbon. Serve the sauce, still warm, over the bread pudding.

APPLE GOLDEN-BROWN BETTY

SERVES 6 TO 8

Classic betty gets even better when all or part of the crumb topping comes from cornbread. A homey dessert for fall, it will perfume the entire house as it bakes.

Eat it hot with ice cream, for dessert; or cold, for breakfast, with plain yogurt. It can be made with pears instead of, or in addition to, apples; or, add a handful of fresh cranberries to the apple slices for bright bursts of flavor. Any leftovers can be reheated, but it's also good cold.

A DIFFERENT KIND OF SWEET CORN

Need further proof of corn's iconic nature? What other vegetable do you know that is mimicked in a confection? Made of sugar, water, and corn syrup (of course), with fondant and marshmallow whipped in for texture, candy corn is tinted in three different colors and poured, color by color, into kernel-shaped molds. It's been around since the 1880s and has, like "Indian" corn and corn shucks decorating front porches, always been associated with harvest time, which became transmuted into decorating for Halloween and trick-or-treating somewhat later.

Candy corn was possibly the invention of a home cook—no one knows for sure—but its first commercial manufacturer was the Wunderle Candy Company of Philadelphia. However, the Goelitz Confectionery Company of Cincinnati, founded by German immigrant Gustav Goelitz, is the longest ongoing maker of the tri-colored triangular kernels. Goelitz began candy corn production in 1898 and still makes it today.

According to the National Confectioners Association, candy manufacturers in total sold more than 20 million pounds of candy corn in 2001. Each kernel has 3.5 calories.

If you are using a very sweet cornbread, cut the sweetening back by a tablespoon or two. If, on the other hand, your crumbs are less sweet, add an extra tablespoon or two of apple juice concentrate.

Vegetable oil cooking spray

1½ cups dry, stale cornbread crumbs, finely crumbled (if you don't have enough, extend them with crumbs of other types of bread, or semi-crushed cornflakes)

½ cup brown sugar

¼ cup white sugar

1¼ teaspoons ground cinnamon, preferably Saigon or canela (see Pantry, page 348)

¼ teaspoon ground allspice

¼ teaspoon ground ginger

⅛ teaspoon ground cloves

A few gratings of nutmeg

7 to 8 (about 3 pounds) apples (Rome, Empire, Cortland, Greening, Braeburn, or Golden Delicious, or a combination), peeled, cored, and sliced in ⅓-inch-thick wedges

2 lemons, halved

⅓ cup frozen apple juice concentrate, thawed

½ cup (1 stick) butter, chilled

Accompaniments: ice cream, custard sauce, plain yogurt, or whipped cream

1. Preheat the oven to 375°F. Spray a shallow 8½-by-11-inch glass or enamel baking dish with oil. Set aside.

2. Toss together the crumbs, sugars, and spices in a medium bowl. Set aside.

3. Place the apple slices in a second medium bowl. Squeeze the lemons over the apples, with a strainer set over the bowl to catch the seeds. Toss the apples well to distribute the juice.

4. Sprinkle 2 tablespoons of the crumb mixture on the bottom of the prepared dish. Then scatter half the prepared apples over the crumb mixture. Pour the apple juice concentrate over the apples in the dish, then scatter on a layer of about half of the remaining crumb mixture. Dot about half the butter across this layer. Top with the remaining apple slices, followed by the remaining crumbs. Dot the remaining butter over the top.

5. Cover the dish tightly with aluminum foil and bake until the apples are quite tender, 35 to 40 minutes. Remove the foil from the dish, crank the heat up to 400°F, and let the dish bake until the top crumbs are deeply golden and crisp, about 10 minutes more. Serve, warm but not hot, with a dollop of the creamy accompaniment of your choice.

VERY LEMONY CORNMEAL POUND CAKE

MAKES 1 LARGE, 2 MEDIUM, OR 3 SMALL LOAVES

E veryone who bakes has a favorite pound cake. This is mine—and it knocked the one that *had* been my favorite clear out of the ballpark. I now consider this the ultimate pound cake: It is dense without being heavy, fine-grained but with the pleasant gritty crunch only cornmeal confers, straightforward but with a quite extraordinary depth of flavor. It's too good to cover up with a lot of complex sauces and toppings: fresh raspberries and lemon sorbet at the very most. But just as is, with a good cup of coffee or hot, strong, unsweetened black tea—perfection. As one of my tasters, Christy Wickham, remarked as she went back for a third slice, "This could be dangerous."

While the cake is by no stretch of the imagination low-fat, the fat content here has been reduced considerably from the classic pound cake.

Vegetable oil cooking spray

1 cup sifted unbleached white flour, plus extra for dusting the pan

¼ cup cornstarch

1 teaspoon baking powder

¼ teaspoon salt

¼ teaspoon baking soda

1½ cups stone-ground yellow cornmeal, plus extra for dusting the pan

2 lemons, preferably organic

½ cup reduced-fat (not fat-free) sour cream

¾ cup buttermilk

1 teaspoon pure vanilla extract

6 eggs, separated

¼ teaspoon cream of tartar (optional)

1¾ cups sugar

¾ cup (1½ sticks) butter, at room temperature

¾ cup packed light brown sugar

1. Preheat the oven to 350°F. Spray one large, two medium, or three small loaf pans with oil. Sprinkle the pan(s) very well with a combination of flour and cornmeal, shaking out the excess.

2. Sift the flour, cornstarch, baking powder, salt, and baking soda together into a large bowl. Stir in the cornmeal. Set aside.

3. Grate the zest from the lemons, placing it in a small bowl. Then cut the lemons in half and squeeze their juice through a strainer (to catch the seeds) over the grated zest. Whisk in the sour cream, buttermilk, and vanilla. Set aside.

4. Place the egg whites (see Beating Egg Whites, pages 186–187) in a clean, high-sided bowl, with the cream of tartar if you have it. Using an electric mixer with clean beaters set on a medium speed, begin to beat the egg whites. When the whites are in soft cloudlike peaks, turn the speed up to high and begin adding ½ cup of the sugar, 2 tablespoons or so at a time, beating until the whites form stiff peaks. Set aside, but don't wash the beaters. Work as quickly as you can from here on out, so the whites will stay fluffy.

5. Using the electric beaters set on medium, beat the butter in a medium bowl, until it is creamily fluffy. Gradually beat in the remaining 1¼ cups white sugar and all the brown sugar, a quarter cup or so at a time, slowly increasing the mixer speed to high. It should take 4 or 5 minutes, no more, for all the sugar to be added and the mixture to become lighter and fluffier.

6. Beat the egg yolks into the butter and sugar mixture one at a time, mixing well after each addition. Add the lemon mixture, beating until it's all well combined. Stop the mixer and add the flour mixture, mixing it in on low speed just until combined (longer beating will toughen the cake).

7. Using a rubber spatula and working with about a third of the egg whites at a time, fold the whites gently into the batter.

8. Immediately, transfer the batter to the prepared pan or pans. Bake the large pan for 60 to 70 minutes, the smalls for 45 to 55. Test the center of the cake(s) with a toothpick; pound cakes, being so dense, are notoriously finicky about being truly done all the way through. The toothpick should come out clean, no bits of batter stuck to it.

9. Let the pound cake(s) cool in the pan(s), set on a rack, for about 10 minutes. Cut around the edges of each cake with a thin-bladed knife, and let stand for another 5 minutes. Turn each pan upside down, and reverse out the cake, giving the bottom of the pan a sharp rap. Quickly place the loaf or loaves right side up on the rack and let them complete cooling, at least 40 minutes more.

Miss Kay's Dark Secret Cornmeal Cake

MAKES 12 SQUARES

Here is a truly wonderful quick cake, with an elusive—indeed, addictive—quality. What makes it transcendent? A secret ingredient: cocoa. This isn't a chocolate cake, mind you; instead, in the mysterious synergy that makes cooking ever-surprising, the cocoa quietly melds the spices and fruit into what may be one of the best speedy cakes I know, taught to me by my beloved early culinary mentor, Miss Kay, oh, my gosh, nearly forty-five years ago. It has been adapted, I think improved, by the cornmeal's crunchy graininess.

When I say quick and speedy: get familiar with this recipe, and you can knock it out in 15 to 20 minutes, plus baking time. Great for drop-ins or unexpected company, and you probably have everything you need on hand. Serve it, warm, with freshly brewed coffee or a tall glass of cold milk.

Amazingly, this cake is eggless. If you've been looking for a cake batter the bowl of which your kids can lick with impunity (as in the pre-possible-salmonella-in-eggs days), this is it. And the dairy ingredients can easily be replaced with vegan counterparts. More great news: It can easily be halved, making a perfect 9-inch round cake.

Vegetable oil cooking spray

1¼ cups unbleached white flour

¼ cup stone-ground yellow cornmeal

1 cup sugar

2 tablespoons unsweetened cocoa

1 teaspoon baking soda

½ teaspoon salt

¾ teaspoon ground cinnamon, preferably canela or Saigon (see Pantry, page 348)

½ teaspoon freshly grated nutmeg

¼ teaspoon ground allspice

1 cup unsweetened applesauce

½ cup buttermilk

¼ cup (½ stick) butter, melted, or mild vegetable oil

⅔ cup raisins

½ cup chopped toasted walnuts, (optional)

Confectioners' sugar, for sifting (optional)

1. Preheat the oven to 350°F. Spray an 8-by-11-inch baking dish with oil, and set aside.

2. Sift together the flour, cornmeal, sugar, cocoa, baking soda, salt, cinnamon, nutmeg, and allspice into a large bowl.

3. Combine the applesauce, buttermilk, and melted butter in a medium bowl. Whisk well.

4. Stir the wet mixture into the dry mixture, using as few strokes as possible. Stir in the raisins and nuts, if using, with a few additional strokes, then transfer the batter to the pan.

5. Bake until the cake tests clean, 40 to 45 minutes. Dust with sifted confectioners' sugar, if you like, and serve warm.

PLAYING DRESS-UP

Lay a paper doily across the top of a baked cake, and sift confectioners' sugar evenly over the cake onto the doily. Then lift the doily carefully, straight up, and voilà! You'll have a lacy powdered sugar pattern.

This is one of those tricks I am always sure everyone in the world knows, yet when I bring a cake finished in this manner to a community potluck or some such, people are always asking me, "How did you *do* that?"

DARK, EXTRA-GINGERY GINGERBREAD, WITH DARRA'S HOT CITRUS SAUCE

MAKES 9 SQUARES

This almost-classic hot-water gingerbread is very dark, very moist, and heady with molasses and spice, including, if you like, fresh or crystallized ginger. Using a measure of that New World marvel—gritty stone-ground cornmeal—gives the sweet, spicy cake a pleasing touch of texture.

Delicious in its own right, especially when served warm, I think gingerbread needs a little something to set off its intense flavors. Whipped cream is a classic choice, and good; so is ice cream; so is a baked apple with a little custard sauce. But! Late in my lifelong gingerbread love affair I found the ultimate combination: gingerbread with a warm citrus sauce. It's an alliance I'd heard of but disputed; I couldn't mentally taste the pairing. But Darra Goldstein's description, in

The Vegetarian Hearth, her book on cold-weather vegetarian cooking, was ecstatic enough to get me to try it. Now I wouldn't dream of having this gingerbread any other way.

Vegetable oil cooking spray

1 egg

⅓ cup brown sugar, packed

1 tablespoon white sugar

½ cup dark molasses, preferably blackstrap

6 tablespoons (¾ stick) butter, melted

1 tablespoon peeled, finely chopped fresh or crystallized gingerroot (optional but very, very good)

1¼ teaspoons ground ginger

¾ teaspoon ground cinnamon, preferably Saigon or canela (see Pantry, page 348)

¼ teaspoon ground cloves

¼ teaspoon freshly grated nutmeg

⅛ teaspoon salt

1 teaspoon baking soda

¼ teaspoon baking powder

¾ cup plus 1 tablespoon unbleached white flour

¼ cup stone-ground white cornmeal

½ cup boiling water, preferably filtered or spring

Darra's Hot Citrus Sauce (recipe follows)

1. Preheat the oven to 350°F. Spray an 8-by-11-inch baking pan with oil.

2. In a food processor, combine the egg and the sugars. Stir in or buzz in the molasses and butter. When smooth, add the fresh or crystallized ginger, if using, and pulse a few times.

3. Add the ground ginger, cinnamon, cloves, nutmeg, salt, baking soda, baking powder, flour, and cornmeal to the food processor, along with (carefully) the boiling water. Pulse a few times, scrape the sides, then pulse again. You don't want to overprocess, just to get everything combined. The batter will be very thin.

4. Pour the batter into the prepared pan and bake until the cake tests clean, 30 to 35 minutes. Allow the cake to cool for at least 15 minutes before cutting into it. Serve still warm with the hot citrus sauce spooned over each piece.

Darra's Hot Citrus Sauce
Makes about 1½ cups

¾ **cup white sugar**

¼ **cup plus 2 tablespoons brown sugar**

2 tablespoons cornstarch

Finely grated zest of 2 oranges, preferably organic

¾ **cup freshly squeezed orange juice, from 1 to 2 oranges**

3 tablespoons freshly squeezed lemon juice

Dash of salt

1 tablespoon butter

1½ **tablespoons mild honey**

Mix the sugars with the cornstarch in a medium saucepan, preferably nonstick. Gradually whisk in the orange zest and the juices, whisking hard to get the cornstarch incorporated properly and to avoid lumps. Add the salt, butter, honey, and 1 cup plus 2 tablespoons water, and bring the mixture to a boil over medium heat. Cook, stirring often, until the sauce thickens and clears, about 5 minutes. Serve hot, over the warm gingerbread.

Pantry
Ingredient Glossary and Tidbits

I like to think of this pantry section—part glossary, part how-to—as a *lagniappe*—a little something extra. (In New Orleans, a lagniappe is the bonus item a merchant offers the purchaser to sweeten the deal.) Here, the "something extra" is more information, which I hope will help you with shopping for, using, and storing some of the ingredients called for in this book. I threw in a few opinions and techniques, too, for good measure.

Apple cider syrup: Essentially apple cider that has been boiled down into a sweet, flavorful syrup, it has been used as a sweetener since colonial times. It can be purchased at www.countrystoreandgardens.com.

Baking powder: The baking powder–containing recipes in this book were tested using double-acting baking powder. This familiar leavening agent has an eventual shelf life, after which its ability to raise baked goods decreases. Test an older baking powder's vigor by dissolving a teaspoon of it in a half-cup of hot water. If the solution foams and fizzes, your BP is still good to go.

Baking soda: Baking soda starts to react and release carbon dioxide gas as soon as it is moistened. After adding baking soda to a batter, make sure to bake the batter immediately. Like baking powder, it does have a shelf life, so if your box, especially a long-opened one, is dusty, test it, too, as above.

Better: I make "Better," my own delicious instead-of-straight-butter mixture, which I use as a spread as well as in cooking—almost anywhere butter is called for (the exceptions being butter cookies and pie crusts). Why bother? Better spreads like a dream on toast, bread, or muffins, even straight from the fridge. It has a higher smoke point than plain butter, which means Better is better for sautéing, because it's less likely to burn. And it tastes every bit as good as butter. It's also more healthful than straight butter, and *much* more healthful (as

well as far better tasting) than margarines with hydrogenated fats or trans fats.

The following recipe makes quite a lot, but it freezes perfectly. Depending on the number of people in your family and their butter consumption, one batch can last in the freezer 4 to 6 months.

BETTER
MAKES 4½ CUPS

1 pound (4 sticks) salted butter, preferably organic, at room temperature
2½ cups any mild, slightly sweet, buttery oil (I like to combine almond oil, avocado oil, and macadamia nut oil, but canola oil's not bad)
1¾ teaspoons fine sea salt (or to taste)

Combine everything in a food processor and buzz until smooth, scraping the sides of the work bowl occasionally. Transfer the Better into smaller tightly covered containers, and freeze all but one of them. Thaw as needed. It will keep in the refrigerator for about 2½ months.

Butter: When I call for butter in a recipe, I generally use salted butter because I personally am not wild about the taste of most of the unsalted commercial butter widely available. It's almost always made from cultured (soured) cream, which to me is always a little off. Whether the salt in salted butter offsets or hides that particular soured flavor, or whether it in some way preserves the butter from further souring, I don't know. I just know I find most supermarket unsalted butters objectionable.

However, if you have access to butter churned from sweet cream (local regional dairies sometimes offer it, and it is usually quite a bit pricier than conventional butter, but its flavor is heavenly in comparison), do try it and see what you think.

If you do choose unsalted butter in any of the recipes here, since they were tested with salted butter, remember to add just a teeny bit of extra salt, no more than a few grains, to the dry ingredients.

Buttermilk: Once the by-product of churning butter from sour milk, these days it is a thick, creamy-tasting (even when low-fat or skim) cultured milk. It is used as the acid ingredient in many, many cornbreads, especially those from the southern region of the United States. It's also, often, eaten with Southern-style cornbread; the bread is crumbled into a bowl or glass, the buttermilk poured over it, and you eat it with a spoon, as one would eat cereal and milk (which it is, of course, in a fashion).

When buying buttermilk, look for one that has two ingredients: milk and culture. (This type is sometimes sold as Bulgarian buttermilk.) Inferior buttermilks have a long list of unpronounceable ingredients, though they will work in a pinch.

If you don't have buttermilk on hand, substitute plain yogurt (a variety whose sole ingredients are milk and yogurt cultures, usually lactobacillus and acidophilus) and thin the yogurt slightly by whisking in a little water (say, for the equivalent of 1 cup of buttermilk, use ¾ cup plain yogurt plus ¼ cup water). Another substitute: 1 cup of regular milk, whole or reduced-fat, with ½ teaspoon white vinegar, cider vinegar, or lemon juice stirred in.

Powered buttermilk is available at virtually all supermarkets, and it's pretty good. (It's used in the Toasted Sesame Multigrain Pancake Mix on page 212.) Reconstitute it according to package directions.

Buttermilk, soy: Vegans or the lactose-intolerant can easily make a buttermilk substitute by putting 1 tablespoon lemon juice in the bottom of a liquid measuring cup, and topping off to 1 cup with plain, unflavored soy milk. Stir a few times with a fork. It will thicken slightly. Use wherever dairy buttermilk is called for; it works perfectly. See also **Vegan ingredients, substitutions for.**

Cake flour: A very heavily bleached low-gluten wheat flour, preferred by some for the extreme lightness it gives cakes. Being no great fan of refined products or extreme lightness in baked goods, I have found a happy compromise: a combination of cornstarch (which is gluten-free) and either unbleached white flour or whole wheat pastry flour. To make it, sift together ¾ cup plus 2 tablespoons unbleached white or whole wheat pastry flour, plus 2 tablespoons cornstarch.

Canela cinnamon: See **Cinnamon.**

Cinnamon: As beloved an American as the apple pie it typically seasons, cinnamon is cinnamon—right? Wrong. There's a reason I usually specify "canela or Saigon" when I call for cinnamon. What Americans call "cinnamon" is actually several different related spices.

The cinnamon tree, *Cinnamomum zeylanicum*, is native to Sri Lanka (formerly Ceylon), and has long been cultivated in India as well. (Because Christopher Columbus set off on his voyages in search of spices, particularly cinnamon, it was wishful thinking that made him label the people he found here "Indians," to everyone's lasting confusion.)

The spice above is true cinnamon, usually called "canela," "mexicali cinnamon," or "Ceylon" cinnamon in the U.S. It's the tree's fragrant, soft inner bark. Hand-harvested, rolled into papery, easily shattered reddish brown rolls, called quills, its flavor is delicate but persistent, naturally distinctly sweet, and a little warm in the mouth. In Britain, Australia, and many European countries, *this spice and only this* may be legally labeled "cinnamon."

But in America, it's legally permitted to allow cassia, a more harshly flavored but less expensive Chinese relative of cinnamon, to be labeled cinnamon. Though similarly flavored, cassia (*C. aromaticum*) is thicker, tougher, and has a pronounced, slightly bitter or acrid undernote along with the sweet warmth. It's often used in savory Asian dishes like Chinese "red-braised" foods. A stick of cassia is much harder to break in two than true cinnamon, and its rolls curl inward toward each other, scroll-like.

Throughout this book I have specified canela or Saigon cinnamon. *Huh—Saigon?* How did Saigon jump in here? Well, just to further complicate matters there is a third variety of cinnamon, *C. loureirii*, which is Vietnamese. Its quills scroll inwards like those of cassia sticks, but are thinner and smaller, and its flavor is like an extra-rich version of canela, with a sweet floral twist to its fragrance and taste.

I get my cinnamons—both canela/Ceylon, and Saigon/Vietnamese—from www.kalustyans.com.

Cornmeal, colors of: Corn, and hence the meal made from it, comes in almost every color of the rainbow, but yellow, white, and blue cornmeal are the most readily available, thus the most familiar. Although cornmeals are identical in some ways (you can substitute a cup of stone-ground white cornmeal for a cup of stone-ground blue, allowing you to switch among the colors of meals you use in a particular recipe), there are differences beyond the visual. Some are indisputable: yellow cornmeals (and, if you can find them, red cornmeals) are higher in beta-carotene than white; blue cornmeals have the highest protein content of all cornmeals.

But the more important differences are aesthetic. A particular color of meal in each recipe is specified because it is traditional to that recipe and, in some cases, to the part of the world in which the recipe originates. Subtle flavor differences somehow suit certain sets of ingredients, and there are just obvious affinities: for example, a blueberry muffin just *should* be made with blue cornmeal (which can be purchased at www.wareaglemill.com or www.bobredmill.com).

To some of the descendants of the original corn planters, these color differences have spiritual significance; they are the symbolic alphabet of Zuni and Hopi cosmology, and human's place in it. North is yellow, west is blue, east is white, and south is red: The universe's story is told in corn. See also **Cornmeal, whitecap flint.**

Cornmeal, grinds of:

Cornmeal, bolted: A processed cornmeal that contains the germ but not the bran. It's a bit more nutritious than degerminated cornmeal, but it still does not count as a whole grain.

Cornmeal, enriched, degerminated: This meal is made from corn that has had its germ removed to improve the cornmeal's shelf life (the germ contains high levels of oil, which can spoil over time). Because it is fortified with synthetic versions of the vitamins and minerals lost during processing, it's called "enriched." In my view, this doesn't cut it. Period. But this is the one you will find in every American supermarket.

Cornmeal, grits: Coarsely ground cornmeal, often used for cooked hot breakfast cereal or polenta. Like all grain products, grits can be refined (whiter,

uniform, degerminated, quick-cooking, available in virtually every American supermarket), or whole-grain and artisanal (stone- or water-ground, coarse, irregular, full of flavor and texture, slower to cook, far more nutritious). The latter is my preference (no surprise), and I have used it for testing the recipes in which coarse-ground meal is called for.

Cornmeal, high-lysine: Because traditional cornmeal was notoriously lacking in lysine, which is one of the essential amino acids (vital building blocks of protein), a hybrid dent corn was selectively bred to compensate for this in the 1970s. This was considered a huge nutritional breakthrough at the time, and there was quite a fad over it in health-food circles. But the buzz has since faded, for Americans as a rule get plenty of lysine from other sources. However, its taste is sweet and good, and it has a slightly longer shelf life than many other whole-grain corn products. If you come across it, by all means give it a try.

Cornmeal, masa harina: see **Masa harina.**

Cornmeal, polenta: The Italian name for grits, above. Unlike American grits, however, which may be white, grits for polenta are almost always golden-yellow and usually are served as a side dish or main dish with something savory, at lunch or dinner, not as a hot sweetened breakfast cereal. A versatile staple in Italian cooking, polenta also shows up, under different names, in some perhaps unexpected cuisines, including Romanian, Argentinean, and Brazilian. It's also become popular in America. An exception to the yellow polenta rule: Anson Mills, in Columbia, South Carolina, makes a delicious white polenta, in addition to yellow and a special rustic coarse polenta from an Italian corn variety (see www.anson mills.com for products).

Read your polenta labels: Some varieties are more quick-cooking than others, though even the so-called instant takes about fifteen minutes.

In an Italian grocery or specialty store, you may run across a product called *polenta taragna*, which is the characteristic golden yellow but speckled with tiny bits of something darker. That something is coarsely ground buckwheat, and its haunting, distinct nutty-toasty-grainy flavor is very special as part of polenta. It is cooked the same way as all-cornmeal polenta.

Cornmeal, self-rising: This is enriched, degerminated cornmeal to which salt, baking powder, and baking soda have been added, saving the cook the time needed to add these three ingredients. I don't generally like it for the same reasons I don't generally like any non–whole-grain grain product. However, a few of the recipes in this book do call for it, because that is the way they were given to me and they were just too tasty to leave out. If you want to make your own self-rising cornmeal, just substitute the following for the commercial kind: 1½ cups stone-ground yellow cornmeal plus 1 teaspoon baking powder, ½ teaspoon baking soda, and ½ teaspoon salt.

Cornmeal, stone-ground or water-ground: This is just what it sounds like, cornmeal that is made by grinding dried corn between two large stones. When the grinding stones are powered by water, as in a streamside mill, it is sometimes called water-ground. I strongly urge you to use stone-ground cornmeal instead of its less expensive steel-ground cousin because it just tastes more like *corn* than the steel-ground meal does; it's richer in flavor and nutrients because it retains more of the hull and the germ, and it does not reach the high (and flavor-killing) heats of commercial steel-roller mills. Also, stone grinding means that the particles of ground corn are inconsistent: This is what gives good cornbread the characteristic grittiness it must have.

Stone-ground cornmeal is more perishable, so for longer life, especially in hot weather, be sure to store it in an airtight container in the fridge or freezer. It will last there for 2 to 3 months.

Cornmeal, whitecap flint: The key ingredient in Rhode Island jonnycakes, whitecap flint cornmeal is ground from the corn variety of the same name, which is notoriously difficult to grow and just as difficult to grind. If you do not live in or near Rhode Island, you can order whitecap flint cornmeal from Gray's Grist Mill (www.graysgristmill.com) or Kenyon's Grist Mill (www.kenyonsgristmill.com), both located in the Ocean State.

Corn syrup: This sweet, sticky liquid is made from cornstarch and contains mostly glucose. It's available in dark and light, with flavor variations loosely parallel to those of dark brown or white sugar. Although corn syrup is different from the high-fructose corn syrup that is widely used to sweeten soft drinks and has been getting much bad press lately, it is still a processed sugar, and too much of it has all the drawbacks of too much of any sugar. While corn syrup is sometimes used in baking to create a moister crumb, you'll find only one bottle of corn syrup in my pantry, used once a year: when I make pecan pie at Thanksgiving.

Creamed corn (sometimes called cream-style corn): Originally, creamed corn was fresh corn scraped from the cob and cooked in its own milky juices with a little heavy cream. Today, however, this product has come to be a thick, somewhat sweet canned mixture of corn kernels, sugar, cornstarch, and salt. Canned creamed corn finds its way into quite a few cornbread recipes, where it adds considerable moisture to the finished breads. If you prefer the idea of using fresh creamed corn, you can make

it from scratch. Simply buzz together in a food processor about 2 cups corn kernels, cut from 3 or 4 ears of fresh corn (see Shuck and Jive, page 49), with ½ cup milk and 1 tablespoon each of honey and cornstarch. This makes an amount equal to one 14.75-ounce can.

Eggs: Whenever possible, try to purchase eggs from local free-range chickens fed an organic diet. (The eggs are more flavorful as a rule, have brighter yellow yolks, and have more of the healthful antioxidant beta-carotene.) Or try "natural" eggs from the supermarket or natural foods store; several larger egg companies now guarantee their eggs are from "cage-free" hens (not the same as free-range, however) fed an "all natural, vegetarian diet enriched with DH Omega-3 and Vitamin E."

Egg replacers: Due to their unique properties in the kitchen, in some recipes eggs are problematic to replace. This is an issue both for those who are allergic to them, and for vegans. While powdered egg replacers (such as Ener-G), crumbled tofu, applesauce, and ground flaxseeds are often offered as alternatives, in an (egg)shell, I don't think any of these works as well as the real thing, at least not in baking. (You can, however, make a darned good scrambled tofu for breakfast if you are so inclined.)

Because we had the occasional can't-eat-eggs guest back in the days when Ned and I owned and ran our inn, I developed my own, homemade egg replacer for baking, which I called Eggscellence. It's a dry mix that you reconstitute as needed. In any *non-custard-y* baked-good or griddled recipe calling for one or two whole (unseparated) eggs, Eggscellence (recipe below) works as well as the real deal; my tasters literally could not tell the difference between the fabricated and real eggs in a blind tasting of muffins (they could with every other common egg substitute mentioned above). And oh my goodness, did I ever make some vegans and egg-allergic folks happy! Muffins, cookies, brownies, yeast breads, as well as cornbread: If the original recipe calls for 1 to 2 eggs, this works like a charm. If it calls for 3, it usually works. But if the recipe calls for 4 or more, pick a different, less eggy recipe. And don't, certainly, try it as a substitute in a recipe where eggs dominate. No quiches or soufflés, for instance. In the recipes in this book, it will work just fine in almost any cornbread except the spoonbreads, the three-layer-custard cornbreads, and the custardy dessert bread puddings.

Eggs do a lot of things in baked recipes: they emulsify (bind and incorporate ingredients into one another smoothly); add structure as the dish bakes (high heat firms up proteins); leaven or lighten just a bit; and add moisture, flavor, richness, and color. Eggscellence mimics these functions. It uses soy flour for protein, potato and/or tapioca starch for binding, and baking powder for leavening. The last and most unusual ingredient called for is xanthan gum. This, like the potato or tapioca starch, is another gluten-free carbohydrate, but in addition to binding, it adds volume, emulsifies, and gives a little egg-like viscosity. It is a natural product from a microorganism called *Xanthomonas campestris*.

Most importantly, Eggscellence is reconstituted at the time of use with water *and* liquid lecithin, a bright, golden fatty substance found both in egg yolks and soybeans. The lecithin emulsifies and enriches flavors, and also adds a bit of color. (Refrigerate liquid lecithin once you've opened the bottle.)

These ingredients may sound (okay, *are*) a little esoteric, but I can buy them all at my local natural foods co-op. If you can't, order them from www.bobsredmill.com or www.kingarthur flour.com. You can omit the xanthan; you can use all tapioca starch or all potato starch if you wish (though I think the combo of all three is best). It still comes out far tastier than all the other egg substitutes, including the commercial ones (she said immodestly). But do use the liquid lecithin in reconstituting: No substitutions there. This dry mix is sufficient to substitute for about 21 eggs, but the dry mix keeps indefinitely, so you just reconstitute it as you need it.

EGGSCELLENCE DRY MIX

MAKES ABOUT 2 CUPS

1 cup potato starch
¾ cup tapioca flour
¼ cup full-fat soy flour
1 tablespoon baking powder
2 tablespoons xanthan gum (optional)

Combine all the dry ingredients in a medium bowl, stirring or whisking thoroughly to combine. Store in a tightly-covered, labeled jar or zip-top bag in a cool place, or in the freezer.

To reconstitute Eggscellence

For each egg called for in a recipe, combine the following in a small bowl: 1½ tablespoons Eggscellence mix, 1½ tablespoons water, and 1 teaspoon liquid lecithin. Combine the dry mix with the wet very well, whipping with a fork or mini whisk. Add reconstituted Eggscellence to a recipe when the eggs are called for.

Flour, corn: Corn flour (often seen in British cookbooks) and cornstarch (the American equivalent) are one and the same—a fine white powder, nearly all starch, ground from the endosperm of the corn plant. It is most often mixed with a liquid and used as a thickening agent in sauces and puddings, although it's used in the occasional cookie recipe for the extreme tenderness it can add, and as a way to fabricate **cake flour** (see entry). It is a refined, not whole-grain, product.

Gluten: The protein component of wheat, which gives yeast-risen breads their distinct texture and which is "developed," or strengthened, through kneading. Some grains besides wheat have a little gluten (rye, barley); others are wholly gluten-free (corn, rice, quinoa). It is

because corn lacks gluten that yeast-risen cornbreads always contain either wheat flour or a few tablespoons of straight wheat gluten, often sold as "vital wheat gluten." The latter is a fine, slightly granular powder, sold at most natural foods stores and through King Arthur Flour's mail-order catalogue (www.kingarthurflour.com). It compensates for the lack of gluten in cornmeal and makes it possible to get a nice rise out of cornmeal-centric yeast breads.

"Green" corn: The old-fashioned name for corn eaten as a fresh vegetable, as opposed to in its dry ground form, cornmeal or masa. In other words, "green" corn is corn on the cob—yellow, white, or bicolor . . . not green in color (except for its husks) at all.

Hominy: This is whole "alkaline" corn (also known as posole). Whole corn kernels are soaked in a mild lye solution (see **nixtamalization**) until the outer skins soften enough to release the kernels from within. Although it's possible to buy dried hominy and cook it yourself, it is more readily available already cooked and in the can, typically in the international or Latino foods section of the supermarket. Lest you think that something out of a can is bound to have lost out in the translation, let me assure you that this is not the case. Canned hominy is simply cooked hominy, much as canned beans are simply cooked beans—it's not a case where, as with canned green beans or spinach, the whole character of the food is lost in the canning process. Occasionally you'll find hominy/posole canned in various sauces or stews. Avoid those. You want the plain kind, white or yellow (I prefer white).

Honey: Any mild, liquid honey can be used in the occasional cornbread in which honey is called for. Mild honeys include clover, wildflower, and orange blossom. However, for eating *with* hot cornbread (and butter), good, strong, dark buckwheat honey has its loyal Yankee partisans.

If your honey is crystallized, warm it to re-liquefy, either in a small saucepan or by running the bottle under hot water.

"Indian" corn: The contemporary common name for the bright, lovely, multihued ears of corn, dried on the stalk and gathered together with their still-attached husks, used strictly for decoration in the fall. The name is a misnomer: Columbus was wholly mistaken about the world he had arrived at, which most decidedly was *not* India, as he thought. Moreover, since all types of maize are native to the Americas and cultivated by its original residents, *all* types of corn are "Indian."

Nonetheless, go to any American farmstand in September or October, ask for "Indian corn," and these decorative ears are what you'll get.

"Indian" meal: The early American name for cornmeal. This was sometimes just shortened to "Indian" (old cookbooks will say, "add a cup of indian," lowercase i) and sometimes spelled just "injun" as in New England Rye'n'Injun bread (page 162).

Maize: Another of corn's many names, derived from its original, Native American name *mahiz*. When friendly Arawak Indians rowed out from what's now the island of Hispaniola to greet Columbus and company, they bore gifts of welcome, including mahiz. In Taino, the Arawak language, mahiz means "life-giver." The Spanish adapted this to *maíz* and the English speakers to *maize*.

Maple syrup: Occasionally, maple syrup is called for in a particular cornbread. According to USDA regulations, maple syrups are classified by "grade." Each grade has its own characteristic flavor, color, and ideal usages, but, unlike marks in school, an A is not better than a B, just different.

There are four grades of maple syrup.

Grade A Light Amber, sometimes called Fancy Grade (and, in Canada, No. 1 Extra Light), is very light in color, almost the shade of apple juice. Mild and delicate, it's usually the first made in sugaring season and is excellent on pancakes, especially buckwheat.

Grade A Medium Amber is a little darker and has a more intense maple flavor. This is the most widely available grade of syrup, the one you're likely to find in most supermarkets. Made a little later in sugaring time, it, too, is great used on waffles, French toast, and pancakes, and it is okay for cooking.

Grade A Dark Amber is still darker. Its more pronounced maple flavor emerges later in sugaring season, giving you more bang for the buck. Although it is great as a table syrup, its special qualities make it worthwhile to use in cooking: The maple-ness, not just the sweetness, comes through loud and clear.

Grade B, the darkest, strongest, and thickest, is sometimes called cooking syrup and is a late-season product. Some do like it as table syrup, but it is truly the premium cooking syrup; its essence-of-maple taste shines recognizably and beautifully in pies, cakes, muffins, mousses, bread puddings, and even in sweet-savory glazes and barbecue sauces.

Masa harina: Quite different from regular cornmeal, masa harina is ground from cooked, wet nixtamalized (see **nixtamalization**) corn, which is then dried to flour. It's used in making corn tortillas and tamales, and sometimes to thicken sauces (some chilies are traditionally masa-thickened). Masa has a distinctive, easily recognizable taste, grain-like, not sweet. Its texture, however, is powdery or floury, not grainy. Masa harina keeps better than stone-ground sweet cornmeal.

Just to make things extra confusing, *masa harina* also sometimes refers to the wet basic dough mixed up from dry masa harina. If you live in or near a Latino neighborhood, you may be able to buy fresh masa harina, which has a consistency almost like that of Play-Doh.

Mesquite meal/flour: A texture-y flour ground from the seedpods of the mesquite tree, it's almost too good to believe: rich, with haunting undernotes of flavor—a bit nutty, yet reminiscent of chocolate and cinnamon. Buff-brown in color, slightly granular, and very sweet (though low on the glycemic index and high in protein) it

has become one of my favorite unusual ingredients to play with: I'll use ¼ to ⅓ part mesquite meal to replace the equivalent amount of wheat flour in many cake or cookie recipes, and I find I can then cut back considerably on the sugar. Order it from www.cocinadevega.com.

Molasses: The thick syrup that is produced by boiling the sweet juices extracted from sugarcane, it is available in three varieties: light (very sweet, less flavorful); dark (some sweetness, richer flavor); and blackstrap (bitter, with a darker, deeper flavor; the most nutritious of the three). I usually use "dark"; if I prefer a particular one in a recipe, I'll note it.

Nixtamalization: The process by which corn is alkalinized to make **masa harina** and **hominy** or posole, usually through the addition of lime (the mineral, not the citrus fruit) or culinary ash, which is made from burning particular trees or woody plants until only ash remains. This process was developed by Native Americans, and the types of trees and bushes that have been used vary by region and tribe (traditionally, for instance, Navajos used mostly juniper, while Hopis preferred chamisa bush). Nixtamalization confers a great many nutritional and culinary benefits, although it's uncertain for which of these benefits, if any, it was originally developed. What we do know is that alkalinizing achieves several purposes: It loosens the hulls from the corn; swells the corn kernels to easily two or three times their previous size; makes the corn much easier to grind; adds infinitely more variation in flavor, form, and culinary properties; intensifies the color of the corn; and, most important, makes it easier to digest and far more nutritious.

This last piece is crucial if corn is your staple food, the main source of calories you take in (as is true throughout much of Mexico, Central America, and Africa, and used to be true in the southern United States and northern Italy). If it *is* your staple food and it has not been nixtamalized, you are at major risk for the terrible and deadly disease pellagra, caused by a niacin deficiency. So while we don't know how or why the nixtamalizing process was first developed, we continue to reap its lifesaving benefits while also enjoying the haunting mineral flavor it imparts.

For more about this amazing Native American technology, please visit this book's website, www.cornbreadgospels.com.

Oils: Most cornbread recipes contain some fat, sometimes of a couple of different varieties. While many old-time cornbreads were originally made with bacon drippings, person after person has told me, "Yeah, I grew up with it that way, but I've switched to oil now; even my granny has." My preference for vegetable oil is any fresh, mild-tasting oil, my three favorites being corn, canola, and peanut (not roasted peanut). Most often I use **Better,** see entry, either on or in the cornbread, too.

Posole: see **Hominy.**

Quick breads: If a bread is leavened, or raised, with baking powder and/or baking soda, it is called a quick bread (because it does not need the long rise time of **yeast**-leavened breads). Most cornbreads are quick breads, as are muffins, biscuits, scones, and most pancakes.

Rapadura: see **Sugar.**

Raw or unrefined sugar; see **Sugar.**

Sorghum: A sweet, sticky, dark syrup much loved in the South. Though sometimes called "sorghum molasses," it's not molasses, and has a distinctive, mellower flavor, with none of the slightly bitter aftertaste of unrefined molasses. Sorghum is made from pressed sorghum cane; molasses (see entry) from sugar cane. If you can't find sorghum, use molasses instead. Sorghum is, however, available in the gift shops of Cracker Barrel restaurants, as well as at www.smokiesstore.org.

Soy milk: A creamy milk made from soybeans, it is available plain or flavored and is an excellent substitute for dairy milk. For recipes, use the same amount of soy milk as dairy, and use plain (unflavored; not, say, vanilla). If the recipe calls for the dairy milk to be heated, do the same with the soy.

Succanat: see **Sugar.**

Sugar (unrefined and less refined): Nutritionally speaking, sugar is pretty much sugar. However, like anything else, it can be organic or not, refined to a greater or lesser degree, and processed so that it ends up in different forms. Thus, you get slightly different results depending on which sugar you choose. Note "slightly"—just use white or conventional brown sugar if you don't have any of these on your kitchen shelf.

Rapadura/succanat: With brown, small grains (not exactly crystals), it is made from evaporated sugarcane juice (it is also sometimes sold under this name). It deepens the color of baked products, adds a little texture, and has a flavor like conventional brown sugar with a little more personality. It is the least-refined, closest-to-its-natural-state sugar.

Turbinado or raw sugar: A pleasant off-white instead of pure snow white, turbinado is slightly less refined than white sugar and comes in crystals a bit larger than conventional white sugar. It dissolves into a batter seamlessly (like white sugar) but is far superior when you want to create something with sparkle: Just sprinkle a bit on top of the batter before it goes into the oven. I like it a lot in streusel toppings for sweet muffins in particular.

See also **Corn syrup, Honey, Maple syrup,** and **Molasses.**

"Sweet milk": An archaic term which, these days, only turns up in some cornbread recipes. It means, simply, regular, fresh milk, as opposed to cultured buttermilk, yogurt, or sour milk.

Turbinado: see **Sugar.**

Vegan ingredients, substitutions for: Almost all but the spoonbread cornbreads can be made vegan. See the entries in this glossary under **Buttermilk, soy; Soy milk;** and **Eggscellence** (which any vegan baker will use much more frequently than just here). For butter, simply substitute vegetable oil or, if you prefer, vegan margarine; cheese may either be omitted or be replaced by your favorite soy- or rice-based quasi-cheese.

Yeast, types of: Yeast, a single-cell fungus, is a culinary change agent. It changes grape juice into wine, wine into vinegar, milk into cheese. And it also makes breads (other than **quick breads**) rise. Yeasts work their magic by multiplying and being fruitful. They need food (sugar and starch), warmth, and moisture to breed. The conversion of their food into carbon dioxide, and eventually alcohol, is called fermentation. It's the small bubbles of carbon dioxide created as the yeasts reproduce, trapped in the **gluten** structure, that makes breads rise. Here are the types of yeast available:

Baker's yeast, dry: Small beige granules, dry yeast comes in ¼-ounce packets or loose, in larger amounts, in a jar (if you buy it in a jar, refrigerate the jar after opening it, and write the date of opening on the label in permanent marker; use the yeast within 6 months of opening it). *Regular dry yeast*, which is what the recipes in this book were tested with, takes the conventional amount of time to raise bread (individual recipes will give you an idea of how long this is). *Rapid* or *quick-rising yeast* takes a little more than half of the time of regular dry yeast to make bread rise.

Both types are common and can be found in any supermarket.

Baker's yeast, fresh or compressed: Because it's perishable, fresh yeast is harder to find, but it is quite delightfully lively. It comes in small square foil-wrapped cakes, and you'll sometimes find it in the refrigerator case of larger supermarkets and natural foods markets, as well as at some baking supply stores. The squares of fresh yeast are grayish, and you crumble them into the warm liquid in the recipe, at the same point at which you'd pour or stir in the dry yeast. One cake of fresh yeast equals one packet of dry yeast. Check its expiration date, and use fresh yeast within 5 days of bringing it home.

Nutritional yeast: Vying with "prune" as the least tasty-sounding name for a really good food, nutritional yeast is a variety of the nutrient-rich yeast used to ferment beer. This variety is specifically grown for its excellent savory flavor (somewhat like Parmesan cheese) as well as its super-high B-vitamin complex content, rather than for leavening. (Brewer's yeast, for beer making, is nutritious but decidedly untasty; it is quite bitter.) Bread will not rise if you substitute nutritional yeast for baker's yeast, so don't. However, corn-lovers should have some on hand,

because there is nothing, and I mean *nothing*, better on hot buttered popcorn than a major sprinkle of nutritional yeast. Some enlightened independent movie theaters actually keep a jar at the concession stand for popcorn patrons to sprinkle to their heart's content. Sometimes sold as "good-tasting nutritional yeast," it's available in bulk and sometimes in bags at your local natural foods market.

Yeast, methodology for, in bread-baking: Most homemade yeast breads are made by one of two methods, straight dough or sponge.

In the straight dough method, all or most of the ingredients are combined at one time to make a dough that rises once, twice, or three times, according to the recipe, and is then baked (every so often a straight dough recipe will hold back an ingredient like raisins or nuts to be kneaded in before the last rise).

In the sponge method, *some* of the flour, liquid, and yeast are combined and allowed to set and rise before being stirred down, at which point the remaining ingredients are stirred in to make a dough. This is allowed to rise as per the individual recipe, and then is baked. Some sponges are put together only an hour or two before they get made into dough; other sponges are allowed to ferment overnight, which gives them a tangier and, in the view of some, more flavorful (because of the yeast's longer fermentation) and better textured bread.

Zea mays: Corn's scientific name.

Conversion Tables

Approximate Equivalents

1 stick butter = 8 tbs = 4 oz = ½ cup

1 cup all-purpose presifted flour or dried bread crumbs = 5 oz

1 cup granulated sugar = 8 oz

1 cup (packed) brown sugar = 6 oz

1 cup confectioners' sugar = 4½ oz

1 cup honey or syrup = 12 oz

1 cup grated cheese = 4 oz

1 cup dried beans = 6 oz

1 large egg = about 2 oz or about 3 tbs

1 egg yolk = about 1 tbs

1 egg white = about 2 tbs

Please note that all conversions are approximate but close enough to be useful when converting from one system to another.

Weight Conversions

U.S.	METRIC	U.S.	METRIC
½ oz	15 g	7 oz	200 g
1 oz	30 g	8 oz	250 g
1½ oz	45 g	9 oz	275 g
2 oz	60 g	10 oz	300 g
2½ oz	75 g	11 oz	325 g
3 oz	90 g	12 oz	350 g
3½ oz	100 g	13 oz	375 g
4 oz	125 g	14 oz	400 g
5 oz	150 g	15 oz	450 g
6 oz	175 g	1 lb	500 g

Liquid Conversions

U.S.	IMPERIAL	METRIC
2 tbs	1 fl oz	30 ml
3 tbs	1½ fl oz	45 ml
¼ cup	2 fl oz	60 ml
⅓ cup	2½ fl oz	75 ml
⅓ cup + 1 tbs	3 fl oz	90 ml
⅓ cup + 2 tbs	3½ fl oz	100 ml
½ cup	4 fl oz	125 ml
⅔ cup	5 fl oz	150 ml
¾ cup	6 fl oz	175 ml
¾ cup + 2 tbs	7 fl oz	200 ml
1 cup	8 fl oz	250 ml
1 cup + 2 tbs	9 fl oz	275 ml
1¼ cups	10 fl oz	300 ml
1⅓ cups	11 fl oz	325 ml
1½ cups	12 fl oz	350 ml
1⅔ cups	13 fl oz	375 ml
1¾ cups	14 fl oz	400 ml
1¾ cups + 2 tbs	15 fl oz	450 ml
2 cups (1 pint)	16 fl oz	500 ml
2½ cups	20 fl oz (1 pint)	600 ml
3¾ cups	1½ pints	900 ml
4 cups	1¾ pints	1 liter

Oven Temperatures

°F	GAS MARK	°C	°F	GAS MARK	°C
250	½	120	400	6	200
275	1	140	425	7	220
300	2	150	450	8	230
325	3	160	475	9	240
350	4	180	500	10	260
375	5	190			

Note: Reduce the temperature by 20°C (68°F) for fan-assisted ovens.

INDEX